This book is sent to you for review with the compliments of

University of Toronto Press

New Institutionalism: Theory and Analysis

Edited by André Lecours

Cloth	0802039006	$65.00	£42.00	Publication:	18-Jun-05
Paper	0802048811	$29.95	£20.00	Publication:	18-Jun-05

World Rights

OUTSIDE OF CANADA DOLLAR PRICES ARE IN US DOLLARS

Please send two copies of the review and, if possible, a copy of the issue in which it appeared to the Head Office address, attention Review Coordinator.

UNIVERSITY OF TORONTO PRESS - HEAD OFFICE:
10 St Mary Street, Suite 700, Toronto, ON, M4Y 2W8   Fax: (416) 978-4738
CANADIAN, US, AUSTRALIAN,
and R.O.W. (excluding Europe) ORDERS can be sent to:
University of Toronto Press, 5201 Dufferin Street, North York, ON, M3H 5T8
Tel: 800-565-9523 / (416) 667-7791 / Fax: 800-221-9985 / (416) 667-7832
US ORDERS can be sent to:
University of Toronto Press, 2250 Military Rd, Tonawanda, NY, 14150
Tel: (716) 693-2768 / Fax: (716) 693-7479
EUROPEAN ORDERS can be sent to:
NBN International, Estover Road, Plymouth, PL6 7PY England
Faxed orders: 44 (0) 1752 202333. E-mail: orders@nbninternational.com

NEW INSTITUTIONALISM:
THEORY AND PRACTICE

Edited by André Lecours

New institutionalism is one of the most influential approaches in con-temporary political science. In this collection of essays, top scholars in the field offer important contributions to new institutionalist theory, engaging in debates about structure and agency, state-society relations, institutional creation and change, preference formation, and the com-plicated web of relationships between institutions, culture, ideas, iden-tity, rationality, and interests. From an analytical point of view, the essays examine how the state and political institutions shape a variety of political phenomena and outcomes, namely, nationalism, demo-cratic transition, party aggregation, policy networks, war and peace, international recognition, sovereignty, and specific public policies.

One of the unique features of the book is that it offers institutionalist analysis in the sub-fields of political science: comparative politics, pub-lic policy, and international relations. Also included are chapters explor-ing the institutionalist approach within both the English and French Canadian traditions in political science. This ambitious and comprehen-sive work addresses the complex issues involved in new institutionalist research and debate in North America and abroad, and makes a major contribution to the growing literature in the field.

(Studies in Comparative Political Economy and Public Policy)

ANDRÉ LECOURS is an assistant professor in the Department of Political Science at Concordia University.

Studies in Comparative Political Economy and Public Policy

Editors: MICHAEL HOWLETT, DAVID LAYCOCK, STEPHEN MCBRIDE, Simon Fraser University

Studies in Comparative Political Economy and Public Policy is designed to showcase innovative approaches to political economy and public policy from a comparative perspective. While originating in Canada, the series will provide attractive offerings to a wide international audience, featuring studies with local, subnational, cross-national, and international empirical bases and theoretical frameworks.

Editorial Advisory Board

For a list of books published in the series, see p. 365.

EDITED BY ANDRÉ LECOURS

New Institutionalism
Theory and Analysis

UNIVERSITY OF TORONTO PRESS
Toronto Buffalo London

© University of Toronto Press Incorporated 2005
Toronto Buffalo London
Printed in Canada

ISBN 0-8020-3900-6

Printed on acid-free paper

Library and Archives Canada Cataloguing in Publication

New institutionalism : theory and analysis / edited by André Lecours.

Includes bibliographical references.
ISBN 0-8020-3900-6

1. Political sociology.   2. Social institutions.   I. Lecours, André, 1972–

JA76.N49 2005   306.2   C2005-900162-3

University of Toronto Press acknowledges the financial assistance to its publishing program of the Canada Council for the Arts and the Ontario Arts Council.

University of Toronto Press acknowledges the financial support for its publishing activities of the Government of Canada through the Book Publishing Industry Development Program (BPIDP).

Contents

Acknowledgments

I would like to thank Linda Cardinal for having invited me, in early 2001, to edit a special issue of the journal *Politique et Sociétés* on new institutionalism. It is this invitation, along with discussions with Miriam Smith, that gave me the idea for this book.

Thank you to the two anonymous reviewers who read the first version of this collection. Their comments were most helpful.

I want to acknowledge the financial contribution of the Faculty of Arts and Science of Concordia University and the Social Sciences and Humanities Research Council of Canada.

Special thanks go to my wife Natasha, whose help and support was needed for the realization of the project.

AL

Contributors

Daniel Béland is assistant professor of sociology at the University of Calgary. A political sociologist studying state-building and comparative social policy, he is the author of *Une Sécurité libérale?* as well as numerous articles in scholarly journals among them *West European Politics, Journal of Public Policy, Policy and Politics, Canadian Journal of Sociology,* and *Journal of Social Policy.*

Linda Cardinal is professor of political science at the University of Ottawa, where she holds the University of Ottawa Research Chair on la Francophonie and Public Policy. From 2002 to 2004, she held the Craig Dobbin Chair in Canadian Studies at University College Dublin (Ireland). She has published widely on linguistic minorities as well as on issues of identity and citizenship in Canada. Author of *Chroniques d'une vie politique mouvementée: L'Ontario francophone de 1986 à 1996,* she is the co-editor of *From Subjects to Citizens: A Hundred Years of Citizenship in Australia and Canada.* From 2001 to 2004, she was the editor of *Politique et Sociétés,* the journal of the *Société québécoise de science politique.*

Alexandra Dobrowolsky is associate professor of political science at Saint Mary's University. She is the author of *The Politics of Pragmatism: Women, Representation and Constitutionalism in Canada* and *Women Making Constitutions: New Politics and Comparative Perspectives* (with Vivien Hart). She has written numerous articles and chapters relating to issues of representation, citizenship, mobilization, social policy, and democracy.

Mamoudou Gazibo is assistant professor of political science at Université de Montréal. He is the co-author of *La politique comparée, fondements, enjeux et approches théoriques* and the author of several articles on new institutionalism, conflicts, and democratization in Sub-saharian Africa. He has been awarded grants from the Fonds Québécois de la recherche sur la société et la culture (FQRSC), the Agence universitaire de la francophonie, and the Social Sciences and Humanities Research Council of Canada (SSHRC). Currently he is working on the electoral-management bodies of West African new democracies.

Siobhán Harty is assistant director, Social Policy Directorate, Policy and Strategic Direction Branch, Social Development Canada (SDC). Previous to this she was a lecturer in the Department of International Politics, University of Wales, Aberystwyth, where her teaching and research areas were nationalism, citizenship, and European politics. Her work on nationalism and citizenship has been published in *Citizenship Studies, Law and History Review, Comparative Politics*, and the *Canadian Journal of Political Science*, and as chapters in several books. She is the co-author (with Michael Murphy) of *In Defence of Multinational Citizenship* and winner (with Michael Murphy) of the 2004 Legal Dimensions Initiative on Law and Citizenship.

Luc Juillet is associate professor of political science and associate director of the School of Political Studies at the University of Ottawa. His research focuses mainly on issues of environmental policy, democratic governance, and Canadian political institutions. His work has been published in several edited volumes and scholarly journals, including *Society and Natural Resources, Interventions économiques, Government Information Quarterly*, and *Economie et Solidarité*.

André Lecours is assistant professor of political science at Concordia University, Montreal. His primary research interests are nationalism, institutionalist theory, and West European politics. His articles have appeared in various scholarly journals, among them *Nationalism and Ethnic Politics, Space and Polity, Canadian Journal of Political Science, Journal of Multilingual and Multicultural Development, National Identities, International Negotiation*, and *Regional and Federal Studies*.

Hudson Meadwell is associate professor of political science at McGill University. He writes primarily on nations and nationalism. He is the editor (with Axel van den Berg) of *Rationality and the Social Sciences*, and has contributed recent papers to *Studies on Voltaire in the Eighteenth Century* (2003) and *The Myth of the Sacred: The Court and Constitutional Politics in Canada* (edited by Patrick James, Donald Abelson, and Michael Lusztig).

Éric Montpetit is assistant professor of political science at Université de Montréal. His work is on the development of environmental and biotechnological policy in North America and Europe. He is the author of *Misplaced Distrust*, which was selected as a finalist for the 2004 Donner Prize for the best Canadian book in public policy. He has published articles in *World Politics, Governance*, the *Journal of European Public Policy, Comparative Political Studies, Canadian Public Policy*, and *Lien social et politiques*.

Csaba Nikolenyi is assistant professor of political science at Concordia University. His research interests include the causes and consequences of institutional design and party politics in new and non-western democracies, with the focus of his current work being India as well as the post-Communist states of East Central Europe. His articles have appeared in *Party Politics, Canadian Journal of Political Science, Japanese Journal of Political Science*, and *Communist and Post-Communist Studies*.

Jeremy Paltiel is associate professor of political science at Carleton University. He specializes in the politics, government, and foreign policies of Asia (China and Japan) and the politics of development. His published work includes articles in *The China Quarterly* and *The Journal of Chinese Law*, as well as a chapter contributed to *Confucianism and Human Rights* (edited by Weiming Tu and William Theodore de Bary).

Norrin M. Ripsman is associate professor of political science at Concordia University. His primary research interests include the domestic sources of foreign security policy in democratic states, postwar peacemaking, constructing regional stability, and the political economy of national security. He is the author of *Peacemaking by Democracies: The Effect of State Autonomy on the Post–World-War Settlements* and a co-editor (with Jean-Marc F. Blanchard and Edward D. Mansfield) of *Power and the Purse: Economic Statecraft, Interdependence, and International Conflict*.

Denis Saint-Martin is associate professor of political science at Université de Montréal where he teaches public policy and administration. In 2004, he was Fulbright Scholar at the Kennedy School of Government, Harvard University. He is currently on leave to work as senior policy adviser to the Prime Minister of Canada. He has published numerous articles and books in the field of public management, governance, and political ethics. One of his books, *Building the New Managerialist State* (Oxford, re-edited in 2004) won the U.S. Academy of Management Best Book Award in 2002. His new book, *Governance and Ethics in Anglo-Saxon Democracies* (co-edited with Frederick Thompson), will be published in the United States in 2005 by Oxford/Elsevier Press.

Miriam Smith is professor of political studies at Trent University. Her areas of interest are Canadian and comparative politics, particularly social movements and lesbian and gay politics in Canada. She is the author of *Lesbian and Gay Rights in Canada*, as well as a number of articles and book chapters, and co-editor of *New Trends in Canadian Federalism*.

Der-yuan Maxwell Wu is assistant professor in the Department of Public Policy and Administration at National Chi Nan University, Puli, Taiwan. His research focuses on international relations, new institutionalism, public policy, and methodology. His doctoral dissertation, completed at Carleton University and entitled 'Institutional Development and Adaptability: Canada, Taiwan and the Social Construction of "One China,"' is currently being revised for publication.

NEW INSTITUTIONALISM:
THEORY AND PRACTICE

1

New Institutionalism: Issues and Questions

ANDRÉ LECOURS

Renewed attention to institutions in political science over the past ten to fifteen years is a trend that has been widely recognized, discussed, and debated. This effort to emphasize the theoretical importance of institutions, succinctly expressed by slogans such as 'bringing the state back in' and 'structuring politics,' typically is associated with a school that has come to be known as new institutionalism.[1] New institutionalists have made the case for giving institutions analytical primacy, but substantial disagreements remain over how institutional analysis should be carried out. New institutionalism has its critics. Some have suggested that it suffers from theoretical and conceptual confusion, lacks explanatory power, or simply represents nothing new in the discipline.[2] These debates have involved primarily American scholars. This is hardly surprising since the development of new institutionalism finds its roots in the particular trajectory of political science in the United States. Institutions were marginalized in American political science during the 1960s and 1970s because of their association with a formal-legal style of scholarship, retrospectively dubbed 'old institutionalism,' which was criticized for being descriptive, a-theoretical and parochial. Society-centred approaches came to be seen as more likely to yield generalizations and enable comparisons. Specifically, and in the context of the behaviouralist movement, institutions were seen as being anathema to deductive logic, quantification, and grand theorizing. Thus, a focus on institutions was criticized as contrary to the good and proper study of political science; indeed, contrary to the scientific study of politics. In reaction to this new orthodoxy in U.S. political science, the new institutionalist movement emerged and, as a consequence, engaged American academics in particular.[3] Early new institutionalists focused on the United States: its social policies,[4] economic policies,[5] union politics,[6] and so forth.

Of course, new institutionalism also appeals to political scientists elsewhere. Europeans have made significant contributions to its literature.[7] In the European case, new institutionalism embodies continuity rather than rupture. European political science never experienced a struggle to 'bring back the state' because the state had never been abandoned.[8] Thus, new institutionalism for European scholars tends to stem from its closeness with their own political science tradition.

But what about Canadian political scientists? They have not been heard very much in the debates surrounding new institutionalism, nor have they been particularly likely to explicitly refer to this perspective when conducting their empirical investigations despite the fact that most of them are familiar with it.[9] The nature of the Canadian political science tradition probably contributes to explain this situation. Institutions have generally been taken seriously in this tradition which, despite having never fully taken the behavioural turn, had its own theoretical aspirations. Arguably more theoretically minded than its European counterpart but sceptical towards the possibility and desirability of formulating nomothetic statements devoid of institutional references, Canadian political science may be, generally speaking, too close to new institutionalism to view it as something different than current practice. The flip side of this coin is that Canadian political scientists are in a unique position to contribute to the theoretical debate on the place of institutions in political science or, in other words, to discuss new institutionalism and to think of novel ways of using the approach.[10]

This does not mean that there is a distinct Canadian version of new institutionalism the way there may be a separate French school, for example.[11] Much like their American colleagues, Canadian new institutionalists hold a diversity of perspectives on institutions. Nevertheless, it can be said that new institutionalism in Canada tends to be historical institutionalism, whereas in the United States it is about evenly divided between the rational choice and historical streams.

Canadian scholars have, independently of their particular perspective, a contribution to make to the new institutionalist literature in political science. The objective of this book is to offer them an opportunity to make this contribution. The authors are not, for the most part, specialists of Canadian politics, although some of them have drawn from Canada as an empirical case study. All of the contributors are scholars working in Canada and/or Canadian-trained. They represent a variety of specializations, empirical interests, and theoretical inclinations – some perhaps more historical, some more sociological, and others more rationalist. The authors were not chosen to reflect or build a specific perspective, or to articulate a Canadian version of the new institutionalism. They were simply asked to think creatively about institutions and institutionalist theory in political science in order to fully take advantage of their particular expertise.

A significant feature of this book is that the contributions to it cover virtually all of the main fields within political science. This is significant because initially the presence in political science of new institutionalism was felt in the area of public policy analysis and, in the case of rational choice institutionalism, in the study of American legislative bodies. Indeed, these trends still hold true today despite the fact that the new institutionalist perspective is used by an increasing number of comparative politics specialists. In this context, this book adds an element of diversity to the literature on new institutionalism. In addition to offering cutting-edge research in the area of public policy through discussions of social learning and policy networks, the book tackles traditional comparative politics issues such as nationalism, democratic transitions and party systems from a new institutionalist perspective and examines new institutionalism in light of Canadian political science. In this book new institutionalism confronts international relations, discussing institutionalist trends in this field and exploring possibilities for empirical applications.[12] This is something of a rarity, considering the disciplinary divide in political science between international relations and comparative politics / public policy. This book would seem to suggest – by example – that one of the contributions of new institutionalism could be to break down intradisciplinary walls by engaging all political scientists in a debate over the place of institutions in political analysis.

Finally, this book wrestles with the 'big questions' that accompany new institutionalism. As a research program, new institutionalism pushes certain types of questions onto the agenda of political science. The questions themselves, of course, are not new; rather they tend to involve classic debates: What are institutions? What is their impact on action? How are institutions formed and transformed? What methodological and epistemological positions best suit institutional analysis? New institutionalists may not have been the first to formulate these questions but they are giving them renewed importance. In addition, new institutionalism often has some original answers to these questions, or, at least, poses them in a new and different way. At the same time, new institutionalism rarely offers coherent perspectives as it struggles with the very issues it raises. Internal diversity represents a major dimension of the debates that follow.

What Are Institutions?

The question of definition inevitably comes up with new institutionalism. Society-centred approaches are not as acutely confronted with it, because their analytical leverage rests on individuals, groups, classes, gender categories, social movements, or some other realm of civil society. New institutionalism argues that political analysis is best conducted through a focus on institutions or, more specifically, when starting off with institutions. In this context, it becomes important to know exactly what institutions are. This issue was not problematic, or indeed problematized, by the 'old institutionalism': institutions were material structures. They were constitutions, cabinets, parliaments, bureaucracies, courts, armies, federal or autonomy arrangements, and in some instances, party systems. In other words, institutions referred to the state or, more exactly to 'government.' As far as society-centred approaches even think of institutions, that is also the way they are usually conceptualized, although more often implicitly rather than explicitly, everything else being considered societal.

This materialist definition is accepted by great many new institutionalists. In their book entitled *Structuring Politics*, Steinmo et al. spoke of electoral rules, party systems, the structure of relationships between branches of government, and trade unions.[13] This is close to the strict materialist definition articulated by the 'old institutionalism,' although trade unions and, to a lesser extent political parties, would probably have been considered societal organizations. But this position is not shared by all new institutionalists. Rational choice institutionalists depart somewhat from this definition by focusing more squarely on the 'rules of the political game,' which tend to be associated with material structures but in themselves represent less tangible parameters. For many rational choice institutionalists, the important question is not so much what institutions are but what they represent: an equilibrium.[14]

A more significant departure from the materialist definition consists in conceptualizating institutions in terms of norms and values.[15] This was the avenue chosen by March and Olsen in their book, *Rediscovering Institutions*, where they defined institutions as collections of interrelated rules and routines.[16] The meaning of institutions was, therefore, contested from the very first days of the new institutionalist movement, and it still is. Following March and Olsen, sociological institutionalists go the furthest in defining institutions in a non-materialist fashion, when they speak of beliefs, values, and cognitive scripts.[17] From this perspective, institutions can be seen as 'mythic' in the sense that they internalize, as they are formed, elements of the cultural and normative contexts.[18] Historical institutionalists are generally closer to the view that institutions are formal structures, although some have brought ideas into their framework.[19] Typically, historical institutionalists tend to view ideas in terms of norms and values whose importance are a function of the material institutions from which they emanate, while sociological institutionalists conceptualize them as cognitive frameworks separate from formal structures.[20]

The issue of definition is crucial. Kathleen Thelen is right in saying that the most fundamental divide within the new institutionalism features the materialist versus the normative or ideational views of institutions.[21] Of course, there is something to be said for both types of definition. The normative or ideational definition responds to a standard criticism of new institutionalism: the idea that a focus on formal structures leads to a narrow and simplistic perspective on politics. It can be argued that this definition is more likely than the materialist one to produce analyses offering a multidimensional treatment of politics. Thus, normative or ideational definitions counter, at least partly, objections relating to what new institutionalism ignores. The materialist definition has the advantage of analytical clarity because it involves an ontology where institutions and society are more clearly distinct. This is not to say that state structures and other material institutions are not shaped by society, but that their existence is not as dependent upon a society-based mechanism of institutional reproduction as culture or ideas. Indeed, the normative or ideational definition paints a picture in which state and society are really close, even almost indistinguishable, and in which the ontological line, which is apparently central to the analytical position of new institutionalism, becomes blurred. This is problematic if it is seen as diluting the logic of new institutionalism. Extending the notion of institutions beyond formal structures – and this is where this debate within new institutionalism becomes significant for political science as a whole – may serve to bridge the gap between institutionalist approaches (in the traditional materialist sense) and approaches emphasizing norms, values, culture, and ideas.

Institutions and Action

The central theoretical argument of new institutionalism is that institutions shape action.[22] New institutionalists argue that theorizing in political science must take into account that action does not occur in an institutional vacuum. In emphasizing the theoretical importance of institutions, new institutionalists reject two perspectives on the relationship between institutions and action. The first takes institutions to be a reflection of societal forces, whatever their exact nature (socio-political, economic, cultural, ideological, and so on). This view is disputed because it depicts institutions as 'neutral,' adjusting mechanically to changes in society so as to continually embody the current balance of power or cultural-ideological landscape and as always being solely at the receiving end of social change. The second perspective that is criticized by new institutionalists considers institutions to be purely instruments that can readily be manipulated by actors. This position is considered inadequate because it is seen as exaggerating the extent to which actors can use institutions to serve their political objectives or, more generally, for purposes of problem-solving. New institutionalists suggest that such a view marginalizes the constraints on action which result from the very existence of institutions. Perhaps more importantly, they argue that both this instrumentalist and the 'societal reflection' perspectives ignore the possibility that institutions themselves can have effects on political outcomes. New institutionalism puts forward the idea that institutions represent an autonomous force in politics, that their weight is felt on action and outcomes. It suggests that political analysis is best served by taking institutions as the starting point. Or, methodologically speaking, new institutionalism advocates using institutions as independent or, at least, key intervening variables.

In adopting such a position, new institutionalists inevitably pose the question of structure and agency. New institutionalism is arguably the approach to politics that currently engages most explicitly with this dilemma and, in this context, has considerable influence in the way this debate is restructured and re-articulated in political science. At the broadest level, new institutionalism gives the discipline of political science a 'structuralist turn' by focusing on the impact of institutions on action, rather than the other way around. More specifically, new institutionalism raises three types of questions that relate to the issue of structure and agency. These are: What are the mechanisms through which institutions shape action? What is the extent of the weight of institutions on agents? What is the depth of institutional influence on political processes, or put in other words, is the weight of institutions felt only on strategies or also on preferences?

These three questions are not answered in the same way by all new institutionalists. The issue of how institutions affect agency is approached in two different ways. The first emphasizes path dependency, which at the broadest level, 'refers to the causal relevance of preceding stages in a temporal sequence.'[23] Path dependency is the idea that once institutions are formed, they take on a life of their own and drive political processes. From this particular perspective, most often associated with historical institutionalism, when an event occurs is as important as what this event is. The concept of path dependency, more specifically, involves the idea that 'once a country or a region has started down a track, the costs of reversal are very high. There will be other choice points, but the entrenchments of certain institutional arrangements obstruct an easy reversal of the initial choice.'[24] Path dependency, thus, involves not only an analytical focus on institutions but contingency and unpredictability, as well. Indeed, institutions really have a logic of their own, and therefore, their creation and development result in consequences unplanned for and unforeseen by political actors.[25]

A second way that new institutionalists approach the issue of how institutions affect agency is from the perspective that institutions shape action because they offer opportunities for action and impose constraints. This perspective, stressed first and foremost by rational choice institutionalists (although not ignored by historical institutionalists), suggests that the weight of institutions is felt on outcomes in so far as that weight affects individual and collective decisions. In this context, the theoretical importance of institutions stems from their mediating effect on the calculations of actors, and new institutionalism becomes an 'institutional incentives'[26] or a 'choice-within-constraints' approach.[27]

An interesting framework that is inspired by rational choice institutionalism is Fritz Scharpf's actor-centred institutionalism.[28] For Scharpf, the analytical consideration of institutions serves to reduce reliance on assumptions on the part of the researcher. Actor-centred institutionalism features constellations of actors, that is, players with specific capabilities, perceptions, and preferences whose interactions follow different patterns, or modes, depending on the institutional setting. Rational choice institutionalism has also inspired other analytical frameworks, for example, those featuring the concept of 'veto points' or 'veto players.'[29] Veto players are actors whose approval, by virtue of a particular institutional configuration, is necessary for bringing about change. Their existence is recognized by all involved, which means that veto points or players mould and shape actors' strategies.

The second question, concerning the extent of the weight of institutions on agency – or the level of structuralism involved in institutional analysis – is also discussed in at least two different ways. New institutionalists more rationalist in their perspective on the nature of the relationship between institutions and agents argue that political processes are really driven by actors. They argue that institutions represent a context for action rather than an autonomous force per se. Path dependency suggests that institutions have a more overwhelming influence and that the autonomy of actors may be severely limited by the logic of institutional development and reproduction.[30]

Structuralism appears to be even stronger when institutions are conceptualized in terms of ideas, culture, and norms, as in the case of sociological institutionalism and some versions of historical institutionalism, because ideas, culture, and norms are internalized by actors.[31] James March and Johan Olsen[32] were central figures in launching the new institutionalist movement. They have developed powerful arguments about structure and agency, in which they contend that behaviour is driven by elements other than utility calculations, which include internalized principles and values, cultural features, identity, and habit. To the 'logic of consequences,' where actors behave in accordance with expected results, they substitute the 'logic of appropriateness,' where actors behave so as to conform to existing rules or values. Rationality itself is viewed, not only as 'bounded,'[33] but as constructed by the cultural environment.[34] Mark Granovetter has expressed a similar idea with his concept of 'embeddedness,' borrowed from Karl Polanyi,[35] which holds that action is shaped not merely by the institutional context but embedded in it.[36] Consequently, actors may not even be able to conceive of alternatives to their usual behaviour.[37] This sociological institutionalism situates action within such a very broad societal context that some have argued that it comes close to cultural theory.[38]

The issue of the depth of institutional influence ties into the first two questions. For the more rationalist-minded new institutionalists, the impact of institutions is felt strictly on strategies. The interests and preferences of actors are formed independently of the specific institutional environment; they follow a logic of power maximization. In other words, the formation of preferences and the definition of objectives occur, in analytical terms, before any institutional weight is felt. The question of preference formation, therefore, remains unanswered. This has led some scholars to suggest borrowing from sociological institutionalism for a theory of the origins of preferences.[39] From a sociological institutionalist perspective, as well as from a historical institutionalist one, institutions affect not only strategies and interests, but also patterns of relationships between actors,[40] preferences, objectives, identities,[41] and indeed, the very existence of actors. From this angle, institutions do not simply represent constraints or embody opportunities for action; institutions are central markers in the process of preference formation. Hence, institutions are involved in every dimension of politics, and they shape political processes every step of the way.

New institutionalists do not all conceptualize the interactions between structure and agency in the same way. However, there seems to be one common aspect of their treatment of the relationship between institutions and action: the emphasis is on a dynamic of continuity rather than change. New institutionalists typically suggest that actors adapt their behaviour to existing institutional frameworks, thereby legitimizing institutions and favouring institutional continuity. As a consequence, the possibilities for change may be limited because this institutional continuity produces repetitive behaviour on the part of actors. From this perspective, institutional change becomes a precondition for political change.

Institutional Change

New institutionalists are more comfortable in explaining continuity rather than change because the logic of their approach focuses on institutional reproduction rather than transformation. New institutionalists argue that institutions embody the societal situation prevailing at the time of their birth because, once created, they have autonomy from society and their development follows a largely independent pattern. Moreover, institutions tend to generate 'positive feedback' or 'increasing returns' which act as mechanisms of reproduction.[42] As a result, institutions adapt imperfectly and with much delay to whatever occurs in society, and they resist change.

To account for change, institutional and otherwise, new institutionalists use several different arguments. One focuses on exogenous shocks. This approach suggests that international events (such as wars and global financial crises), in disturbing the unfolding of domestic processes, break the cycle of institutional reproduction, and thereby open up opportunities for – if not force – institutional transformations and political change. With this explanation, the logic of path dependency, positive feedback, and re-enforcing mechanisms does not have to be altered, but change occurs as a result of a force which is not incorporated into the theoretical perspective per se. Consequently, the notion of exogenous shock questions the ability of new institutionalism to handle change. It also rests on the debatable empirical argument that domestic change always has external roots.

Some new institutionalists, primarily those of the rational choice stream, have adopted a more utilitarian view of institutional change. They suggest that 'institutions are demanded because they enhance the welfare of rational actors'[43] and are transformed when they become dysfunctional or yield sub-optimal results. In this conceptualization, institutional change is the result not of a mechanism of adjustment that is endogenous to the institutions, but rather the product of a strategic decision on the part of actors. For example, Elinor Ostrom has argued that the 'tragedy of the commons' or 'common-pool resource' situations often trigger the creation of institutions for the purposes of securing commitments on the part of actors and enforcing rules.[44] Rationalists would say that the source of institutional change is to be found in the institutions themselves, more specifically, in their dysfunctional or sub-optimal character; however, change in the institutional environment is really linked to actors.

Other new institutionalists, mainly sociological institutionalists, tend to view institutional change in terms of convergence. The key idea here is isomorphism, meaning that coexisting institutions, more specifically, institutions in a similar domain, tend to look alike whatever the differences in their immediate environment.[45] DiMaggio and Powell identified three mechanisms that lead to institutional isomorphism: coercion, which involves explicit pressures from other institutions, as well as from the cultural environment; mimesis, where standardization ensues from uncertainty; and norms, which legitimize autonomy.[46] Institutional isomorphism is coherent with the new institutionalist emphasis on the theoretical importance of institutions because it situates the mechanism of institutional change within the institutions themselves. Isomorphism involves a limited, indeed one-dimensional, perspective on change because it cannot tackle differenti-ation-oriented change.[47] From the sociological institutionalist perspec-tive, this type of institutional transformation is best understood through the concept of legitimacy: institutions do not necessarily crumble when they lose efficiency, as argued by rational choice institu-tionalists, but rather when they no longer are in tune with dominant social and cultural codes.[48] Institutions can, therefore, survive even if they engender sub-optimal outcomes.

An interesting theory of political change has recently been put forth by Robert C. Lieberman,[49] who argues that neither institutionalist nor ideational approaches, on their own, are very effective in accounting for political change because of their bias for stability, regularities, and recurrence. Lieberman suggests that politics might be conceptualized as a set of orders, rather than as a single and coherent political order. Political change could then be viewed as emerging from frictions between these orders. If, as Lieberman does, we can envisage institu-tional and ideational orders, change can be theorized as a mechanism of adjustment between institutions and ideas.[50]

A related approach to change focuses on the discrepancy between an existing sociopolitical situation and the one embodied by an institution or, more generally, by the institutional context; when this discrepancy becomes too great, institutions undergo transformations so as to bring them closer to the current societal reality. This explanation puts the institutional landscape, more specifically its particular historical grounding, at the centre of change, although it departs somewhat from the new institutionalist idea that institutions are autonomous from society. Here, new institutionalists would argue that this autonomy is not complete and that at some point society can force institutional re-arrangements.

Karen Orren and Stephen Skowronek have formulated an 'intercur-rence' approach to change that involves focusing on tensions emanat-ing from the institutions themselves.[51] These historical institutionalists postulate that such tensions necessarily exist because institutions are created in different historical periods and tend to embody the socio-political outlook at the time of their birth. Tension derives from the juxtaposition of various institutions which have distinct, even contra-dictory, patterns of development and reproduction. In other words, institutions grounded in different historical periods and carrying with them different interests and identities coexist uneasily. Here again, a mechanism of adjustment is triggered when the tension becomes too important. From this angle, however, the tension exists within an institutional landscape rather than between institutions and society, and the adjustment emanates from the institutions themselves and not from society.

Historical institutionalism, like its rational choice and sociological counterparts, has a bias in favour of order and stability. It also puts great emphasis on timing and sequences.[52] From this angle, historical institutionalism holds potential for explaining change[53] without having to resort to elements exogenous to the approach, such as external shocks, or to agency. Thus, there is some potential for explaining change without escaping the logic of the approach through a focus on tensions between sets of institutions or between institutional orders and various sociopolitical processes.

Methodological and Epistemological Issues

What are the methodological and epistemological consequences of adopting an approach to politics that centres on institutions? New institutionalism is a theoretical enterprise; its objective is not to describe institutions and how they work but rather to explain political outcomes and make attempts towards generalization. New institutionalism is fundamentally different from previous forms of institutional analysis, namely, the 'old institutionalism,' which were primarily concerned with understanding the workings of institutions. Despite a common aim at generating explanations and building theory, new institutionalists are not united on how to proceed with an institutional analysis[54] and on the extent to which the formulation of general propositions is possible and desirable.

New institutionalists who conceptualize the impact of institutions on political processes in terms of path dependency, primarily historical institutionalists, typically start their inquiry with empirically directed research questions relating to differences in outcomes through time and/or space. From the spatial/cross-national perspective, the idea is to explain why common events, processes or socioeconomic situations lead to different outcomes in different countries or regions. For example, why do similar social policies across states produce contentious politics only in some cases? From a temporal angle, the objective is to

explain why an unfolding process yields a certain outcome at a particular point in time. For example, why has a revolution happened when
it did? To explain these puzzles, historical institutionalists look at differences between institutional frameworks which are grounded in
time-specific national, sub-national or continental history. In this context, the generalizations put forward are of the 'middle-range' variety,
that is, they tend to be bound by spatial and temporal parameters.

As a matter of methodology, historical institutionalists employ techniques of periodization, that is, they divide history into 'slices.' Evan
Lieberman has usefully distinguished between four such stategies[55]:
With the institutional origins strategy scholars compare periods before
and after the creation of an institution. With the institutional change
strategy the focus is on the moments that correspond to substantial
and discrete changes in the institutions. The exogenous shock strategy
involves comparing periods before and after the occurrence of a major
international event. The rival cause strategy examines continuity in the
context of non-institutional change.

For new institutionalists who view institutions from a more rationalist perspective, the methodological process is deductive. Outcomes are
considered to be puzzling when they do not appear to flow logically
from rational behaviour or, in other words, when they do not conform
to the expectations specified by a general theory. Institutions are introduced to provide a link between rationality and the puzzling or surprising outcome. The argument here is that the outcome can be explained in
terms of rational behaviour if it is recognized that institutions affect the
strategic calculations of actors. This does not imply that in political analysis to make room for institutions limits the range of theories. On
the contrary, because here institutions are conceptualized as strategic
constraints, rather than historical structures, they do not obstruct the
elaboration of a general theory. Methodologically, rational choice institutionalists seek to model strategic micro-level behaviour.[56] Using this
method, they look for settings, such as legislatures, in which there are
'coherent strategic actors operating in well-bounded contexts where
choices are clearly identifiable and payoffs relatively transparent.'[57]

The different positions within new institutionalism, of course, reflect
a larger debate in political science. It is not surprising that rational
choice institutionalists contend that the more historically minded institutionalists produce 'configurative studies' which they find too heavy
on empirical (historical) details. Rational choice institutionalists themselves are criticized for sacrificing nuance in producing theories that

are at a very high level of abstraction. Some have suggested that this dichotomy is essentially false and that, on the contrary, new institutionalists increasingly are building bridges between these methodological and epistemological poles.[58] It is true that the two positions tend to be crudely laid and that the new institutionalist literature is currently struggling with this divide. However, it is important to recognize the 'story' of those embracing each of these views: they are not new institutionalists who have decided to follow different methodological/epistemological paths but rather scholars with distinct and well-defined orientations who have developed a theoretical interest for institutions. In other words, methodology and epistemology is as fundamental to their scholarship as the theoretical implications of institutions. This serves to further highlight the diversity within new institutionalism and begs the question of the consequences of this multi-faceted nature.

The Many Faces of New Institutionalism: Implications and Consequences

It is often said that new institutionalism is not a coherent and unified theoretical school but rather that it includes several 'branches' or 'streams' which developed in relative isolation to each other. Typically, three such branches are identified: historical, rational choice, and sociological.[59]

Historical institutionalism emerged as a reaction to behaviouralism. As the branch that can be associated with the idea of path dependency,[60] it views the impact of institutions on action more in terms of unintended consequences than strategic constraints. Historical institutionalism generally uses the notions of external shock or institutional tension to explain institutional change and creation. It produces historically grounded generalizations and middle-range theorizing. Rational choice institutionalism grew out of the work of rational choice theorists who were increasingly emphasizing the importance of institutions in the strategic calculations of actors.[61] It defines institutions in materialist terms, or as rules governing the political game, and views them primarily as offering opportunities and imposing constraints.[62] Institutional change, in this view, occurs when institutions become dysfunctional or yield sub-optimal results, at which point actors make the conscious decision to remodel them. Rational choice institutionalism seeks to produce general theories of politics. Sociological institutionalism arose out of organization theory.[63] Institutions are here defined in terms of norms, values, culture, and ideas.[64] Sociological institutionalism focuses on the cognitive, rather than the historical or strategic, dimension of institutions. Power relationships are entangled in this cognitive institutional web rather than manifested in individual behaviour.[65] Institutions are internalized by actors. In other words, institutions shape the perceptions of actors and through this mechanism lead to behaviour that favours the reproduction of institutions.

To some the new institutionalist world is even more complex than described so far. B. Guy Peters submits that there are seven streams within new institutionalism.[66] In addition to the historical, rational choice, and sociological, he sees another four: the normative, empirical, interest representation, and international branches. The normative institutionalism of Peters is subsumed by other authors under sociological institutionalism. However, Peters argues that the normative institutionalism, which he associates with the work of James March and Johan Olsen, stresses the normative aspect of institutions while sociological institutionalism emphasizes their cognitive dimension.[67] The empirical branch, according to Peters, focuses heavily on the consequences of different systems of government (parliamentary versus presidential) in the hope of finding out which 'works better.'[68] The institutionalism of interest representation takes political parties and interest groups as its institutional variables. Finally, Peters presents an international institutionalism, which is simply institutionalist theory applied to international relations, primarily through the notion of regimes.

Despite their differences, the 'traditional' and the Peters typologies make a similar argument, that is, that there is great diversity within new institutionalism. This heterogeneity is disturbing for many scholars, both for those looking at new institutionalism 'from the outside' and for new institutionalists themselves. Reflecting on new institutionalism involves some consideration of its branches. In this context, two questions tend to come up. First is the issue of a 'theoretical core.' Can it be said that the different branches of new institutionalism share a theoretical core? Or, as Peters has asked, is there really only one or are there many new institutionalisms? Second is a concern regarding the possibility of bringing all these different streams closer together. Is a synthesis possible? In other words, do the streams have enough in common to be merged as one single approach?

Most would argue that, indeed, new institutionalism has a theoretical core.[69] Their argument is simple. All three streams (or seven, for Peters) see institutions as the single most important variable in explaining politics. It is true that historical, rational choice, and sociological institutionalists alike give great theoretical importance to institutions and hold the position that political analysis is best conducted when starting off with institutions. Is sharing this position enough to constitute a theoretical core, despite the fact that the streams have different, sometimes divergent, views on the nature of institutions, their impact on action and on the processes that lead to their creation, transformation, and reproduction? In the broadest sense, yes, it is. At the same time, sharing a theoretical core need not mean that there is one single new institutionalism. It is more accurate to say that there exists many new institutionalisms, and not primarily because of differences on specific theoretical points relating to institutions. More fundamental is the fact that the three main streams of new institutionalism are located in distinct intellectual traditions: traditional-historical political science, rational choice theory, and sociology. As such, institutions represent a *meeting point* in the evolution of these traditions, not their full convergence. From a broad perspective, which considers everything that underpins these intellectual traditions, institutions represent too narrow a common basis to speak of one single approach.

Several authors have recently suggested that the differences between the branches of new institutionalism, more particularly historical and rational choice institutionalism, are not as important as they appear.[70] This exercise serves to advocate, implicitly if not explicitly, a greater dialogue, perhaps even a synthesis, between the branches.[71] However, if one recognizes that the various versions of new institutionalism are grounded in fundamentally different intellectual traditions, the idea of a meaningful dialogue, and even more that of a synthesis, appears greatly problematic.[72] These traditions embody different methodological and epistemological positions, as we have already discussed, but also distinct ontologies and assumptions about politics.[73] Rational choice institutionalism is an extension of rational choice theory.[74] It cannot, therefore, stray from rationalism, voluntarism, and an ontological emphasis on actors.[75] For rational choice institutionalists, an institution is simply an equilibrium, that is, 'a regular behavior pattern sustained by mutual expectations about the actions that others will take.'[76] In discussing 'new institutionalism,' although they are really talking about rational choice institutionalism, Ingram and Clay contend that a fundamental behavioural assertion is that 'actors pursue interests by making choices within constraints.'[77] Meanwhile, the very existence of historical institutionalism stems from a reaction to the popularity and perceived 'excesses' of behaviouralism. Drawing from traditional, some would say Weberian political science, historical institutionalism is a rejection of the notion that politics is the end result of sequences of strategic decision-making. Instead, historical institutionalists prefer to view politics as the complex set of relationships between actors and ontologically prominent institutions and, thus, the realm of the contingent and the unplanned. Sociological institutionalism is grounded in organization theory and consequently has very little rationalism and voluntarism. The focus is on the routinizing psychological effects of common cultural frameworks. Sociological institutionalists would contend that where you stand (in terms of preferences, interests, positions, and finally, action) usually depends on where you sit (the normative environment and prevalent cognitive scripts). Sociological institutionalism is not very compatible with rational choice assumptions,[78] which makes the theoretical link between these two streams of new institutionalism very tenuous indeed.[79]

The debate among these various streams of new institutionalism is important because, as Thomas Koelble has stated, 'it goes to the heart of the basic problem of social science: how do we explain the things people do? [...] How much weight ought to be given to the individual and to the institutional context within which decisions are made and to the larger environmental factors such as culture, social norms, and conventions?'[80] Nevertheless, the absence of unity within new institutionalism and the obstacles in the way of any effort towards a synthesis should not be deplored. There are different ways of conducting institutional analysis, and all of them bring their own insight to the study of politics. Indeed, this diversity of new institutionalism is what gives it tremendous scope and capacity to add to our understanding of a great many very different processes. Moreover the fact that new institutionalism is plural, heterogenous and, in all likelihood, irreducibly differentiated, has not prevented it from carrying a strong theoretical message and, as demonstrated by the considerable literature and interest it has generated, from proving quite influential in political science.

The remaining chapters of this book are a testament to this influence of new institutionalism. The various parts highlight how the new institutionalist approach structures theoretical discussions of many key questions in political science (Part 1); how it can provide a reading of the scholarship in Canadian political science (Part 2); and how it features into the sub-fields of comparative politics (Part 3), public policy (Part 4) and international relations (Part 5).

Notes

1 Peter Evans, Dietrich Rueschemeyer, and Theda Skocpol, *Bringing the State Back In* (Cambridge: Cambridge University Press, 1985); Sven Steinmo et al., *Structuring Politics: Historical Institutionalism in Comparative Perspective* (Cambridge: Cambridge University Press, 1992). For a more recent discussion, see Paul Pierson and Theda Skocpol, 'Historical Institutionalism in Contemporary Political Science,' in Ira Katznelson and Helen V. Milner (eds.), *Political Science: State of the Discipline* (New York: Norton, 2002), 693–721.
2 Michael J. Gorges, 'New institutionalism and the EU,' *West European Politics* 24 (2001), 152–68; Fiona Ross, 'Forty Years of 'Muddling Through': Some Lessons for the New Institutionalism,' *Swiss Political Science Review*, 6 (2000), 41–4; Matthew S. Kraatz and Edward J. Zajac, 'Exploring the Limits of the New Institutionalism: The Causes and Consequences of Illegitimate Organizational Change,' *American Sociological Review*, 61 (1996), 812–36; Gabriel Almond, 'The Return to the State,' *American Political Science Review*, 82 (1988), 853–74.
3 On the emergence of new institutionalism, see David Brian Robertson, 'The Return to History in American Political Science,' *Social Science History*, 17 (1993), 1–36.
4 Ann Shola Orloff and Theda Skocpol, 'Why Not Equal Protection? Explaining the Politics of Social Spending in Britain, 1900–1911, and the United States, 1880s–1920,' *American Sociological Review*, 49 (1984), 726–50; Ann Shola Orloff, 'Gender in Early U.S. Social Policy,' *Journal of Policy History*, 3 (1991), 249–81.
5 Elizabeth Sanders, 'Industrial Concentration, Sectional Competition, and Antitrust Politics in America, 1880–1914,' *Studies in American Political Development*, 1 (1986), 142–214; Donald Brand, *Corporatism and the Rule of Law: A Study of the National Recovery Administration* (Ithaca: Cornell University Press, 1988).
6 Victoria C. Hattam, 'Economic Visions and Political Strategies: American Labor and the State,' *Studies in American Political Development*, 4 (1990), 82–129.
7 For example, Ellen M. Immergut, *Health Politics: Ideas and Institutions in Western Europe* (Cambridge: Cambridge University Press, 1992); Colin Hay and Daniel Wincott, 'Structure, Agency and Historical Institutionalism,'

Political Studies, 46 (1998), 951–7; Bruno Théret, 'Institutions et institution-nalismes: vers une convergence des conceptions de l'institution?,' in Michèle Tallard, Bruno Théret, and Didier Uri (eds.), *Innovations institution-nelles et territoires* (Paris: L'Harmattan, 2000), 25–58.

8 See Jack Hayward, 'Between France and Universality: From Implicit to Explicit Comparison,' in Hans Daalder (ed.), *Comparative European Politics: The Story of a Profession* (London: Pinter, 1997), 147.

9 There are, of course, exceptions. See, e.g., Jane Jenson, 'Les réformes des ser-vices de garde pour jeunes enfants en France et au Québec: une analyse his-torico-institutionnaliste,' *Politique et sociétés*, 17 (1998), 183–216; Denis Saint-Martin, 'The New Managerialism and the Policy Influence of Consultants in Government: An Historical-Institutionalist Analysis of Britain, Canada and France,' *Governance: An International Journal of Public Policy and Administra-tion*, 11 (1998), 319–56; Siobhán Harty, 'The Institutional Foundations of Sub-state National Movements,' *Comparative Politics*, 33 (2001), 191–210; André Lecours, 'Regionalism, Cultural Diversity and the State in Spain,' *Journal of Multilingual and Multicultural Development*, 22 (2001), 210–26.

10 A major contribution to the development of new institutionalism in Canada was the work by Michael Atkinson (ed.), *Governing Canada: Institutions and Public Policy* (Toronto: Harcourt Brace Jovanovich, 1993.) I thank an anony-mous reviewer for pointing that out.

11 Bruno Palier and Giuliano Bonoli, 'Phénomènes de *path dependence* et réformes des systèmes de protection sociale,' *Revue française de science poli-tique*, 49 (1999), 399–420; Patrick Hassenteufel and Yves Surel, 'Des poli-tiques publiques comme les autres? Construction de l'objet et outils d'analyse des politiques publiques,' *Politique européenne*, no. 1 (2000), 8–24; Théret, 'Institutions et institutionnalismes.'

12 The field of international relations has its own tradition of institutionalist and structuralist analysis: regime theory, neo-realism, and, arguably, constructivism. However, new institutionalism has rarely been explicitly discussed in regard to international relations. There are two exceptions, both of them from the sociological institutionalism perspective: Martha Finnemore, 'Norms, Culture, and World Politics: Insight from Sociological Institutionalism,' *International Organization*, 50 (1996), 325–47; James G. March and Johan P. Olsen, 'The Institutional Dynamics of International Political Orders,' *International Organization*, 52 (1998), 943–69.

13 Steinmo et al., *Structuring Politics*, 2.

14 See the discussion in Sue E. Crawford and Elinor Ostrom, 'A Grammar of Institutions,' *American Political Science Review*, 89 (1995), 582–3.

15 Donald D. Searing also speaks of roles, that is, 'conceptions of how typical

people in typical positions [...] are expected to behave.' See 'Roles, Rules, and Rationality in the New Institutionalism,' *American Political Science Review*, 85 (1991), 1239.

16 James March and Johan P. Olsen, *Rediscovering Institutions, The Organizational Basis of Politics* (New York: Free Press, 1989), 21.

17 W. Richard Scott, *Institutions and Organizations* (Thousand Oaks: Sage, 2nd ed., 2001).

18 Vivien Lowndes, 'Varieties of New Institutionalism: A Critical Appraisal,' *Public Administration*, 74 (1996), 185.

19 Peter A. Hall, 'Policy Paradigms, Social Learning, and the State: The Case of Economic Policymaking in Britain,' *Comparative Politics*, 25 (1993), 275–96; Judith Goldstein, *Ideas, Interests, and American Trade Policy* (Ithaca: Cornell University Press, 1993).

20 John L. Campbell, 'Institutional Analysis and the Role of Ideas in Political Economy,' *Theory and Society*, 27 (1998), 377–409.

21 Kathleen Thelen, 'Historical Institutionalism in Comparative Politics,' *Annual Review of Political Science*, (1999), 380n12.

22 New institutionalism is reminiscent of the 'political opportunity structure' approach to social movement usually associated with Sidney Tarrow. See, e.g., *Power in Movement* (Cambridge: Cambridge University Press, 1998). See also, Edwin Amenta and Yvonne Zylan, 'It Happened Here: Political Opportunity, the New Institutionalism, and the Townsend Movement,' *American Sociological Review*, 56 (1991), 250–65.

23 Paul Pierson, 'Increasing Returns, Path Dependence, and the Study of Politics,' *American Political Science Review*, 94 (2000), 251–67.

24 Margaret Levi cited in ibid., 252.

25 See Kenneth Dyson, 'EMU, Political Discourse and the Fifth French Republic: Historical Institutionalism, Path Dependency and "Craftsmen" of Discourse,' *Modern and Contemporary France*, 7 (1999), 179–96.

26 Elinor Ostrom, Larry Schroeder, and Susan Wynne, *Institutional Incentives and Sustainable Development: Infrastructure Policies in Perspective* (Boulder: Westview Press, 1993).

27 Paul Ingram and Karen Clay, 'The Choice-within-Constraints New Institutionalism and Implications for Sociology,' *Annual Review of Sociology*, 26 (2000), 525–46.

28 Fritz W. Scharpf, *Games Real Actors Play: Actor-Centered Institutionalism in Policy Research* (Boulder: Westview Press, 1997).

29 George Tsebelis, 'Decision Making in Political Systems: Veto Players in Presidentialism, Parliamentarism, Multicameralism, and Multipartyism,' *British Journal of Political Science*, 25 (1995), 289–315.

30 Simon J. Bulmer, 'New Institutionalism and the Governance of the Single European Market,' *Journal of European and Public Policy*, 5 (1998), 365–86.

31 Julia Black, 'New Institutionalism and Naturalism in Socio-Legal Analysis: Institutionalist Approaches to Regulatory Decision-Making,' *Law and Policy*, 19 (1997), 51–93.

32 'The New Institutionalism: Organizational Factors in Political Life,' *American Political Science Review*, 78 (1984), 734–49; *Rediscovering Institutions: The Organizational Basis of Politics* (New York: Free Press, 1989); *Democratic Governance* (New York: Free Press, 1995).

33 Herbert Simon, *Administrative Behaviour* (Glencoe: Free Press, 1957).

34 Paul J. DiMaggio, 'The New Institutionalisms: Avenues of Collaboration,' *Journal of Institutional and Theoretical Economics*, 154 (1998), 700.

35 Karl Polanyi, *The Great Transformation* (Boston: Beacon, 1944).

36 Mark Granovetter, 'Economic Action and Social Structures: The Problem of Embeddedness,' *American Journal of Sociology*, 3 (1985), 481–510.

37 Thomas A. Koelble, 'The New Institutionalism in Political Science and Sociology,' *Comparative Politics*, 27 (1995), 235.

38 Gunnar Grendstad and Per Selle, 'Cultural Theory and the New Institutionalism,' *Journal of Theoretical Politics*, 7 (1995), 5–27.

39 Ingram and Clay, 'Choice-within-Constraints,' 529. Ingram and Clay point to the work of Walter W. Powell and Paul J. DiMaggio. See *The New Institutionalism in Organizational Analysis* (Chicago: University of Chicago Press, 1991).

40 Hongwu Ouyang, 'The PRC's New Elite Politics: The New Institutionalism Perspective,' *Issues and Studies*, 34 (1998), 1–21.

41 Jeffrey Haydu, 'Workplace Governance, Class Formation, and the New Institutionalism,' *Mobilization: An International Journal*, 3 (1998), 69–88.

42 See Paul Pierson, 'When Effect Becomes Cause: Policy Feedback and Political Change,' *World Politics*, 45 (1993), 595–628; and 'Increasing Returns, Path Dependence, and the Study of Politics.'

43 Robert H. Bates, 'Contra Contractarianism: Some Reflections on the New Institutionalism,' *Politics and Society*, 16 (1988), 393.

44 Elinor Ostrom, *Governing the Commons: The Evolution of Institutions for Collective Action* (Cambridge: Cambridge University Press, 1990).

45 Walter W. Powell and Paul J. DiMaggio, 'The Iron Cage Revisited: Institutional Isomorphism and Collective Rationality in Organizational Fields,' *American Sociological Review*, 48 (1983), 147–60.

46 Ibid., 150–4.

47 An additional criticism of isomorphism is that it does not specify the mechanism of change. See Paul M. Hirsch, 'Sociology without Social Structure:

Neoinstitutional Theory Meets Brave New World,' *American Journal of Sociology*, 102 (1997), 1702–23.

48 Johan P. Olsen, 'Garbage Cans, New Institutionalism, and the Study of Politics,' *American Political Science Review*, 95 (2001), 195.

49 Robert C. Lieberman, 'Ideas, Institutions, and Political Order: Explaining Political Change,' *American Political Science Review*, 96 (2002), 697–712.

50 Ibid., 702.

51 See 'Beyond the Iconography of Order: Notes for a "New Institutionalism,"' in Lawrence C. Dodd and Calvin Jillson (eds.), *The Dynamics of American Politics: Approaches and Interpretation* (Boulder: Westview Press, 1994), 311–30; and 'Institutions and Intercurrence: Theory Building in the Fullness of Time,' in Ian Shapiro and Russell Hardin (eds.), *Nomos XXXVIII Political Order* (New York: New York University Press, 1996), 111–46.

52 Paul Pierson, 'Not Just What, but *When*: Timing and Sequence in Political Processes,' *Studies in American Political Development*, 14 (2000), 72–92.

53 Lieberman, 'Ideas, Institutions, and Political Order,' 704.

54 Philip Ethington and Eileen McDonagh, 'The Eclectic Center of the New Institutionalism: Axes of Analysis in Comparative Perspective,' *Social Science History*, 19 (1996), 467–77.

55 Evan S. Lieberman, 'Causal Inference in Historical Institutional Analysis: A Specification of Periodization Strategies,' *Comparative Political Studies*, 34 (2001), 1017–23.

56 Pierson and Skocpol, 'Historical Institutionalism in Contemporary Political Science,' 716.

57 Ibid.

58 Thelen, 'Historical Institutionalism in Comparative Politics.'

59 See, e.g., Peter A. Hall and Rosemary C.R. Taylor, 'Political Science and the Three New Institutionalisms,' *Political Studies*, 44 (1996), 936–57; Ellen M. Immergut, 'The Theoretical Core of the New Institutionalism,' *Politics and Society*, 26 (1998), 4–34.

60 Paul Pierson, *Dismantling the Welfare State? Reagan, Thatcher, and the Politics of Retrenchment* (Cambridge: Cambridge University Press, 1994); 'The New Politics of the Welfare State,' *World Politics*, 48 (1996), 143–79.

61 George Tsebelis, *Nested Games: Rational Choice in Comparative Politics* (Berkeley: University of California Press, 1989).

62 Barry R. Weingast, 'Rational-Choice Institutionalism,' in Ira Katznelson and Helen V. Milner (eds.), 660–92.

63 Powell and DiMaggio, *The New Institutionalism*.

64 Frank Dobbin, *Forging Industrial Policy: The United States, Britain, and France in the Railway Age* (New York: Cambridge University Press, 1994).

65 Rosa Mulé, 'New Institutionalism: Distilling Some "Hard Core" Proposi-
    tions in the Works of Williamson and March and Olsen,' *Politics*, 19 (1999),
    149.

66 See *Institutional Theory in Political Science: The 'New Institutionalism'* (Lon-
    don: Continuum, 1999).

67 Ibid., 103.

68 The following would probably qualify: Kent Weaver and Bert Rockman
    (eds.), *Do Institutions Matter? Government Capabilities in the United States and
    Abroad* (Washington: Brookings Institution, 1993).

69 Peters, *Institutional Theory*, 149–50; Immergut, 'The Theoretical Core.'

70 Thelen, 'Historical Institutionalism.'

71 See, e.g., Mary C. Brinton and Victor Nee, *The New Institutionalism in Sociol-
    ogy* (New York: Sage, 2001).

72 DiMaggio, 'The New Institutionalisms,' 699.

73 Hay and Wincott, 'Structure, Agency and Historical Institutionalism.'

74 Elinor Ostrom, 'Rational Choice Theory and Institutional Analysis: Toward
    Complementarity,' *American Political Science Review*, 85 (1991), 237–43.

75 Keith Dowding, 'The Compatibility of Behaviouralism, Rational Choice
    and "New Institutionalism,"' *Journal of Theoretical Politics*, 6 (1994), 105–17.

76 Sue E. Crawford and Elinor Ostrom, 'A Grammar of Institutions,' *American
    Political Science Review*, 89 (1995), 583.

77 Ingram and Clay, 'Choice-within-Constraints.'

78 See, e.g., the critique by Jonathan Bendor, Terry M. Moe, and Kenneth W.
    Shotts, 'Recycling the Garbage Can: An Assessment of the Research Pro-
    gram,' *American Political Science Review*, 95 (2001), 169–90.

79 For a different opinion, see Arash Abizadeh, 'Informational Constraints
    and Focal Point Convergence: Theoretical Implications of Plurality-Rule
    Elections for the New Institutionalism,' *Rationality and Society*, 13 (2000),
    99–136.

80 Koelble, 'The New Institutionalism in Political Science and Sociology,'
    231–2.

Part 1

Theoretical Reflections on New Institutionalism

The first part features theoretical discussions of new institutionalism. It tackles questions about the nature of institutions, the process of institutional change, the dynamic of structure-agency relationships, the methodology and epistemology of institutionalist analysis, and the relationship between institutions and other analytical variables and concepts, such as rationality, strategy, interests, identities, and culture.

These contributions are critical of at least some aspects of new institutionalism, namely its vague conceptualization of institutions, its weakness in providing an explanation for change coherent with its own logic, and its poor integration of ideational forces as well as, in the case of historical institutionalism, interest-related considerations. The contributions seek to address these weaknesses by bringing new theoretical insight into the institutionalist framework or by reframing it entirely.

In the first chapter, Daniel Béland suggests that the 1990s have witnessed a reintegration of societal elements into the original institutionalist framework. While he views this intellectual shift has having been positive for historical institutionalism, Béland argues that the approach is still in need of a more complex understanding of the relationship between ideas, interests, and institutions. As an alternative to using culturalism and rational choice theory for integrating ideas and interests with institutionalist analysis, Béland suggests drawing from the work of French sociologist Pierre Bourdieu. Two of Bourdieu's theoretical concepts appear particularly useful: 'field,' which refers to 'an arena of enduring battle for power between social actors,' and 'habitus,' which is the product of a learning process corresponding to the internalization of the field's rules. The 'political field' represents the rules of the political game; it is a highly structured realm (both institutionally and ideationally) that shapes actors' perceptions, preferences and interests. The habitus reflects the field's structure, and links ideas, interests, and institutions to individual behaviour.

In her chapter, Siobhán Harty develops a conceptualization of institutional change from an *institutionalist* perspective. She argues there are two preconditions for institutional change: the loss of legitimacy of existing institutions and the calculations by actors that, in their time horizon, the benefits of institutional change will outweigh the costs. She recognizes that these are not sufficient conditions for institutional change, since actors who consider institutions illegitimate and who calculate that change would benefit them often fail to bring about change. In this context, she argues that two variables could explain change: 'windows of opportunity,' that is, the political context, and resources. Harty invites Canadian scholars to clarify the relationship between these variables, and to develop an institutionalist theory of institutional change, through studies of the country's recent institutional transformations. She leads the way by applying her framework to the cases of aboriginal self-government and judicial activism.

In the next chapter, Hudson Meadwell questions the theoretical distinctiveness of new institutionalism. For Meadwell, historical institutionalism cannot easily be differentiated from non-institutionalist approaches, because its concepts (critical junctures, unintended consequences, path dependency, and so on) are often used by scholars who do not present themselves as institutionalists. Also, Meadwell argues that historical institutionalists rarely specify a particular combination for their analytical focus on structures, cultures, organizations, and time. Moreover, the seemingly more solid argument that historical institutionalism's distinctiveness stems from a conception of preference formation as endogenous to institutions represents a contested statement about ontology. In this context, new institutionalism could be understood simply as an approach that emphasizes constraint; it is therefore not far removed from rational choice theory. Meadwell concludes by suggesting that strategic rationality should be central to political analysis even if one accepts the presence of principled commitments.

2

Ideas, Interests, and Institutions: Historical Institutionalism Revisited

DANIEL BÉLAND

Historical institutionalism is based on the assumption that a historically constructed set of institutional constraints and feedbacks structure the behaviour of political actors and interest groups during the policy-making process.[1] As stated by Theda Skocpol, 'this approach views the polity as the primary locus for action, yet understands political activities, whether carried by politicians or by social groups, as conditioned by institutional configurations of governments and political party systems.'[2] Such a *structural* approach of politics recognizes the autonomy of the political arena while directly taking into account the impact of previously enacted measures on policymaking. In contrast with sociological and rational choice institutionalisms, historical institutionalism focuses on asymmetrical power relations as well as the impact of long-term institutional legacies on policy-making.[3]

The present chapter has two main objectives: studying older and more recent theoretical developments that have favoured a gradual reintegration of societal factors with historical institutionalism; suggesting that Pierre Bourdieu's field theory may contribute to a more coherent incorporation of these factors while providing interesting insights about inequality and actors' preferences. Historical institutionalism, as formulated during the 1980s, could not provide social scientists with a complete explanation concerning the origins and the content of key political decisions. Although keeping the assumption that the political domain has some autonomy from the rest of society, recent scholarship has demonstrated the need for a more complex understanding of the relationship between ideas, economic interests, and political institutions.[4] Using the case of social policy development to illustrate these theoretical developments, how is it possible to formally take into account the structuring role of ideas and economic interests within a historically informed institutionalist framework? Yet this more complex historical institutionalism still lacks theoretical consistency since it does not include a coherent, unified set of assumptions about the nature of social inequality and the origin of actors' preferences and strategies. Bourdieu's theoretical contribution could help institutionalist scholars frame a more coherent structural model aimed at explaining policy outcomes while taking into account the interaction between ideas, interests, and institutions. Distinct from culturalism and rational choice theory, Bourdieu's account offers important insights about social inequality and the relationship between micro-level individual behaviour and macro-level structures – insights that could significantly enrich historical institutionalism. In this context, the present chapter represents an attempt to initiate a dialogue between two theoretical traditions that are rarely linked in current theoretical debates about politics and policymaking: historical institutionalism and Bourdieu's field theory.

An Institutional Perspective

Before exploring the basic assumptions of historical institutionalism, it is relevant to discuss briefly two macro-societal approaches that tend to reduce the political arena to simply a mirror of socioeconomic interests and cultural values. Then it will be possible to more clearly understand the specificity of the institutionalist model imagined as an alternative to societal reductionism. The key issue at stake is the autonomy of the political domain and its relationship with social and economic forces.

Among socioeconomic approaches, neo-Marxism is probably the most influential one. From a neo-Marxist perspective, economic inequality and class mobilization structure the political arena and determine policy outcomes.[5] In the area of social policy analysis, the 'Social Democratic model' (Korpi and Esping-Andersen) illustrates the neo-Marxist perspective. This model shows, for example, that Scandinavian welfare states offer more generous and universal benefits than do European and North American countries because of the exceptional influence of the local labour movement. Korpi and Esping-Andersen proceed from the argument that social policy outcomes are, for the most part, determined by the struggle between labour and capital. A strong correlation is to be found between the societal strength of labour (membership, cultural, and political unity within the movement) and the welfare state's level of comprehensiveness. In other countries, for example the United States, where the labour movement is divided and has limited membership, social policies are generally residual and limited in their scope.[6]

Another theoretical perspective that tends to reduce politics and policymaking to simply a reflection of forces that are external to the society is the culturalist approach as developed by Seymour Martin Lipset and Louis Hartz, among others.[7] Their contention is that the political life of every country is framed by a historically constructed set of 'national values.' These values consist of expectations and taken-for-granted assumptions about economic and social realities. Thus, from this perspective, normative differences may explain cross-national variations in economic, military, and social policies. Shared normative beliefs reduce the number of options available to policymakers. Widely shared identities and values structure a society's political behaviour and policy outcomes,[8] for example, with regard to social policy issues. This culturalist approach argues that there is a causal link between the socioeconomic perceptions of the population and legislative outcomes.[9] Furthermore, the shape of the specific welfare state reflects that state's set of shared values, as can be measured using surveys.[10]

Historical institutionalism, emerging in the 1980s, is now considered to be a powerful alternative to the societal approaches. In the area of social policy, scholars such as Ellen Immergut, Ann Orloff, and Theda Skocpol have criticized societal assumptions by examining the impact of political institutions and policy feedback on the development of the welfare state.[11] The initial objective of historical institutionalism was to 'bring the state back in.' Recognition of 'state autonomy' and the analysis of 'state capacities' are primary steps in this process.[12]

In order to show that 'independent goal formation occurs,' Skocpol and her collaborators first published several articles about the New Deal and the elaboration of the 1935 Social Security Act in the United States. Considering the 'recalcitrant socio-economic circumstances' of the 1930s, those interested in studying 'state autonomy' and 'state capacities' perceived the enactment of the Social Security Act as a relevant case study. The fact that several culturalist and neo-Marxist studies focused on state formation and social classes during the New Deal provided institutionalist scholars with an opportunity to frame an alternative vision of the relationship between state and society.[13] Against Marxist claims, institutionalist authors showed that key legislation enacted during the New Deal did not merely reflect the interests of the capitalist class. Bureaucrats and elected politicians were seen to enjoy a significant degree of political autonomy from interest groups and social movements. State actors could not be considered to be mere servants of a social class. Instead, as autonomous political actors, they had their own interests and strategies and their own ability to pursue them without reliance on a particular social class.[14] Against the claims of culturalists, authors like Skocpol argued that reference to broad national values was insufficient to explain specific political decisions. Culturalist arguments seemed too vague to be useful in analysing concrete political and policymaking processes.[16]

During the second half of the 1980s, scholars such as Skocpol and Orloff transformed historical institutionalism into a more complex framework centred less on 'state autonomy' per se than on the structuring impact of formal administrative and political institutions on policymaking. This evolution towards a more integrated, policy-centred model is well described in Skocpol's *Protecting Soldiers and Mothers*. According to Skocpol, 'This approach views the polity as the primary locus of action, yet understands political activities, whether carried out by politicians or by social groups, as conditioned by the institutional configurations of governments and political party systems.'[16] Instead of focusing on 'state autonomy,' Skocpol now frames a broader model of institutional structuring that focuses on four different factors: '(1) the establishment and transformation of state and party organization ... (2) the effects of political institutions and procedures on the identities, goals, and capacities of social groups ... (3) the "fit" – or lack thereof – between goals and capacities of various politically active groups, and the historically changing points of access and leverage allowed by a nation's political institutions; and (4) the way in which previously established social policies affect subsequent politics.'[17]

During the 1990s, many social scientists adopted a similar historical and institutional approach to politics. Antonia Maioni analysed the impact of political party systems on policy outcomes in her study of the political history of public health insurance policy in Canada and the United States.[18] She found that the Canadian political system favours the arrival of third parties that pressure mainstream parties and affect policy outcomes. Maioni concluded that the constant influence of the Co-operative Commonwealth Federation (CCF), which later became the New Democratic Party (NDP) throughout the post–Second World War era (at both the provincial and the federal levels) was instrumental in the enactment of legislation enabling universal public health insurance in Canada. While in the United States the labour movement integrated the heterogeneous democratic 'Roosevelt coalition,' Canadian labour unions supported the CCF/NDP, which was able to directly pressure the two dominant parties to implement bold economic and social reforms at all levels of government. From this perspective, the political mobilization of labour unions can be understood only through the lens of the party system.

Courts can also be instrumental in shaping economic and social interests. Concerning the United States, William Forbath, Victoria Hattam and other scholars have demonstrated how the anti-labour attitude of the U.S. Supreme Court directly shaped labour's political strategies at the beginning of the twentieth century. In face of the strong opposition from the courts to an ambitious agenda for social and political reform, most American unions finally embraced 'pure and simple trade unionism,' with its emphasis on collective bargaining at the expense of political involvement that favoured broadly improved social programs and economic regulations.[19] The ideas developed by the likes of Forbath, Hattam, and Maioni are at odds with the assumptions that ground the social democratic model. For these authors, political institutions such as courts and party systems structure the political battlefield as well as the strategies of interest groups.

In order to better understand how political institutions shape labour and interest group behaviour, institutionalists also used the concept of veto player.[20] Generally speaking, 'a veto player is an individual or collective actor whose agreement is required for a change in policy.'[21] In her analysis of the politics of health care reform, for example, Immergut demonstrated that the structure of the Swiss federal system explains why it is that physicians in Switzerland enjoy greater political influence than do their colleagues in France and Sweden. Even though physicians in all three countries are equally well organized, its decentralized polity and referendum procedures give Switzerland's doctors for greater opportunities to veto health insurance and other policies that they deemed were harmful to their interests.[22] In short, 'political institutions shape (but do not determine) political conflict by providing interest groups with varying opportunities to veto policy.'[23]

Next, institutionalist scholars turned to the concept of policy feedback to describe what structuring impact policies that were previously enacted might have on policymaking. This concept really makes institutionalism 'historical' because it shows how policymakers have to take into account the vested interests created by well-established programs. Policy feedback is also linked with social learning, which refers to the process by which politicians and bureaucrats evaluate the performance of well-established policies.[24] Through the process of social learning, existing policies shape the perceptions and the strategies of all the political actors. When they enact new legislation, actors have to take into account the institutionalized policy legacy of decisions made decades or even centuries earlier. In short, present-day politicians have to live with the decisions of their predecessors.[25]

Within the institutional approach, Paul Pierson certainly has the most elaborated views on the role of policy feedback in the domain of social policy studies. In examining the 'new politics of the welfare state,' Pierson describes how 'retrenchment' is a risky undertaking for politicians who face the 'armies of beneficiaries' who emerged in the aftermath of the postwar expansion of the welfare state. Welfare states create vested interests that favour the reproduction of the current institutional logic(s). From this perspective, welfare state development is largely path dependent. Inspired by the work of the economist Douglass North, Pierson argued that significant path-altering processes are seldom to be seen because politicians never take the risk of alienating themselves from powerful constituencies that are 'attached' to the social programs that were implemented decades ago. Instead, politicians adopt strategies of blame-avoidance which tend to perpetuate institutional inertia. These strategies reflect the institutional constraints that result from policy feedback related to previously enacted policies.[26]

The concepts of policy feedback and veto player are powerful intellectual tools used to further our understanding of the institutional obstacles and 'windows of opportunity' that shape the behaviour of political actors. More generally, new institutionalist scholars have succeeded in demonstrating that the political arena is a structured, yet autonomous, historical reality that cannot be reduced to social and economic interests. This theoretical perspective sheds a light on the 'rules of the game' governing political life.

Ideas, Interests, and Institutions

An increasingly subtle understanding of the relationship between ideas, economic interests, and political institutions has emerged since the early 1990s to transform historical institutionalism into a powerful theoretical toolbox for explaining political outcomes. This intellectual shift has been achieved through a reintegration of societal elements into the original institutional framework, which has never been rooted in the idea 'that institutions are the only causal force in politics.'[27]

Scholars have explicitly attempted to move beyond two significant problems with the original institutionalist approach: (1) the rather unsophisticated understanding of the relationship between policymaking and private economic interests, and (2) the somewhat unsatisfactory discussion of policy ideas as they are related to institutional structuration.[28] Analysis of these two issues leads to a discussion of the relationships among policy ideas, socioeconomic interests, and political institutions.

As discussed earlier, institutionalist scholars reject the neo-Marxist idea that powerful economic interests directly shape policy outcomes. From an institutionalist perspective, party systems and political institutions mediate and transform these interests. Without rejecting this idea, some institutionalist scholars argue that socioeconomic interests also create constraining rules of the game in the area of public policy. For example, Daniel Béland and Jacob Hacker have claimed that to understand how well-established, structured, private 'vested interests' influence policymakers through the process of 'social learning' one needs to extend the concept of policy feedback to the private sector.[29] Concerning the development of the welfare state, it seems essential to demonstrate that policymakers' and political movements' conceptualization of private welfare institutions has had a strong impact on the politics of health care reform in the United States.[30] For example, labour unions never fully supported President Harry Truman's attempt to create a national health insurance system because of the hopes raised by the rapid development of private health insurance. In the context of postwar economic prosperity, the confidence of the population and of most of the political class in the virtues of the private sector apparently reduced the need for such a statist model.[31] More importantly, the growing private insurance sector created new, institutionalized constraints for policymakers as private companies and beneficiaries organized to protect their interests in the political arena. This logic was largely reinforced by 'checks and balances' and the absence of party discipline in Congress. These interest groups could individually pressure elected officials to block the enactment of threatening health insurance bills. Institutionalist scholars already know that economic interests and political institutions are closely related, but considering policy feedback from the private insurance sector could help them to understand better the relationship between the economic and the political fields. Without denying the autonomy of the political domain, one should recognize that the political rules of the game *also* reflect feedback effects emanating from the private sector. Yet it is essential to acknowledge that the private sector is also shaped by public policies.[32] Public policies affect private ones, and vice versa. This dialectic illustrates that the autonomy of politics cannot be understood in terms of its isolation from economic forces. Further institutionalist research on economic policy and business power in welfare state development provides more ground for this claim.[33]

Although the traditional institutionalist approach does well in explaining why legislative proposals fail or succeed in a specific context, the traditional concept of social learning seems too limited to adequately explain the struggle between policy options during the process of agenda-setting. For this reason, institutionalist scholars like John Campbell, Peter Hall, and Margaret Weir have systematically studied the role of ideas in policymaking, paving the way towards more rigorous study of ideational processes in institutionalist analysis.[34] In the domain of economic policy, Hall has demonstrated that it is not only possible but essential to understand the origin and the nature of policy paradigms if political decisions are to be better understood. For Hall, a policy paradigm is a 'framework of ideas and standards that specifies not only the goals of policy and the kind of instruments that can be used to attain them, but also the very nature of the problems they are meant to address.'[35] Being both technical and ideological, paradigms constitute the pragmatic world view of politicians and social movements who fight within institutional structures. Policy paradigms are not abstract ideas floating in the air but structured entities grounded in the institutional logic of the political arena. Within that arena, political actors embrace specific paradigms that reflect their world view and their political strategies. More importantly, paradigms are often framed in the 'parapolitical sphere,' which is located at the interstices of business, government, and academia.[36] In modern society, the parapolitical sphere is highly institutionalized through the establishment of think tanks and academic research institutes which are generally autonomous from political parties and the state.[37]

Beyond social learning and policy paradigms, institutionalist scholars could further extend their analysis of ideas through the study of agenda-setting.[38] According to Kingdon, the concept of agenda refers to 'the list of subjects or problems to which governmental officials, and people outside of government closely associated with those officials, are paying some serious attention at any given time.'[39] Consequently, agenda-setting is the process that narrows the 'set of conceivable subjects to the set that actually becomes the focus of attention.'[40] The study of agenda-setting must take into account policy feedbacks from previously enacted institutions[41] as well as the manner in which policymakers frame their proposals to increase popular support, before and after their enactment.[42] Framing processes, then, transcend the boundaries of agenda-setting, as it is associated with relatively stable symbolic repertoires. In these, political actors find rhetorical tools aimed at convincing the population to support the policy options they put forward.

Bringing in Field Theory

In many ways, Pierre Bourdieu's field theory provides scholars with interesting insights concerning the political rules of the game, as well as the articulation between these structures, individual behaviour, and social inequality. An alternative to culturalism and rational choice theory, Bourdieu's theory explores the relationship between micro-level individual behaviour and macro-level structures. This structural approach to individual behaviour could significantly enrich historical institutionalism. According to Peter Hall and Rosemary Taylor, historical institutionalism is not grounded in a coherent answer to the following question: How do institutions affect the behaviour of individuals? These two authors rightly argue that two distinct, but generally implicit, visions of the relationship between individual behaviour and political institutions cohabitate within historical institutionalism: the 'calculus approach,' which is close to rational choice theory, and the 'cultural approach,' which is close to sociological institutionalism.[43] At the most general theoretical level, historical institutionalism lacks coherence because of such an eclectic attitude towards the articulation between self and political structures. Although the work of Bourdieu is not centred on political institutions per se, his theoretical model offers a coherent perspective on the relationship between self and structures that is, nevertheless, rooted in assumptions compatible with historical institutionalism: the political field is an autonomous yet highly structured, historically constructed order that shapes political actors' preferences and strategies.[44] As I will argue, this model can contribute to the understanding of the relationship between ideas, economic interests, and political institutions in political processes, while offering an illuminating framework to systematically understand actor's preferences and strategies as they are related to formal institutions and informal rules of the game. This is especially true of the concepts of capital, field, and habitus, which point to the structuring impact of cultural structures (ideas) and social inequality (interests) on individual behaviour without simply returning to either culturalism or neo-Marxism – two societal approaches that are not fully compatible with institutionalist assumptions about the autonomy of the political arena.

In Bourdieu's language, the concept of field refers to a highly stratified system of power relations regulated according to its internal rules. The field is always an arena of enduring battle for power between social actors. Bourdieu considers society as the imbrications of many different fields: religious, academic, artistic, political, and so on. Every field is structured by its central goal, as well as the 'rules of the game' that actors must follow to achieve this goal. Fields create also what is perceived as the 'interest' of actors struggling for power and success within its established rules: 'Every field, as a historical product, generates the interest which is the precondition of its functioning. This is true of the economic field itself, which, as a relatively autonomous space obeying its own laws, and endowed with its own specific axiomatics linked to an original history, produces a particular form of interest, which is a particular case of the universe of possible forms of interest. Social magic can constitute more or less anything as interesting, and establish it as an object of struggle.'[45]

In this theoretical context, the political field, like any other field, can be considered as a socially constructed set of goals and rules that shape the actors' perceptions. These actors have some autonomy, which reflects the autonomy of the field itself from other fields in society. For Bourdieu, the modern political field is actually based on the opposition between the 'passive' citizens who form most of the population, and a class of professional politicians and bureaucrats who have the symbolic power to rule over the political field and social order at large. Yet the political field itself, like every field, is an arena of competition: 'The political field is thus the site of competition for power which is carried out by means of a competition for the control of non-professionals or, more precisely, for the monopoly of the right to speak and act in the name of some or all of the non-professionals.'[46] In this context, non-professionals are transformed into consumers of 'political products' offered by professional politicians and their machines. This remark points to the enduring inequality between those who take political decisions and those who have little or no direct control over legislative outcomes.

To succeed in a specific field, actors must mobilize different kinds of capital, a concept that refers to the tools allowing them to gain more power and symbolic recognition. Here, it is essential to understand that Bourdieu's concept of capital differs from Marx's purely economic vision. Beyond economic capital, Bourdieu defines four other types of capital: social (connections), cultural (useful linguistic and cultural skills), symbolic (prizes and recognition), and political (political legitimacy). Extensively discussed in only a few of Bourdieu's papers, political capital 'is a form of symbolic capital, *credit* founded on *credence* or belief and *recognition* or, more precisely, on the innumerable operations of credit by which agents confer on a person (or an object) the very powers that they recognize in him (or it).'[47] In other words, political capital is the power enjoyed by professional politicians as it 'is derived from the trust (expressed in a form of credit) that a group of followers places in them.'[48] From Bourdieu's perspective, this power must be highly institutionalized to reproduce itself: 'The delegation of political capital presupposes the objectivation of this kind of capital in permanent institutions, its materialization in political "machines," in jobs and instruments of mobilization, and its continual reproduction by mechanisms and strategies.'[49] Yet the political field, like any other field, is about domination and unequal access to capital. In this context, the political field is internally stratified and, more importantly, it is grounded in the exclusion of most citizens from policymaking processes. Only a limited number of citizens and interest groups are granted constant, direct access to policymakers. Both social and economic capital play a significant role in the allocation of political resources.

At this point, one should note that the concept of 'political field' is distinct from the one of 'polity' commonly used in political science and, more specifically, institutionalist scholarship.[50] As opposed to 'polity,' political field implies that, while politics forms an autonomous level of reality, it is also grounded in social logics present in other fields of action. In this context, the study of the political field can explicitly draw on sociological knowledge about other fields – and society at large – instead of studying politics from a more restricted perspective. For example, cultural, economic, or social capital transcends the political field. This means that scholarship about other fields – and Bourdieu's field theory itself – could directly contribute to our understanding of the specific logic of the political field, as it is frequently analogous (but not identical) to the one prevailing elsewhere in society. The political field has a specific nature, yet general field theory could prove useful to understand it as forms of capital exist in – and circulate between – different fields, and across society. Furthermore, the understanding of the goal-oriented 'practical reason,' as it exists in other fields, could help scholars to capture what is specific about political strategies and domination.

Before criticizing the blind spot about the structuring role of political institutions in Bourdieu's theory, it is essential to link the concepts of field and capital to the one of habitus. This is necessary because habitus represents a conceptual alternative to rational choice theory, an approach that is unable to shed light on the social origin of individual preferences, which are generally taken for granted in the study of economic and political behaviour.[51] As opposed to rational choice theory, field theory and, more precisely, the concept of habitus, allow scholars to better grasp individual behaviour as it reflects the practical reason of actors who develop a 'taste for the game' (*illusio*) through socialization. At the same time, habitus transcends mere culturalism, as this concept explicitly refers to competition and strategic knowledge.

In *Questions of Sociology*, Bourdieu defines the *habitus* as the 'product of conditionings that tends to reproduce the objective logic of those conditionings while transforming it.'[52] In other words, 'habitus is the shared mode of perception, judgment, and behavioural dispositions of a category of people, particularly a class.'[53] This concept is related to the fact that when actors learn the rules of the game, they actually learn – often implicitly – how to behave and think in order to succeed in a specific field. The result of this learning process is the habitus, which constitutes the link between one's behaviour and the field's structures. In this context, the habitus is the integration of the rules of the game with one's perceptions and strategies. The habitus both reflects the structure of the field and shapes one's behaviour. Furthermore, habitus formation is directly related to social inequality as some individuals, because of their specific class, gender, and ethnic background, have a greater access to different forms of capital that may help them to successfully master the rules of the game and compete within a specific field.

The concept of habitus is particularly useful because it breaks with the strict opposition between micro- and macro-structures, between self and society. Moreover, it moves analysis beyond the abstractness of 'rational choice' and the consensual vision of culturalism, where emphasis on 'shared values' potentially hides domination. Habitus is also distinct from the Marxist concept of ideology, which traditionally depicts dominant economic, social, and political ideas as mere tools of capitalist domination. Although Bourdieu acknowledges the power of capitalist forces in advanced industrial nations, he understands that domination and social struggles cannot be reduced to economic interests. As we will see, the concept of habitus can, indeed, contribute to a more accurate analysis of the relationship between ideas, interests, and institutions that is coherent with basic institutionalist assumptions.

Another interesting concept in Bourdieu's work points to the relationship between ideas and social inequality: symbolic violence. This concept refers to the imposition by powerful actors of identities and normative models that are constructed to be inferior or superior to others. Symbolic violence points to the impact of ideational forces that both reflect and reinforce social inequality and concrete power relations within a specific field and in society at large. Actors competing within the political field produce symbolic violence as enacted policies impose social categories such as 'criminal,' 'welfare beneficiary,' or 'illegal immigrant.' Bureaucratic policy implementation tends to reinforce these categories, or even create new forms of symbolic violence through exclusionary practices based on class, ethnic, and gender differences. Moreover, political discourse itself is a significant source of symbolic violence, just as frames that justify particular political options frequently define a social group or a political entity as inferior, dangerous, or incompetent. Recurring political debates over nationalism, illegal immigrants, and ethnic minorities provide grounds for this claim. The concept of symbolic violence thus shows how ideas are directly related to social inequality, as representations emanating from the political field affect social and symbolic hierarchies across society. In terms of societal feedback, common social representations about inequality also affect political discourse and policymaking.

At this point, it seems appropriate to acknowledge the limitations of the concepts of field and habitus as framed in Bourdieu's work. Then, I will show how these concepts can take a new meaning – and transcend these limitations – if placed into the context of historical institutionalism.

One can identify two main limitations in Bourdieu's framework. On the one hand, Bourdieu does not systematically take into account formal political institutions when defining the 'political field.' In fact, he defines the rules of the game in mostly cultural and symbolic terms. From an institutional perspective, however, it is possible to relate this concept to institutional logics while preserving its basic meaning as a competitive and highly structured system of power relations based on domination. Political institutions play an active role in shaping the symbolic rules of the game that reproduce power domination within the field. On the other hand, the concept of habitus is too rigid to reflect the tensions within the self and, more importantly, intellectual and ideological innovation at the individual's level. In fact, the habitus shall be considered as a fragmented set of behavioural dispositions that never perfectly reflect the rules of the game.[54] Considering their ambiguity, each actor has a socially constructed, yet individual, interpretation of the field's logic. This autonomy of the social actor favours the emergence of new ideas and strategies that often lead to political and social change, that is, to the gradual transformation of the field's rules. The 'reproduction' of social and political order is probably more plastic than Bourdieu argues.[55] Despite these remarks, Bourdieu's concepts of field, habitus, and political capital could prove useful to those interested in studying 'political structuration.'[56] Furthermore, Bourdieu's theory could help to explore how the institutional rules of the game (field) are closely tied to ideas (habitus) and interests (capital).

The concepts of field and habitus show that structuration is not only about formal political institutions and previously enacted policies. The logic of the political field is institutional but also symbolic and cultural. When not conceived as a deterministic and rigid framework, the concept of habitus can shed new light on political choices by linking ideas, interests, and institutions at the actor's level. As mentioned earlier, the habitus reflects the institutional rules in the sense that actors struggling within a specific field internalize the rules of the game mostly through social interaction and practical experience. The knowledge and the internalization of these rules are instrumental in their success within the field. Yet beyond formal political institutions, political actors must take into account non-written rules that reflect the relationship between the political field and other components of society. Because the political field is not totally isolated from the economic field, for example, political actors must consider economic ideas and interests in order to exploit them at the political level. Indirectly, vested interests in the economic field structure the policymaking process in the sense that political actors shall gain support from economic groups that have enough economic and social capital to affect political outcomes. Political struggles reflect social inequality, and individual preferences, as well as strategies, stem from one's habitus, which embodies the political field's cultural and institutional logics. This is not to say that political actors are 'servants' of the private sector, but that their political habitus is also grounded in an understanding of the economic and cultural environment of the political field. In a way, this is a form of social learning that structures this field. This is not about pure 'external constraint,' but an 'internal understanding' of the environment aimed at reproducing symbolic domination and conceiving winning political strategies. From the standpoint of the political field, economic interests and cultural values have a political meaning. In this context, policy ideas and paradigms mobilized by elected politicians take into account the rules of the game prevailing in other fields when these can affect electoral outcomes. Political structuration is not only about formal rules and policy feedback. It is closely related to political actors' perception of economic interests and ideological trends that can have an impact on the struggles within the political field (for example, economic cycles and recessions directly affect political actors as they develop credit-claiming or blame-avoidance strategies). Policymaking thus reflects social inequality and symbolic domination, a fact rarely acknowledged by culturalists. At the ideological level, political actors tend to adapt ideas coming from other fields in order to gain more symbolic power to legitimize their proposals. They also rely on 'policy entrepreneurs' who build bridges between the academic, economic, and political fields.[57] Simultaneously, the paradigms mobilized by bureaucrats and elected officials are rooted in political assumptions; they often serve their perceived interests as they reflect the field's rules of the game. From this perspective, political interests cannot be separated from the field's structuring norms and institutions. As a matter of fact, the political field's institutionalized goals frame political actors' interests and preferences. These interests and preferences have no substance outside the political field, and they cannot be reduced to the abstract model of rationality generally associated with rational choice theory.

An example of this complex set of interactions between ideas, interests, and institutions is the enactment of the 1935 Social Security Act in the United States.[58] President Roosevelt and his advisers – in the name of fiscal equilibrium – imposed a model of social insurance explicitly based on the insurance techniques developed in the private sector. As Raymond Richards suggests, Roosevelt probably discovered insurance principles in 1921, when he became vice-president of the Fidelity and

Deposit Company of Maryland. Because of this job, he made close ties with a manager of Metropolitan Life. Through these connections, Roosevelt became familiar with the principles of insurance.[59] As a fiscal conservative, Roosevelt wanted workers to 'purchase' their own security instead of depending on taxpayers' money. He also saw social insurance as a way to establish some sort of contractually 'earned rights' that would protect the social insurance system against future political attack.[60] The influence of private actuarial models on Roosevelt and the New Dealers is a significant example of 'policy transfer' from the economic to the political field. Of course, this transfer was aimed at serving Roosevelt's electoral and policy goals within the political field. Given the prestige of private insurance companies in American society, the reference to actuarial principles was a way to legitimize a measure that could help Roosevelt please his constituencies while protecting this measure against attacks formulated in the name of 'capitalist values.' The reference to the private sector appears as a convenient way to justify a public policy that serves politicians' strategies. Facing ideological as well as institutional constraints, they frame their strategies and act upon a habitus that reflects structural patterns within and between the fields.

Conclusion

As stated in the introduction, the present chapter represents a modest attempt to survey theoretical developments that have favoured a gradual reintegration of societal factors into historical institutionalism. The second objective of the chapter is to inaugurate a fruitful dialogue between historical institutionalism and Bourdieu's field theory, two well-known approaches that are rarely discussed together in current theoretical debates about politics and policymaking.

While preserving the basic assumptions of historical institutionalism, it seems relevant to extend the idea of structuration beyond formal political institutions and policy feedback; policy ideas and economic interests appear as key factors that structure the political actors' autonomous strategies. Furthermore, Bourdieu's concepts of field and habitus can prove useful in the theoretical articulation of ideas, interests, and institutions within the context of historical institutionalism. At the theoretical level, one must recognize that structuration concerns ideas and interests, as well as formal political institutions. In addition to acknowledging the autonomy of political actors, Bourdieu's concept of field shows how political life has a specific logic, reflecting the institutional 'rules of the game,' while showing feedback effects from other fields. An alternative to culturalism, neo-Marxism, and rational choice theory, Bourdieu's theoretical account offers many useful insights about symbolic violence, social inequality, and the relationship between micro-level individual behaviour and macro-level institutions.

More theoretical discussion is needed in order to break the opposition between institutional and societal approaches. In the future, it could be relevant to frame empirical case studies in order to fully discuss the approach drafted in this chapter. Theoretical work on politics is not an end, but the starting point, of historical and sociological analysis. Conceptual frameworks such as the one sketched in the present chapter are only aimed at preparing the ground for theoretically informed comparative and historical studies. Without these studies, it will prove impossible to fully grasp the concrete meaning of political structuration.

Notes

Many ideas discussed in this essay were first outlined in Daniel Béland, 'Néo-institutionnalisme historique et politiques sociales: Une perspective sociologique,' *Politique et sociétés*, 21 (2002), 21–39, and Daniel Béland and Jacob S. Hacker, 'Ideas, Private Institutions, and American Welfare State "Exceptionalism": The Case of Health and Old-Age Insurance in the United States, 1915–1965,' *International Journal of Social Welfare*, 13 (2004), 42–54. I wish to thank Jacob S. Hacker, Angela Kempf, André Lecours, and two anonymous reviewers for their comments on previous drafts of this chapter.

1 According to Peter Hall and Rosemary Taylor, there are three types of 'institutionalism': historical, sociological, and rational choice. Although these approaches share some basic assumptions, they form three distinct perspectives on politics and policy: Peter A. Hall and Rosemary C.R. Taylor, 'Political Science and the Three Institutionalisms,' *Political Studies* 43 (1996): 936–57. This chapter deals only with historical institutionalism.
2 Theda Skocpol, *Protecting Soldiers and Mothers: The Political Origins of Social Policy in the United States* (Cambridge, Mass.: Harvard University Press, 1992), 41.
3 Hall and Taylor, 'Political Science and the Three Institutionalisms,' 940–1.
4 On the theoretical relationship between ideas, interests, and institutions,

see Bruno Théret, 'Institutions et institutionnalismes: vers une convergence des conceptions de l'institution?' in Michèle Tallard, Bruno Théret, and Uri Didier (eds.), *Innovations institutionnelles et territoires* (Paris: L'Harmattan, 2000).

5 Ralph Miliband, *Marxism and Politics* (Oxford: Oxford University Press, 1977) and G. William Domhoff, *Who Rules America? Power and Politics* (Boston: McGraw-Hill, 4th ed., 1998).

6 Gösta Esping-Andersen, *Politics against Markets: The Social Democratic Road to Power* (Princeton, NJ: Princeton University Press, 1985); Walter Korpi, *The Democratic Class Struggle* (Boston: Routledge and Kegan Paul, 1983).

7 Seymour Martin Lipset, *Continental Divide: The Values and Institutions of the United States and Canada* (New York: Routledge, 1990); Louis Hartz, *Liberal Tradition in America: An Interpretation of American Political Thought since the Revolution* (Boston: Harvest Book, 1991). For a critique of the culturalist perspective concerning nationalism, see André Lecours, 'Theorizing Cultural Identities: Historical Institutionalism as a Challenge to the Culturalists,' *Canadian Journal of Political Science*, 33 (2000), 499–522.

8 John L. Campbell, 'Ideas, Politics, and Public Policy,' *Annual Review of Sociology*, 28 (2002), 24.

9 For example, Daniel Levine, *Poverty and Society: The Growth of the American Welfare State in International Comparison* (New Brunswick, NJ: Rutgers University Press, 1988). On this issue, see Theda Skocpol, 'Thinking Big: Can National Values Explain the Development of Social Provision in the United States? A Review Essay,' *Journal of Policy History*, 2 (1990), 425–38.

10 In his book the *Continental Divide*, Lipset himself formulates this type of analysis in order to explain major policy differences between Canada and the United States, 136–51.

11 For example, Ellen M. Immergut, 'The Theoretical Core of Institutionalism,' *Politics and Society*, 26 (1998), 5–34; Sven Steinmo, Kathleen Thelen, and Franck Longstreth (eds), *Structuring Politics: Historical Institutionalism in Comparative Analysis* (New York: Cambridge University Press, 1992); Skocpol, *Protecting Soldiers and Mothers*; Ann Shola Orloff, *The Politics of Pensions: A Comparative Analysis of Britain, Canada, and United States, 1880–1940* (Madison: University of Wisconsin Press, 1994); Ellen M. Immergut, *Health Politics: Interests and Institutions in Western Europe* (Cambridge: Cambridge University Press, 1992); Antonia Maioni, *Parting at the Crossroads: The Emergence of Health Insurance in the United States and Canada* (Princeton, NJ: Princeton University Press, 1998); Paul Pierson, *Dismantling the Welfare State? Reagan, Thatcher, and the Politics of Retrenchment* (Cambridge: Cambridge University Press, 1994); Sven Steinmo, *Taxation and Democracy:*

Swedish, British, and American Approaches to Financing the Modern State (New Haven: Yale University Press, 1993).

12 Theda Skocpol, 'Bringing the State Back In: Strategies of Analysis in Current Research,' in Peter B. Evans, Dietrich Rueschemeyer, and Theda Skocpol (eds.), *Bringing the State Back In* (Cambridge: Cambridge University Press, 1985), 9

13 See Skocpol, 'Thinking Big.'

14 Edwin Amenta, *Bold Relief: Institutional Politics and the Origins of Modern American Social Policy* (Princeton, Princeton University Press, 1998); Theda Skocpol and John Ikenberry, 'Expanding Social Benefits: The Role of Social Security,' *Political Science Quarterly*, 102 (1987), 389–416; Theda Skocpol and Edwin Amenta, 'Did Capitalist Shape Social Security?' *American Sociological Review*, 50 (1985), 572–5.

15 Skocpol, 'Thinking Big.'

16 Skocpol, *Protecting Soldiers and Mothers*, 41.

17 Ibid.

18 Maioni, *Parting at the Crossroads*.

19 William E. Forbath, *Law and the Shaping of the American Labor Movement* (Cambridge, Mass.: Harvard University Press, 1991), and Victoria C. Hattam, *Labor Visions and State Power: The Origins of Business Unionism in the United States* (Princeton: Princeton University Press, 1993).

20 George Tsebelis, 'Decision Making in Political Systems: Veto Players in Presidentialism, Parliamentarism, Multicameralism, and Multipartyism,' *British Journal of Political Science* 25 (1995), 289–315.

21 Stephen J. Kay, 'Unexpected Privatizations: Politics and Social Security Reform in the Southern Cone,' *Comparative Politics*, 31 (1999), 403–22.

22 Immergut, *Health Politics*.

23 Kay, 'Unexpected Privatization,' 406. See also Daniel Béland, 'Does Labor Matter? Institutions, Labor Unions, and Pension Reform in France and the United States,' *Journal of Public Policy*, 21 (2001), 153–72.

24 Hugh Heclo, *Modern Social Politics in Britain and Sweden: From Relief to Income Maintenance* (New Haven: Yale University Press, 1974); Randall Hansen and Desmond King, 'Experts at Work: State Autonomy, Social Learning and Eugenic Sterilization in 1930s Britain,' *British Journal of Political Science* 20 (1999), 77–107.

25 For example, Skocpol, *Protecting Soldiers and Mothers*.

26 Paul Pierson: 'The New Politics of the Welfare State,' *World Politics*, 48 (1996), 143–79; 'Increasing Returns, Path Dependence, and the Study of Politics,' *American Political Science Review*, 94 (2000), 251–67.

27 Hall and Taylor, 'Political Science and the Three New Institutionalisms,' 942.

28 One could also argue that the work of feminist scholars like Theda Skocpol and Ann Orloff has enriched historical institutionalism's vague assumptions about inequality. Theda Skocpol, *Protecting Soldiers and Mothers*, and Ann Shola Orloff, 'Gender and the Social Rights of Citizenship: The Comparative Analysis of Gender Relations and Welfare States,' *American Sociological Review*, 58 (1993), 303–28.

29 Béland and Hacker, 'Ideas, Private Institutions.'

30 Jacob S. Hacker, *The Divided Welfare State: The Battle over Public and Private Social Benefits in the United States* (Cambridge: Cambridge University Press, 2002).

31 Colin Gordon, 'Why No Health Insurance in the U.S.? The Limits of Social Provision in War and Peace, 1941–1948,' *Journal of Policy History*, 9 (1997), 277–310.

32 In the United States, for example, the impact of tax credits on private social policy has been widely discussed. Beth Stevens, 'Blurring the Boundaries: How the Federal Government Has Influenced Welfare Benefits in the Private Sector,' in Margaret Weir, Ann Schola Orloff, and Theda Skocpol (eds.), *The Politics of Social Policy in the United States* (Princeton: Princeton University Press, 1988), 123–48; Frank Dobbin and Terry Boychuck, 'Public Policy and the Rise of Private Pensions: The U.S. Experience Since 1930,' in Michael Shalev (ed.), *The Privatization of Social Policy? Occupational Welfare and the Welfare State in America, Scandinavia and Japan* (London: Macmillan, 1996), 104–35; Teresa Ghilarducci, *Labor's Capital: The Economics and Politics of Private Pensions* (Cambridge, Mass.: MIT Press, 1992); Steven Sass, *The Promise of Private Pensions: The First Hundred Years* (Cambridge, Mass.: Harvard University Press, 1997).

33 Jacob S. Hacker and Paul Pierson, 'Business Power and Social Policy: Employers and the Formation of the American Welfare State,' *Politics and Society*, 30 (2002), 277–325; Peter A. Hall, 'Policy Paradigms, Social Learning, and the State: The Case of Economic Policymaking in Britain,' *Comparative Politics*, 25 (1993), 275–96.

34 On this issue, see Campbell, 'Ideas, Politics, and Public Policy'; Hall, 'Policy Paradigms'; Margaret Weir, *Politics and Jobs*, (Princeton, NJ: Princeton University Press, 1992).

35 Hall, 'Policy Paradigms,' 279.

36 On the concept of 'parapolitical sphere,' see Janet R. Horne, *A Social Laboratory for Modern France: The Social Museum and the Rise of The Welfare State* (Durham: Duke University Press, 2002).

37 For a general discussion concerning the political impact of think tanks, see Donald E. Abelson, *Do Think Tanks Matter? Assessing the Impact of Public*

Policy Institutes (Montreal: McGill-Queen's University Press, 2002); James G. McGann and Kent Weaver (eds.), *Think Tanks and Civil Societies* (New Brunswick, NJ: Transaction Publishers, 2000); Diane Stone, Andrew Denham, and Mark Garnett (eds.), *Think Tanks across Nations: A Comparative Approach* (Manchester: Manchester University Press, 1998).

38 In recent years, some institutionalist scholars have increasingly studied agenda-setting processes in their empirical research. Kent Weaver, 'Public Pension Reform in the United States,' paper presented at the workshop Social Policy Responses to Population Ageing in the Globalization Era, Hokkaido University, Japan, March 2003.

39 John W. Kingdon, *Agendas, Alternatives, and Public Policies*, 2nd ed. (New York: Harper Collins, 1995), 3.

40 Ibid.

41 Weir, *Politics and Jobs*, 18.

42 On frames, see Campbell, 'Ideas, Politics, and Public Policy.'

43 Hall and Taylor, 'Political Science and the Three Institutionalisms,' 938.

44 Pierre Bourdieu, 'Questions de politique,' *Actes de la recherche en sciences sociales*, 16 (1977), 55–89, and 'Political Representation: Elements for a Theory of the Political Field,' in John B. Thompson (ed.), *Language and Symbolic Power* (Oxford: Polity Press, 1991), 171–202.

45 Pierre Bourdieu, *In Other Words: Essays Towards a Reflexive Sociology* (Stanford: Stanford University Press, 1990), 88.

46 Bourdieu, 'Political Representation,' 190.

47 Ibid., 192.

48 Daniel Schugurensky, 'Citizenship Learning and Democratic Engagement: Political Capital Revisited,' *Proceedings of the 41st Annual Adult Education Research Conference*, 2–4 June, Vancouver, AERC, 2000, 417–22.

49 Bourdieu, 'Political Representation,' 196.

50 In her book *Protecting Soldiers and Mothers*, Skocpol indeed defines historical institutionalism as a 'polity-centred' (and not 'state-centred') analysis.

51 Even proponents of rational choice theory recognize this inescapable theoretical problem. Debra Friedman and Michael Hechter, 'The Contribution of the Rational Choice Theory to Macrosociological Research,' in Donald McQuarie (ed.), *Readings in Contemporary Sociological Theory: From Modernity to Post-Modernity* (Englewood Cliffs, NJ: Prentice-Hall, 1995). As Bourdieu notes in *Pascalian Meditations*, rational choice theory is the expression of a 'scholarly mind' that projects its abstract way of thinking upon the social word. Moreover, this approach reflects the symbolic domination of economics within social sciences, as rationality is generally defines in eco-

nomic terms. Pierre Bourdieu, *Pascalian Meditations* (Stanford: Stanford University Press, 2000).

52 Pierre Bourdieu, *Sociology in Question* (London: Sage, 1993), 86.

53 Roberta Garner, 'Pierre Bourdieu,' in Roberta Garner (ed.), *Social Theory: Continuity and Confrontation* (Peterborough: Broadview Press, 2000), 374.

54 For a critical discussion of Bourdieu's concept of *habitus*, see Bernard Lahire, *L'homme pluriel. Les ressorts de l'action* (Paris: Nathan, 1998).

55 Another danger with the concept of field is to perceive it as an ahistorical construction, as a stable set of rules that seldom change; fields change over time when facing external choc or internal anomie.

56 In the English-speaking sociological literature, the concept of structuration is developed in the work of Anthony Giddens, *The Constitution of Society: Outline of the Theory of Structuration* (Cambridge: Polity Press, 1984).

57 On the concept of policy entrepreneur, see Kingdon, *Agendas, Alternatives, and Public Policies.*

58 Béland and Hacker, 'Ideas, Private Institutions.'

59 Raymond Richards, *Closing the Door to Destitution: The Shaping of the Social Security Acts of the United States and New Zealand* (University Park: Pennsylvania State University Press, 1994), 138.

60 Mark H. Leff, 'Taxing the "Forgotten Man": The Politics of Social Security Finance in the New Deal,' *Journal of American History*, 70 (1983), 359–79.

3

Theorizing Institutional Change

SIOBHÁN HARTY

The claim that 'institutions matter' for structuring social and political outcomes might make intuitive sense. It has provoked widespread debate, however, in the social sciences about the merits of institutional over more established forms of analysis. An initial impediment to assessing the relative advantages of new institutionalism for political science was the difficulty in distinguishing between its various forms and identifying its research agenda. In an influential article that provided a great service to the discipline, Peter Hall and Rosemary Taylor drew out the distinctions between historical, rational choice, and sociological institutionalism and attempted to map out their respective research agendas by linking the genesis of each school to a reaction against the dominance of behaviouralism in the social sciences.[1] But while Hall and Taylor stressed the differences among the three schools in order to argue for increased interchange, political scientists were left wondering whether there was an explicit overarching theoretical concern that could allow us to judge the contributions of new institutionalism on their own merits. Immergut responded to these concerns by arguing that new institutionalism is part of an institutionalist tradition rooted in the work of Rousseau, the theoretical core of which is related to scholars' preoccupation with 'the difficulties of ascertaining what human actors want when the preferences expressed in politics are so radically affected by the institutional contexts in which these preferences are voiced.'[2] Compared with classic behavioural approaches or the social determinism of Marxism, in reaction to which it emerged, new institutionalism analyses the influence of institutions – as either independent or intervening variables – on the formation of preferences and patterns of collective action. To the extent that institutions do indeed matter – which in itself is a question for both theoretical and empirical investigation – one of new institutionalism's chief merits has been to problematize preference formation and to show that actors' strategic action is often planned in response to specific institutional contexts. An emerging case-study literature has attempted to demonstrate the importance of institutions for explaining political outcomes, but generally speaking, the absence of a clearly stated methodology in new institutionalism makes it difficult to categorize a study as being 'institutionalist.'[3]

Out of these earliest debates about the merits of new institutionalism emerged one clear point: it would not be possible to study the influence of institutions on preference formation, identity construction, strategic action, and decision-making unless institutions themselves were stable and durable. Whether one is engaged in a longitudinal, cross-national comparison of the evolution of workers' rights or a detailed examination of the role played by legislative rules on the voting patterns of parliamentarians, one assumes institutional continuity. This is one important reason for which new institutionalism studies have tended to focus on liberal, western democracies: situations of institutional stasis and stable decision rules facilitate the examination of the role of institutions more readily than do situations of institutional instability or breakdown. But this assumption has meant that the first generation of theoretical and case-study literature in the new institutionalism, while focusing on the effects of institutions, has virtually ignored institutions themselves. The origin of institutions remains under-theorized and, more crucially for assessing the merits of new institutionalism, the notion of institutional change is not problematized in the literature. While institutional collapse has been a focus of investigation in the study of domestic politics, it has most often been examined in the context of *regime* collapse.[4] The possibility of institutional change is the Achilles' heel of new institutionalism: If it can be proven that institutions are not as stable and continuous as new institutional theorists claim, then new institutionalism's potential for explaining preference formation, discursive practices, and strategic action will clearly diminish. Moreover, as assumptions about institutional stability in the developed west have underwritten a whole literature on democratic transitions[5] and the institutional reconstruction of post-conflict states,[6] the theoretical implications of such a finding would extend beyond new institutionalism itself.

Indeed, the most recent critiques of new institutionalism have focused precisely on the question of institutional change. Actually, there are two critiques: first, critics of new institutionalism argue that by its very nature, new institutionalism should include a self-contained theory of institutional genesis and change that does not rely on references to exogenous forces. This first critique is aimed at what is perceived to be a general lack of coherence in new institutional theory. Second, critics challenge that institutions might not be as stable and permanent as new institutionalism claims. The second critique is empirical: while there may be theoretical reasons for supposing that institutions are stable, they are not supported by evidence from the real world. The 'default' position in new institutionalism is that institutions are durable; there are theoretically compelling reasons – which will be examined below – to believe that this is the case. However, if it can be shown empirically that institutions are not as durable as new institutionalism theorists claim (the second critique), then the argument for a theory of institutional change (the first critique) would be strengthened. As I will argue below, the empirical critique is in the developmental stage; nevertheless, its proponents are marshalling considerable evidence in support of their claims.[7] Therefore, new institutionalist scholars will need to face up to the problem of coherence. In this chapter, I suggest how they might do so.

Neither critique is exclusively the work of new institutionalism's detractors: even scholars who are at the forefront of new institutionalism admit that compared with their work on social and political outcomes, they 'have made far less progress in treating institutions as themselves important objects of explanation.'[8] As many new institutionalism scholars recognize, it is time to pause and reflect on this lacunae in the burgeoning literature that now labels itself 'institutionalist': before we can be sure that institutions explain outcomes, we need to be clearer about the nature of institutions themselves. The type of institutional change with which new institutionalism must concern itself is related to primary decision-making structures, not policy change. As Kenneth Shepsle has argued, there are 'grounds for maintaining a distinction between changes in institutions and rules of the game on the one hand, and changes in outcomes that take place under a specific regime of rules and institutions on the other.'[9] Canadian political scientists are ideally placed to contribute to current debates on institutional change and to the theoretical development of new institutionalism itself as there have been several recent examples in Canada of the type of institutional change that results in new rules of the game. In this chapter, I examine the creation of self-governing aboriginal communities and compare this process with constitutional changes taking place in western Europe. The emergence of new governing units has not only produced new decision-making institutions, but it has also altered the scope of existing ones. The second example to be considered is the controversial issue of judicial activism and judicial supremacy in the twenty years since the introduction of the Canadian Charter of Rights and Freedoms. This issue, which touches directly on questions of democracy and decision-making, is mirrored in the European context by the intervention of the European Court of Justice (ECJ) in the political affairs of the member states of the European Union (EU) through the judicial supremacy of EU law. These events have not been examined or analysed as instances of institutional change, yet such a perspective could illuminate the processes which have led to these outcomes, thereby informing a general theory of institutional change. It is beyond the scope of this chapter to provide such a theory. Rather, the purpose of this chapter is more modest: to clarify the terms of the debate on institutional change; to sketch out the main elements which would need to figure in a theory of institutional change; and to suggest how Canadian political scientists might engage in genuinely comparative work in order to make a significant contribution to the development of such a theory.

Defining the Debate: Institutions and Institutional Stasis

A chief problem with any discussion of institutional change is the lack of consensus on what constitutes an institution. As Hall and Taylor noted, new institutionalism 'does not constitute a unified body of thought,'[10] a fact which is evident from the different ways in which new institutionalists define institutions. Historical institutionalists are concerned with the rules and conventions emanating from formal organizations, which would include not only decision-making institutions but also organizations for collective action. Rational choice institutionalists view institutions as a set of rules and information that promote 'gains from exchange' by reducing the costs associated with the pursuit of individual rationality in strategic interactions. Finally, sociological institutionalism views institutions as the embodiment of 'symbols, scripts and routine' which act as filters through which actors interpret their situation, their particular place in it, and the most appropriate course of action for whatever decision faces them. As sociological institutionalism is not as prominent in political science as historical and rational choice institutionalisms, I focus the remainder of the discussion on these last two. According to these two schools of new institutionalism, the following qualify as institutions: (1) decision-making and bargaining structures that distribute resources; (2) rules and procedures that govern access to power; and (3) rules and measures to monitor and enforce compliance. Peter Hall's definition is often used to capture these three points: Institutions are 'the formal rules, compliance procedures, and standard operating procedures that structure the relationship between individuals in various units of the polity and economy.'[11]

Hall focused on the organizational qualities of domestic institutions for the way in which they process societal demands through the political system.[12] Similarly, Immergut describes the theoretical core of new institutionalism as the black box between political demands and ultimate outcomes.[13] The type of institutions that figure in Immergut's 'black box' are characterized by their stability and continuity over time; that is, the rules and procedures by which they are constituted do not change with any regularity. Institutional stasis is not an assumption that is unique to new institutionalism; it underwrites many approaches and theories in political science. Modernization theory, for example, is built on the assumption that the construction of stable, liberal democratic institutions that conform to the rule of law is the end point on a continuum that progresses from traditional to modern society. In his 1968 classic, *Political Order in Changing Societies*, Samuel P. Huntington argued that the relationship between political participation (which is itself determined by socioeconomic development) and political institutionalization determines political stability in a state.[14] But the stability of which Huntington and others wrote in their comparisons of the developed and developing worlds is rooted in a much earlier literature on the political theory of liberalism and the construction of governments. In the works of Locke, Mill, Montesquieu, and Rousseau, which became the foundation for modern democratic theory, the rule of law tamed the law of nature and created the stable institutional environment that allowed commerce and the market to flourish. The study of pluralist, consociational, and social democracies in the developed West is built on the premise that, whatever the form of political representation, social and political order requires stable decision rules. The literature on transitions from authoritarian rule might use 'contingency'[15] to explain the pacted nature of democracy in these cases, but it stakes the success of democratization on the ability of new institutions to demonstrate to losers that they can be winners the next time the democratic game is played. In other words, the benefits of democratization – certainty, predictability and economic growth – are predicated on stable institutions founded on the rule of law. The possibility of bringing together 'winners' and 'losers' to share power in post-conflict settings, such as civil or ethnic wars, is similarly predicated on the existence of stable democratic institutions that can distribute power and resources in a relatively equal manner. Much of recent democratic theory and the literature on institutions in comparative politics is concerned with which institutional designs can best guarantee stability, promote access for all, and provide the most equitable distribution possible of power and resources.[16]

Compared with these other approaches and areas of investigation in political science, new institutionalism is unique for attempting to theorize institutional stasis. None of the literatures and approaches referred to above has much to say about this topic. There is an implicit functionalism present in the literature on consociationalism and the reconstruction of post-conflict states: power-sharing institutions exist because actors have determined in advance that these are what they need in order to be able to create a stable political environment for governing. In other accounts, 'stability' is presented as an objective measure that is derived from cross-national empirical investigations that are part of a longer tradition in political science of identifying the 'determinants of democracy.'[17] In this literature, institutional stability is treated as part of a complex of factors that make democracy work.[18]

In new institutionalism, institutional stability is less a fact derived from empirical measures than a theoretical supposition. New institutionalist theorists have two main explanations for institutional stability: historical institutionalists refer to 'path dependency' while rational choice institutionalists rely on 'voluntary agreements.' Pierson has noted that 'it is increasingly common for social scientists to describe political processes as "path dependent" by which they mean, in a general sense, that "history matters."'[19] That is, the timing and sequence of even the smallest of events can have enduring and large consequential effects on the development of political life. For new institutionalist theorists working in political science, path dependency means that institutional choices made at critical junctures in the past can be more important for explaining political outcomes than relatively recent events, even when these are 'big.' To take a hypothetical example, although no one would dispute that the events of 9/11 were big, they are possibly less significant for explaining the recent emergence of security measures in North America and the EU than earlier 'small' events. The historical trajectory of the emergence of citizenship laws in these states – some of which have promoted loyalty and assimilation while others have made integration of minorities impossible – might better explain why governments are now scrambling to do something to protect their citizens from potential terrorists in the short term while attempting to create more inclusive citizenship laws for the longer term. The problem, in other words, did not emerge on 9/11; it has long been in existence because of particular choices about the rules for membership in these societies made at critical junctures in the past but which have been out of step with changes in patterns of global migration beginning in the 1960s.

The continued salience of these past choices derives from the concept of 'increasing returns': once initial start-up costs are made and learning and adaptation have taken place, the cost of switching paths, which would entail a new investment of time and resources in the short term, exceeds the benefit of staying the course. There are increasing returns for continuing along the same path given the sunken costs and the way in which actors have adapted to a particular institutional constellation: it is not only the institution itself which is at issue but also the social and political networks that it has spawned. As a result of this positive feedback loop, actors become 'locked-in' to their original institutional choices so that there is now a single equilibrium, whereas multiple equilibria might have existed at the point of departure. The outcome is institutional stasis or a clear inertia in the face of institutional change. Because institutions embody power asymmetries between different political actors, institutional stasis is still likely even in cases where a weaker actor seeks change. The study of politics is replete with marginalized, underprivileged, and minority groups who seek change but do not have the means to achieve it.[20] Indeed, new institutionalism maintains that formal political institutions are 'change-resistant' because they have built-in barriers to reform. Political stability requires that the actions of political players be predictable over time; institutional continuity guarantees predictability.

Institutional continuity, according to historical institutionalists, should not be interpreted as an indication of efficiency or optimality. The institutions on our political landscape – formal political institutions, in particular – are rarely efficient, and critics can imagine a range of alternative designs to make institutions more optimal. Rather, institutional continuity is an indicator of the prohibitive costs of switching to a design that had been presented as an option at an earlier point in time. By contrast, rational choice institutionalists do view institutional stability as a sign of continued efficiency. Institutions, in this variant of new institutionalism, are quasi contracts emanating from the voluntary agreements among actors having roughly equal amounts of power. The parties to the contract assume that actors operate using a strategic calculus that is motivated not only by their preferences but also by their assessment of how other actors will behave. In order to avoid the sub-optimal outcomes that result from the pursuit of individual rationality – as exemplified by the Prisoner's Dilemma – a form of predictable and complementary behaviour that is defined by a specified range of options and alternatives is required. Institutions, by structuring interactions in this way and providing much needed decision-making and enforcement rules, allow actors to capture the 'gains from exchange' that would otherwise be lost. Both rational choice institutionalists and their critics often refer to the functionalism of rational choice explanations for the creation of an institution: it is 'purpose-built' to assist actors in realizing benefits through cooperation and, 'if [it were] subject to a process of competitive selection, it [would] survive primarily because it provides more benefits to the relevant actors than alternate institutional forms.'[21]

There are two ways of approaching the question of institutional change in rational choice institutionalism. First, accounts of rational choice institutionalism that emphasize functionalism would argue that when there are unintended consequences associated with the functioning of a particular institution, then that institution is no longer performing the function for which it was originally created. In such cases, actors will seek to change the institution. An alternative approach would be to argue that it is theoretically possible in rational choice institutionalism for some of the benefits derived from an institution to be related to the same 'increasing returns' that historical institutionalists study. That is, even if there are unintended policy consequences from an institution over the long term, actors might have adapted to the institution itself in such a way that it would be too costly to create a new institution. The advantage of this second view is that 'rather than explaining the institution by the functions it would provide for the actors at the time, the institution is explained as the result of self-interested actors making instrumental choices based on their understanding of the effects of their decisions on their own goals.'[22]

In summary, although historical and rational choice institutionalists have different definitions of institutions, they both assume, for theoretical reasons, institutional stasis. In this sense, new institutionalism joins a long tradition in comparative politics in positing institutional stasis as a condition for stable political and social outcomes. However, where new institutionalism differs from other approaches in the subfield is that it problematizes institutional stasis and attempts to explain it using the arguments outlined above. Furthermore, new institutionalism depends on institutional stasis in order to be able to test for the effects of institutions on the behaviour of social and political actors and for explaining differences in outcomes across cases. But, as the next section details, the assumption about institutional stasis is now being challenged both from within and without new institutionalism.

Reviewing the Debate on Institutional Change:
New Institutionalists and Their Critics

The most recent critics of new institutionalism have challenged the idea of institutional stasis from both an empirical and a theoretical perspective. The empirical critique maintains that while it might be theoretically possible to postulate conditions for institutional stasis, the empirical reality is that institutions are not as change resistant as new institutionalists claim. If this is true, then theories of institutional stasis need to be modified. Presently, when institutional change does take place, new institutionalists draw on exogenous factors as explanations. However, as critics point out, the need to do so points to an incoherence in new institutionalism: the idea of 'increasing returns' suggests that institutional change is unlikely because it is too costly. Costs are understood not only in terms of the material risks associated with the uncertainty of new institutions, but also in terms of the transition costs associated with learning new institutional rules and regulations, on the one hand, and adapting to these, on the other. But critics charge that if institutional change takes place despite these assumed costs, then new institutionalism theory needs to be able to explain change through reference to the nature of institutions themselves. I refer to this as the 'coherence critique.' The possibility that certain exogenous shocks reduce, suspend, or eliminate the costs associated with change does not seem plausible.

The coherence critique is directed at the posited source of institutional change. As we saw above, the concept of path dependency makes it difficult to theorize about endogenous sources of change. The earliest literature on institutions in international relations and comparative politics was concerned with establishing institutional stability through arguments about either institutional 'breadth and depth'[23] or path dependency. When change was considered at all, two dominant features characterized the literature: first, change is generally assumed to be of a critical nature, and second, change is episodic. Borrowing from Stephen Jay Gould's model of 'punctuated equilibrium,' theorists argue that periods of institutional equilibrium – marked by stasis and 'lock-in' – are interrupted by sudden, critical events that disrupt a stable environment by creating opportunities for innovation and change. For the most part, the types of crises are international in scope and appear to force change upon actors. International relations scholars, in particular, refer to 'triggers' that destabilize the international system: wars, terrorism, geopolitical conflicts, global economic crises, and so on. There is not much reference to agency in this discussion of change; instead, actors appear to react to events not of their own making in an attempt to restore system-wide stability. Institutional change is the means they use to restore order. In comparative politics, there has until recently been even less discussion of institutional change. However, in line with an established tradition in the sub-field, the emphasis has similarly been on exogenous macro-structural forces that reconfigure material interests. The episodic nature of change explains the timing of the realignment of classes, groups, or sectors and the emergence of new coalitions for change.[24]

Critics are right to point to the fact that the reliance on exogenous forces to explain institutional change tends to discredit new institutionalism theorizing: just as new institutionalism can explain the origin and persistence of institutions through reference to the characteristics of institutions themselves, so should it be able to explain institutional change through reference to endogenous factors. However, it is worth considering the possibility that in some cases the line between exogeneity and endogenity is in fact blurred. An exogenous shock might emerge in response to factors that are endogenous to an institutional system. Thanks to globalization, the institutional setting in which states are operating is increasingly complex and multilayered with the result that it is difficult to distinguish between internal and external environments. For example, in the context of multilevel governance in the European Union, is an institutional development at the European level exogenous or endogenous to institutions at the sub-state level?

We know from the extensive literature on multilevel governance that the political and policy links between the sub-state and the supra-state levels are increasingly developed: it is not unlikely that a directive from Brussels might force a change upon a regional governing institution. Indeed, in multilevel institutional settings, we might expect to find plenty of examples of 'nested games': institutional change at the sub-state level is a response to political developments at the European level that are nested within, say, regional party politics.[25]

The reliance on critical junctures to explain change does not satisfy some new institutionalist theorists either. Kathleen Thelen raises the point that many institutions persist in the face of exogenous shocks or broad macro-historical transformations.[26] Extending this observation further, she maintains that while these institutions persist, they have been marked by subtle changes over time: 'institutional stability,' Thelen hypothesises, 'may include a major dose of institutional adaptation.'[27]

This is a new spin on a debate in the literature over what constitutes institutional change. Critics of new institutionalism charge that there is far more institutional change than is assumed by new institutionalist theorists (the 'empirical critique'), but the types of change that these critics examine are incremental, amounting either to a reform or revision of existing institutions. New institutionalist theorists presume that if institutional change does occur, it is motivated by the need to reduce uncertainty of outcomes linked to existing institutions. Uncertainty can be the result of unintended consequences or a change to the environment in which an institution is located (possibly because of an exogenous shock). Incremental change is similarly believed to be motivated by the need to reduce the uncertainty connected with existing institutions. However, this type of change is more likely to be a form of institutional adaptation because institutions are reformed or revised in response to an environmental factor rather than substituted with new institutions. Incremental change rarely ushers in a completely new set of decision rules but rather adjusts existing rules at the margins, perhaps by changing the procedure of decision-making rather than the rules for decision-making. While incremental change is not without consequence – even some procedural changes can alter the distribution of power – it is less likely that such change will result in a radically new redistribution of resources when compared with changes in decision-making rules.

If incremental change and institutional adaptation are taken to be examples of institutional change, then arguments against the assumption about institutional stability in new institutionalism are easily constructed. For example, Gerald Alexander argues that *'revising* formal political institutions appears not to generate such high costs [as new institutionalists claim]'[28] and offers several examples of institutional designs from among the consolidated democracies of the developed West that are contested and ultimately revised or reformed.[29] When revision or reform is taken as evidence of change, then it can readily be argued that there is less political predictability than presumed by path dependency arguments and therefore, there are increased opportunities for institutional change. Arguing against this position, Shepsle has countered that there is an important distinction between binding and non-binding constraints (rules). By relaxing any non-binding constraints, a change may have taken place but it is more cosmetic than substantial in that it produces only a very small effect. To relax a binding constraint, on the other hand, would produce a more concrete change with a larger effect on the distribution of power. In the end, institutional change must refer to the binding constraints by which decisions are made if the study of institutional change is to have any bite at all.

Another possible line of argument is suggested by Thelen's observation that institutional stability might include institutional adaptation: the reason that institutions are durable is that actors manage to adapt them to changes in the surrounding environment. She suggests two types of adaptation: layering and conversion. The former 'involves the partial renegotiation of some elements of a given set of institutions while leaving others in place,' whereas the latter refers to redirecting institutions to new purposes.[30] Over time, a series of small adaptations might amount to a substantial change to the original institution but the extent of the change might only be appreciated in hindsight or, it might not be noticed at all, if the constituency that the institution was originally intended to serve no longer exists. Few theorists could dispute Thelen's argument that there are forms of change that fall far short of the complete substitution or replacement of one institution by another. Indeed, institutional layering and conversion are non-controversial forms of institutional change because they largely pass unnoticed: actors use the existing rules of the game to bring about change. They might push these rules to the limit or bend them here and there, but they do not operate outside them. Indeed, institutions are a resource for actors seeking incremental change: by using the existing institution as a base, they might be able to secure the outcome they are after without having to introduce new institutions. The result would be institutional stability and continuity, even if political outcomes were affected.

To sum up this section, there is a difference of opinion in the literature over what constitutes institutional change. Actually, the debate is over degrees of change: is reform change or something else? Does a series of reforms – adaptation – amount to change or is it evidence of institutional continuity and stability? The answers to these questions are beyond the scope of this chapter: I flag them here because until they are debated and resolved, a theory of institutional change will not be possible. It is also worth cautioning that the debate should be resolved so that we can renew the original purpose of new institutionalism, which is to study political outcomes, not to write histories of particular institutions. With that in mind, the next section moves to consider how institutional change can be explained. Different theoretical proposals have been advanced in response to this challenge; when some of these are combined, we have the beginnings of a theory of endogenous institutional change.

Elements of a Theory of Institutional Change

The starting point for a theory of endogenous institutional change is to identify *why* certain actors would seek change despite the benefits of 'staying the course' that are implied by path dependency arguments. Moreover, 'an institutional regime impounds a great deal of information about how political games are played and what can be expected' – information which acts as a deterrent to change.[31] One argument has been that actors will seek change when existing institutions are somehow discredited or delegitimized.[32] From a normative perspective, there is a strong tradition in liberal democratic theory that maintains that justifiable political authority requires that governing institutions, and in particular decision rules, be viewed as legitimate by a substantial majority of the population.[33] But even when pockets of the population view institutions as illegitimate and campaign against them, political authority can be challenged. We can think of various factors that would give rise to a condition whereby a portion of the population withdraws its support for governing institutions, thereby deeming them illegitimate. Some actors might begin to push the existing rules of the game to the limit, thereby creating uncertainty for other actors. Or, an institution might no longer redistribute resources in an equitable way, prompting the protests and defection of any disadvantaged groups. Still another option might be a shift in the preferences of some actors, which cannot be accommodated by existing institutions. In all of these cases, and other similar ones, actors are forced to re-examine the usefulness of existing institutions.

Simply to reach the conclusion that existing institutions are no longer credible does not, however, mean that they can easily be changed. Many sub-state nationalist movements have long charged that state structures are illegitimate because they discriminate against their rights to representation and the public use of their culture. Moreover, where such movements openly reject the state's authority, the state cannot easily claim that citizen loyalty is the basis of its sovereign legitimacy. Despite the existence of state structures that sub-state nationalists deem 'illegitimate,' the long history of sub-state nationalism makes clear that such movements have not met with much success when it comes to replacing the centralized state authority with their preferred institutional alternatives. Compared with state actors, sub-state nationalist actors are relatively weak; consequently, their straightforward preference for change is not sufficient for bringing it about. Therefore, we need to consider other factors beyond actors' motives, such as opportunities and resources.

Accordingly, the second step in building a theory of institutional change is to establish *when* actors are most likely to be able to initiate change. In other words, what conditions facilitate change? A standard argument is that actors are most likely to be able to initiate institutional change when they are presented with an opportunity to do so. Recent arguments by comparative political scientists maintain that actors can initiate change in response to 'windows of opportunity' that are presented in the form of *either* international *or* domestic triggers. According to Andrew Cortell and Susan Peterson, 'every environmental trigger – whether a crisis or non-crisis – creates the opportunity for structural change if it discredits existing institutions or raises concerns about the adequacy of current policy-making processes.'[34] To large-scale international triggers for change are added domestic ones, such as a change of government following a democratic election, demographic change, or social conflict. Although the type of change introduced by non-crisis triggers tends to be incremental in nature, Cortell and Peterson hold that non-crisis triggers are just as likely to 'dismantle or alter institutional configurations'[35] as are crisis-driven triggers.

In positing domestic triggers, Cortell and Peterson borrow John Kingdon's 'windows of opportunity' to argue that advocates for change – Kingdon's 'policy entrepreneurs' – use these opportunities to push forward their agendas for change.[36] The advantage of this approach is that institutional change can come on the heels of non-crisis triggers. The disadvantage of this approach is that it relies on environmental triggers, which are necessarily exogenous to the institutions that actors seek to change.[37] Therefore, this explanation will fail to satisfy fully new institutionalism's critics.

Every attempt at theorizing institutional change seems to get stuck at this point: unless there is a trigger – either domestic or international – that reduces the costs associated with change and cancels out the increased returns associated with path dependency, there is no easy explanation for the timing of institutional change. Therefore, much of the literature on institutional change has focused on identifying those opportunities that allow actors to pursue relatively low-cost opportunities to change institutions. However, there is an alternative theoretical path, which is to focus on *how* actors can pursue change. The emphasis here is placed on resources as opposed to opportunities.[38] In his study of the transformation of Swedish social democracy beginning in the 1960s, Mark Blyth argued that Swedish business started to view the institutions of the Swedish model as discredited after Swedish 'labor experienced increasing returns to continued participation while business suffered diminishing returns once labor became institutionally powerful enough to challenge businesses' rights of ownership.'[39] Two points are crucial here: first, power asymmetries were changed through the institutions themselves and, second, a straightforward cost-benefit analysis was the basis for a change in business's view of the legitimacy of the institutions of the Swedish model. According to Blyth, there was no environmental trigger – no opportunity – that initiated the process of change. Instead, actors drew exclusively on their resources to initiate change. As I argued above when discussing Thelen's contribution to 'how institutions' evolve, institutions themselves can act as resources. Therefore, in seeking to explain institutional change, it might be possible to focus exclusively on resources and the ability of actors to deploy these in order to implement their agendas for change.

The advantage of a resource-based approach is that it moves the focus of investigation from questions of the form – exogenous or endogenous – of institutional change to a sustained examination of the costs of institutional change. Examinations that focus on 'triggers' do not adequately explain how triggers reduce costs. However, resource-based explanations necessarily focus on costs. Resources are not here limited to power and money. Blyth's important contribution to the debate on institutional change is to argue for ideational factors at this juncture. Presumably, the final objective when initiating a process of institutional change – or, seeking to implement one's agenda for change – is to arrive at a set of new institutions. But in deciding on the form of these new institutions, actors rely on ideas. In the case of Swedish business, these were neo-liberal ideas, which had already gained currency elsewhere in the developed West. Ideational factors do not discount the importance of material and structural forces, but they fill an important gap in the literature by giving some additional substance to the concept of resources, at the same time as they make explicit the new preferences and interests of actors seeking institutional change.

New ideas can be costly, however. Any discussion of ideational factors must be able to show that in seeking institutional change actors weigh up the costs of change – which include propagating the new ideas – against the costs of staying the course. This is a difficult, if not impossible, task, which would rely on the use of counterfactuals: we can never know with certainty what opportunity costs would be associated with pursuing one option over another, since other factors could conceivably intervene to affect overall costs. Nevertheless, the important point is that actors themselves must make these calculations and make their strategic decisions based on their best estimates. Blyth's account of Swedish business's decision to initiate institutional change does not include a discussion of these estimates and, as an attempt to stake out a general explanation for institutional change, fails to convince. For example, Swedish business decided to withdraw unilaterally from the corporatist institutions of the Swedish model, but Blyth makes no reference to any penalties associated with this move. Similarly, the process of introducing neo-liberal ideas in Sweden was 'long, expensive, and difficult.'[40] Therefore, it would useful to know whether business absorbed these costs because it expected neo-liberalism would return long-term benefits that would eventually balance its accounts or because it believed in these ideas at all costs. In short, ideational factors tell us how actors introduce new institutions, but they do not provide the whole picture. Therefore, in focusing on resources to explain institutional change, scholars must give some consideration to how resources are spent.

Path dependency theorists are right: moving from one path to another is costly, and actors will only undertake to do so once they have made some calculations about the uncertainty (due to the loss of legitimacy of the institutions) associated with staying on the present path and the expected long-term gains associated with moving to a new path. Ideational factors are clearly important in helping us understand the nature of the new path but, as the Swedish case makes clear, at the bottom of ideational factors are certain assumptions about the redistribution of resources. Therefore, in theorizing the possibility of institutional change, we need to consider the length of actors' time horizons versus the costs of making a change. That is, if actors have a long time horizon they might be willing to absorb the cost of making an institutional change. They calculate that institutional change will result in higher aggregate returns over the long run. By contrast, a short time horizon – which is normally assumed when dealing with political actors – would mean that institutional change, which is costly, is unlikely. To pick up on an earlier discussion, this is why the distinction between incremental and institutional change is so important: in the end, a decision to initiate change will be based on actors' time horizons, the balance between short- and long-term benefits, and transition costs. Incremental change is most likely to result in short-term benefits most of the time and will therefore be pursued by actors with short time horizons. The start-up and transition costs are unlikely to be high in cases of incremental change, while the learning effects are bound to be negligible. Actors are, after all, revising or reforming existing institutions: many, if not most, rules of the game will remain the same.

To summarize: there is an emerging theory of institutional change in the literature on new institutionalism, which can be assembled from several recent contributions to the ongoing debate about change by new institutionalists and their critics. As it currently stands, the elements of the theory are as follows:

1. There are two preconditions for endogenous institutional change:
   a. 'Loss of legitimacy': Refers to the discrediting or delegitimization of existing institutions. Actors no longer view an institution as legitimate when it fails to guarantee certainty or when decision rules systematically and regularly discriminate against them.
   b. 'Cost calculation': A calculation by actors of the likely short and

long-term costs and benefits of change which factors in actors' time horizons.
2. Two independent variables explain institutional change:
   a. 'Windows of opportunity' (the timing of change): Some political climates are more favourable to change than others. Actors' agendas for change might accelerate during propitious periods and stall under adverse environmental conditions. In the absence of a window of opportunity, the pursuit of institutional change will likely be costly. These costs can be reduced when actors can take advantage of windows of opportunity (i.e., they are mobilized and 'ready to go').
   b. Resources (the means to change): These can be of a non-material or material nature. For the former, actors will be unable to advance their agendas for institutional change unless they have concrete ideas about the form of the new institutions that they seek to set up. Ideas are also necessary in order to build coalitions for change in democratic societies. Implementing ideas in the form of new or reformed institutions requires material resources, such as funds for campaigning around the new ideas or for absorbing any short-term losses associated with seeking change.

The elements of a theory of institutional change outlined above resemble those found in the synthetic approach to social movement theory that emerged in the mid-1990s: mobilizing structures and processes, political opportunity structures, framing processes, collective identity, and repertoires of contention.[41] The resemblance underscores the heavy doses of agency and structure that are present in new institutionalism: our political environment – of which institutions are a part – shapes the realm of the possible and how we organize and mobilize largely determines whether or not we will be successful in our political goals. Second, this resemblance reminds us that bringing about institutional change – whatever the degree – is ultimately a political act. We already have many models of political mobilization: do we need a completely new one to explain institutional change? The answer would be 'yes' only if we judged that the study of institutional change should be a field of study in its own right, but 'no' if it was felt that institutional change is only important insofar as it challenges the theoretical presupposition of established theories in comparative politics. Again, this is not a debate that can be resolved here although this chapter has leaned more towards the latter view.

Studying Institutional Change: Canada in Comparative Perspective

Let's assume that a theory of institutional change is required. How can Canadian political scientists contribute to this task? The move towards a genuine theory of institutional change requires a series of comparative investigations to which Canadian political scientists are ideally placed to contribute. Canada itself is something of a laboratory of examples of recent institutional change. Moreover, these changes are instances of a more globalized phenomenon, creating the opportunity for comparative perspectives. Two examples of institutional change stand out: the extension of self-government to certain aboriginal groups and the question of judicial supremacy. I consider each of these below and suggest that the significance of these examples of institutional change is best understood in a comparative light.

Self-government for Aboriginal Peoples

Claims to self-government on the part of aboriginal peoples in British settler societies are part of a process of removing colonial institutions that aboriginals view as illegitimate. The principal reasons for this illegitimacy are extensively discussed in the literature and only need to be referred to here: state institutions do not reflect the core values of aboriginal communities, and the governing relationship between aboriginal peoples and the state was not voluntarily entered into by the former. Sub-state national groups have made very similar arguments about the lack of legitimacy of state institutions on their territory. Claims for self-determination necessarily involve creating new decision-making institutions for self-government by members of the community. Where the acquisition of these institutions does not require secession, aboriginal communities and sub-state national groups view these institutions as a net gain for members of the community. Sometimes, the gain is cast in non-material terms: freedom, cultural preservation, and so forth. In material terms, the ability of these communities to make decisions about how to spend their resources is also viewed as a net gain even if some monies are originally lost because of changes to the fiscal relationship between the state and the community. For example, aboriginal Canadians have enjoyed an exemption from various forms of tax which, in most cases, will be lost with self-government. Despite real fears of fiscal responsibility on the part of both these communities and the federal government, aboriginal communities view financial management as a challenge that is inherent to self-government and which they must face. Evidence for the way in which these groups have calculated the costs and benefits of self-government is readily available. Similarly, this evidence is available for the cost-benefit analyses performed by several key constituencies within sub-state national groups, such as political parties and sectoral or professional associations.

The introduction of aboriginal self-government in Canada in recent years is mirrored by new constitutional relations between states and sub-state national groups in Europe. To date, there is no theoretical explanation for these forms of institutional change. We do not know (1) why certain groups have been successful in having their demands for self-determination met while others have not; (2) why states which historically have resisted change have now consented to devolving political authority to sub-state communities; and (3) why many of these changes have occurred in the last ten to twenty years when sub-state nations and aboriginal groups have been campaigning for decades if not centuries. As per the theoretical outline above, two explanatory factors suggest themselves. First, the answers to these various questions could have something to do with timing and opportunities. These opportunities might be case-specific, but they are just as likely to be common to several cases: for example, the end of the Cold War has reduced security risks and therefore the need to consolidate power in a central authority. Furthermore, processes of integration at the interstate level, particularly in Europe, have reconfigured sovereign relations between the state and supranational organizations, on the one hand, and sub-national organizations, on the other. It is possible that self-government at the sub-state level is an outcome of these processes.[42]

Second, these questions might also be answered by considering the role of resources. For example, it could be argued that important ideational factors related to developments in liberal theory are key for explaining new forms of self-government at the sub-state level. According to these new ideas, the stability of liberal democratic states is no longer threatened by claims to group-differentiated rights. Moreover, multiple and competing national identities and loyalties within the state's boundaries are no longer considered to be a recipe for state disintegration. In Canada, aspects of these new ideas were disseminated through the Royal Commission on Aboriginal Peoples, but the main proponents of many of these ideas – and their ideas themselves – are also well known in European circles.[43] Therefore, a comparative investigation of the way in which these ideas have influenced both the mobilization and strategies of aboriginal and sub-state national groups as well as governments' responses to their demands might yield important results. Such an investigation must make clear what forms of decision rules are implicit in such ideas.[44] As discussed above, selling ideas requires material resources; therefore, any comparative inquiry must also take these into account. It might transpire that whatever the cross-national popularity of new liberal ideas about national identities and loyalties, some groups might have failed to have these ideas implemented because they lacked the material resources to make their case.

Judicial Activism: The Role of the Supreme Court in Canadian Federalism since the Charter

One hotly debated theme among Canadian political scientists has been that of judicial activism since the promulgation of the Canadian Charter of Rights and Freedoms.[45] Critics of the Charter argue that in its Charter decisions the Court has championed national values at the expense of provincial values and in so doing has threatened the balance between parliament, the judiciary, and the provinces. As one scholar has noted, because 'Canada is a federal system, Charter review has serious implications for the level of policy diversity evident in Canada and the ability of provincial governments to pursue policy agendas that reflect the priorities of provincial societies.'[46] Studies of the Charter have underscored how the enforcement of a national legal document in a federal state can work against some of the principles underpinning the institutions of federalism itself. In the Canadian case, there is a potential conflict between the application of universal rights in a country that has allowed regional diversity through federalism. Whether or not Charter critics are correct about the way in which the Court has sought to promulgate certain values since 1982 is, in part, an empirical question that others have attempted to resolve.[47] However, beyond the numbers and figures lie more important questions related to institutional change in a democratic setting: Has the arrival of the Charter paved the way towards a form of judicial supremacy via an erosion of parliamentary supremacy? In other words, is the Court, whose members are unelected, the keeper of the Constitution at the expense of democratically elected members of parliament? From an institutional perspective, the rise of judicial supremacy might be the result of a perception on the part of judges after 1982 that the institution of Canadian federalism – which privileged provincial rights and parliamentary supremacy – was discredited because provincial and federal parliaments were unwilling to legislate in accordance with new principles contained in the Charter.

Similar questions and concerns have been raised within the European Union in relationship to the European Court of Justice. Indeed, judicial activism has been a key topic for investigation in studies of European integration[48] and is a frequent object of examination in the debate between neo-functionalists and liberal intergovernmentalists.[49] The ECJ, like other international tribunals, started its life as a weak institution operating in the murky waters of international law. Since its inception, the ECJ has managed to transform itself into one of the most powerful institutions on the European landscape, having the power to declare national law illegal when it contradicts European Union law. By establishing the judicial supremacy of EU over national law through the doctrine of 'direct effect' – by which EU law creates rights that can be claimed through national courts – the ECJ could influence the policy agendas and policymaking processes of national governments. One school of thought in the field of EU studies argues that the ECJ enjoys sufficient legal autonomy to be able to push forward its agenda for European integration against the wishes of member states.[50] Institutionally, the ECJ might have sought to do so, beginning in the 1960s, because the emerging principles associated with the European Community Treaty – which has created a community of unlimited duration with its attendant institutions – were not properly respected by national courts and member governments. The principle of state sovereignty and the judicial supremacy of national law were discredited as a result.

According to one school of thought, the establishment of judicial supremacy (Canada) or the supremacy of EU law would amount to a net gain for the courts by allowing them to consolidate both judicial and political power.[51] But assuming that there has been some move away from parliamentary supremacy in both cases, we need to be able to explain how this has happened. One potential explanation would focus on the opportunities presented to the judiciary with the introduction of new legal documents negotiated by political actors: the federal parliament, in the case of the Charter, and the intergovernmental conferences, in the case of the European Union treaties. This is a fairly one-dimensional explanation that would benefit from some further consideration of the resources available to judges. The principle of judicial independence is one important resource that, hypothetically, could make it relatively easy for the court to pursue its agenda for change in each of the two cases. This agenda would be informed by ideas related to universal principles and, in the EU, the 'four freedoms.'

But the story is more complicated than this: Justices are not the only interested parties in the new era of policymaking ushered in by the Charter or the supremacy of EU law. For Canada, James Kelly has introduced the concept of 'Charter activism' in recognition of the fact that 'multiple forms of activism, and not simply its judicial manifestation, structure the Charter's relationship to Canadian democracy.' In his estimation, democratic activism, judicial activism, and legislative activism serve as countervailing forces which, on balance, ensure constitutional supremacy in Canada. Kelly's research suggests that to resolve the debate about the supposed judicial supremacy in Canada, we cannot ignore the resources available to other actors, such as bureaucrats, legislators, and citizens.[52] Kelly's criticism of existing work on judicial activism and the Charter – that it is overly focused on the judiciary – could well be made of studies of the ECJ. Compared with research that has been done on the Canadian case, we know very little about how national parliaments (or even regional ones) and interested groups in civil society have responded to the establishment of the supremacy of EU law.[53]

Conclusion

Recent criticism of new institutionalism has focused on the question of institutional change. Two aspects in particular have forced new institutionalist scholars to consider more carefully the merits of new institutionalism for explaining social and political outcomes. First, critics have charged that there are more instances of institutional change in the political world than new institutionalism, with its assumptions about path dependency and institutional stasis, allows. However, this criticism relies primarily on examples of institutional reform and revision, and there is an ongoing debate in the literature over whether reform, adaptation, and evolution constitute change. Therefore, the argument for a theory of institutional change based on empirical reality is not yet conclusive. Nevertheless, a second criticism of new institutionalism is that for reasons of coherence, it should be able to explain institutional change without resorting to the use of exogenous forces.

The argument that path dependency is a valid argument for institutional stasis that can only be challenged by factors from outside the argument itself is neither theoretically compelling nor easily defensible. For these reasons, new institutionalist theorists need to give some thought to the development of an endogenous theory of institutional change.

New institutionalist scholars have taken some steps towards addressing both criticisms. In fact, the debate about what constitutes change has opened up the door to a theory of endogenous institutional change. Recent efforts will no doubt evolve through a continued dialogue over both criticisms, but the utility and relationship of such a theory to new institutionalism needs to be clearly explicated. By drawing on existing research on why institutions change, this chapter posited some elements of a theory of institutional change by specifying the conditions under which it could occur and two possible explanatory factors that can bring it about. By way of illustration, two contemporary examples of institutional change from the Canadian and European contexts were examined using the theoretical outline developed. Canadian political scientists are engaged in important investigations of institutional change, although the terms of inquiry are rarely cast in this light. I have attempted to direct their attention to genuinely comparative research on institutional change – to which they can bring their considerable research experience to bear – and the broader issue of theory building in new institutionalism.

Notes

1 Peter A. Hall and Rosemary C.R. Taylor, 'Political Science and the Three New Institutionalisms,' *Political Studies*, 43 (1996), 936–57.
2 Ellen M. Immergut, 'The Theoretical Core of the New Institutionalism,' *Politics and Society*, 26 (1998), 25.
3 However, a recent attempt to specify such a methodology for historical institutionalism can be found in Evan S. Lieberman, 'Causal Inference in Historical Institutional Analysis: A Specification of Periodization Strategies,' *Comparative Political Studies*, 34 (2001), 1011–35.
4 The contributors to Juan J. Linz and Alfred Stepan (eds.), *The Breakdown of Democratic Regimes* (Baltimore: Johns Hopkins, 1978) examine the role of political actors in breakdowns and as such make regimes the dependent variable. By contrast, in *Subversive Institutions: The Design and Destruction of Socialism and the State* (Cambridge: Cambridge University Press, 1999),

Valerie Bunce makes regime collapse the dependent variable and institutional design (as well as certain international opportunities) the independent variable.

5 Philippe Schmitter, Guillermo O'Donnell, and Laurence Whitehead (eds.), *Transitions from Authoritarian Rule*, 3 vols. (Baltimore: Johns Hopkins, 1986); Samuel P. Huntington, *The Third Wave: Democratization in the Late Twentieth Century* (Norman: University of Oklahoma Press, 1991); Adam Przeworski, *Democracy and the Market: Political and Economic Reforms in Eastern Europe and Latin America* (Cambridge: Cambridge University Press, 1991); Alfred Stepan and Cindy Skach, 'Constitutional Frameworks and Democratic Consolidation: Parliamentarism and Presidentialism,' *World Politics*, 46 (1993), 1–22; Barry R. Weingast, 'The Political Foundations of Democracy and the Rule of Law,' *American Political Science Review*, 91 (1997), 245–63; Adam Przeworski, Michael Alvarez, José Cheibub, and Fernando Limongi, *Democracy and Development: Political Institutions and Well-Being in the World, 1950–1990* (Cambridge: Cambridge University Press, 2000).

6 There is an emerging literature on the importance of domestic governing institutions for stabilizing post-conflict settings by promoting certainty. See Barbara Walter, 'Designing Transitions from Civil War: Demobilization, Democratization, and Commitments to Peace,' *International Security*, 24 (1999), 127–56; John McGarry (ed.), *Northern Ireland and the Divided World: The Northern Ireland Conflict and the Good Friday Agreement in Comparative Perspective* (Oxford: Oxford University Press, 2001); Andrew Reynolds (ed.), *The Architecture of Democracy: Constitutional Design, Conflict Management and Democracy* (Oxford: Oxford University Press, 2002); Philip Roeder and Donald Rothchild (eds.), *Powersharing and Peacemaking* (forthcoming).

7 Aside from the literature that is cited elsewhere in this chapter, other scholarly efforts to address institutional change include, W.W. Powell and D.L. Jones (eds.), *How Institutions Change* (Chicago: University of Chicago Press, forthcoming); and the recent Joint Sessions Workshop of the European Consortium for Political Research (ECPR) on *Institutional Theory: Issues of Measurement and Change*, Edinburgh, 28 March to 2 April 2003, convened by Uwe Serdült and B. Guy Peters.

8 Paul Pierson, 'The Limits of Design: Explaining Institutional Origin and Change,' *Governance: An International Journal of Policy and Administration*, 13 (2000), 475.

9 Kenneth Shepsle, 'A Comment on Institutional Change,' *Journal of Theoretical Politics*, 13 (2001), 321.

10 Hall and Taylor, 'Political Science and the Three New Institutionalisms,' 936.

11 Peter A. Hall, *Governing the Economy: The Politics of State Intervention in Britain and France* (Oxford: Polity Press, 1986), 19.

12 I include policy networks as part of this process although other scholars view such networks as institutions in and of themselves. In opposition to this perspective, I would argue that such networks operate within existing institutions and as such play by the rules of these institutions. For the view that policy networks are institutions, see Andrew P. Cortell and Susan Peterson, 'Altered States: Explaining Domestic Institutional Change,' *British Journal of Political Science*, 29 (1999), 177–203.

13 Immergut, 'The Theoretical Core,' 25.

14 Samuel P. Huntington, *Political Order in Changing Societies* (New Haven: Yale University Press, 1968).

15 See especially, Guillermo O'Donnell and Philippe Schmitter, *Transitions from Authoritarian Rule: Tentative Conclusions about Uncertain Democracies* (Baltimore: Johns Hopkins, 1986).

16 Cass Sunstein, *Designing Democracy: What Constitutions Do* (Oxford: Oxford University Press, 2001).

17 Seymour Martin Lipset: 'Some Social Requisites of Democracy; Economic Development and Political Legitimacy,' *American Political Science Review*, 53 (1959), 69–105; 'The Social Requisites of Democracy Revisited,' *American Sociological Review*, 59 (1994), 1–22; Tatu Vanhanen, *Prospects of Democracy: A Study of 172 Countries* (London and New York: Routledge, 1997); Arend Lijphart, *Patterns of Democracy: Government Forms and Performance in Thirty-Six Countries* (New Haven: Yale University Press, 1999).

18 Lisa Anderson (ed.), *Transitions to Democracy* (New York: Columbia University Press, 1999); Robert D. Putnam, with Robert Léonardi and Rafaella Nanetti, *Making Democracy Work: Civic Traditions in Modern Italy* (Princeton: Princeton University Press, 1993).

19 Paul Pierson, 'Increasing Returns, Path Dependence and the Study of Politics,' *American Political Science Review*, 94 (2000), 251–2.

20 We will examine some of the conditions which might facilitate change for such groups below.

21 Hall and Taylor, 'Political Science and the Three Institutionalisms,' 945.

22 Gary Miller, 'Rational Choice and Dysfunctional Institutions,' *Governance: An International Journal of Policy and Administration*, 13 (2000), 540.

23 Stephen Krasner, 'Sovereignty: An Institutional Perspective,' *Comparative Political Studies*, 21 (1988), 66–94.

24 For example, Ronald Rogowski, *Commerce and Coalitions* (Princeton: Princeton University Press, 1989). For a selection of case studies that analyse institutions as meso-level factors for explaining political outcomes, see Sven

Steinmo, Kathleen Thelen, and Frank Longstreth (eds.), *Structuring Politics: Historical Institutionalism in Comparative Analysis* (Cambridge: Cambridge University Press, 1992).

25 I thank an anonymous reviewer for having pointed out this relationship between exogeneity and endogeneity.

26 Without disagreeing with Thelen's observation, it is interesting to note that consistent with 'punctuated equilibrium' explanations of change generally, she does not suggest a role for agency. Maybe some institutions persist in the face of exogenous shocks because political actors work hard to ensure that they do. Conversely, institutional change in the face of the same shock could be due to actors seizing the opportunity to innovate.

27 Kathleen Thelen, 'How Institutions Evolve: Insights from Comparative Historical Analysis,' in James Mahoney and Dietrich Rueschemeyer (eds.), *Comparative Historical Analysis in the Social Sciences* (Cambridge: Cambridge University Press, 2003), 225.

28 Gerald Alexander, 'Institutions, Path Dependence, and Democratic Consolidation,' *Journal of Theoretical Politics*, 13 (2001), 257. Emphasis added.

29 See also, Gerald Alexander, *The Sources of Democratic Consolidation* (Ithaca: Cornell University Press, 2001).

30 Thelen, 'How Institutions Evolve,' 225–6.

31 Shepsle, 'A Comment on Institutional Change,' 325.

32 Mark Blyth, 'The Transformation of the Swedish Model: Economic Ideas, Distributional Conflict, and Institutional Change,' *World Politics*, 54 (2001), 1–26; Cortell and Peterson, 'Altered States.'

33 See the argument and references to the broader literature in Helena Catt and Michael Murphy, *Sub-State Nationalism: A Comparative Analysis of Institutional Design* (London: Routledge, 2002), Chapter 6.

34 Cortell and Peterson, 'Altered States,' 185.

35 Ibid., 179.

36 John Kingdon, *Agendas, Alternatives, and Public Policies* (New York: Harper Collins, 2nd ed., 1995).

37 It might be possible to view an electoral change as an endogenous change. Nevertheless, Cortell and Peterson are not advancing a theory of endogenous change but rather examples of domestic (as opposed to international) triggers; theirs is an argument for considering sources of incremental (as opposed to episodic) change.

38 Approaches that examine opportunities do not ignore resources but they do tend to conceive of them in relationship to the position that actors occupy in an organizational structure.

39 Blyth, 'The Transformation,' 2.

40 Ibid., 25.
41 See Doug McAdam, John D. McCarthy, and Mayer N. Zald (eds.), *Comparative Perspectives on Social Movements: Political Opportunities, Mobilizing Structures, and Cultural Framing* (Cambridge: Cambridge University Press, 1996) and Sydney Tarrow, *Power in Movement: Social Movements, Collective Action and Politics* (Cambridge: Cambridge University Press, 1994). I thank an anonymous reviewer for drawing this fact to my attention.
42 Michael Keating, *Nations against the State: The New Politics of Nationalism in Quebec, Catalonia and Scotland* (London: Macmillan, 1996).
43 See the collaborative work of Europeans and North Americans on questions of multinational states in Alain-G. Gagnon and James Tully (eds.), *Multinational Democracies* (Cambridge: Cambridge University Press, 2001).
44 Will Kymlicka, *Multicultural Citizenship: A Liberal Theory of Minority Rights* (Oxford: Oxford University Press, 1995); Catt and Murphy, *Sub-State Nationalism*.
45 F.L. Morton, 'The Effect of the Charter on Canadian Federalism,' *Publius*, 25 (1995), 173–88; Peter H. Russell, Rainer Knopff, and Ted Morton, *Federalism and the Charter: Leading Constitutional Decisions* (Ottawa: Carleton University Press, 1990); Christopher P. Manfredi, *Judicial Power and the Charter: Canada and the Paradox of Liberal Constitutionalism,* (Toronto: Oxford University Press, 2nd ed., 2001).
46 James B. Kelly, *Governing with the Charter: Legislative and Judicial Activism and the Intentions of the Framers* (Vancouver: UBC Press, forthcoming). See also, James B. Kelly 'Bureaucratic Activism and the Charter of Rights: The Department of Justice and Its Entry into the Centre of Government,' *Canadian Public Administration*, 42 (1999), 476–511.
47 James B. Kelly: 'The *Charter of Rights and Freedoms* and the Rebalancing of Liberal Constitutionalism in Canada, 1982–1997,' *Osgoode Hall Law Journal*, 37 (1999), 625–95; 'Reconciling Rights and Federalism during Charter Review: Re-examining the Centralisation Thesis, 1982–1999,' *Canadian Journal of Political Science*, 34 (2001), 321–56.
48 Renaud Dehousse, *The European Court of Justice: The Politics of Judicial Integration* (New York: St Martin's Press, 1998); Karen Alter, *Establishing the Supremacy of European Law: The Making of an International Rule of Law in Europe* (Oxford: Oxford University Press, 2001); Derek Beach, *Between Law and Politics: The Relationship between the European Court of Justice and EU Member States* (Copenhagen: DJØF, 2001); Lisa Conant, *Justice Contained: Law and Politics in the European Union* (Ithaca: Cornell University Press, 2002).
49 For the debate, see Simon Hix, 'Approaches to the Study of the EC: The

Challenge to Comparative Politics,' *West European Politics*, 17 (1994), 1–30; Andrew Hurrell and Anand Menon, 'Politics Like Any Other? Comparative Politics, International Relations and the Study of the EU,' *West European Politics*, 19 (1996), 386–402; and Simon Hix, 'CP, IR and the EU! A Rejoinder to Hurrell and Menon,' *West European Politics*, 19 (1996), 802–4. See also, Karen Alter, 'Who Are the "Masters of the Treaty"? European Governments and the European Court of Justice,' *International Organization*, 52 (1998), 121–48.

50 Anne-Marie Burley and Walter Mattli, 'Europe before the Court: A Political Theory of Legal Integration,' *International Organization*, 47 (1993), 41–76.

51 For a recent attempt to explain the rise of judicial supremacy generally, see Carlo Guarnieri and Patrizia Pederzoli, *The Power of Judges: A Comparative Study of the Courts and Democracy* (Oxford: Oxford University Press, 2002).

52 A recent attempt to balance judicial-focused studies of the Charter can be found in Janet L. Hiebert, *Charter Conflicts: What Is Parliament's Role?* (Montreal: McGill-Queen's University Press, 2002).

53 One exception is Karen Alter and Jeannette Vargas, 'Explaining Variation in the Use of European Litigation Strategies: European Community Law and British Gender Equality Policy,' *Comparative Political Studies*, 33 (2000), 452–82.

4

Institutions and Political Rationality

HUDSON MEADWELL

In this chapter, I present an argument about institutions and political rationality. My goal is to question some of the conventional ways in which institutional theories are set up as alternatives to rational choice theory in political analysis. Institutional theories, I will argue, do a poor job of clarifying our theoretical options. Thus, while my perspective on political analysis is influenced by theories of rational choice, the purpose of this chapter is not to argue for the superiority of rational choice institutionalism over other varieties of institutionalism.

This goal is pursued in the following ways. First, many rational choice theorists shy away from any discussion of *nature*, even the nature of politics. They prefer a methodological defence of rational choice theory that does not imply any commitments about nature or ontology. My interest in rational choice theory in this chapter is not strictly methodological. Rather, my interest is theoretical, because of what I take to be the nature of politics.

Second, a consequence of this approach, as I will argue shortly, is that distance is established between economic theory and political analysis. Too much of applied rational choice theory in political analysis privileges economics. It puts politics in the service of the economy. In establishing this distance, I emphasize the importance of individual *commitments* in political action. I find an important place for calculation in politics, not in spite of these commitments, but because of the conflicts generated by disagreement over commitments. This feature of politics is invariant across different institutions. Finally, calculation, the 'business of figuring out how to attain some end that you value,'[1] structures action in general, and stands in a conceptual rather than empirical relation to action. I use the term 'rational' in an evaluative rather than empirical sense.[2]

Let me begin by summarizing the point of view that underlies the arguments to follow. (1) Politics is a process. (2) There are two fundamental analytical moments in political analysis: macro-moment(s) and micro-moment(s). (3) Micro- and macro-moments are linked analytically through the specification of mechanisms.[3] (4) There are two general and dominant types of mechanisms; following Manski, I term them endogenous effects and correlated effects.[4] This is a dualist point of view. Political analysis cannot be reduced to the macro or micro, nor to a single type of mechanism.

Issues in the Institutional Analysis of Politics

I raise two issues to open with: the place of institutionalism in the broader array of theories of politics and definitions of institutions. I argue that it is not clear where institutionalism fits, and that this problem is associated with how institutions are defined.

As a starting point, let us assume that there are institutional theories of politics. This assumption implies that there is a contrasting class of theories that are not institutional. Otherwise, if institutional theories exhaust the theoretical space, we do not need to, and should not, qualify those theories as institutional because, in this case, there are no theories of politics which are not institutional. In fact, the literature on institutions is ambiguous between these two positions: (1) all theories of politics are institutional and (2) institutional theories of politics are a subset of theories of politics, which implies that there are political theories that are not institutional.

Let us consider some of the implications of position (2). How would we describe and partition the contrasting class? For example, are there macro-theories of politics that are not institutional? Are there cultural theories of politics that are not institutional? Are there structural theories that are not institutional? Or, are all of these simply different varieties of macro-theory? If they are, then the fundamental contrast is not between *institutional* and *non-institutional* theories; rather it is a contrast between *macro* and *micro* theories of politics and the correlated distinction between structure and agency.

In other words, if we want to claim that the contrast is between institutional and non-institutional, then we need to clearly discriminate among macro-phenomena such as institutions, organizations, struc-tures, and cultures. However, I think it is obvious that institutional the-orists do not do this very well at all, in part because their definitions of institutions are unreasonably broad. And their definitions are as broad as they are because, in fact, institutional theorists are interested in spec-ifying constraints on choice, whether these constraints are cultural, structural, or organizational. 'Institutions' in institutional analysis have become a proxy for anything that constrains human action, as long as that constraint is conventional. The clear implication, because of the implied contrast ('non-institutional' theories), is that, in the con-trast class, choice is unconstrained. And this is a further indication that institutional analysis is obscuring our understanding of our theoretical options. I do not know of any theory of politics that presumes strict voluntarism and unconstrained choice.

Institutional analysis in politics currently comes in three forms: his-torical, sociological, and rational choice.[5] This classification is problem-atic in two different ways corresponding to how the theoretical space can be partitioned. Suppose there are theories of politics that are not institutional. How is this contrasting class to be understood? If it is strictly disjoint, then it cannot contain any theory that is sociological, historical, or choice-theoretic (rational choice); moreover, it cannot con-tain any theories that are institutional. Now suppose that there are, for example, sociological theories of politics that are not institutional, or rational choice theories that are not institutional. If there are, then why partition this theoretical space into sociological institutionalism and sociological 'non-institutionalism' (for example)? And surely there are such sociological theories, for example, unless 'institution' is defined so broadly as to include structures or organizations. Why not simply specify a 'sociological' theory of politics?

Now suppose that these three varieties of institutionalism exhaust the theoretical possibilities because there are no theories of politics that are not institutional. How discriminating are the descriptions of these three forms of institutional analysis? My suggestion is that they perform poorly in this regard. Consider historical institutionalism. A typical argument about how this theory or approach is constituted would point to its emphasis on asymmetrical power relations, critical junctures, unintended consequences, and sequencing effects.[6] Here is the problem, however. Is everyone who assumes the existence of asymmetrical power relations in politics an historical institutionalist? Further, many of the remaining characteristics of historical institutionalism can be specified using dynamic theories of choice, such as those of Thomas Schelling[7] or Susanne Lohman[8] – theories that are not usually described by their users as institutionalist and which, on the face of it, most people would associate with some form of rational choice analysis. In other words, the characteristics attributed to historical institutionalism do a poor job of discriminating between historical institutionalism and other theories that do not claim to be institutionalist.

What might discriminate between dynamic theories of choice that are sensitive to power asymmetries, on the one hand, and historical institutionalism? One possible argument is that the features that constitute individual choice (say, beliefs, desires, and preferences) are *endogenous* to institutions. Taking this tack has two problems, however. First, dynamic theories of choice are in fact also endogenous; they are theories of 'reinforcing endogenous effects.'[9] Second, endogeneity of choice is typically associated with sociological institutionalism. If we take it on board, we destabilize the distinction between historical and sociological institutionalism. Now the alternatives boil down to just two.[10]

In fact, the controversy here is ancient: Is the social ontologically prior to the individual? A positive answer to this question is the background claim that helps to make the argument about endogeneity persuasive. It is not a coincidence that the endogeneity argument is associated in the first instance with *sociological* institutionalism. Variations on this argument have been deeply embedded in sociology at least since Emile Durkheim (although he was more of a structuralist than an institutionalist. More on this distinction below). In fact, they have been so embedded that occasionally individuals appeared to disappear altogether from social theory.[11]

Recall that we made this move towards endogeneity in order to make good our desire to effectively discriminate between historical institutionalism and a dynamic theory of choice. We have apparently succeeded but, in the process, we are left with two types of institutionalism.

Moreover, as I noted, institutionalists have no special claim on endogeneity. There is a response to their move, which is to claim that institutions are themselves endogenous to choice. In the strong version of a game theoretic research program, for example,[12] everything is endogenous, and everything endogenous is chosen. Thus, endogeneity is not a solution; rather, it is a problem. To invoke it to defend some version of institutionalism is to invite its use to defend some version of individualism.

We are left in an impasse, having taken sides in an essentially contested debate about ontology.[13] For example, a countermove to the claim that institutions are endogenous to choice, and therefore to individual actions, is to claim that individuals are social constructions.[14]

Note as well, however, that this game theoretic research program is not strictly equivalent to rational choice institutionalism, although game theoretic concepts and analyses seem to be core to rational choice institutionalism. A game theorist is not necessarily an institutionalist. Another problem is therefore broached, which raises further doubts about this tripartite division of theoretical options (historical, sociological, and rational choice institutionalism), and indeed about the usefulness of the theoretical label, 'institutionalism.'

We have used the example of historical institutionalism to make this point: A description of historical institutionalism either discriminates poorly, or it is essentially contested. The standard version of historical institutionalism (HI) discriminates poorly between HI and other theories. A version that discriminates more effectively (the endogeneity version) is essentially contested.

We have just questioned how varieties of institutionalist analysis can be distinguished one from the other. The upshot of this exercise is to imply that institutionalism per se provides a poor way of distinguishing our theoretical options. There is a reason why institutionalism performs poorly in this regard. It is not clear what institutionalism means.

More directly, institutionalism seems to be ubiquitous because it trades on features of political and social life, and the theories that have been developed to analyse that life, which can be identified and described without invoking institutions or institutionalism. What is described as institutional analysis is for the most part the analysis of structures, cultures, organizations and time.

We are left with two ways of understanding institutionalism. One is to understand institutionalism as a systematically specified analytical combination of these features of political and social life, a combination that cannot be reduced to any of these features. Another, rather different way would be to understand institutionalism as marking off a place in macro-analysis (note that those features of political and social analysis specified above do not refer to persons or individuals) that becomes relevant only as the importance of structures, cultures, organizations, and time are exhausted.

The definitions of institutionalism that I will discuss below seem to be more consistent with the first version. The problem, however, is that they draw rather indiscriminately on these features (structures, cultures, and so on). As a result, there is no systematically specified combination of these features that constitutes institutionalism. Sometimes it is structures that count, on other occasions it is cultures; on still others, institutions seems to be no more (nor less) than organizations. Sometimes structures are cultures and vice versa.

Further, path dependence and closely related notions of increasing returns and punctuated equilibria, which have become connected to institutional analysis, do not strike me as obviously (or as exclusively) institutionalist arguments. The concepts of time and equilibrium, on which these second-order concepts depend, are too general for institutionalists to claim as their own, even if they often invoke them. For example, a concept central to historical institutionalism and its interest in time, punctuated equilibrium, is drawn from evolutionary theory.[15]

Moreover, most historical institutionalists (but not all, see the discussion of Pierson below) have ignored the obvious implication: appropriate use of this concept outside of its original locus requires an evolutionary theory of politics and society. For the purposes of some historical institutionalists, moreover, any such evolutionary theory would have to be specified without including strategy or strategic interaction. Recall, further, that Stephen Jay Gould and Nils Eldridge, like typical natural scientists interested in evolution, studied time spans measured in thousands of years, and longer. By comparison, the time span of interest to a typical historical institutionalist is a cross-section.

Let me now consider two influential definitions of institutions. First, institutions are the 'formal rules, compliance procedures, and standard operating practices that structure the relationship between individuals in various units of the polity and economy.'[16] Peter Hall continued, stating that 'the term "organization" will be used here as a virtual synonym for "institution."'[17] Recall that this definition was put in service of a comparative analysis of 'the political dimensions of economic management' – an 'approach to political analysis that stresses the ways in which *institutions* structure state-society relations and the direction of policy.' Hall then identified 'five sets of *structural* variables' that were most important for national economic policy: 'the *organization* of labor, the organization of capital, the organization of the state, the organization of the political system, and the *structural* position of the country within the international economy.'[18] There is no clear distinction here among key concepts. Judging by Hall's usage of terms, we could jettison his concept of institutions and still retain most if not all of his empirical conclusions and his theoretical approach to political-economic management in capitalist democracies. More directly, what we would lose in this account if we never invoked 'institutions'?

Hall's definition and empirical arguments are tied to a specific historical problem and context, the world of rational-legal states and mature capitalism – the densely organized and bureaucratized world described by Max Weber in which hierarchy characterizes most organization, whether of the state, political parties, trade unions, or firms. On this point, consider the content of the volume on historical institutionalism edited by Sven Steinmo, Kathleen Thelen, and Frank Longstreth.[19] The subject matter is the political economy of the modern welfare state, and historical institutionalism is elaborated around this important but rather narrow focus. If historical institutionalism is a theory of anything in this volume (and its practitioners do not want to go so far as to call it a theory, preferring 'approach' or 'perspective'), it is a theory, not of politics in a general sense, but of the welfare state.

Another influential definition was developed for more general purposes. 'Institutions are the rules of the game in a society or, more formally, are the human devised constraints that shape human interaction. In consequence, they structure incentives in human exchange, whether political, social, or economic.'[20] Douglass C. North distinguished institutions and organizations, thus distinguishing the rules of the game from the players,[21] and he also included under institutions both formal and informal constraints. He understood the latter loosely as cultural constraints, referring to values and norms as 'informal institutions.'

So, in separating institutions and organizations, North made the former concept more distinctive. Yet his treatment of values and norms as institutions, even if informal institutions, simply introduced a different form of ambiguity. 'If values are just as much institutions as formal structures, what isn't an institution?'[22] Values, furthermore, have a peculiar quality. As part of a motivational set, they enable rather than constrain action, and the existence of different values provokes disagreement and conflict. How can values have these qualities and still be construed as rules of the game or as constraints?

North's more general definition suited his purposes, which were different from Hall's. In comparison with North's interest in economic performance over *la longue durée*, Hall worked on a conjunctural cross-section of time. North comes much closer to posing as his concern the general problem of social order – how is social order possible at all? However, in making economic performance his central concern, politics and culture come to take on a functional cast because they are interpreted according to the contributions they make to economic performance. The problem of social order then is reduced to a problem of economic order. Hall's cross-sectional analysis is not prone to the same problem as long as political institutions and organizations are not treated as existing only to solve problems of economic production and exchange. A final difference: The chunk of time that concerns North may be more compatible with evolutionary forms of explanation than the cross-section that concerns the typical analyst of contemporary capitalist performance.

Can we, at this stage, identify what motivates these various approaches to institutions, despite their differences? It seems to be this: An institution is anything that constrains human action, as long as that device is conventional, that is, not natural. (For example, genetic makeup might be said to constrain action, but genes are not conventional and therefore are not institutional.) This accounts for the tendency to lump together and to move back and for among these features: structures, cultures, organizations, and time. All of these features are more or less on the same footing because hypothetically they share the same quality. As a consequence, there is little effort to distinguish them. The emphasis is on constraint, virtually any kind of constraint as long as it is not natural, rather than choice. In the limiting case, individuals or persons do not need to be independently specified; there are, for example, only structural locations or organizational roles or collective meanings, and social reproduction proceeds without choice. Thus what appears to motivate institutionalism as a critical enterprise is some form of full-blown voluntarism in which there is choice without constraints.

I believe that the motivation that underlies institutionalism draws on at least three related claims or worries. More directly, first, given the rather wide range of constraints that are invoked, one image that is implied is of radically undersocialized individuals who have internalized no prescriptive beliefs, no values, and no non-instrumental cognitive beliefs whatsoever. Individuals are empty vessels, pre-social entities; they are isolated, atomistic monads. This is particularly the case in sociological versions of institutionalism, under which the language of institutionalism is a way to reassert in different words the priority of the social.

Thus, any argument that modifies this picture by introducing structure, culture, or organization – that is, assumes that individuals are socialized, is 'institutionalist.' This sets up a situation where critics can be dismissed because, by this definition of institutionalism, a critic must hold to the position that individuals who choose have not been socialized. The implication, in other words, is that a position critical of institutionalism that simultaneously allows for socialization *and* choice (particularly along egoistic, instrumental lines) is incoherent. Of course, this dismissal will be credible only when critics are full-blown and thoroughgoing voluntarists, or if the incoherence of this critical position can be demonstrated. A second claim (or worry) might also be present. It is simply that the egoistic impulses of undersocialized or presocialized individuals must be restrained.

I suspect, as well, that there is a third concern that runs through some of the work on institutionalism. It is that there is a little too much *hubris* – a disdain for limitations and a failure to understand our situation as moderns – in some political and social political theory. We need to recognize how we are limited by forces larger than ourselves, by the weight of our pasts,[23] and how, as a consequence, many of our choices are at the margins. I am sympathetic to this point. There is hubris in modernity. Yet I fail to see how this agreement implies a commitment to *institutionalism*. Rather, what this position commits me to methodologically is a form of dualism that recognizes the separate importance of macro- and micro-moments in political analysis and the importance of specifying mechanisms that link these moments.

Something like this third concern runs through some of the literature on historical institutionalism, especially in the ways that these theorists have developed the concept of path dependence. In particular, the work on path dependence turns the methodological vice of endogeneity into a theoretical virtue. What I call a 'strict' version of path dependence has this simple form: 'Path dependence involves three phases: the first is the critical juncture in which events trigger a move toward a particular path out of at least two possibilities; the second is the period of reproduction, that is, the period in which positive feedback mechanisms ... reinforce the movement along one path; and finally the path comes to an end when new events dislodge the long-lasting equilibrium ... every path begins and ends with a critical juncture.'[24]

In this strict version, it is acknowledged that change cannot be explained endogenously. Rather change is associated with the specification of some exogenous variable or event, that is, a variable or event that is not caused by those variables and events that are associated with reproduction.[25] The dynamic of change must come from outside the system of variables that cause the process of reproduction.

There are, however, looser versions of path dependence as well that want to argue that institutional change, up to and including a change of paths, can occur without an exogenous shock so that both reproduction and change are built into the logic of institutions. Thelen has suggested that institutions are structured by both mechanisms of reproduction (such as increasing returns) and mechanisms of change. The latter include institutional layering (that enables innovation at interstices – those points where institutions intersect or come up one against the other) and institutional conversion (when an institution is converted to new purposes).[26] What is notable about this tack is that everything continues to rest on institutions and institutions alone. In effect, change becomes consistent with path dependence and historical institutionalism simply by increasing the number of institutions (so, for example, one institution is layered over another).

The larger issue is that these kinds of modifications may eventually so water down the concept of path dependence that historical institutionalism loses its distinctiveness. The problem with path-dependent historical institutionalism is that the strict version is not fully persuasive, and versions that are more persuasive have this quality precisely because they are less distinctive (less 'strict'). This dilemma is nicely presented in the work of Richard Deeg.[27] Thelen illustrates the problem when, in concluding her argument, she states that institutional change is connected to 'political contestation.'[28] Further, if as Deeg argued, increasing returns must be captured through political mobilization,[29] the concept of path dependence has lost most of its independent analytical power. A path should have deterministic properties.[30] If returns are not automatic but must be captured, if institutional change is a consequence of 'political contestation,' then we are in the presence of rather familiar political processes of mobilization and counter-mobilization.[31]

Pierson's point of departure is in using the economic literature on increasing returns to describe the mechanisms that drive endogenous reproduction in path-dependent historical processes.[32] In doing so, Pierson eschewed evolutionary theory and thus distances his arguments from the literature on punctuated equilibria (that I referred to earlier).[33] The literature on increasing returns is economic, and the mechanisms that generate increasing returns, not surprisingly, are broadly utilitarian.[34] They are: fixed costs, learning effects, coordination effects, and adaptive expectations.[35] 'Underlying these mechanisms is the assumption that actors choose particular institutions and choose to reproduce them so long as they see it in their interest to do so, and this determination is based on a cost-benefit analysis of alternative choices.'[36] I am reminded here of Randall Calvert's[37] point that 'human motivations include an ineradicable kernel of self-interest.'

Evidently, in this work on path dependence and historical institutionalism, we are not that far away from a form of rational choice analysis. More directly, if 'path dependence is [nothing more than] a way to narrow conceptually the choice set and link decision-making through time,'[38] then it is not exclusively the intellectual property of historical institutionalism (at least as the latter is typically understood in political science and sociology).

Pierson's work is sophisticated but it, too, is ambiguous about change within path dependence. 'Change [on a path] continues,' argued Pierson, 'but it is bounded change – until something erodes or swamps the mechanisms of reproduction that generate continuity.'[39] Notice that his explanatory language here is metaphorical (something 'erodes' or 'swamps' something fairly stable, as a wind erodes a rock formation or a flood swamps a town), whereas Pierson's treatment of increasing returns was more precise. He resists referring to that 'something' as an exogenous shock, but his alternative is vague: 'We should expect, however, that these change points often occur when new conditions disrupt or overwhelm the specific mechanisms that previously reproduced the existing path.'[40]

While Pierson drew on an important literature in economics, he is careful to distinguish politics and economics, as he applies this literature to the political world. He believes that increasing returns, in fact, have more relevance in politics than they do in economics because of the 'character of the political world'. 'The prevalence of increasing returns processes is indeed a defining feature of politics.' There are four features of politics that make these processes prevalent: the central role of collective action, the density of institutions, the existence of political authority, and the complexity of politics. Do these features, however, predict uniquely to processes of increasing returns?

Suppose, for example, that there are other defining qualities of politics, other than increasing returns, equally consistent with collective action, organization, authority, and complexity. We could then say that Pierson's argument in favour of increasing returns (and thus path dependence and historical institutionalism) is underspecified because we could take these features (collective action and so on) on board without committing to increasing returns and, thus, to path dependence or historical institutionalism.

In fact, according to Pierson, there is one fundamental feature of politics that underpins those other features discussed above: 'The fundamental feature of politics is its preoccupation with the provision of public goods' (p. 257). Although not narrowly functionalist, this understanding of politics puts politics in the service of the modern capitalist market. The purpose of politics is to supply those goods that cannot be efficiently supplied by the market. Pierson makes a linkage between this feature and another political fact: 'In politics, the consequences of my actions are highly dependent upon the actions of others' (p. 258).

Politics, in other words, rests on interdependent choice, which is to say that politics has a *strategic* structure. I believe that this is an important feature of politics; however, the free-rider problem is not the only collective action problem in politics, nor is it necessarily the most fundamental. Pierson has not directly addressed this issue. Rather, he argues that the only problem of strategic interaction in politics is the problem of free-riding. However, since strategic interaction is separable from free-riding, an alternative formulation of the character of the political world that incorporates strategic interaction, but that does not make the problem of free-riding central, will be available.

The reasons why strategic interaction is important in politics are independent of free-riding. More generally still, strategic interaction in politics, and thus *political rationality*, does not entail that politics exists to serve the economy. The latter is the implication of Pearson's claim about the fundamental character of politics – politics solves problems that cannot be solved by competitive markets. To analyse political rationality, however, is not to study the political prerequisites of economic relations, whether it is public good provision or positive transaction costs that require 'solutions.' Such accounts of politics privilege economic production and exchange. Rather, my interest is in political disagreement, which does not depend on an economic theory of politics, and my interest is in a kind of political rationality that is implied by disagreement.

Why, for example, would an actor attempt to assess constraints and opportunities in a field of political competition and conflict? A political actor is considering how to devise a program and frame his or her actions in order to achieve goals, whether we are talking about a classic type of political entrepeneur, for example, or a motivated activist. There is a moment in politics, a decisive moment, that implies this kind of political rationality. These actors may have commitments to prescriptive beliefs or to non-instrumental cognitive beliefs; they may be principled actors with identities, for example. Still, if they want to engage in politics, they have to think instrumentally; they have to try to assess the probable consequences for maximizing support and minimizing opposition of various alternative political strategies. And thinking instrumentally in these contexts implies strategic thinking because of the interdependence of choice.

A condition of scarcity and conflict underpins this perspective on politics. There is more than one principle in the world; there is more than one identity. If not all identities and principles can be satisfied simultaneously, there is scarcity and conflict. Interaction under this condition still implies the formation of strategies and the choice of tactics as actors seek to achieve their ends. It implies as well the interdependence of choice. In other words, even when we grant those sorts of commitments that are emphasized by some of the critics of rational choice theory, I find an important place for rational action, not in spite of the existence of these commitments, but *because* of the conflict generated by disagreement over commitments.[41]

An understanding of politics that privileges the provision of solutions to free-riding as the central feature of politics needs more justification. Too many questions are begged. The problem of free-riding implies some agreement about the value of a public good to start with, before the incentives to misrepresent preferences become relevant, because there can be two kinds of non-contributions to collective outcomes. One kind of non-contribution does not reveal individual preference. This non-contribution is free-riding. My defection does not reveal my preference.[42] Non-contributions, however, also can be preference-revealing. This kind of non-contribution is not free-riding. Disagreement is not defection.

There are two different problems here: free-riding and division. They should be separated. In an analysis of constitutional choice, Douglas Heckathorn and Steven Maser made this separation. They suggested that individuals typically face a choice between the 'comparatively anarchic' status quo and multiple, conflicting forms of order. Failure to reach agreement under these circumstances 'may result not merely from the failure to deal effectively with free-riders (the *defection problem*) ... but also from failure to agree upon a mutually acceptable allocation of concessions (the *division problem*).'[43]

Adam Przeworski made a related argument when he criticized Olson's treatment of the free-riding problem facing workers. He argued that workers are in a Prisoners' Dilemma because of the interdependence of their private and rival consumption, before and independently, of any action that would result in providing goods that are non-rival in consumption, that is, before and independently of free-riding. Przeworski continued, in pointing to the problem of preference aggregation: 'If individuals are in a situation in which the particular state of the world that is best for them is simultaneously the best for all, then indeed their "common" interests can be represented simultaneously. But if individuals compete with each other, then their "common" group interests are no longer the same as their serial, particular interests.'[44]

These authors are pointing to the conflation of collective choice and free-riding. Przeworski, in particular, went to the heart of the matter because he challenged the canonical source on free-riding – Mancur Olson's *The Logic of Collective Action.* Pierson's arguments, as do many others, drew on the work of Olson without acknowledging the problems.

Olson made an analogy between groups and markets, arguing that the provision of a public good in a latent group is like individual maximization in a competitive private goods economy.[45] First, Olson's analogy begged the question of public good provision in a latent group because the presence of a public good is presupposed in the analogy. This is so because the private goods economy is not completely decentralized, even in competitive equilibrium. The price system of competitive economies are efficient signals only so long as there are no incentives to steal. These incentives tend to zero when exclusion is enforced, which requires a monitoring and enforcement regime – which is itself a public good.

Further, Olson also argued that privileged groups are to oligopolies as latent groups are to competitive markets.[46] In his analogy, Olson allowed the number of agents to increase. This size variable is a central distinguishing feature of latent groups. In the analogy to oligopolies, competition increases as the number of agents increases and demand therefore *reveals* preference. But in the latent group, demand is not preference-revealing. For the analogy between latent groups and competitive markets to hold, demand in the latent group must be preference-revealing. By definition, however, demand for public goods does not reveal preference.

Olson's work, therefore, is not enough to motivate an argument that the fundamental feature of politics is the solution of free-riding problems. And without this argument, we do not have a reason to accept

Pierson's claim that increasing returns and path dependence are defining features of politics. Pierson's understanding of politics is economistic but political contestation, collective choice, and the division problem are not intrinsically economic phenomena. Further, if politics does not solve the division problem, there may be no problems of free-riding to worry about.

Conclusion

Here, then, is one point of view about institutional analysis in politics. I have not canvassed in this chapter all that could be said about structures, cultures, organizations, and time, nor have I discussed all of the work that passes as institutionalist. But the work that I have discussed is central and influential. Clearly, the issues that institutionalists are grappling with are central to political analysis. As we move forward, many of the concerns that motivate institutionalists will continue to be relevant and their arguments will be important. However, the problems I have raised tend to point in one direction: Institutionalism is not yet an effective way of distinguishing our theoretical options.

I have made two more general points. First, politics is an activity that has as a constitutive feature strategic interaction. Second, even when I grant the kinds of political commitments that are emphasized by the critics of rational choice theory, I find an important place for rational action in political analysis. It is often the case that a forced choice is expected between two positions: strategy without commitments or commitments without strategy. It is a false choice.

In making these points, I have moved some degrees away from a methodological defence of rational choice theory. And I have established some distance between economic theory and political analysis, in part, by emphasizing the relevance of commitments in political interaction.

Notes

1 Candace Vogler, *Reasonably Vicious* (Cambridge, Mass.: Harvard University Press, 2002), 231.
2 Thus there may be cognitive limits on calculation that affect the matching of means and ends, but such limitations do not mean that action is not calculative. Precisely because there is a calculative structure to action, action is criticizable according to how means match ends.

3 See in particular, Peter Hedström and Richard Swedberg (eds.), *Social Mechanisms: An Analytical Approach to Social Theory* (Cambridge and New York: Cambridge University Press, 1998).

4 Charles F. Manski, *The Identification Problem in the Social Sciences*. (Cambridge, Mass.: Harvard University Press, 1995).

5 See Peter A. Hall and Rosemary C.R. Taylor, 'Political Science and the Three New Institutionalisms,' in Karol Soltan, Eric M. Uslaner, and Virginia Haufler (eds.) *Institutions and Social Order* (Ann Arbor: University of Michigan Press, 1998).

6 Taylor and Hall, 'Political Science and the Three Institutionalisms,' 19–20; Paul Pierson, 'Increasing Returns, Path Dependence, and the Study of Politics,' *American Political Science Review*, 94 (2000), 251–67; James Mahoney, 'Path Dependence in Historical Sociology,' *Theory and Society*, 29 (2000), 507–48; Kathleen Thelen, 'How Institutions Evolve: Insights from Comparative-Historical Analysis,' in James Mahoney and Dietrich Rueschemeyer (eds.), *Comparative-Historical Analysis* (Princeton, NJ: Princeton University Press, 2003).

7 Thomas C. Schelling, *Micromotives and Macrobehavior* (New York: W.W. Norton, 1978).

8 Susanne Lohman, 'The Dynamics of Informational Cascades: The Monday Demonstrations in Leipzig, Germany,' *World Politics*, 47 (1994), 42–101. Note that this particular example involves mobilization processes over a short time frame. The point is that time in this type of model is non-linear, and there are many other elaborations, similar to Lohman's, that cover longer time frames.

9 Manski, *The Identification Problem*, 128.

10 Compare with Colin Hay and Daniel Wincott, 'Structure, Agency and Historical Institutionalism,' *Political Studies*, 46 (1998), 951–7.

11 Consider Durkheim on the sacred, Parsons on systems, or Foucault on discipline. See also Dennis Wrong, *The Oversocialized Conception of Man* (Rutgers, NJ: Transaction Books, 1999); Randall Collins, 'The Microfoundations of Macrosociology,' *American Journal of Sociology*, 86 (1981), 984–1014.

12 For a more detailed discussion of endogeneity and game theory, see Hudson Meadwell and Axel van den Berg, 'Conclusion,' in Axel van den Berg and Hudson Meadwell (eds.), *The Social Sciences and Rationality: Promise, Limits and Problems* (Rutgers, NJ: Transaction Books, 2004). Unlike endogeneity within institutionalism, which produces (to put it in simplified terms) the problem of too little choice, the problem of endogeneity within game theory is rather different (again to simplify) – there is too much choice.

13 For further discussion, see Axel van den Berg and Hudson Meadwell,

'Introduction,' in van den Berg and Meadwell, *The Social Sciences and Rationality*.

14 For example, Thomas C. Heller, Morton Sosna, and David Welberry (eds.), *Reconstructing Individualism* (Stanford: Stanford University Press, 1986); Craig Calhoun, 'The Problem of Identity in Collective Action,' in Joan Huber (ed.), *Macro-Micro Linkages in Sociology* (Beverley Hills and London: Sage, 1994), 61.

15 Stephen Jay Gould and Nils Eldredge, 'Punctuated Equilibria: The Tempo and Mode of Evolution Reconsidered,' *Paleobiology*, 3 (1977), 115–51; Stephen Krasner, 'Approaches to the State: Alternative Conceptions and Historical Dynamics,' *Comparative Politics*, 16 (1984), 223–46.

16 Peter A. Hall, *Governing the Economy: The Politics of State Intervention in Britain and France* (Oxford: Polity Press, 1986), 19.

17 Ibid., 19.

18 Ibid., 259; emphasis added.

19 Sven Steinmo, Kathleen Thelen, and Frank Longstreth (eds.), *Structuring Politics: Historical Institutionalism in Comparative Perspective* (Cambridge: Cambridge University Press, 1992).

20 Douglass C. North, *Institutions, Institutional Change and Economic Performance* (Cambridge: Cambridge University Press, 1991), 3.

21 Eric M. Uslaner, 'Field of Dreams: The Weak Reeds of Institutional Design,' in Soltan et al., *Institutions and Social Order*, 102.

22 Ibid., 103.

23 Notice that there is a somewhat different way to make this point which is almost its flipside – that our decisions are at the margins because we are at the mercy of contingent events (the 'exogenous shocks' of some versions of historical institutionalism). Either way, the point is that we have less control over the world than we might think we have. However, this claim is then ambiguous between two different positions: Either there is too much meaning in our lives, or too little.

24 Richard Deeg, *Institutional Change and the Uses and Limits of Path Dependency: The Case of German Finance*, Max Planck Institute, Discussion Paper, (2001), 8.

25 Note that from a different point of view, an exogenous shock provides an opportunity to conduct a natural experiment, allowing the comparativist to move some degree beyond a quasi-experimental research design.

26 Kathleen Thelen, 'How Institutions Evolve.' On 'change at the interstices,' see also the theoretical introduction in Michael Mann, *The Sources of Social Power*, vol. 1 (Cambridge and New York: Cambridge University Press, 1986).

27 Richard Deeg, 'Institutional Change and Path Dependency: The Case of

German and Italian Finance,' in Wolfgang Streeck and Kathleen Thelen (eds.), *Continuity and Discontinuity in Institutional Analysis*, forthcoming; Deeg, *Institutional Change*.

28 Thelen, 'How Institutions Evolve,' 231.

29 Deeg, *Institutional Change*.

30 Mahoney, 'Path Dependence and Historical Sociology.'

31 Jack Knight, *Institutions and Social Conflict* (Cambridge and New York; Cambridge University Press, 1992).

32 Note this difference: Pearson's work is more directly about *process* than about institutions.

33 Pierson, 'Increasing Returns,' 253, n5.

34 Mahoney, 'Path Dependence,' 516.

35 Pierson, 'Increasing Returns,' 253–7.

36 Deeg, *Institutional Change*, 10.

37 Randall L. Calvert, 'Explaining Social Order: Internalization, External Enforcement or Equilibrium,' in Soltan et al., *Institutions and Social Order*, 134.

38 North, *Institutions, Institutional Change*, 98–9; parenthetical material added.

39 Pierson, 'Increasing Returns,' 265.

40 Ibid., 266.

41 This perspective on politics is not sociologically centric. It focuses, not on typical actors from large populations, but on atypical actors – atypical because they are mobilizers rather than the mobilized. At first glance, this may seem to impose limitations on the identification and analysis of political rationality. The implicit focus here is on actors who are relatively pivotal because they are actively involved in politics. I do not want to *assume*, however, that rationality falls away as we move outside this subset of actors. Rather, I have simply marked off a minimum place for political rationality in larger processes of interaction among and between pivotal actors and non-pivotal actors by focusing on the importance of rational action among those motivated enough to become involved actively in politics.

42 For example, Theodore Groves and John Ledyard, 'Optimal Allocation of Public Goods: A Solution to the Free-Rider Problem,' *Econometrica*, 45 (1977), 783–809.

43 Douglas Heckathorn and Steven Maser, 'Bargaining and Constitutional Contracts,' *American Journal of Political Science*, 31 (1987), 142–68.

44 Adam Przeworski, 'Marxism and Rational Choice,' *Politics and Society*, 14 (1985), 379–410.

45 Mancur Olson Jr, *The Logic of Collective Action: Public Goods and the Theory of Groups* (Cambridge, Mass.: Harvard University Press, 1965), 50, 9.

46 Olson, *The Logic of Collective Action*, 49–50.

Part 2

Institutionalist Theory in Canadian Politics

The second part looks at new institutionalism in light of the study of Canadian politics, both its English and French language components.* Here, the authors examine to what extent the field of Canadian politics has an institutionalist tradition and how this tradition compares with new institutionalism. They also assess the impact of the new institutionalist movement on contemporary research on Canadian politics.

At the broadest level, the two contributions in this part ask how state-society relations and the impact of institutions on action have been conceptualized in scholarship on Canadian politics. They highlight differences in the treatment of institutions by Canadian politics specialists, but also find near consensus on key questions. Institutions tend to be defined in terms of formal structures. Epistemological and methodological positions are closer to those of historical institutionalism than those of either sociological or rational choice institutionalism. This part also unveils differences between the theoretical importance of institutions in the English- and French-Canadian tradition: there is less of an institutionalist legacy in Quebec because scholars there have traditionally been preoccupied with normative questions focusing on changing Canadian federalism.

In this part's first chapter, on institutionalism in the study of Canadian politics in English Canada, Miriam Smith distinguishes between four styles of institutional analysis: empirical, which consists in describing how institutions work; normative, which is preoccupied with

---

* Historically, Quebec scholars wrote in French, but they increasingly write also in English. In many cases, they publish primarily in English. This is blurring the line between English and French language scholarship on Canadian politics.

the purpose they are supposed to serve; explanatory, which focuses on accounting for political outcomes through a focus on institutions; and sociological, which explores state-society linkages. Smith sees in the work of such scholars as J.R. Mallory, Alan Cairns, and Richard Simeon strong explanatory and sociological features, but she argues that the empirical and normative styles of institutional analysis have overall been most prominent. The normative dimension, she submits, has been particularly salient because of the historical linguistic cleavages which had political scientists such as Cairns discuss institutions in a perspective of national unity. Smith also suggests that the explanatory and sociological styles have been more central to the generation of Canadian politics specialists writing in the 1980s and 1990s, particularly those working on federalism, public policy, and the Charter. She sees this development as following the rise of historical institutionalism in comparative politics and suggests that an emphasis on these explanatory and sociological dimensions is positive for Canadian political science because it can improve debate and understanding between scholars of the two language groups.

In the following chapter, Linda Cardinal explores institutionalism in the French-Canadian and Quebec scholarship on Canadian and Quebec politics. She finds that this tradition is rather weak, although some early scholars, for example, Jean-Charles Bonenfant, were interested, much like their English-Canadian counterparts, in federalism. She notes that this first generation of Quebec political scientists was particularly concerned with change and that, consequently, their discussions of institutions had a strong normative dimension. Cardinal then explains how, in the 1960s and 1970s, institutionalist analysis was largely abandoned in favour of systemic and structuralist approaches only to be brought back in the 1980s and 1990s. Overall, the trajectory of institutions in French-Canadian political science is roughly comparable with that of the discipline in English Canada, with the difference that society-centred approaches have historically been more pervasive in Quebec. Moreover, Cardinal suggests that the peculiarity of Quebec's political situation means that political analysis, institutionalist or not, is often guided by a preoccupation with normative issues. In this context, new institutionalism, with its bias towards institutional continuity, could sit uneasily with political science in Quebec.

5

Institutionalism in the Study of Canadian Politics: The English-Canadian Tradition

MIRIAM SMITH

Over the past twenty years, there has been a theoretical trend towards 'bringing the state back in' to comparative politics. This trend – a reaction to the perceived lack of analysis of the state in comparative politics during the post–Second World War period – has been termed the 'new' institutionalism to distinguish it from the formal-legal study of political institutions that dominated political science in the Anglo-American world prior to the war. In the post-1980 period, this new institutionalism has developed into a fertile research agenda in comparative politics, particularly in studies of American and comparative political development and policy studies. New institutionalism has often been divided into historical and rational choice variants,[1] although recent developments in historical institutionalism suggest important links between the two.[2] It has also been linked to institutionalism in sociology, particularly in Britain, where a sociologically based institutionalism is important as a theoretical approach in organization theory and policy studies.[3]

In English-speaking Canada,[4] political institutions have never been out of fashion in the study of Canadian politics. As elsewhere in the English-speaking world, political science before the Second World War was largely concerned with the formal-legal description of political institutions, although, in the study of Canada, this competed with the influence of the political economy tradition, as exemplified in the writing of Harold Innis.[5] Throughout the 1960s, 1970s, and early 1980s, the Canadian politics field in English-speaking Canada retained its institutional focus, often conceptualizing political developments such as province-building, Quebec nationalism, Aboriginal nationalisms, and multiculturalism in terms of political institutional reform. The crisis of

Canadian 'unity' was, in part, read as a crisis of political institutions that required a constitutional solution. Thus, even before 'historical institutionalism' was a glint in Theda Skocpol's eye,[6] students of Canadian politics in English-speaking Canada were steeped in, trained in, and even (one might say) obsessed with the central importance of political institutions in Canadian political life. In this chapter, I set out to explore this unique English Canadian institutionalist tradition, to provide a selective history of its emergence and development as reflected in key texts drawn from different historical periods, and to compare developments in the study of Canadian politics with developments in the broader field of comparative politics.[7]

Throughout the chapter, I examine the literature on Canadian politics by distinguishing four types of institutionalist analysis. These types are by no means mutually exclusive and, indeed, almost all of the texts discussed in this chapter engage with at least two of the four types. The main purpose of the chapter is not to defend or advocate for one style of analysis over another, although, in the concluding section, I suggest that an empirical, explanatory, and sociological style of institutionalist analysis is more likely to build bridges between political scientists from different traditions across the Canada-Quebec divide in the field of Canadian politics. Rather, the goal here is to distinguish styles of institutionalist analysis which may provide benchmarks for comparing and contrasting the various literatures of Canadian institutionalism over time and for comparing these texts to the main tenets of historical institutionalism in comparative politics.

The first dimension of institutionalist analysis is the task of describing political institutions in formal-legal terms. This type of analysis reflects the origins of some branches of political science in the discipline and practice of law. The second dimension is the normative and pragmatic task of assessing how well political institutions work according to some defined standard. Such standards may naturally be contested and may reflect particular interests or particular conceptions of what political institutions are supposed to do and the ends they are supposed to serve. Examples here would include the evaluation of the extent to which Canadian political institutions are democratic or the extent to which they work to ensure 'national unity.' A third dimension of institutionalist analysis is the explanatory task which is central to historical institutionalism in comparative politics, namely, taking political institutions seriously as independent variables that potentially shape policy and political outcomes. In this type of analysis, the main goal is not description or normative evaluation, although both of these may occur as by-products or implications of the task of explanation. For example, historical institutionalist work on social policy provides explanations of U.S. social policy development that clearly imply an underlying ideological or normative preference for certain public policies, such as, for example, a bias in favour of the welfare state.[8] However, in explanatory work, these normative considerations are implications rather than priorities of the analysis.

The fourth dimension, also common in historical institutionalism, is what I term the 'sociological' dimension. This means that taking political institutions seriously as potentially independent variables in social science explanation does not require that institutions be divorced from the social and economic contexts in which they operate. The sociological dimension calls attention to the ways in which institutions are connected to and are part of the societies in which they operate. Much of the best historical institutionalist work has precisely problematized the state-society linkage. For example, Margaret Weir and Theda Skocpol's work demonstrates how political institutions and policy legacies shape the preferences and strategies of collective actors such as groups or class organizations such as unions. In turn, the mobilization of these collective actors shapes policy outcomes in a feedback loop across time.[9] This type of analysis highlights the importance of anchoring political institutions in society, and in not using the focus on the state as an excuse for ignoring society.

Most institutionalist analyses contain some mix of these four types of analysis. This chapter will demonstrate how the English Canadian literature on Canadian politics mixes these types of institutionalist analysis and how this mix compares to the style of historical institutionalist analysis. While historical institutionalism in comparative politics tends to focus on the explanatory and sociological dimensions of institutionalism, the Canadian literature has tended to focus on the descriptive and normative dimensions. The descriptive and normative style of institutionalist analysis is alive and well in Canadian political science in the contemporary period, although, in certain sub-fields of the literature, such as policy studies, the explanatory and sociological demonstrations of institutionalist analysis have been highlighted, often with systematic attention to the comparative dimension.

In the first section of the chapter, I provide a brief disciplinary history of the interaction between formal-legal institutionalism in English Canadian political science and the political economy tradition, with particular attention to J.R. Mallory's *Social Credit and the Federal Power in Canada*, which is a key text in the development of a distinctive English Canadian institutionalism.[10] In the second section of the chapter, I survey developments in the work of the 1960s and 1970s from scholars such as Donald Smiley, Alan Cairns, and Richard Simeon. Their work poses many of the same questions as American-style 'new' institutionalism, but contains a strong and explicitly normative component that reflects the crises of Canadian federalism over the period in which they are writing. In the third section of the chapter, I evaluate the ways in which the powerful legacy of English Canadian institutionalism has interacted with the rise of historical institutionalism in comparative politics over the 1980s and 1990s. I argue that, in some areas of the Canadian politics field, English Canadian scholars have adhered to descriptive and normative dimensions of the English Canadian institutionalist tradition while others have built bridges to the comparative literatures, especially in the area of policy studies.[11]

Political Economy and Political Institutions: The Emergence of an English Canadian Political Science

In the prewar period, the study of politics in Canada, as elsewhere in the English-speaking world, was often approached as a branch of law or economics, and confined to the analysis of formal institutional and constitutional arrangements. Examples of this in the study of Canadian politics are J.G. Bourinot's 1895 text,[12] R. MacGregor Dawson's 1947 text,[13] and J.R. Mallory's 1971 text[14] on Canadian politics and government. These texts centred on the formal, legal, and conventional aspects of the operation of Canadian political institutions. This formal-legal approach is often contrasted to behaviouralism, which arose in political science in the United States and elsewhere after the Second World War. Formal-legalism in its early incarnations had a strong normative component as Canadian government texts such as Bourinot's were intended to be scholarly manuals of citizenship.[15] These texts reflected the constitutional fact that Canadian political institutions were nested within the colonial system as well as the deeply held political support for the British Empire in English-speaking Canada prior to the war. Bourinot began his text with a description of Imperial government, namely, the operation of the British political system and its control over Canada, before moving on to describe the Dominion government, the provinces, and the government of schools across the provinces and territories of Canada as they were in 1895 in all their (sectional) religious diversity. Similarly, Dawson situated Canadian government within the context of the British inheritance, which he largely viewed in a positive light.

Formal-legal institutionalism is usually contrasted with the behaviouralism that succeeded it after the Second World War. The behavioural revolution, as its name implies, focused on the actual behaviour of political actors rather than on the dry legalities of political institutions. The contrast between behaviouralism and formal-legal institutionalism has not been as well drawn in Canadian political science as in U.S. political science because the formal-legal (especially constitutional) aspects of political institutions have long been a central focus of study in Canada and because the gap between the formal operation of political institutions and the living realities of constitutional conventions meant that scholars of Canadian political institutions could never ignore the actual behaviour of the political actors such as political parties. Moreover, throughout the postwar period, American political science was caught up in a process of the professionalization of academic life and in the institutionalization of funding relationships which steered the study of politics in a 'scientific' direction, at times in the service of the power of the American state.[16] Naturally, these influences were less keenly felt in the life of Canadian political science.

Although the behavioural revolution was weaker in Canada than in the United States, formal-legal institutionalism was strongly influenced early by the uniquely Canadian project of political economy. Formal-legal institutionalism coexisted alongside the first wave of Canadian political economy, especially during the early postwar period. This can be seen in the fact that, at universities such as Toronto and McGill, the departments that would later become 'political science' departments were called departments of 'political economy' and the *Canadian Journal of Political Science* was the *Canadian Journal of Economics and Political Science*. These important connections between economics and political science contributed to the development of the unique if neglected bridge between political economy and institutionalist analysis in Canadian political science. Indeed, the development of political economy indirectly served as an important mechanism in moving the study of politics in a more analytical and less descriptive direction. As represented by scholars such as H.A. Innis, the first wave of Canadian political economy provided a theoretical rather than a descriptive approach to explaining Canadian history and development. In masterworks such as *The Fur Trade in Canada*,[17] Innis pointed to the distinctive features of Canadian economic development compared with similar country cases and argued that Canadian development could not be understood apart from the imperial political and economic system of which Canada was a part. A standard critique of Innis's work is that he did not pay much attention to political actors or political institutions and that he did not see much room for agency in his presentation of Canadian development. Indeed, much of Canadian political economy during both its initial phase during the Innis era and during its revival in the late 1960s and 1970s under the banner of the 'new political economy' suffered from those lacunae. It was only in the 1980s that agency began to be seriously debated in the Canadian political economy tradition.[18] Even in the 1980s, Canadian political economy did not see political institutions as important structuring forces in determining economic and political outcomes; indeed, the distinctive feature of Canadian political economy as an intellectual trajectory was precisely its privileging of the forces of economic and social development. Even in the most recent generations of Canadian political economy, no attention has been paid to political institutions or to historical institutionalism, despite its seeming relevance to at least some of the questions of political economy.[19]

Yet, the Canadian political economy tradition had an indirect effect on the development of approaches to the study of Canadian political institutions in English Canada. Canadian political economy suggested that social scientists should approach their subject matter analytically, seeking to explain developments, as well as to describe them. Moreover, Canadian political economy suggested that developments in society and economy were important for politics. Politics did not occur in a vacuum. The state and its institutions were part of a complex of power that was shaped by the forces of economic and social development with which political economy was principally concerned. Canadian political economy was interested in the society end of the state-society divide. And, society was exactly what was absent in the early formal-legal descriptions of Canada's political institutions. Not only were the early works unconcerned with analysis of political institutions, that is, the explanatory focus of social science, but the formal-legal approach neglected the exploration of the dynamic relationships between political institutions and social structures. Even if Canadian political economy did not emphasize the agency of political actors or the importance of Canadian political institutions, it indirectly exemplified several of the types of institutionalist analysis set out earlier, namely, an awareness of the structuring power of economic and social development (or 'the sociological dimension') and an emphasis on the task of explanation. Those interested in the study of Canadian political institutions did not always pick up the tools of analysis provided by political economy. One early scholar who did was J.R. Mallory in his early work on Social Credit in Alberta.

J.R. Mallory's *Social Credit and the Federal Power*

J.R. Mallory is often classified with R. MacGregor Dawson as a formal-legal institutionalist.[20] Yet, Mallory's *Social Credit and the Federal Power* is a conveyor belt by means of which the central contentions of Canadian political economy in the Innis period were translated from the study of economic history into the study of political institutions. It moves beyond descriptive institutionalism to engage with explanatory, sociological, and normative styles of analysis. In *Social Credit*, Mallory's concern was with the way in which political institutions responded to or shaped the transition from individualism to collectivism, as he put it, or, as we might put it, the shift from classical liberalism to Keynesian interventionism.[21] One of the key aspects of this state-society relationship for Mallory was the relationship between the courts and society. During the interwar period, a series of rulings from Canada's highest court of appeal of the period, the Judicial Committee of the Privy Council (JCPC), created institutional obstacles to federal policy by placing responsibility for many important levers of social and economic policy in the hands of the provinces. While the court's decisions were lauded by many Quebecers for maintaining the principles of federalism, the social democratic English Canadian left decried them as impeding effective action by the federal government, the only level of government that could deal with the economic crisis, in the left's view. Mallory's analysis was sympathetic to the view of the left and pragmatically concerned with solving the 'crisis of federalism.' However, his analysis went beyond the stock condemnations of the JCPC in seeking to understand why the court acted as it did and how social change shaped legal decision-making.

According to Mallory, as governments undertook intervention in society and the economy, the groups threatened by such intervention used the courts to resist the pressure. Judges tended to look favourably on the resistor group because their training and background inclined them in that direction. So, submitted Mallory, groups that had been able to 'shift the burden of unfavorable market conditions on to less sheltered groups' cloaked 'economic motives in a concern for the public interest by raising doubts as to the powers of the legislature to enact laws to which they objected.' This strategy, he argued, was naturally most effective 'where the legislature whose jurisdiction they were defending was the least favorable to economic regulation or the least able to make its regulation effective.' Frequently, Mallory observed, cases challenging federal authority to regulate were brought by litigants seeking to avoid economic regulation and their objection was less to the constitutional law than to the substance of economic regulation.[22] As collectivism arose in the late nineteenth and early twentieth centuries, the courts, whose traditional tasks were 'the narrow interpretation of statutes and the application of the rules of the common law affecting private right,' came to be charged with completely different tasks, namely, 'the shaping of the constitution of a federal state.'[23] The division of powers set up by the JCPC decisions fairly reflected pre-1914 Canadian society in which social policy, such as it was in that period, was seen as a purely local concern.[24] However, as Mallory argued, these decisions set up Canadian federalism for the 'twenty years' crisis' of the interwar period, in which the effects of Canada's transition to industrialization transformed the world of the early JCPC decisions beyond recognition. Industrialization accelerated the decentralization of Canadian federalism. Then the Depression and rise of Keynesian economic theory 'cut the ground almost completely from under the Canadian federal system'[25] because the tools and mechanisms of Keynesian economic policies could not be implemented at the provincial level. Mallory argued then, that the JCPC decisions of the 1930s, such as the Bennett New Deal cases which hamstrung Parliament, were reached because of the Privy Council's unwillingness to embrace the interventionist state advocated by Keynesians.[26]

Mallory's focus on specific dimensions of political institutions, namely, courts and their decisions, in relation to the changing social and economic fabric of Canadian society, provides an example of a sociological approach to the study of the impact of political institutions. Political institutions such as courts must be understood in relation to society and society itself must be understood as something that is composed of more than individuals. Instead, it must be understood as a structured set of power relationships, as suggested by the political economy approach. Further, Mallory paid attention to the 'role of ideas' (that is, the rise of collectivism as a system of political values) in his work, a theme of later institutionalist work. As such, he provided a bridge – albeit a neglected bridge – between Innis and the postwar discussion of political institutions of federalism.

The Postwar Legacy: Smiley, Cairns, and Simeon

The work of Donald Smiley, Alan Cairns, and Richard Simeon reflects a new stage in the development of English Canadian institutionalism. These scholars, who contributed to political science over the postwar period, during which the behavioural revolution had its greatest impact on Canadian political science, were concerned with the same issues of state-society relations as was Mallory. Their approaches reflect diverse responses to English Canadian interpretations of the institutional developments of the postwar period, in particular, the rise of executive federalism and the various rounds of constitutional amendment that took place in the wake of the Quiet Revolution.

Donald Smiley

Donald Smiley's *Canada in Question* and *The Federal Condition in Canada*, among other writings, were major texts in the study of Canadian federalism and political institutions. Among the political institutions that Smiley explored in these texts are federalism, constitutional development, and the role of executive, legislatures, and the judiciary in relation to federalism and constitutional debates. Smiley clearly distinguished his approach from that of the descriptive institutionalism of R. MacGregor Dawson's vintage. However, the way in which he distinguished this is telling. He observed that Dawson's text (revised by Norman Ward through many editions) neglected the 'consequences of these structures of power for the welfare of the Canadian peoples, the responses of governments to their needs and desires, political stability and so on.'[27] Much of Smiley's work is explicitly engaged in normative analysis, evaluating institutions as a means to the end of nation-building. Smiley's own preference – for a federal government that can articulate a sense of one national community (not two) against continentalism, regionalism, and nationalism – is crystal clear in his work.[28] Further, rather than viewing society and economy as 'structures of power' in the political economy tradition, political institutions were the only structures of power for Smiley. Hence, he was not able to theorize about the relationships between structures of social or economic power and structures of institutional power. Although Smiley did discuss what he termed 'analytical perspectives' on the development of Canadian federalism and constitutionalism, and included the American institutionalist approach as epitomized in his view by the works of Skocpol and Nordlinger, he was not interested in using these perspectives to explain policy or political outcomes. In Smiley's work political institutions were evaluated as a means to certain ends that are held to be good – 'rational' public policy, liberal democratic values, and a strong federal government.[29] With regard to liberal democratic values, Smiley pointed out that the division of powers between two orders of government helps to prevent either order of government from abusing its authority, that competition between the two levels of government helps to protect civil liberties, and that federalism is better suited to reflecting the public's preferences when these are unequally distributed on a regional basis.[30] Smiley explained the rise of executive federalism – a concept that he described over the course of many of his writings – in terms of the rise of Quebec nationalism and the shifting preferences of federal and provincial elites over the postwar period, and he criticized the intergovernmental infighting that he saw as a necessary feature of executive federalism. He argued that intergovernmentalism institutionalized conflict and impeded effective public policy. However, the emphasis was on the ways in which intergovernmentalism impedes public policy, not on the causal relationships between institutions and elite behaviour.[31] Thus, of the four types of institutionalist analysis, Smiley emphasized pragmatic or normative analysis at the expense of an explanatory political science. In his later writings, he certainly viewed political institutions in relation to the social and economic context but, unlike Mallory, he did not draw on this to pose explanatory questions about state-society relations.

Alan Cairns

In Alan Cairns's work, we find some of the most highly developed arguments about the impact of political institutions on Canadian society and about the relationships between society and political institutions. Cairns has argued both sides of the state-society divide; in some of his work, he has argued that institutions shape society and in other work, he has argued that outcomes that appear to be caused by or brought about by the operation of political institutions, in fact, have deeper sources in the surrounding society. Cairns's classic contribution on the 'society' side of the debate was his interpretation of the JCPC in the 1971 landmark article 'The Judicial Committee.'[32] In this article, Cairns objected to the normative obsession of the JCPC critics and recalled the sociological dimension of the analysis of political institutions found in the work of Mallory. Cairns argued that the workings of political institutions – in this case, courts – reflected the diversity of Canadian society and, in particular, the place of Quebec in Canada. This sociological approach may seem to be at odds with the Cairns of another landmark contribution, 'Governments and Societies of Canadian Federalism,'[33] in which he argued that sociological approaches to politics had come to dominate Canadian political science during the behavioural revolution at the expense of an understanding of the impact of provincial governments as institutional and bureaucratic actors, concerned to build up their power and authority. The process of building provincial state power was intertwined with political culture, according to Cairns, because strong provincial actors had every interest in defining and reinforcing provincial political cultures. While Cairns defined political cultures as provincial in this text, his arguments about the ways in which political institutional complexes build political identity is an approach that is quite similar to the 'new' institutionalism.

This institutional emphasis was carried on in Cairns's work on the Charter and the constitutional debate in which he argued that the Meech Lake and Charlottetown rounds of constitutional discussion were shaped by Charter politics. According to Cairns, the Charter created political-institutional openings for new political actors – especially non-governmental and non-territorial actors – to involve themselves in constitutional debates. These groups gained constitutional standing and an exploitable foothold in constitutional negotiation as a result of the institutional change wrought by the Charter. Further, Cairns argued, it was not just Charter *groups* that were drawn into constitutional discussion as a result of the new status given to non-provincial, non-territorial rights-based political identities by the Charter. It was *citizens* who were constitutionally empowered by the political-cultural effects of the Charter.[34] Superficially, it might appear that Cairns contradicted himself over the course of his writings, arguing, first that societies shape institutions and then arguing against the 'sociological approach' in arguing that institutions shape societies. The fact that Cairns has made arguments on both sides of the question of 'state v society' does not mean that there is inconsistency in his position; his willingness to consider both sides of the question demonstrates one of the key features of the institutionalist approach in the study of Canadian politics. Cairns argued that institutions are 'embedded' in society and that one cannot understand institutions and their impact without placing them in a societal context. One cannot begin by understanding one side or the other of the equation as necessarily more important than the other.

Again, taken superficially, this may appear to be somewhat similar to early works in historical institutionalism. Founders of the literature such as Skocpol have argued that, as middle range theory, the institutionalist approach takes no position on the question of whether state or society is more important. Indeed, arguably, one of the reasons for the great success of the historical institutionalist variant of new institutionalism, as championed by leading scholars such as Skocpol, is that it avoids grand theories of society or of the relationship between state and society. Rather, the research program of historical institutionalism has stressed the importance of working at the middle range of theory and of developing claims about the impact of institutions and their legacies. While historical institutionalism recognizes that there are power relationships in society, it does not attempt a grand theory of such relationships; rather it examines how the power relationships operate on a case-by-case basis. Yet, historical institutionalism studies tend to find that institutionalist and policy legacies are important to shaping policy outcomes.[35]

Similarly, in Cairns's work, the focus is on the institutions and their impacts, not on social forces and their impact. Even when Cairns argues that the social context is important in shaping institutional and political outcomes (as in 'The Judicial Committee'), he does not begin by analysing society, but by analysing the JCPC. This in contrast to the historical sweep of Mallory who described changes in the Canadian economy and society in the nineteenth and twentieth centuries as a backdrop for the discussion of public policy and judicial decisions. Cairns's work is strongest in the normative and explanatory areas and weakest in its lack of developed focus on social forces or economic and social context, namely, the sociological approach.

Richard Simeon

Richard Simeon has made an important contribution to the study of political institutions in English Canadian political science. This contribution begins with *Federal-Provincial Diplomacy*[36] and carries on through a key later (co-authored) work, *State, Society and the Development of Canadian Federalism.*[37] These two books are somewhat different in their theoretical emphasis and orientation, and the differences between them constitute a critique (although a very respectful one) of the normative dimension of English Canadian institutionalism that runs through the literature. *Federal-Provincial Diplomacy* is an intensive examination of the process of federal–provincial negotiation during the 1960s over the Canada Pension Plan, federal-provincial tax agreements, and the Constitution (1967–1971). The postwar period saw the rise of executive federalism as a mechanism for resolving the structural problems of the Depression era. Executive federalism permitted the federal and provincial governments to collaborate in the development of policy. Whether centralized or decentralized, the federal system operated by a process of negotiation which Simeon memorably termed 'federal-provincial diplomacy.' The work also reflects a technocratic emphasis on how to make policies work across the federal system and how to produce good public policy, which is reflective of the postwar period of prosperity. This technocratic emphasis recalls the normative and pragmatic dimension of institutionalism in the study of Canadian politics. At the same time, however, the book documents the first reactions of the federal government to the rise of Quebec nationalism and foreshadows later constitutionalism and federalism debates in its account of the position and bargaining strengths of the Quebec government in the pension, taxation, and constitutional debates.

Simeon's three cases are used to highlight the importance of interstate federalism, namely, the government-to-government relationships of executive federalism that are so important in the operation of the Canadian federal system. Simeon focused his attention on the behaviour of the political and bureaucratic elites in the decision-making process and explored the sources of their power and effectiveness in intergovernmental negotiation. He has also been interested in the 'how' question – how does executive federalism work? – as well as in the policy outcomes that are produced by the system. Simeon highlighted the heavy weight of institutions in shaping the processes through which decisions are made. As such, he argued that political institutions shape policy outcomes by foreclosing certain paths of policy choice and by determining the players who will have access to the table. One of Simeon's most important insights concerns the way in which 'interest groups,' as he called them, would be able to access the decision-making process of executive federalism. Essentially, Simeon provides an alternative to the multiple-crack hypothesis common in studies of American federalism and interest group behaviour which suggests that groups will have greater access and political influence in federal systems because they can step up to bat at two levels of government, rather than one, that is, if groups fail to exercise influence at one level of government, they may try at the other level, and even play the two levels of government off against each other in pursuit of their policy goals.[38]

Instead, Simeon pointed out that executive federalism privileges governmental elites in the negotiating process and that groups are simply barred from participation. Therefore, their interests must be represented by governments themselves, and Simeon does not theorize about why some government may represent certain interests and not others. He pointed out that the provincial governments in the pension negotiations were very far from consistently championing the interests of business, for example, and that the provinces varied greatly in the extent to which they consulted interest groups at all in formulating their positions. And, as Simeon made clear, interest group points of view could be easily sacrificed by governments in pursuit of other goals.[39]

In sum, many of the arguments of this rich and complex work connect up very nicely with the claims of the new institutionalism. In particularly, Simeon's emphasis on what has been more recently termed 'path dependency' is echoed in comparative institutionalist theories. Simeon's elites are not mechanical rational actors since their perceptions are viewed as shaping the negotiating process in very important ways. The interests and strategies of political actors in Simeon's account cannot be read off from any objectively existing conditions, but, rather have to be defined and perceived by the actors in keeping with the contemporary constructivist spirit. As with Mallory, Simeon's work stands the test of time in providing a compelling portrait of Canadian political institutions during an important historical period. In his approach to understanding the behaviour of political actors and elites and in tying policy decisions to institutional factors, Simeon's approach presages the concerns of the comparative institutionalists of the 1980s and after. In this sense, Simeon's work may be considered as a piece of evidence in the battle over the relative 'newness' of new institutionalism. In this debate, proponents of pluralist and behavioural approaches from the 1950s to the 1970s defended themselves from Skocpol's charge of excessive societal focus by pointing to the many works of comparative politics throughout the pre-1980s period that had focused on political institutions as a causal variable. Simeon's book could in this sense be considered as part of the evidence of the institutionalist orientation of political science prior to the rise of new institutionalism.[40]

As Simeon's work developed over time, he became more interested in broadening the explanatory terrain of the society-state relationship. In his overview and quasi-critique of Smiley's contribution to the study of Canadian federalism, Simeon pointed out a series of flaws with the literature on Canadian political institutions. This article in itself stands as a useful summary of the strengths and flaws of English Canadian institutionalist approaches. He argued that Smiley's work does not give a good account of non-territorial interests in Canadian federalism. Published in 1989, Simeon called attention to the relative neglect of class or economic forces in Smiley's account of Canadian federalism. He argued that students of Canadian federalism and political institutions had become too bound up in the constitutional events of the day at the expense of the analysis of the longer term developments. Work on Canadian federalism and political institutions has been insufficiently comparative, too theoretically eclectic, insufficiently causal, not sufficiently interested in hypothesis-testing, and insufficiently attentive to social forces. In essence, Simeon argued that work such as Smiley's (although his remarks on this were written in the form of a 'we' as if he referred to his own work as representing part of this tendency) has not paid sufficient attention to economics and society and concluded that 'we have made little progress in theorizing state-society linkages.'[41] In later works, such as *State, Society and the Development of Canadian Federalism*, Simeon himself attempted to redress these shortcomings of the Canadian literature. With co-author Ian Robinson, Simeon evaluated the history of Canadian federalism in terms of major comparative approaches to state-society relations including public choice theory, political culture, institutionalism, and political economy. This is an important book in terms of the scope of its theoretical ambitions, and it offers many fresh interpretations of the evolution of Canadian political outcomes in terms of the balance between institutions and societal forces. For example, Simeon and Robinson's interpretation of the interwar play of social and political forces and political institutions follows Mallory's interpretation, but in a more sophisticated interpretation that draws in the question of party politics and electoral coalition-building.

Simeon's work grapples at one time or another with all of the types of institutionalist analysis included here. If *Federal-Provincial Diplomacy* is strong on the technocratic and normative evaluation of public policy, it also centres on explanatory research questions and provides a theoretical approach to these questions, based on the behaviour of governmental actors engaged in the process of interstate negotiation. What is absent in *Federal-Provincial Diplomacy* is the sociological dimension; yet, in the later work, *State, Society,* Simeon and Robinson explicitly evaluated political economy, along with political culture, public choice theory, and statism as theoretical approaches to explaining the evolution of Canadian federalism. While *State, Society* does not provide a comprehensive explanation of political outcomes over time, it provides an explanatory template for analysis which, rather than privileging either the institutional or the sociological side at the outset of the analysis, evaluates each approach on its own terms.

After Historical Institutionalism

The rise of comparative historical institutionalism in the early 1980s had ambiguous effects on the English Canadian literature in the Canadian politics field. In some areas of the literature, it is as if historical institutionalism never existed. In other areas – particularly in studies of federalism and public policy and of the impact of the Charter – the literature sporadically engaged in explanatory and sociological institutionalist analysis.

The good old-fashioned English Canadian tradition of pragmatic, normative, and descriptive formal-legal institutionalism remains alive and well. This tradition has broadened and deepened, emphasizing the behaviour of political actors (especially elite actors) in the institutional context. However, for the most part, these thick descriptions lack any explicit engagement with the comparative institutionalist literatures. Studies such as Donald Savoie's *Governing from the Centre*,[42] and David E. Smith's *The Invisible Crown*, go beyond formal-legal institutionalism by focusing, in Savoie's case, on the ways in which political and bureaucratic elites operate within the complex of formal-legal institutions and, in Smith's case, on the way in which the Crown structures the organization of Canadian political power. These works retain the traditional focus on normative questions, such as the evaluation of how well Canadian political institutions work. These studies are not fundamentally concerned with explanatory questions, nor do they anchor the study of Canadian political institutions within the context of either explanatory or sociological institutionalism. Indeed, they are noteworthy for their exclusion of society and social forces from consideration in their presentation of Canadian political power.[43] Smith and Savoie are representative of a large body of scholarship in the study of Canadian politics which continues to work within the bounds of formal-legal and normative institutionalism, leavened with a healthy post-behavioural appreciation for the role of political actors, especially the elite actors in the political system. Other fine examples would include Herman Bakvis on the regionalized cabinet, John Courtney on party conventions, Andrew Heard on constitutional conventions, and David Docherty on Parliament.[44] In these works, the goal is to describe institutional developments and to assess the pragmatic or normative implications of institutional arrangements.

Yet, there have been some important works that have applied historical institutionalism to Canada in ways that draw on the comparative literature in framing the research questions and engage in the explanatory and sociological types of institutionalist analysis. In policy studies, Keith Banting, Sylvia Bashevkin, Michael Atkinson, William Coleman, and Grace Skogstad have all made important contributions. These scholars have undertaken policy analysis that explains policy outcomes by paying attention to the impact of institutions. Further, their work has also placed Canada in comparative context, whether in comparisons between the organizational forms of business associations across developed countries[45] or comparing agricultural policies.[46] Coleman, for example, has systematically examined the role of policy communities in the policymaking process, a set of networks that occur at the intersection of organized social forces and political institutions. His work on business and politics, for example, maps out the complex relationships between business associations and the state and demonstrates the ways in which relationships of causal influence vary across policy areas and economic sectors.[47] Coleman and Skogstad's edited collection on policy communities and policy networks examines the policy process across sectors ranging from labour market policy to fisheries, based on an explanatory and sociological style of analysis in which political institutions are viewed as actual or potentially independent variables that structure the choices of other political actors, such as organized interests. Bashevkin's comparative analysis of the evolution of women's movements in the neo-conservative era emphasizes the intersections of ideas and institutional structures in determining outcomes for women and for the success of women's movements.[48]

The analysis of political institutions is placed in the context of broader political and economic developments – whether the structure of market systems or the policy networks that define the discursive space of debates over public policy.[49]

The study of the impact of federalism on public policy – long a concern of Canadian institutionalist writings – took a turn in a less normative and more explanatory direction in a new generation of work on Canadian federalism. Banting's book on income security[50] examines the extent to which federalism has acted as a barrier restraining social policy development in the income security area, and Canada has increasingly appeared as a case study in the comparative consideration of this question.[51] Antonia Maioni's important comparative work on the historical origins of the Canadian and American health care systems also falls into this camp.[52] And, Kenneth McRoberts, picking up on the work of Banting and Cairns, has surveyed the extent to which federalism structures the policy process and the configuration of societal influences on policymaking.[53]

Another area of the contemporary literature in which institutionalist analysis has been undertaken is in Charter studies. The entrenchment of the Canadian Charter of Rights and Freedoms in the Canadian Constitution in 1982 constitutes one of the few significant formal-legal changes to the Constitution since the act of Confederation itself. As such, it provides an opportunity to examine the ways in which formal, constitutional changes in political institutions affect policy outcomes and the organization of social forces.[54] The literature on the Charter is understandably enormous, and most of it revolves around questions that recall the descriptive and normative traditions of intuitionalist analysis. In Richard Sigurdson's review of the early Charter literature, in 1993, he pointed out that the Charter was seemingly disliked by scholars whom he called 'Charterphobes' of both the left and the right.[55] From the left, the Charter was seen as potentially demobilizing progressive groups through engagement with the thoroughly liberal and individualistic paradigm of law. In addition, a focus on Charter rights was inimical to the success of class-based claims.[56] From the right, the Charter was condemned as inimical to liberal constitutionalism, as undercutting the potential for political negotiation and compromise, which is essential to democracy, by casting issues in the stark black-and-white terms of rights discourse.[57] Right-wing Charter critics have argued that the Charter has provided an access point for minority groups and minority points of view which would not have achieved their policy goals without the help of the courts.[58] In the same vein, Leslie A. Pal's *Interests of State* argues that the Canadian state undertook a policy of supporting certain 'public interest groups' as a direct and indirect consequence of federal policies aimed at shoring up national unity.[59] These scholars have often claimed that their approach is institutionalist in that it privileges the independent effects of institutions on the ways in which social forces mobilize themselves in politics and, in the case of Pal, there has been an extensive engagement with some of the comparative debates on institutionalism.[60] Whatever the claims made for this literature in the name of an explanatory style of institutionalist analysis, much of it is in fact engaging in a normative debate over the legitimacy of judicial review or over the role of the state in privileging 'minority'[61] groups. The literature ignores the sociology of group politics, that is, the rootedness of collective actors in societal power relationships. The purpose of invoking 'institutionalism' in the analysis is not to frame explanatory research questions about the types of impacts that political institutional changes have on the policymaking process or the impact of institutional change on group politics, but, rather, to condemn state policies and judicial decision-making on specific issues that have privileged the traditionally marginalized in Canadian society such as women, linguistic minorities, and ethnocultural minorities.[62] Once again, then, a normative style of institutionalist analysis has dominated the literature at the expense of an explanatory or sociological approach.

Conclusions

Both English Canadian political discourse and political science have been engaged with 'redesigning the state' to an extent perhaps unparalleled in other industrialized democracies.[63] There has been no need for a 'new' institutionalism in the study of Canadian politics because institutionalism was never 'old' or neglected to the extent that it was in the United States during the behavioural revolution. Just as electoral competition and political discourse have revolved around national division and regionalism, so too political science has concentrated on the unique set of federal institutions that regulates these conflicts. During the Depression era, debates on redesigning political institutions revolved around the role of the courts in relation to the federal division of powers and the capacity of the federal state to undertake economic and social interventions in response to the economic crisis. During the postwar years, the problems of 'redesign' were deemed largely solved through the mechanisms of executive federalism. This brief moment of postwar complacency was shot down by the rise of modern Quebec nationalism during the 1960s and an assertive western regionalism during the 1970s. The constitutional crisis unleashed twenty-five years of institutionalist analysis, largely devoted to attempting to solve the constitutional 'problem.'

The explanatory project of an empirical social science, as represented in theoretical approaches such as historical institutionalism in comparative politics, is weakly rooted in the English Canadian side of the Canadian politics field. Of the four types of institutionalism sketched at the beginning of the chapter – the descriptive, the normative, the sociological, and the explanatory – English Canadian institutionalism has an in-built tendency to constantly tilt back towards the normative and descriptive dimensions. Even in the contemporary period in which the constitutional issue is in abeyance in federal politics, the literature continues with its pragmatic emphasis on how our political institutions can work better as conceptualized in terms of a subjectively defined standard of 'democracy,' social cohesion, 'national unity,' or cultural survival in the face of globalization. In fact this normative dimension has been linked to that perennial anglo- and franco-Canadian theme – survival.[64] As Cynthia Williams and Doug Williams state in a fairly typical example, 'the genius of the Canadian experiment ... is to be found in the unique arrangement of political institutions and the ways in which they have been used to activate, enhance, and sometimes jeopardize a shared sense of political nationality and destiny.'[65] Or, as Cairns put it, 'do our constitutional arrangements contribute to our unity or our disunity?'[66]

While the normative debates of the literature have resulted in some important contributions in institutionalist analysis, the style of institutionalist analysis that has dominated the English Canadian literature has also cut off debates between anglophone and francophone scholars. Aside from the linguistic and cultural barriers between the scholarly communities, the focus on a normative style of institutionalist analysis creates barriers to scholarly debate and understanding. Although debates on political values are important, especially for political theorists who are explicitly called upon to discuss such questions, they may create problems for the research community. If scholars are seemingly required to agree with some normative standard or to valorize a particular definition of citizenship prior to engaging in the debate or conducting analysis, they may be less interested in and less willing to engage in the projects of scholarly communication across the profound divide of fundamental values or even primordially defined identities. The style of normative institutionalist analysis, which begins with a concern for 'national unity' in English Canada's terms, deploys an assumption that may be anathema to some francophone scholars. In contrast, the explanatory and sociological styles of analysis permit scholars to pose causal questions and to make links between political institutions, policy outcomes, and organized social forces in ways that do not depend on accepting particular values and do not require that the research community subscribe to a particular goal prior to undertaking analysis, even if normative implications may ultimately flow from the analysis.

The differences between the explanatory and sociological styles of institutionalism in comparative politics and the largely descriptive and normative styles of institutionalism in the study of Canadian politics have been bridged in the work of some of the scholarship by Mallory (*Social Credit*), Cairns ('Governments and Societies'), and Simeon, even if, with the exception of Simeon, these contributions are not presented as comparative politics. Yet, the student of comparative institutionalism who wishes to apply the approach to Canada as a case study could profitably engage with these works as examples of explanatory analysis. The sociological style, stemming from the political economy tradition, is especially strong in Mallory's *Social Credit* and in Simeon and Robinson's *State, Society.* That English Canadian institutionalism has not made more use of the political economy tradition and that political economy in Canada has not been engaged with or has been seemingly uninterested in explanatory explorations of the relationships between political institutions and the economic and social power relationships is to be regretted. Yet, it is perhaps not surprising that political economy – a project of the English Canadian social democratic left – and English Canadian institutionalism – a product of the muddling, middling, liberal centre – have not met up much in the scholarly enterprise. In English Canadian political science, ultimately, debates on values have dominated the scholarly and intellectual enterprise at the expense of an empirical and comparative social science.

Notes

A previous version of this chapter was published as 'Héritage institutionnaliste de la science politique au Canada anglais,' *Politique et Sociétés*, 21 (2002),

113–38. I would like to thank Linda Cardinal, André Lecours, and the anonymous referees for their very helpful comments on the first draft of this chapter, and Maya Berbery for suggesting many useful editorial revisions. Financial support for the ongoing research project of which this chapter is a part was provided by the GR-6 Fund of Carleton University and the Social Sciences and Humanities Research Council of Canada.

1 Kathleen Thelen and Sven Steinmo, 'Institutionalism in Comparative Politics,' in Sven Steinmo, Kathleen Thelen, and Frank Longstreth (eds.), *Structuring Politics: Historical Institutionalism in Comparative Analysis* (Cambridge: Cambridge University Press, 1992), 1–32.

2 Paul Pierson, 'Increasing Returns, Path Dependence, and the Study of Politics,' *American Political Science Review*, 94 (2000), 251–68, suggests that links between 'historical' and 'rational choice' institutionalism may increasingly define this literature.

3 Colin Hay and Daniel Wincott, 'Structure, Agency and Historical Institutionalism,' *Political Studies*, 46 (1998), 951–7.

4 Throughout this chapter, I use the terms 'English-speaking Canada' or 'English Canada' as labels of convenience. A rapidly declining share of the 'rest of Canada' population outside Quebec is not even of 'British,' let alone 'English' origin. I believe that we will shortly need to agree on a new term.

5 Alan C. Cairns, 'Alternative Styles in the Study of Canadian Politics,' *Canadian Journal of Political Science*, 7 (1974), 108–9.

6 Theda Skocpol's seminal condemnation of society-based approaches such as neo-Marxism, structural-functionalism, and pluralism in American political science was published in the introduction to her first book, *States and Social Revolutions: A Comparative Analysis of France, Russia, and China* (Cambridge: Cambridge University Press, 1979), 7–32.

7 Another text, which gives a different interpretation of some of the same material presented here, is Alexandra Dobrowolsky, 'The Charter and Mainstream Political Science: Waves of Practical Contestation and Changing Theoretical Currents,' in David Schneiderman and Kate Sutherland (eds.), *Charting the Consequences: The Impact of Charter Rights on Canadian Law and Politics* (Toronto: University of Toronto Press, 1997), 303–42.

8 Some well-known institutionalists have also offered more partisan politics works as well, which make the normative underpinnings of historical institutionalism clear. For example, Theda Skocpol, *Boomerang: Clinton's Health Security Effort and the Turn against Government in U.S. Politics* (New York: W.W. Norton, 1996).

9 Margaret Weir and Theda Skocpol, 'State Structures and the Possibilities for "Keynesian" Responses to the Great Depression in Sweden, Britain, and the United States,' in Peter Evans, Dietrich Rueschemeyer, and Theda Skocpol (eds.), *Bringing the State Back In* (Cambridge: Cambridge University Press, 1985), 107–63.

10 Cairns, reviewing Mallory's textbook on Canadian government, acknowledged that, although Mallory's approach in the text was that of the formal-legal institutionalist, with all the weaknesses of this approach, Mallory did explore the 'interaction between institutions and society.' Ironically, the tendency to discuss this interaction is greater in Mallory's *Social Credit* (published in 1954) than in a text on Canadian government (published in 1971). See Cairns, 'Alternative Styles,' 108.

11 Recent developments in Quebec political science have also resulted in new linkages between Quebec and English Canadian political science in comparative politics to the extent that, in the contemporary period, it is often difficult to clearly distinguish the two as intellectual currents. See Linda Cardinal, 'Le néo-institutionnalisme et la science politique au Québec,' paper presented at the Société québécoise de science politique conference, Université Laval, Quebec, May 2002.

12 J.G. Bourinot, *How Canada Is Governed: A Short Account* (Toronto: Copp Clark, 1895).

13 R. MacGregor Dawson's text was first published in 1947, and revised through subsequent editions up to 1987, latterly by Norman Ward. The first edition was R. MacGregor Dawson, *The Government of Canada* (Toronto: University of Toronto Press, 1947). The last edition was Norman Ward, *Dawson's The Government of Canada* (Toronto: University of Toronto Press, 6th ed., 1987). For many years, this was the standard textbook in Canadian politics and government in English-speaking universities.

14 J.R. Mallory, *The Structure of Canadian Government* (Toronto: Macmillan, 1971). This text was also reissued in subsequent editions.

15 Bourinot began his text by explaining that his book is 'intended to be understood by all classes of people' and went on to state that 'the first duty of the citizens in every country is to make themselves thoroughly acquainted with the nature and operation of the system of government under which they live' (p. v).

16 David M. Ricci, *The Tragedy of Political Science: Politics, Scholarship, and Democracy* (New Haven and London: Yale University Press, 1984).

17 H.A. Innis, *The Fur Trade in Canada: An Introduction to Canadian Economic History* (New Haven: Yale University Press, 1930).

18 Gregory Albo and Jane Jenson, 'Relative Autonomy: A Contested Concept,'

in Wallace Clement and Glen Williams (eds.), *The New Canadian Political Economy* (Montreal and Kingston: McGill-Queen's University Press, 1989), 180–211.

19 A representative sample of political economy work is found in Wallace Clement and Leah Vosko (eds.), *Changing Canada: Political Economy as Transformation* (Montreal and Kingston: McGill-Queen's University Press, 2003).

20 In my view, this classification is a stereotype, based on defining Mallory's approach solely on his Canadian politics text. See Cairns's treatment of Mallory in 'Alternative Styles,' 109.

21 Mallory, *Social Credit*, 32.

22 Ibid.

23 Ibid., 37

24 Ibid., 38.

25 Ibid., 41.

26 Ibid., 54.

27 Donald V. Smiley, *Canada in Question: Federalism in the Seventies* (Toronto: McGraw-Hill Ryerson, 1972), and Donald V. Smiley, *The Federal Condition in Canada* (Toronto: McGraw-Hill Ryerson, 1987), 11.

28 Smiley, *Federal Condition*, 22–34. See also Richard Simeon, 'We Are All Smiley's People,' in David P. Shugarman and Reg Whitaker (eds.), *Federalism and Political Community: Essays in Honour of Donald Smiley* (Peterborough: Broadview, 1989), 414–15.

29 Smiley, *Federal Condition*, 11–22.

30 Ibid., 16–17.

31 Donald V. Smiley, 'An Outsider's Observations of Federal-Provincial Relations among Consenting Adults,' in Richard Simeon (ed.), *Confrontation or Collaboration: Intergovernmental Relations in Canada Today* (Toronto: IPAC, 1979), 105–12.

32 Alan C. Cairns, 'The Judicial Committee and Its Critics,' *Canadian Journal of Political Science*, 9 (1971), 301–45.

33 Alan C. Cairns, 'The Governments and Societies of Canadian Federalism,' *Canadian Journal of Political Science*, 10 (1977), 695–725.

34 Alan C. Cairns, 'The Charlottetown Accord; Multinational Canada vs Federalism,' in Douglas E. Williams (ed.), *Reconfigurations: Canadian Citizenship and Constitutional Change* (Toronto: McClelland and Stewart, 1995), 280–314. See also Alan C. Cairns, 'A Defense of the Citizens' Constitution Theory: A Response to Ian Brodie and Neil Nevitte,' *Canadian Journal of Political Science*, 26 (1993), 261–8.

35 Of many examples, Theda Skocpol, *Protecting Soldiers and Mothers: The Political Origins of Social Policy in the United States* (Cambridge: Harvard

University Press, 1992), and Paul Pierson, *Dismantling the Welfare State: Reagan, Thatcher, and the Politics of Retrenchment* (Cambridge: Cambridge University Press, 1994).

36 Richard Simeon, *Federal-Provincial Diplomacy: The Making of Recent Policy in Canada* (Toronto: University of Toronto Press, 1972).

37 Richard Simeon and Ian Robinson, *State, Society and the Development of Canadian Federalism* (Toronto: University of Toronto Press, 1990).

38 Other works which evaluated the 'multiple crack' hypothesis with reference to Canada are: Richard Schulz, 'Interest Groups and Intergovernmental Negotiation: Caught in the Vise of Federalism,' in Peter Meekison (ed.), *Canadian Federalism: Myth or Reality?* (Toronto: Methuen, 1977); David Kwavnick, 'Interest Group Demands and the Federal Political System,' in A. Paul Pross (ed.), *Pressure Group Behaviour in Canadian Politics* (Toronto: McGraw-Hill 1975); M.W. Bucovetsky, 'The Mining Industry and the Great Tax Reform Debate,' in A. Paul Pross (ed.) *Pressure Group Behaviour*, and Hugh Thorburn, *Interest Groups in the Canadian Federal System* (Toronto: University of Toronto Press, 1985).

39 Richard Simeon, *Federal-Provincial Diplomacy*, 280–3.

40 Gabriel Almond, 'The Return to the State,' *American Political Science Review*, 82 (1988), 853–74.

41 Simeon, 'Smiley's People,' 415–16.

42 Donald Savoie, *Governing from the Centre* (Toronto: University of Toronto Press, 1999).

43 By this, I do not mean to cast aspersions on the high quality of this work.

44 Herman Bakvis, *Regional Ministers: Power and Influence in the Canadian Cabinet* (Toronto: University of Toronto Press, 1991); John Courtney, *Do Conventions Matter? Choosing National Party Leaders in Canada* (Montreal and Kingston: McGill-Queen's University Press, 1995); Andrew Heard, *Canadian Constitutional Conventions: The Marriage of Law and Politics* (Oxford: Oxford University Press, 1991); and David C. Docherty, *Mr Smith Goes to Ottawa: Life in the House of Commons* (Vancouver: University of British Columbia Press, 1997).

45 William D. Coleman, 'Federalism and Interest Group Organization,' in Herman Bakvis and William M. Chandler (eds.), *Federalism and the Role of the State* (Toronto: University of Toronto Press, 1987), 171–87.

46 William D. Coleman and Grace Skogstad, 'Neo-Liberalism, Policy Networks and Policy Change: Agricultural Policy Reform in Australia and Canada,' *Australian Journal of Political Science*, 30 (1995), 242–63.

47 William D. Coleman, *Business and Politics: A Study of Collective Action* (Montreal and Kingston: McGill-Queen's University Press, 1988).

48 Sylvia Bashevkin, *Women on the Defensive: Living through Conservative Times* (Toronto: University of Toronto Press, 1998).

49 William D. Coleman and Grace Skogstad, 'Policy Communities and Policy Networks: A Structural Approach,' in William D. Coleman and Grace Skogstad (eds.), *Policy Communities and Public Policy: A Structural Approach* (Mississauga: Copp, Clark, Pitman, 1990). See also Grace Skogstad, 'Globalization and Public Policy: Situating Canadian Analyses,' *Canadian Journal of Political Science*, 33 (2000), 805–28.

50 Keith G. Banting, *The Welfare State and Canadian Federalism* (Montreal and Kingston: McGill-Queen's University Press, 1982).

51 Paul Pierson and Stefan Leibfried, *European Social Policy: Between Fragmentation and Integration* (Washington: Brookings Institution, 1995), and Kent Weaver and Bert Rockman, *Do Institutions Matter? Government Capabilities in the United States and Abroad* (Washington: Brookings Institution, 1992).

52 Antonia Maioni, *Parting at the Crossroads: The Emergence of Health Insurance in the U.S. and Canada* (Princeton: Princeton University Press, 1998).

53 Kenneth McRoberts, 'Federal Structures and the Policy Process,' in Michael M. Atkinson, *Governing Canada: Institutions and Public Policy* (Toronto: Harcourt Brace, 1993), 149–78.

54 Miriam Smith, *Lesbian and Gay Rights in Canada: Social Movements and Equality-Seeking, 1971–1995* (Toronto: University of Toronto Press, 1999).

55 Richard Sigurdson, 'Left- and Right-Wing Charterphobia in Canada: A Critique of the Critics,' *International Journal of Canadian Studies*, 7–8 (1993), 95–116.

56 Michael Mandel, *The Charter of Rights and the Legalization of Politics in Canada* (Toronto: Thompson, 2nd ed., 1994).

57 Christopher P. Manfredi, *Judicial Power and the Charter* (Toronto: Oxford University Press, 2nd ed., 2001).

58 F.L. Morton and Rainer Knopff, *The Charter Revolution and the Court Party* (Peterborough: Broadview Press, 2000).

59 Leslie A. Pal, *Interests of State: The Politics of Language, Multiculturalism, and Feminism in Canada* (Montreal and Kingston: McGill-Queen's University Press, 1993).

60 F.L. Morton and Rainer Knopff, *The Charter Revolution and the Court Party* (Peterborough: Broadview Press, 2000). Pal makes similar claims in *Interests of State*, 19–41.

61 Women, of course, are not a minority, although the right-wing literature uses the term 'feminist' in a pejorative sense to imply that 'feminists' do not represent women. See, for example, Pal's discussion of NAC in *Interests of State*, 233ff.

62 This point is made at length in Miriam Smith, 'Ghosts of the JCPC: Groups Politics and Charter Litigation in Canadian Political Science,' *Canadian Journal of Political Science*, 35 (2002), 3–29.
63 The phrase 'redesigning the state' is taken from the title of Keith Banting and Richard Simeon's edited collection on Canadian constitutional politics, *Redesigning the State: The Politics of Constitutional Change* (Toronto: University of Toronto Press, 1985).
64 Margaret Atwood pointed to the importance of survival as a theme in English Canadian literature in her well-known 1972 literary analysis, *Survival: A Thematic Guide to Canadian Literature* (Toronto: Anansi, 1972).
65 Cynthia Williams and Doug Williams, 'Political Entanglements: Ideas and Identities in Canadian Political Life,' in Alain-G. Gagnon and James Bickerton (eds.), *Canadian Politics: An Introduction to the Discipline* (Peterborough: Broadview Press, 1990), 120.
66 'Editor's Introduction,' in Douglas E. Williams (ed.), *Constitution, Government and Society in Canada: Selected Essays by Alan C. Cairns* (Toronto: McClelland and Stewart, 1989), 13.

6

New Institutionalism and Political Science in Quebec

LINDA CARDINAL

This chapter discusses the conceptualization of institutions and the development of a new institutionalism in political science research in Quebec.[1] Some Quebec political scientists started leaning towards new institutionalism in the 1980s, approximately at the same time as did some of their American, British, and French colleagues.[2] Their work, however, went largely unnoticed, partly because it was competing with an overly abstract and ideological approach to the 'national question' predominant in social sciences in Quebec at the time. In contrast, during the 1990s, new institutionalism became more visible and increasingly popular, especially among a new generation of political scientists – typically those trained in the United States and in English Canada, where the approach has been discussed more extensively.[3] Unlike their predecessors, these researchers seem less concerned with theoretical abstractions and more with the practice of politics and its concrete policy outcomes. This may be explained by the fact that their scholarship developed in the context of debates on the future of the welfare state and the crisis of public finances.

This chapter begins with a brief discussion of the conceptualization of institutions in political science in Quebec. It then looks at the ways in which the study of institutions was dislodged by ideological debates during the 1960s and 1970s. Finally, the chapter sketches the conditions under which the new institutionalist approach came into being in the 1980s. Overall, the chapter provides a critical discussion of old and new institutionalisms in the development of political science research in Quebec. It also identifies areas of inquiry and theoretical questions that still need to be addressed within these institutionalist traditions.

The Study of Institutions

In an article published in 1973 on the status of the profession, W.H.N. Hull wrote that 'the ideal political scientist in Canada is interested in Canadian institutions, and in processes and behaviours at the federal level.'[4] Ten years earlier, Jean-Charles Bonenfant had written that Quebec political scientists, in addition to being concerned with provincial politics, were also interested in Canadian institutions and in particular in investigating nationalism, federalism, and bicameralism.[5] There is no doubt that institutions have always been of particular interest for many Canadian and Quebec political scientists.

However, before the 1980s, Quebec political scientists contributed very few theoretical or empirical studies on institutions or public policy in Quebec, and even fewer from a comparative pespective. In 1950, the directory of political science in Canada prepared by Burton C. Keinstead and Frederick M. Watkins for the United Nations Education, Science, and Culture Organization (UNESCO), mentioned only one Quebecer, Henri Bourassa,[6] who was described as an inspired pamphleteer and journalist. In contrast, for Bonenfant, even though topics like nationalism or federalism were raised in a polemical style by Quebec academics, their approach to politics was not totally lacking in intellectual depth.[7] He argued that as early as 1896, there existed a degree of interest in political theory and the history of ideas in Quebec, a noteworthy example of which was Edmond de Nevers's study on the future of the 'French-Canadian people.'[8] Following de Nevers, in the 1930s and 1940s, Wilfrid Morin, Esdras Minville, and R.P. Richard Arès wrote extensively on nationalism, citizenship, and the federal pact.[9] But Bonenfant was critical of their work. He argued that their attitude towards political institutions was overly influenced by legal approaches and insufficiently concerned with theory. For Bonenfant, the legal study of institutions served to describe rules and functions, while the theory of institutions evaluated the legitimacy of institutions from a normative point of view. It debated politicians' views and their proposals for institutional change. For Bonenfant, only two works corresponded to such theoretical efforts at the time: Léopold Richer's *Notre problème politique* and Édouard Laurent's *Quelle est la nature de l'Acte de 1867?*, both published in the 1930s.[10] These works discussed the nature of Confederation and commented on propositions tabled at the time by the federal government for changes in intergovernmental relations. For these authors, any proposal for change had to be evaluated from the point of view of Quebecers' interests as a people. They also cautioned politicians that any failure to do so could lead to separatist sentiments.

Richer and Laurent, like many others after them, took a normative view on institutions informed by nationalism. In advocating Quebec's interests, they defended the position that Canada was the result of a compromise between two founding peoples, not a creation of Westminster. Over the years, debates on Quebec's autonomy or sovereignty by most Québécois academics have often been conducted from this basic standpoint. To be sure, it is reasonnable to say that since the 1930s, Quebec's tradition of debate on institutions has been predominantly nationalist and decentralist. However, it is not easy to characterize nationalism in Quebec, even then.[11] It would be too simplistic to say that all intellectuals and leaders expressed an exclusively ethnic or cultural nationalism. Henri Bourassa's call for an independent Canada at the turn of the twentieth century is a case in point of a more complex approach to nationalism, whether we call it civic or patriotic. Simply put, Bourassa defined Canada as a political nation – a position which still has much currency among Quebec commentators and intellectuals.[12] He advocated a patriotism which brings to mind the more recent debates on belonging and citizenship in Quebec.[13] Debates on the nature of nationalist and populist discourses during the Duplessis years also point to alternative views of nationalism in Quebec.[14] Studies of pre-Confederation institutions and leaders such as Étienne Parent, Louis-Joseph Papineau, Sir George Étienne Cartier, and the 1837–1838 Patriot Rebellions have also shown the existence of a wide range of ideas: democratic, liberal, or republican coexisting with, or in opposition to, nationalism.[15]

These studies provide institutionalist political scientists in Quebec with new intellectual tools from which to analyse the historical development of institutions and to evaluate more recent ones such as the Canadian Charter of Rights and Freedoms or proposals for a renewed Senate. Political theorists in Quebec whose main research interests lie in the normative debates on pluralism and diversity should also be conscious of this institutionalist heritage.

Nevertheless, there are still very few empirical studies in political science that have taken their inspiration from the institutionalist tradition in Quebec. Stéphane Kelly and Marc Chevier are among the few authors who have built on this tradition,[16] although they discuss actors more than institutions per se. Stéphane Kelly, in particular, suggested a republican interpretation of the role of leaders such as Sir George Éti-enne Cartier or Étienne Parent in Confederation. Using Hannah Arendt's idea of the pariah, Kelly argues that they were mediators between Quebecers and the British Crown, with all the problems that this position entailed. For Kelly, these historical figures were led by ambivalent attitudes towards both cultures, a situation that was con-ducive to corruption. Chevrier is also explicitly republican in his out-look on institutions and has been a strong critic Canadian Charter in Quebec. His work on the Canadian Supreme Court has highlighted the way in which judges rely on monarchical arguments in order to defend their independence from Parliament. Alain Noël's analysis of the use of the prerogatives of power in the development of public policy or Linda Cardinal's study of the role of the executive in promoting the legalization of politics in Canada also belong to this institutionalist tra-dition.[17] Ironically, much of these studies have concentrated on federal institutions and on Canada as a whole. There is still no study of the his-tory of the defunct Upper Chamber in Quebec; neither is there any research on the role of the lieutenant governor or on decision-making more generally.

It is relevant to contrast the original institutionalist tradition in Que-bec with its sister tradition in the rest of Canada. James R. Mallory[18] and R. MacGregor Dawson[19] are the two most important writers of that tradition. They published their major works in the 1930s and the 1940s.[20] However, unlike their Quebec counterparts, they both took a harsh view on any current of thought likely to frustrate the operation of British institutions in Canada. Before them, Sir John George Bourinot had also argued for a strict interpretation of the Constitution as a legislative act from Westminster. According to Alan Cairns, this is because their scholarship was influenced by Canadian nationalism and centrism.

More recently, David E. Smith's studies of the Crown as the first principle of government in Canada and of the Canadian Senate are a reminder of the richness of the English Canadian institutionalist tradi-tion.[21] Debates in political theory and the history of ideas in English Canada have also contributed new and important scholarship for a broader interpretation of institutions. For example, Peter Jay Smith's discussion of republican influences on pre-Confederation debates has shed new light on the idea of political community.[22] In his examination of Confederation debates, Paul Romney has moved away from tradi-tional polarizations and argued that the Canadian federation should be viewed as both a pact between two peoples and between provinces.[23] In keeping with this position, political theorist Will Kymlicka has suggested that Canada is a multinational state. James Tully, for his part, has insisted on Canada's tradition of pluralist federalism and the possibility of intercultural dialogue among Canadians, Quebecers, and Aboriginal peoples.[24] Another example is Robert Vipond's discussion of nineteenth-century debates on the accommodation of linguistic minorities in Canada showing that the monarchy, federalism, and the accommodation of minorities are linked together in ways still unaccounted for. For the same reason, it is also worth mentioning the work of Philip Lawson on the events and debates leading to the adoption of the Quebec Act.[25]

These contributions to the normative debate on institutions have answered Bonenfant's call for a move away from legalistic approaches. Moreover, they now suggest the need for a new dialogue among reseachers. The development of a research agenda that could incorporate their different views in order to find more evidence would be an important next step. But before this is made possible, past normative views on institutions are not to be disgarded because of their more limited and nationalist approaches to Confederation. These views share a conceptualization of institutions as a vehicle for the idea of the common good which is as important today as it was in the 1930s and 1940s. For these institutionalist political scientists, institutions generate civic ties, structure the organization of power in society, and dictate basic ground rules. Moreover, their respect for the Constitution is indicative of a concern that institutional change needs to occur within an institutional framework, not outside of it.

However, Bonenfant also argued that the lack of writings on institutions in Quebec meant that political scientists and intellectuals were not in the same position as their English-Canadian colleagues to influence the direction taken by Canadian federalism. A case in point is the strong presence of English Canadian academics in the work of the Rowell-Sirois Commission (1940). Apart from the contribution of Justice Thibaudeau Rinfret, Esdras Minville, and Léon Mercier-Gouin to the commission, for Bonenfant, English Canadian political scientists were more prepared to leave their imprint on Canadian federalism. Quebec academics had to wait until 1953 and the set up of the Royal Commission of Inquiry on Constitutional Problems in Quebec, the Tremblay Commission, for such a role. As Bonenfant wrote then, 'the time has perhaps come to consider changing institutions, and for that a knowledge of political science and the ability to use political science data are clearly needed.'[26] In addition, in 1956, François-Albert Angers published an appendix to the commission's report entitled *La centralisation et les relations fédérales-provinciales*.[27] Before him, in 1954, Maurice Lamontagne had contributed a work about Canadian federalism, *Le fédéralisme canadien: Évolution et problèmes*,[28] and Bonenfant published on Canadian political institutions.[29] These works are descriptive and worth mentioning for their contribution to the understanding of Canadian federalism.

Lastly, in 1957, in *Problèmes politiques au Québec*, Gérard Bergeron discussed the importance of the 1940 and 1956 royal commissions for the growth of political science in Canada.[30] Subsequent commissions such as the 1963 Royal Commission on Bilingualism and Biculturalism in Canada (B and B Commission) have helped make more accessible the work of some Quebec political scientists to their English Canadian colleagues. The systematic translation in French and English of commissioned research has been important to the study of politics in Canada. Royal commissions are often the only space where French- and English-speaking academics can communicate with each other and exchange their views, as well as present their research findings in either official language. It is also in these forums that the different normative viewpoints that inform their perspectives become more apparent. The polarization between decentralist and centralist nationalist views of Canada is still a dominant feature of these meetings.

Rejection and Return of Institutions

No matter how important the institutionalist heritage may have seemed to be for the study of contemporary politics, there is no doubt that it was severely criticized in the 1960s and 1970s. In Quebec, one of the most important criticisms of institutionalism came from sociologist Louis Maheu. Like Bonenfant, Maheu argued that institutionalism was confined to a descriptive level and that it restricted itself to a treatment of rules, laws, and standards of operation for politics. Moreover, for Maheu, institutionalism naturalized social facts rather than reaching for a higher level of intellectualism. It did not provide a proper understanding of politics and issues of power. He argued that it was necessary 'to study ... society as a system of social action of which political science is a component, as well as government machinery.'[31] He also criticized institutionalism because it said nothing 'of the divergent social interests of groups of actors who belong to the various social layers within the population.'[32] He suggested that social scientists had to search for 'the social entrenchment of the tensions and conflicts that affected relationships among the various government structures.'[33] Thus, in studying relations of power, institutions would no longer be referred to as vehicles for promoting the notion of the common good.

Maheu's views were informed by French sociological theory and systems analysis. But the study of politics in Quebec was also influenced by political economy and structuralist Marxism, another offshoot of French sociological theory. These different approaches all aimed at better understanding issues of power. They focused on inequalities, class, and ideologies, and provided a more radical critique of Quebec politics and institutions. They also helped formulate a politics that would be informed by a national liberation ideology and the call for revolutionary action in order to 'free' Quebecers from the rest of Canada. It was then suggested that Quebecers were oppressed and colonized by English Canada and American capital, as well as by their own elite and the Catholic Church. A good example of a study in this category is Gilles Bourque and Anne Legaré's *Québec: La question nationale*.[34] The works of sociologist Jacques Dofny, Hubert Guindon, Marcel Rioux also stem from that same movement.[35]

Another important approach from which the study of Quebec politics and institutions have been conducted was borrowed from Hartz's theory of fragments – which explained that Quebec's political culture evolved from feudalism and/or absolutism. Simply put, the understanding was that New France had been a fragment of the French *Ancien régime*: the main features of which were absolutism and catholicism. These characteristics, which were supposed to have been congealed in Quebec's 'genetic code,' explained the province's so-called backwardness or incapacity to adapt to change. This resembles a caricature but it was certainly a very efficient one for advocacy purposes. The position provided legitimacy to a political program, popularized by both liberals and sovereigntist politicians at the time, centred on the notion that Quebec had to catch up with the rest of the modern world.

Léon Dion's understanding of Quebec politics and institutions was partly informed by Hartz's views on Quebec. Like many other commentators, he used the expression 'Quiet Revolution' to describe the major cultural and social changes affecting his society at the time. He argued that with the advent of an interventionist state in Quebec, Quebecers had developed a more politicized view of their society. More specifically, he believed that Quebecers were becoming more self-reflective after more than a hundred years of Church domination and ethnic nationalism. As he observed in *La révolution déroutée 1960–1976*, 'in 1960, for the first time perhaps, French Canadians finally decided to take control of their present, through a mysterious communion with their time.'[36]

In 1955, Dion was Laval University's first professor of political science, which at the time only had a sociology and economics component. Early in his career, he became the first president of the Société canadienne de science politique, the ancestor of the Société québécoise de science politique. He was also co-director of the *Canadian Journal of Political Science / Revue canadienne de science politique*. In 1963, Dion worked for the Royal Commission on the Status of Bilingualism and Biculturalism in Canada. In 1973, Dion was also appointed special adviser to the Pépin-Roberts Commission on Canadian Unity.

In his forty years as an academic, Dion published many important books: *Société et politique: La vie des groupes* (1971–1972), *Nationalismes et politique au Québec* (1975), *Québec: The Unfinished Revolution* (1976), *Le duel constitutionnel Canada-Québec* (1995), as well as his trilogy *Québec 1945–2000*. In 1980, he sided with the sovereignists, voting 'yes' to give the government of Quebec the mandate to negotiate a project of sovereignty-association with the rest of Canada without ever becoming a defender of the ideology of separation. He described himself as a tired federalist but voted 'no' during the 1995 referendum. However, unlike the more left-wing activist political scientists of the 1970s and 1980s, Dion aimed at channelling the desire for change through institutions.

Maheu praised Dion, who in 1967 undertook a major study of the legislation on education, namely, Bill 60, which established the Quebec Department of Education.[37] In this study, he examined the structure and organization of power relationships between social agents in the setting up of the new department.[38]

Pierre Elliott Trudeau is another important figure who not only popularized the idea that Quebec was a backward society, but used that notion as the mantra which led to his entry into federal politics. Although he was not a political scientist per se, Trudeau's position in the debate on institutions in Quebec needs to be acknowledged. He contributed many influential works on Quebec politics such as *Le fédéralisme et la société canadienne-française* and *La grève de l'amiante*.[39] Influenced more by the American civil rights movements than by national liberation ideology, he also co-authored in 1965 a manifesto for a just and functional society in which we can find most of his ideas on individual and civil rights.[40]

Guy Rocher, who drew from the work of Alain Touraine and American functionalism, was an important figure in sociology. Rocher, who was concerned with the role of the state in social change,[41] can be seen as the bridge between national liberationists such as Bourque, Guindon, or Rioux, and reformists such as Dion. More precisely, it could be argued that Rocher's outlook was explicitly socialist and centred on Quebec, but his politics was statist and reformist in keeping with the institutionalist heritage. He defended the project of an autonomous and democratic society with socialist leanings in which the state would be the principal agent of change. From this perspective, he viewed the Quebec state as an actor with considerable power.

The combination of systems analysis, Marxism, and Hartz's theory of fragments certainly answered Maheu's call for a more intellectualized social and political science. Although he did not go back to the same French sources, Vincent Lemieux also suggested a shift from institutional analysis towards a more structural analysis of action.[42] Lemieux was especially critical of rational choice approaches. To him, they showed people performing calculations without taking into account the fact that there were laws that placed limits on them. Lemieux was concerned with developing a structural analysis of public policy. He was not at odds with the more abstract turn in political science, but he was certainly not part of the more ideological orientation taken by some of his peers.

According to Alan Cairns, systems thought posed a threat to Canada's institutionalist heritage and to the concept of the common good espoused by it.[43] However, institutionalism did not disappear from the English Canadian academic scene as it did in Quebec. On the contrary, the ongoing debate on the status of Quebec within the Canadian federation required some expertise on the mechanics of federalism and constitutionalism. In the absence of a sustained tradition of writings on institutions in Quebec, English Canadian academics continued to provide most of the literature and data on the topic and to leave their imprint on the direction of Canadian federalism. Trudeau may be the exception, but more because of his direct involvement in Canadian politics than as a result of his academic work. In contrast, the influence of left-wing ideologies and sociological theories in Quebec left an indelible imprint on the discipline and led to the development of a more critical outlook on institutions as loci of power and an engine for the reproduction of inequalities. Until the end of the 1980s, a majority of social and political scientists also accepted that Quebec had been either a backward or tribal society, to use Trudeau's expressions, or a colonized one, to use left-wing terminology. They were part of the same movement of ideas. There were some exceptions such as Philippe Garigue but these were rare. Garigue rejected abstract discussions on the nature of Quebec politics and institutions at the time.[44]

Following the failure of the 1980 Quebec referendum on sovereignty-association, Kenneth McRoberts found that the 'national question' no longer seemed to be as important to Quebec political scientists who were now beginning to move away from the Quebec-Canada debate in order to study other aspects of political life. McRoberts believed that political scientists in Quebec should focus on comparative studies.[45] At the same time, Daniel Latouche complained about the dearth of research within the discipline. Trained at the University of British Columbia, he was probably the first in his cohort to note with regret the loss of interest in institutions and the 'almost total disregard for central decision-making institutions' among Quebec political scientists.[46] Latouche ridiculed those studying municipal elections and voting behaviours. He argued that they should rather study the 'functioning of institutions and ... the role of the Prime Minister.'[47] Latouche challenged political scientists to study institutions once again. Political and social sciences in Quebec had been overpoliticized, and according to André J. Bélanger, 'Quebec political scientists had intellectualized a lot but analysed little.'[48]

New Institutionalism in Quebec Political Science since the 1990s

In 1984, the journal of the Société québécoise de science politique[49] published an article by Réjean Landry on new institutionalist analysis.[50] To our knowledge, it was the first of its kind in Quebec. Landry specialized in the study of public policy. Together with Lemieux, he was among the few to conduct research in this area.[51] However, unlike Lemieux, he did not seem too attracted by structural analysis. Landry's article shows that he was more seduced by the rise of new institutionalism as witnessed in the United States in the area of public policy. New institutionalists were proposing a scientific explanation of people's choices, and this had the potential of providing new insight for explaining the making of public policy. It provided new tools to study the ways in which 'individual choices and behaviour were influenced by the features of the institutions,'[52] a position which may have been attractive to Landry given the state of the discipline at the time. It probably made sense after so many emotional discussions on the future of Quebec in the Canadian federation before the 1980 referendum to use rational choice institutionalism in order to explain decisions. Individual choices had not been an important feature of Marxist sociology or systems analysis. When they were factored in, it was to understand the reproduction of relations of power, rather than change or decision-making. In contrast, rational choice theorists conceptualized institutions as strategic contexts with rules and procedures that determined decision-making and its outcomes. They discussed individual preferences as 'goals that may or may not be consistent with one another, in accordance with values that may differ from the collective assets produced by the institutions.'[53] We were still dealing here with an abstract model, but it seemed more helpful than past approaches had been. In addition, Landry suggested the need for a desegregated concept of the state in order to give more weight to the different levels of intervention and decision-making.

A good example of Landry's application of new institutionalist analysis is his study of Hydro-Québec. He discussed the incentives and constraints that affected decision-makers' choices with respect to the use and sale of Hydro-Québec's excess production.[54] According to Landry, constraints stemming from federal institutional arrangements explained the choice made by Hydro-Québec and the Quebec government to adopt an internal consumption strategy rather than to export. He argued that the decision was not the result of a consciously nationalist strategy, but rather the outcome of a calculation that factored in the constraints imposed by existing institutions.

In 1993, under the editorship of Réjean Landry, the *Revue québécoise de science politique* published a special issue on political science research traditions in which he prepared a major report about the institutionalist approach in Quebec and within the discipline.[55] But institutionalist analysis still did not appear to be very sophisticated,[56] and with few exceptions, Quebec political scientists were not yet conducting many comparative studies.[57]

In contrast, by the end of the 1990s, new institutionalism had become one of the most promising approaches for a more empirically and analytically informed research in Quebec political science. There was also a wider variety of approaches to choose from: historical, sociological, and rational choice institutionalism.

The growing popularity of new institutionalist analysis coincided with the debate on the future of the welfare state. Many academics from the social democratic left concerned with the development of progressive public policies took intense interest in the way in which the more conservative governments coming to power at the time, especially in the United States and in Great Britain, were going to move their own policy agendas ahead. The future of the welfare state was also becoming an important topic in Quebec and the rest of Canada. New institutionalists were concerned with the complex dynamic behind the making of public policy and the possibility of change in times where politics was becoming more and more informed by neo-conservative and neoliberal ideals.

The interest in public policy also called for a new historiography of state intervention, change, and collective action, as Marxist approaches had exhausted their explanatory potential.[58] In contrast, historical and sociological institutionalisms provided new conceptualizations of institutions as structures of political opportunity for groups and proved to be a promising alternative.[59] Discourses, framing processes, and agenda-setting became new areas of research and provided ample insight from which to explain social and political action. Informed by historical and sociological institutionalisms, the study of Québec politics thus led to a new turn in the discipline, less ideological or abstract and more concerned with issues such as the impact of the welfare state on Quebec's civil society, Quebec's capacity for self-development, or the study of public and private governance. In addition, the growing interest of many researchers in the study of democracy and governance led to the study of new issues such as international governance;[60] the domestic politics and international relations of small nations;[61] the democratization of African countries;[62] and comparative public policies.[63] Louis Balthazar's work on the United States and the debate on Quebec's North American identity (*américanité*) are also important indicators of the changes being witnessed in political science at this time.[64]

In addition, the notion of Quebec society as backward was finally formally challenged.[65] Coupled with the new normative debates outlined in the first section of this chapter, the institutionalist turn in the study of politics proved the 1990s to be an important moment for the renewal of the discipline.

Jane Jenson's examination of day-care services in France and in Quebec and her study of natal care policies with Josée Bergeron are exam-

ples of new institutionalist studies in the discipline.[66] Jenson studied
the links between institutions, ideas, and interests in attempting to
understand the politics of day-care services in France and Quebec. She
asked how the actors involved in defining the issues or in setting the
agenda succeeded in influencing the direction taken by day-care policies in both jurisdictions. With Bergeron, Jenson also studied the influence of various groups, looking especially at women's and feminist
groups, on the development of natal care policies in France and Quebec as well. They wanted to explain why women's and feminist groups
have more impact in Quebec than in France. In a similar fashion,
Rachel Laforest and Susan D. Phillips studied the differences between
the volunteer sectors in Quebec and the rest of Canada.[67] They looked
at the redefinition of relations between the state and civil society and
how it gave rise to forms of institutionalization in Quebec that were
very different from the rest of Canada. For them, this can be explained
by looking at the positioning of the actors within their different
regimes of citizenship. They concluded that Quebec groups had more
power and influence over the provincial government than their counterparts in English Canada over the federal government. Comparing
Quebec and Ontario, Éric Montpetit and William Coleman studied the
development of agricultural and environmental policies and the
impact of institutional constraints on the relationship among actors in
the two provinces.[68] Once more, differences between the two regions
were highlighted.

These studies provide a better understanding of the distinctiveness of
Quebec, which seems to be typified more by the strengths of its militant
groups and of the institutions of civil society than by the traditional
political institutions. However, not all studies confirm this view. Dominique Masson and Denis Saint-Martin's discussion of public policy networks has shown how recent governmental transformations in the area
of regional development and employment insurance have had, at times,
a negative impact. They claim that changes in the structure of networks
will influence the future organization and representation of interests
and identities.[69] To be sure, they both argue that the development of
new forms of partnership between the state and civil society will change
the balance of power between groups and highlight the existence of
inequities between them. Thus, changes within the organization of
power can also give rise to new representational conflicts indicative of
the vulnerability of civil society in its relationship to the state. Masson
and Saint-Martin point to the development of a new configuration of

power relations in a citizenship regime riddled with new tensions stemming from a challenge to the existing balance of power. But more areas of public policy such as immigration, language, culture, health, and education, to name a few, need to be investigated and compared before we can make a definite statement on the changing nature of state-civil society relations in Quebec.

Some critics have also argued that Quebec's civil society has been weakened by the development of the welfare state itself, not just because of its recent transformation.[70] For economic historian and governance expert Gilles Paquet, researchers take for granted that Quebec society before the 1960s was backward – this bring us back to the influence of the Hartzian paradigm on the discipline. These researchers' lack of understanding of the province's institutions has negatively influenced their understanding of contemporary civil society. More specifically, for Paquet, enthusiasm for the welfare state stems from this attitude and is not always justified. In contrast, he recalls the importance of pre-1960s institutions such as the Desjardins movement, the equivalent of the credit union movement in the United States. For him, it is an example of Quebec civil society's capacity for innovation and strength, a model of development which preceded the 1960s and which came into existence without the support of the state.

Another area of inquiry for students of new institutionalism has been federalism and nationalism, an abiding concern of past or old institutionalists. The work of André Lecours on nationalism and para-diplomacy is worth mentioning here for its attempt to give a greater historical depth to the advent of Quebec as an actor on the Canadian and international political scene.[71] Moving away from the traditional Canada-Quebec debate, his comparisons with the Basque Country, Flanders, and Wallonia underline the distinct direction taken by Quebec compared with that taken by other small nations. More specifically, Lecours studied the role of federalism conceptualized as an institutional constraint in the development of Quebec's greater presence internationally. With Daniel Béland, he has also looked at the way in which Quebec nationalism structures the development of social policy in Canada in ways that remain unaccounted for.[72]

Luc Juillet is also among those studying federalism from an institutionalist perspective. He has examined the impact of federalism on the development of Canadian policy, mostly in the area of the environment.[73] Briefly, Juillet has argued that federalism does not always facilitate the making of policy. But he has also debated whether it is necessary that environmental policy be unified. Landry's work on Hydro-Québec is also still relevant here but more studies need to be undertaken in order to assess more fully the ways in which federalism and nationalism influence Quebec's capacity to advance its own interests and policy agenda. Noël's more normative and descriptive study mentioned above on the role of the prerogatives of power is also important in developing this research program. It seems timely that past and new institutionalist approaches should come together in order to see how they can inform each other and compensate for their weaknesses. For example, past institutionalists were not as much interested in civil society as the new generation is. This area of inquiry is a welcome addition, especially in the discussion of the state as an institution and of regimes of citizenship. Nevertheless, in both cases, institutions represent the conditions under which change is made possible or constrained. However, new institutionalists have a tendency to be too instrumentalist in their understanding of institutions while the older tradition of institutionalism in Quebec was perhaps not concerned enough with the ways in which institutions constrained the possibility of change. In Quebec, the focus on change calls for more study of the ways in which institutions are also concerned with their own continuity. It has been noted elsewhere that new institutionalists, particularly historical institutionalists, explain continuity better than they explain change.[74] But for Kathleen Thelen, the study of stability and change go hand in hand: 'an understanding of political change is inseparable from and indeed rests on an analysis of the foundations of political stability.'[75] Institutional analysis must concentrate on those political events and processes that can act on institutional mechanisms that play a role in both reproduction and transformation. This approach could provide a useful corrective to the Hartzian perspective on Quebec. In short, new institutionalism advocates are representing change not as an expression of a break between a before and an after, but rather as the expression of a complex articulation of the one to the other. This is a research position which still needs to be discussed with much more depth in Quebec and I would dare to say in English Canada as well.

Conclusion

There is no strong institutionalist heritage in Quebec, but rather a wish, expressed very early by the first generation of political scientists, for more in-depth study of Canadian and Quebec institutions. Our survey shows clearly that the second and third generations of Quebec political scientists did not listen to this appeal from their elders. It is only within the fourth generation of political scientists that the interest in institutional analysis became popular again. But students of new institutionalist analysis in Quebec do not appear to be particularly aware of the existence of a discourse about institutions in Quebec at the end of the nineteenth century. They are more imbued with American and English-Canadian analyses, although their research interests have not been dissociated from issues already debated by their predecessors. The interest in new institutionalism by many political scientists in Quebec also shows that they are providing new and relevant analyses of the nature of public policy in Quebec, Canada, and elsewhere. They have inherited a discipline in great need of empirical studies on institutions, and there is still much room for improvement. At the moment, new institutionalist analysis in Quebec is especially concerned with the future of the welfare state and public policy, but also with Quebec's specific circumstances as a small nation in North America and within the Canadian federation. These questions now lie at the core of the discipline and make it distinctive.

Notes

I would like to thank André Lecours and the anonymous reviewers of this chapter for their comments and suggestions. I would also like to thank Samuel Ouellet Marleau for his assistance. An initial version of this chapter was delivered at the annual meeting of the Société québécoise de science politique at Laval University (Quebec City), 15 May 2002.

1 For another historical overview of new institutionalism in Quebec, see Sarah Fortin, 'New Institutionalism and State Centered Approaches in Quebec and Canada,' Montreal, McGill University, 1994 (unpublished manuscript).
2 For the United States, see Kathleen Thelen and Sven Steinmo, 'Historical Institutionalism in Comparative Polities,' in S. Steinmo, K. Thelen, and Frank Longstreth (eds.), *Structuring Politics* (Cambridge: Cambridge University Press, 1992), 1–32; Theda Skocpol, *States and Social Revolutions* (Cambridge: Cambridge University Press, 1979); James March and Johan Olsen, 'The New Institutionalism: Organizational Factors in Political Life,' *American Review of Political Science*, 78 (1984), 74–9; Peter B. Evans, Dietrich Rueschemeyer, and Theda Skocpol (eds.), *Bringing the State Back In* (New

York: Cambridge University Press, 1985). For France, see François-Xavier Merrien, *L'État-providence* (Paris: Presses Universitaires de France, 1997); Bruno Jobert and Pierre Muller, *L'État en action: Politiques publiques et corporatismes* (Paris: Presses universitaires de France, 1987). For Great Britain and Europe, see Hugh Heclo, *Modern Social Politics in Britain and Sweden* (New Haven: Yale University Press, 1974); Paul Pierson, *Dismantling the Welfare State? Reagan, Thatcher and the Politics of Retrenchment* (Cambridge: Cambridge University Press, 1994).

3 For a discussion of neo-institutionalism in English Canada, see Miriam Smith's chapter in this book.

4 W.H.N. Hull, 'The 1971 Survey of the Profession,' *Canadian Journal of Political Science*, 6 (1973), 89.

5 Jean-Charles Bonenfant, 'Les études politiques,' *Recherches sociographiques*, 3 (1962), 75–82. Also reprinted in Fernand Dumont and Yves Martin (eds.), *Situation de la recherche sur le Canada français* (Quebec City: Presses de l'Université Laval, 1962).

6 His many writings include Henri Bourassa, *Les Canadiens français et l'Empire britannique* (Quebec City: Printer S.A. Demers, 1903). See also André Bergevin, Cameron Nish, and Anne Bourassa, *Henri Bourassa: Biographie, index des écrits, index de la correspondance publique 1895–1924* (Montreal: Éditions de l'Action nationale, 1966).

7 The same observation can be found in François-Albert Angers, 'Naissance de la pensée économique au Canada français,' *Revue d'histoire d'Amérique française*, 15 (1961), 204–29. Reprinted in Gilles Paquet (ed.), *La pensée économique au Québec français* (Cap Saint-Ignace: ACFAS, 1989), 9–27.

8 Edmond de Nevers, *L'Avenir du peuple canadien français* (Paris: H. Jouve, 1896).

9 Wilfrid Morin, *L'Avenir du Canada: Nos droits à l'indépendance politique* (Paris: F. Sorlot, 1938); Esdras Minville, *Le citoyen canadien-français: Notes pour servir à l enseignement du civisme* (Montreal: Fides, 1946); R.P. Richard Arès, *Dossier sur le pacte fédératif: La Confédération, pacte ou loi?* (Montreal: Éditions Ballarmin, 1967 [1941, 1949]).

10 Léopold Richer, *Notre problème politique* (Montreal: Éditions de l'ACF, 1938); Edouard Laurent, *Quelle est la nature de l'Acte de 1867?* (Quebec City: Éditions du Cap-Diamant, 1942).

11 For an overview, see Michel Sarra-Bournet (ed.), *Les nationalismes au Québec du XIXe au XXIe siècle* (Saint-Nicolas: Les Presses de l'Université Laval, 2001); for a contemporary discussion on nationalism in Quebec, see Michel Seymour, *La nation en question* (Montreal: Liber, 2000).

12 See Marcel Côté, 'Que veut maintenant le Québec?' *Policy Options Politiques*,

24 (2003), 56–8. Unfortunately, most studies of Quebec nationalism forget to take notice of this simple fact.

13 For an example of this debate in Quebec, see Jocelyn Maclure, *Le Québec à l'épreuve du pluralisme* (Montreal: Québec Amérique, 2001).

14 For more details, see Gilles Bourque, Jules Duchastel, and Jacques Beauchemin, *La société libérale duplessiste* (Montreal: Les Presses de l'Université de Montréal, 1994); Frédéric Boily, 'Le duplessisme ou le populisme inachevé,' *Politique et Sociétés*, 21 (2002), 101–22.

15 Among these studies, see Yvan Lamonde and Claude Corbo, *Le rouge et le bleu: Une anthologie de la pensée politique au Québec de la Conquête à la Révolution tranquille* (Montreal: Les Presses de l'Université de Montréal, 1999); Jean-Pierre Wallot, 'Révolution et réformisme dans le Bas-Canada (1773–1815),' *Annales historiques de la Révolution française*, 213 (1973), 344–406, and 'La Révolution française au Canada, 1789–1838,' in Michel Grenon (ed.), *Cahiers du Québec* (Montreal: H.M.H. Hurtubise, 1989), 61–104; Fernande Roy, *Histoire des idéologies au Québec au XIXe et au XXe siècles* (Montreal: Boréal, 1993); Pierre Tousignant, 'Problématique pour une nouvelle approche de la Constitution de 1791,' *Revue d'histoire d'Amérique française*, 27 (1973).

16 Stéphane Kelly, *La petite loterie: Comment la Couronne a obtenu la collaboration du Canada français après 1837* (Montreal: Boréal, 1997); Marc Chevrier, 'Le juge constitutionnel et la conservation du régime politique au Canada,' *Politique et Sociétés*, 19 (2000), 65–87.

17 See Alain Noël, 'Without Québec: Collaborative Federalism with a Footnote?' *Policy Matters*, IRPP, 2 (2000), and 'Les prérogatives du pouvoir dans les relations intergouvernementales / Power and Purpose in Intergovernmental Relations,' *Enjeux publics*, 6 (2001); Linda Cardinal, 'Le pouvoir exécutif et la judiciarisation de la politique au Canada: Une étude du Programme de contestation judiciaire,' *Politique et Sociétés*, 20 (2000), 43–65.

18 See the very illuminating testimony of J.R. Mallory, 'Style and Fashion: A Note on Alternative Styles in Canadian Political Science,' *Canadian Journal of Political Science*, 7 (1974), 129–32.

19 Robert MacGregor Dawson, *The Government of Canada* (Toronto: University of Toronto Press, 1947).

20 For more details, see M. Smith's chapter in this book.

21 David E. Smith: *The Invisible Crown: The First Principle of Canadian Government* (Toronto: University of Toronto Press, 1995); *The Canadian Senate in Bicameral Perspective* (Toronto: University of Toronto Press, 2003).

22 Peter J. Smith, 'The Ideological Origins of Canadian Confederation,' in

Janet Ajzenstat and Peter J. Smith (eds.), *Canada's Origins: Liberal, Tory, or Republican?* (Ottawa: Carleton University Press, 1995), 47–79.

23 Paul Romney: 'Provincial Equality, Special Status and the Compact Theory,' *Canadian Journal of Political Science*, 32 (1999) 21–40, and *Getting It Wrong: How Canadians Forgot Their Past and Imperilled Confederation* (Toronto: University of Toronto Press, 1999). For another point of view, see Stéphane Paquin, *L'invention d'un mythe: Le pacte entre deux peuples fondateurs* (Montreal: VLB, 1999).

24 See Will Kymlicka: 'Le fédéralisme multinational au Canada: Un partenariat à repenser,' in Guy Laforest and Roger Gibbons (eds.), *Sortir de l'impasse: Les voies de la réconciliation* (Montreal: IRPP, 1998), 15–55; *Finding Our Way: Ethnocultural relations in Canada* (Toronto: Oxford University Press, 1997); James Tully, 'Le fédéralisme à voies multiples et la Charte,' in Alain-G. Gagnon (ed.), *Québec: État et société* (Montreal: Éditions Québec Amérique, 1994), 125–49; see also his *Strange Multiplicity: Constitutionalism in an Age of Diversity* (Cambridge: Cambridge University Press, 1995).

25 Robert Vipond, *Liberty and Community: Canadian Federalism and the Failture of the Constitution* (Albany: State University of New York Press, 1991); Philip Lawson, *The Imperial Challenge* (Montreal: McGill-Queen's University Press, 1995).

26 Jean-Charles Bonenfant, *Les institutions politiques canadiennes*, 89.

27 François-Albert Angers, *La centralisation et les relations fédérales-provinciales.* Quebec City: Royal Commission of Inquiry on Constitutional Problems, 1956.

28 Maurice Lamontagne, *Le fédéralisme canadien: Évolution et problèmes* (Quebec City: Presses de l'Université Laval, 1954).

29 Jean-Charles Bonenfant, *Les institutions politiques canadiennes* (Quebec City: Presses de l'Université Laval, 1954).

30 Gérard Bergeron, *Problèmes politiques au Québec*: *Répertoire bibliographique des Commissions royales d'enquête présentant un intérêt spécial pour la politique de la province de Québec, 1940–1957* (Montreal: Fédération libérale provinciale (Québec), L'Institut de recherches politiques, 1957).

31 Louis Maheu, 'Les lieux de pouvoir entre la scène politique et les rapports sociaux: Des interrogations en quête d'un cheminement intellectuel,' in Georges-Henri Lévesque (ed.), *Continuité et rupture: Les sciences sociales au Québec* (Montreal : Presses de l'Université de Montréal, 1984), 455–6.

32 Ibid., 456.

33 Ibid., 467.

34 Gilles Bourque and Anne Legaré, *Le Québec: La question nationale* (Paris: Maspero, 1979).

35 Jacques Dofny and Marcel Rioux, 'Les classes sociales au Canada français,' *Revue française de sociologie*, 3 (1962), 290–300; Marcel Rioux, *La question du Québec* (Paris: Editions Seghers, 1969); Hubert Guindon, *Tradition, modernité et aspiration nationale de la société québécoise* (Montreal: Éditions Saint-Martin, 1990).

36 Léon Dion, *La révolution déroutée* (Montreal: Boréal 1998), 45.

37 Léon Dion, *Le Bill 60 et la société québécoise* (Montreal: Éditions HMH, 1967).

38 Louis Maheu, 'Les lieux de pouvoir,' 468.

39 Pierre Elliott Trudeau, *Le fédéralisme et la société canadienne-française* (Montreal: Édition HMH, 1967) and *La grève de l'amiante* (1956) (Montreal : Éditions du Jour, 1970).

40 See his comments in Thomas Axworthy and Pierre Elliott Trudeau (eds.), *Les années Trudeau: La recherche d'une société juste* (Montreal: Le Jour éditeur, 1990).

41 Guy Rocher, 'Le sociologue et le pouvoir ou comment se mêler des affaires des autres,' in *Continuité et rupture: Les sciences sociales au Québec*, 380.

42 Vincent Lemieux, ' Un cheminement en politique,' in Georges-Henri Lévesque et al. (eds.), *Continuité et rupture: Les sciences sociales au Québec* (Montreal: Presses de l'Université de Montréal, 1984), 173–88; see also his 'Pour une science politique des partis,' *Revue canadienne de science politique*, 6 (1972), 487–502; (in collaboration with André J. Bélanger), *Introduction à l'analyse politique* (Montreal: Presses de l'Université de Montréal, 1996); *Décentralisation, politiques publiques et relations de pouvoir* (Montreal: Presses de l'Université de Montréal, 2001).

43 Alan Cairns, 'Alternative Styles,'115.

44 Philippe Garigue, *L'option politique du Canada français* (Montreal: Les Éditions du Lévrier, 1963).

45 Kenneth McRoberts, 'Table-ronde: La sciences sociales aujourd hui,' *Recherches sociographiques*, 26 (1985), 493.

46 Daniel Latouche, 'Science politique et pouvoir: Mais où est donc passé l'héritage,' in *Continuité et rupture: Les sciences sociales au Québec*, 216. He drew attention to only two descriptive studies on institutions at the time, one about the Cabinet published by the Éditeur Officiel in 1979, which consists of a description of formal mechanisms and another, by André Gélinas, about rules, committees, and councils, *Organismes autonomes et centraux* (Montreal: Presses de l'Université du Québec à Montréal, 1975).

47 Daniel Latouche, 'Science politique et pouvoir,' 216.

48 André J. Bélanger, 'Lectures politiques,' *Recherches sociographiques*, 26 (1985), 133. His observation was also shared by Alan C. Cairns in 'Political Science

in Canada and the Americanization Issue,' *Canadian Journal of Political Science*, 8 (1975), 197.

49 The predecessor of *Politique et Sociétés*.

50 Réjean Landry, 'La nouvelle analyse institutionnelle,' *Politique*, 6 (1984), 5–32; See also André Blais, 'Le public choice et la croissance de l'État,' *Revue canadienne de science politique*, 14 (1982), 783–807.

51 See R. Landry, *Introduction à l'analyse des politiques* (Quebec City: Les Presses de l'Université Laval, 1980).

52 R. Landry, 'La nouvelle analyse institutionnelle,' 10.

53 Ibid., 14.

54 R. Landry, 'L'hydro-électricité du Québec: Produire pour consommer ou produire pour exporter?' *Revue Études internationales*, 15 (1984), 95–120.

55 R. Landry, 'Les traditions de recherche en science politique,' *Revue québécoise de science politique*, 23 (1993), 7–19.

56 For an example, see André Blais and Stéphane Dion (eds.), *The Budget Maximizing Bureaucrats: Appraisals and Evidence* (Pittsburgh: University of Pittsburgh Press, 1991). S. Fortin notes that the book contains only one contribution from Quebec: the editors.' The other contributors are either from the United States or from English Canada. See S. Fortin, 'New Institutionalism,' 24.

57 R. Landry, 'Les traditions de recherche,' 15.

58 See Peter B. Evans, Dietrich Rueschemeyer, and T. Skocpol (eds.), *Bringing the State Back In*; Doug McAdam, John D. McCarthy, and Mayer N. Zald (eds.), *Comparative Perspectives on Social Movements* (Cambridge: Cambridge University Press, 1996); Aldon D. Morris and Carol McClung Mueller (eds.), *Frontiers in Social Movement Theory* (New Haven: Yale University Press, 1999).

59 On the concept of political opportunity structure, see Sydney Tarrow, *Power in Movement* (Cambridge: Cambridge University Press, 1994).

60 See Luc Juillet, 'Domestic Institutions and Non-State Actors in International Governance: Lessons from the Migratory Birds Conventions,' in T. Cohn, S. McBride, and J. Zimmerman (eds.), *Grounding Globalization: Relations and Levels of Power in the Global Era* (London: Macmillan and St Martin's Press, 2000), 125–41.

61 See André Lecours, 'Paradiplomacy: Reflections on the Foreign Policy and International Relations of Regions,' *International Negotiation*, 7 (2002), 91–114; See also François Rocher, Christian Rouillard, and A. Lecours, 'Recognition Claims, Partisan Politics and Institutional Constraints: Belgium, Spain and Canada in a Comparative Perspective,' in Alain.-G.

Gagnon and J. Tully (eds.), *Multinational Democracies* (Cambridge: Cambridge University Press, 2001), 176–200.

62 According to Mamoudou Gazibo, interest in the new institutionalist perspective also coincided with democratization movements in various countries, primarily in Africa and Latin America. See M. Gazibo, 'Néo-institutionalisme et démocratisations comparées,' *Politique et Sociétés*, 21 (2002), 139–60.

63 See Daniel Béland, 'Does Labor Matter? Institutions, Labor Unions and Pension Reform in France and the United States,' *Journal of Public Policy*, 21 (2000), 11–52; 'Expertise et politique des retraites: L'influence des *think tanks* aux États-Unis,' *L'année de la régulation*, 4 (2000), 251–74; D. Béland and Alex Waddan, 'From Thatcher (and Pinochet) to Clinton? Conservative Think Tanks, Foreign Models and U.S. Pension Reforms,' *Political Quaterly*, 71 (2000), 202–10.

64 Louis Balthazar and Alfred O. Hero Jr, *Le Québec dans l'espace américain* (Montreal: Québec Amérique, 1999).

65 See Linda Cardinal, Claude Couture, and Claude Denis, 'La Révolution Tranquille à l'épreuve de la 'nouvelle' historiographie et l'approche postcoloniale, une démarche exploratoire,' *Globe: Revue internationale d'études québécoises*, 2 (1999), 75–97. Also, Gilles Paquet, *Oublier la révolution tranquille* (Montreal: Liber, 1997).

66 Jane Jenson, 'Les réformes des services de garde pour jeunes enfants en France et au Québec: Une analyse historico-institutionnaliste,' *Politique et Sociétés*, 17 (1998), 183–216. See also Josée Bergeron and J. Jenson, 'Nation, natalité, politique et représentation des femmes,' *Recherches féministes*, 12 (1999), 83–102.

67 Rachel Laforest and Susan D. Phillips, 'Repenser les relations entre gouvernement et secteur bénévole: À la croisée des chemins au Québec et au Canada,' *Politique et Sociétés*, 20 (2001), 37–68.

68 Éric Montpetit and William D. Coleman, 'Policy Communities and Policy Divergence in Canada: Agro-Environmental Policy Development in Quebec and Ontario,' *Canadian Journal of Political Science*, 32 (1999), 691–715.

69 Dominique Masson, 'Gouvernance partagée, associations et démocratie: Les femmes dans le développement régional,' *Politique et Sociétés*, 20 (2001), 89–116; Denis Saint-Martin, 'Guichet unique et reconfiguration des réseaux d'acteurs publiques: Le cas d'Emploi-Québec,' *Politique et Sociétés*, 20 (2001), 117–39; See also, D. Saint-Martin, *Building the New Managerialist State: Consultants and the Politics of Public Sector Reform in Comparative Perspective* (Oxford: Oxford University Press, 2000).

70 For more details, see Gilles Paquet, 'Duplessis et la croissance économique: Une étude exploratoire,' in Alain-G. Gagnon and Michel Sarra-Bournet (eds.), *Duplessis: Entre la Grande Noirceur et la société libérale* (Montreal, Québec Amérique, 1997).

71 See André Lecours, 'Paradiplomacy'; see also François Rocher, Christian Rouillard, and André Lecours, 'Recognition Claims, Partisan Politics and Institutional Constraints,' 176–200.

72 Daniel Béland and André Lecours, 'The Politics of Territorial Solidarity: Sub-State Nationalism and Social Policy Reform in Canada, the United Kingdom, and Belgium,' *Comparative Political Studies*, forthcoming.

73 Luc Juillet, 'Les politiques environnementales canadiennes,' in Manon Tremblay (ed.), *Les politiques publiques canadiennes* (Ste-Foy: Les Presses de l'Université Laval, 1999), 161–204.

74 Kathleen Thelen, 'Historical Institutionalism in Comparative Politics,' *Annual Review of Political Science*, 2 (1999) 369–404.

Part 3

New Institutionalism in Comparative Politics

The third part of this book features contributions exploring the potential of new institutionalism to shed light on three topics in comparative politics: democratic transitions, nationalism, and party aggregation. The chapter on democratic transitions is a critical assessment of the impact of new institutionalism on that area of research while those on nationalism and party aggregation represent efforts at using new institutionalist approaches to improve our theoretical understanding of these political processes.

The chapters in this part are chiefly concerned with asking how and to what extent institutional analysis can explain change: the first two chapters examine the issue of change through historical institutionalism, while the last one does so using rational choice institutionalism. At the heart of the chapters focusing on historical institutionalism is a preoccupation with the approach's bias for continuity and its tendency to use types of explanations that are outside its theoretical logic to account for sociopolitical change. The chapter that uses rational choice institutionalism is concerned with understanding how institutional transformations shape the strategies of actors in a way that leads to change.

The first chapter, by Mamoudou Gazibo, looks at research on democratic transitions in light of the new institutionalist literature. As Gazibo specifies, the chapter is about neither new institutionalism nor democratization per se; rather, its primary aim is to show how the theoretical and ontological foundations of new institutionalism, especially its historical stream, have permeated works on democratic transitions in the past twenty years. Gazibo argues that the weaknesses of democratization theories, namely, a teleological view of transitions and a tendency to see a democratization process where there often is none, cannot be properly understood without an understanding of the impact of new institutionalism on this field of study. He suggests that new institutionalism's main weakness, its theoretical bias for order as opposed to change, represents an important limitation in its ability to provide insight into democratic transitions. More generally, Gazibo sees the influence of new institutionalism on democratization studies in the tendency of 'transitologists' to conceptualize democracy in formal-institutional terms; to involve, in addition to formal institutional structures, ideational factors linked to institutional learning; and to rely on 'external shocks' or institutional tensions to account for change.

The second chapter suggests that historical institutionalism represents a promising approach for understanding the development of sub-state nationalism. André Lecours argues that political institutions have not been given much theoretical importance by scholars of nationalism who have tended to rely on culture, economic conditions, elites, or macro-processes of state formation. Institutions are not absent from studies on nationalism but they tend to be conceptualized simply as reflections of a social reality or as instruments for the management of cultural diversity. Lecours argues that political institutions are instrumental in shaping processes of identity construction and nationalist mobilization. He suggests using the historical institutionalist concepts of critical junctures, which account for change, and developmental pathways, which involve continuity, to theorize the development of sub-state nationalism. Lecours proposes a conception of critical junctures whereby they are triggered by discrepancies between actual power relationships and those embodied by institutions. He then looks at the Belgian case to show how the rise of nationalist movements is inextricably tied to the structures of the early state and how contemporary institutional changes represent critical junctures that strengthened these movements.

In the third chapter Csaba Nikolenyi looks at the consequences of an institutional change, the passing in 1985 of an Anti-Defection Law, on the party system in India. More specifically, he looks to explain the transition, starting in 1989, from the dominance of the Congress party (either alone or with junior coalition partners) to multipartyism. The case study comes as part of a larger discussion on party system change and party aggregation, that is, the joining of political forces to form parties with a good chance of winning a majority in legislative elections. Nikolenyi argues that, as rational actors, office-seeking politicians will form majority parties if the institutional context provides them with incentives to do so. More specifically, he suggests that party aggregation occurs when a party is large enough to contemplate forming a majority party and when party cohesion and/or discipline is weak so that movement can take place between parties. In the case of India, Nikolenyi suggests, the Anti-Defection Law effectively reinforced party cohesion and, as a consequence, discouraged party aggregation.

7

New Institutionalism and the Crisis of Transitology

MAMOUDOU GAZIBO

The 'carnation revolution' put an end to dictatorship in Portugal in 1974, and launched an era of political renewal in Southern Europe and Latin America. Since then, thanks to the pioneering work of Guillermo O'Donnell and Philippe Schmitter,[1] the study of the transformation of political regimes has resulted in a sub-discipline in political science: democratization studies. These studies concern a 'relatively consensual range of axioms, concepts and hypotheses which have made it possible for politologists to describe, analyze, explain and, occasionally, predict the phases and dynamics leading to the transformation of political regimes.'[2] The term 'democratization studies' refers to the study of the democratization process in general, but in reality we can speak of two distinct sub-disciplines: 'transitology,' which is concerned with *change in the nature of political systems*, and 'consolidology,' which is subsequent to it and deals with the *degree of institutionalization of the rules defining these systems*.[3]

New institutionalism emerged in the early 1980s, about the same time as transitology. The former was the work of authors determined to reintroduce institutional factors into political science (as well as in other disciplines such as economics and sociology) to explain political phenomena long overshadowed by the behaviouralist revolution and the developmentalism of the 1960s and 1970s.[4] This is not a coincidence: not only did the authors of the first works in democratization studies rely on a new institutionalist ontology, but these works, in turn, contributed to the reintroduction of institutions as explanatory factors.

In the studies classified under transitology, the emphasis placed on factors linked with the political has made it possible to avoid explanations too biased towards economics and culture, advanced by authors like Seymour M. Lipset, on the one hand, and Gabriel Almond and Sydney Verba on the other.[5] Thus, a major epistemological and methodological shift has taken place: certain authors have abandoned traditional structural theories and objectivist methods in favour of institutional and strategic models.[6] Without denying the impact of these factors, and using variables of an institutional type[7] in studies on democratization, these authors started placing ever greater emphasis on cognitive factors, on the processes of diffusion of ideas and institutional models, on the inheritance left by institutions of the past, on new institutional architecture, on legal norms, and on the place held by the interests, leadership, and strategic interactions of the political game. However, just as new institutionalism has not escaped criticism,[8] the transitology paradigm is also being put under the microscope after a period of widespread acceptance. Thomas Carothers has provided a synthetic view of the main criticisms addressed to transitology by identifying this sub-discipline's five problematic assumptions: (1) that all countries in transition are evolving towards democracy; (2) that the process follows successive phases of liberalization, transition, and consolidation, an implicitly or explicitly teleological idea, despite recognition of the possibility of regression; (3) insistence on the decisive importance of elections that are not merely factors of legitimization of post-authoritarian regimes, but generate over time deeper democratic reforms; (4) that economic, cultural contexts, etc. are not very important, since democracy can be established anywhere; and, finally (5) the perception that building a democracy is a matter of institutional design.[9]

This chapter deals neither with new institutionalism nor with transitology as such. It attempts, rather, to show how recourse to a new institutionalist ontology and models – specifically historical institutionalism – has influenced the theoretical framework and methodology characteristic of transitology. At the same time, the chapter discusses certain problems arising from connecting the two concepts. Two lines of thought are pursued though they do not, of course, exhaust the subject.[10]

The first relates to the new institutionalist ontology. Although this ontology is complex, and new institutionalism takes multiple forms, democratization studies have explored only certain specific avenues of research, such as formalism and the idea that institutions are full-fledged actors. This narrow interest has led to theoretical and methodological choices giving rise to certain problems, sometimes the very problems the authors involved attribute to former theories.

The second focuses on institutional genesis and change. In other words, transitology deals with what Michel Dobry calls *fluid circumstances*[11] or moments of rapid change.[12] How can historical institutional models, which are mainly models of order and which tend to view institutions as independent variables, serve to explain change and the emergence of democratic institutions? This second point invites comment on the concepts of 'democratic process' and 'democratic transition,' which are not unrelated to the new institutionalist perspective. The latter, contrary to previous theories, as March and Olsen have shown, presents politics as a process rather than a decisional system oriented to output production.[13] In democratization studies, this tenet makes it possible to avoid the reductionism and instrumentalism traditionally associated with the study of political action ; however, the concepts of democratic process and transition lead to a double risk: a teleological tendency (regarding democratization as linear), and methodological imprecision (concerning temporal limits and the quality of the transition).

New Institutionalist Ontology and Its Implications for Transitology

A review of the core assumptions of transitology[14] reveals that, in fact, this sub-field of democratization studies is marked, above all, by historical institutionalism, particularly by the tendency to identify institutions with the organizations, rules, and conventions established by formal organizations.[15]

The works dealing with the first 'third wave' experiences in Southern Europe and Latin America reflect this tendency. They describe the breakdown of democratic institutions,[16] the nature and functioning of the authoritarian regimes which replaced them,[17] and the coming to power of the first democratic regimes.[18] Thus, these writings were mainly interested in the forms of regimes, the diffusion processes, and institutional arrangements. Specifically, analysis models applying to modes of transition, to the impact of pre-existing institutional models, to the consequences of present institutional choices, or to the conditions of the durability of democracy, reflect the influence of this version of new institutionalism.[19] Historical institutionalists focus their inquiries on three types of factors commonly called the three 'I's': political institutions, ideas, and interests.[20] To understand the connection between historical institutionalism and democratization studies, we must look at how each of these 'I's' is put into practice and how the ontology associated with each one is reflected in the core assumptions of transitology. The application of ideas and interest factors is discussed in the second part of the chapter. The discussion of the institutions factor is more relevant here because it points out how the ontology shared by institutionalists affects the conception of democracy.

The 'institutions' factor reflects, in effect, the insistence on formal political institutions and the belief in their structuring capacity. In this respect, implementing democratization studies creates theoretical problems related to formalism and the risk of overdetermination by institutions, as well as methodological problems related to comparison and generalization claims ensuing from the choice of this institutionalist ontology.

The Formal-Institutional Conception of Democracy and its Implications

Generally, transitologists pursue inquiries based on historical institutionalism, whose proponents 'tend to identify institutions with organizations and with the rules and conventions established by formal organizations.'[21] Consequently, they prefer to give 'democratization' a procedural sense, defined by the holding of elections. This option has long enjoyed wide consensus among transitologists. Of course, this is not only a consequence of the historical institutionalist influence. Another potential reason for the formalist tendencies of transition studies is the desire of researchers to avoid setting too high the normative bar for democratization with a susbstantive approach. Guy Hermet, for example, considered that this minimalist sense has two advantages: it provides a better instrument for comparing regimes, as well as democratic foundations which can later be expanded by the granting of economic and social rights.[22] But overall, this perspective engenders two types of problems, related to the same epistemological concern: what are we missing when we study democratization in formal terms?

The first type of problem is related to one of the axioms of transitology, which claims that the existence of democracy is simply the result of *the institutional design and the implementation of the rules of the game.*[23] But does this axiom, which is totally relevant when a democratic regime is introduced for the first time, become heuristic once institutions have been established ? Even in contexts in which this perspective is based (and especially in Latin America), reservations are expressed, linked to the admission that electoralism is inadequate when it is merely a dishonest and superficial process (fallacy of electoralism). The electoral criterion produces what O'Donnell has called 'delegative democracies,' systems in which, once elected, leaders are no longer accountable to the voters and can take any liberties.[24] The rules of electoral process might be followed properly, but more essential changes are not implemented. O'Donnell and Ducatenzeiler have stressed the validity of this criticism. The former quotes Getulio Vargas, to illustrate the shortcomings of electoralism: 'For my friends, everything; for my enemies, the law.'[25] The constitutional states which should characterize democratization never materialize; they are re-placed by the perennial presence of formal institutions. It is perhaps time to admit, as Fareed Zakaria has pointed out, that there is, outside the western world, a clear rift between more and more widespread democratic forms of government and the existence of truly constitutional states and the rule of law that should normally accompany them.[26]

The second type of problem is made particularly evident by the asynchronic dynamics of democratic transitions, although the issues at stake are pervasive in some of the first countries to be involved in such a process. The first democratic experiences of the third wave have taken place in western or 'far western' countries, but in the case of the latter (Latin America), the process has not put an end to social inequality. In Africa and Eastern Europe, many of the countries engaged in democratization at the beginning of the 1990s were states characterized by violence, poverty, and great inequalities. In a larger or more thoughtful perspective on democracy, consideration would have to be given to questions of social inequality, the role of civil society, and the existence of a pluralistic public space. It is legitimate to ask if, in the existing conditions, an institutional and formal explanation is relevant, and whether it can truly account for the phenomena observed.

Aside from the debate on the difference between form and substance, and knowing that new institutionalist theorists themselves admit to having a more complex view of institutions, and given that they do not suffice to explain democratization, the relatively great consensus on the procedural sense, regardless of the timing of democratization, provokes epistemological debate. Aside from the questionable heuristic value of this minimalism, does its analytic validity go beyond transition in the narrow sense, defined by the first free elections? It appears that the institutionalist perspective could suffice at this phase, but it must be completed by other perspectives to explain the process after the initial elections.

Institutional Objectivity and the Subjectivity of Actors: Between
Structuralism and 'Heroic Illusion'

The new institutionalist ontology has allowed political scientists to escape structural-type approaches based on economic or cultural variables, but applying its tools to transitology uncovers a paradox: the risk of structuralism, and its opposite, heroic illusion.

The structuralist tendency emerges from the premises of sociological and historical institutionalism, but we will only deal here with the second. This approach bears the mark of neo-Marxist theorists who see the state as an autonomous actor, not subject to social and economic forces. In transitology, this heritage is exemplified by the success of the *path dependency*[27] and *structural contingency*[28] concepts.

The *path dependency* concept is widely used to describe phenomena of immobility and resistance to change, generated by the pre-existing institutional structure. This perspective holds that innovation or possibilities for democratic reform are determined by the institutional configurations in place prior to the innovation process. Robert Putman, whose perspective is between the cultural and the institutional, expresses this idea by saying that 'most institutional history moves slowly.'[29] Bratton and Van de Walle use this approach to explain different types of transition and to show that the limited possibilities of democratic consolidation in Africa are due, for the most part, to the neo-patrimonial nature of previous political regimes.[30] In the same vein, a number of authors who study democratization in Eastern Europe and Latin America in comparative perspective consider that the kinds of problems actors face depend on the traces left by different types of regimes, either communist or military.[31]

The *structural contingency* concept has been used by Karl and Schmitter in a comparative study of modes of transition. This concept claims that certain structural factors, such as the institutional architecture in which strategic interactions take place, constitute a constraint structure which frames these strategies and limits the range of possibilities in terms of action as well as results. Without denying the existence of room for manoeuvre for actors, this analysis postulates that institutions, by their very existence, channel behaviour in certain directions, precluding many other possibilities.[32]

These two positions – one insisting on the traces of previous institutions, and the other on the limitations imposed by the new institutions – lead to an obvious reification of institutions, but remain faithful to the institutionalists' basic premise: that institutions are more than mere variables in a political process, but in fact the scene of action and the generators of practices.[33] However, given that interaction is structured by institutional frameworks, and that political results depend on the paths already opened by previous institutions, how can transitologists escape the structuralism new institutionalists tried to counter by building the theory which guides them?

If they manage to avoid this problem, they risk going to another extreme: heroic illusion. This is usually what happens during periods of transition and institutional design, as O'Donnell and his colleagues have stated so clearly.[34] Michel Dobry has noted this problem in the works of authors like Przeworski and DiPalma; but he did not make any connections with the new institutionalist ontology of democratization studies. Preoccupied by the central place of uncertainty and contingency in transitology, Dobry saw the problem as the classic opposition between objectivism and subjectivism, and was therefore a little too quick to classify the proponents of uncertainty and contingency as subjectivists. But in fact, this tendency towards heroic illusion springs from two other causes.[35] On the one hand, when transitologists use rational choice institutionalism or the interest-based version of historical institutionalism, as do the two authors quoted above, they are coherent with their theoretical and methodological choices, since they place emphasis on strategy. This does not mean that they disregard structures because the choices are seen as 'more or less rational,' as Dobry himself has noted. On the other hand, aside from the importance of the strategic factor in some versions of new institutionalism, recourse to the actor can be seen as a consequence of the multifaceted nature of this approach. Many new institutionalists suggest that institutional phenomena cannot be explained solely by institutions, which opens the way to using more or less institutional variables.[36] But here, we are already on methodological ground. We will come back later to this recourse to extra-institutional factors, in the discussion on democratic change.

Universalist Methodology and Generalization

Insistence on institutions also causes transitologists to disagree on methodological choices. The latter are related to the desire to generalize and to the challenge of case comparability. When institutions are considered the main explanatory variables, the other contextual variables become less limiting for comparisons, which can therefore be applied more widely.

The choice of this method by transitologists has produced very widely applicable generalizations. Thus, although the core assumptions of transitology were based on Southern European and Latin American experiences, they were later generalized to Africa and Eastern Europe. These generalizations produced concepts and models such as 'the pact model' in the writings of O'Donnell and Schmitter; the 'perils of a presidential regime,' in the work of Juan Linz; and Adam Przeworski's institutionalization model based on the idea of uncertainty.

The universalist ambition found in these models of analysis is especially surprising because it brings to mind the excesses of previous theories like functionalism or developmentalism, which new institutionalists have criticized for their overly general character, a flaw these theorists wanted to avoid in their own doctrines.[37] It is rather strange to find this universalism in these studies based on a formal-institutional definition of democracy. In fact, universalism is mainly linked to actor-oriented theories which, taking rationality as a universal given, elaborate a logic of behaviour not affected by specific contexts.[38] The explanation likely lies in a relatively limited range of institutional models. Contexts aside, the democratic system is represented by a few types of regimes which can be compared using standard measurements, as is done, for example, by the American institute Freedom House.[39] Even without referring to criticism produced by cultural perspectives, this institutional criterion of comparison is questionable. Sartori questioned whether democratic institutions are exportable, underlining the danger of imports which do not take their historicity into account.[40] Bunce has produced a thorough criticism of Schmitter and Karl and of their 'academic imperialism,' denouncing the 'conceptual travels of transitologists and consolidologists,'[41] and insisting on the distinction between universally applicable generalizations and those with a limited scope.[42] Rudolf Tökès has also criticized these writings. He judges them to be too normative, and considers that transitology theories are unsuited for understanding what is happening in the East specifically because neither the strategic nor the institutional variables are comparable, and not so much because of the limited range of models.[43]

This problem seems less connected to new institutionalism than to its application to transitology. When defining democracy, transitologists have not only given priority to the institutional aspect, but they have also reduced the concept of institutions to their formal components, while new institutionalists clearly state that the institutional explanation is complex and does not exclude the other variables.[44] Of course, as previously discussed, the formalist option can be explained by the desire of researchers to find a common ground of analysis trough a more operational definition of democracy.

Epistemological problems also appear when the following two questions are asked: is there a relation between the explanatory frameworks for change used in new institutionalism and the explanatory frameworks associated with democratic transformation? How well are these frameworks, so often constructed to explain institutional stability, able to explain democratic change and the origin of democratic institutions?

Models of Order and Fluid Circumstances: Explanation of Change and the Genesis of Institutions

The issues at stake here are both empirical and theoretical, since they involve critical analysis of the way in which political change is viewed in transitology when transitologists use the tools provided by new institutionalism. A paradox becomes apparent, because some of the crucial theoretical concepts of new institutionalism, such as the path dependency concept or the idea that institutions determine political results, express phenomena associated with structuration, or continuity, rather than phenomena associated with change.[45]

In this sense, despite variations between its different perspectives, new institutionalism, especially historical institutionalism, is dominated by models of order. Given that transitology, on the contrary, studies fluid circumstances, that is, situations characterized by rapid change, it is legitimate to ask to what extent new institutionalism can describe these types of situations. Two issues emerge in this context: the causality of change or of democratic reversal, and the trajectory of democratization.

New Institutionalism and the Explanation of Democratic Change

The explanation of change offered by new institutionalists is insufficiently explored[46] and is probably the element of their theory to be viewed with the greatest caution because of its apparent incompatibility with institutionalist ontology.[47] This explanation is based on the institutional change models proposed by Krasner,[48] who contented that political processes are marked by periods of stability and periods of crisis. The former are characterized by institutional continuity, while the latter are defined, in a somewhat tautological manner, as 'moments when important institutional changes take place, creating bifurcations which lead historical development onto a new path.'[49] Thus, there are two levels of explanation: a descriptive level observed through indicators of bifurcation or change (witnessing, for instance, the passage from one regime to another) and an analytic level which inquires into the causes of bifurcation.

On this analytical level (the more interesting of the two), Hall and Taylor revealed that 'theorists generally insist on the impact of economic crises or military conflicts'; Pedersen has discovered, in the writings of founding authors like Etzioni, Jessop, and March and Olsen, a variety of causes ranging from contradictions inside the institution, to learning processes, to conflict between actors. We can see that despite their different tendencies, new institutionalists use catalysts, in accordance with Krasner's model, which holds that crises are provoked by changes in the external environment.

When we look at the way the onset of different transitions is explained by transitologists, we observe that they all use the same explanatory patterns and factors. As a result, we are always brought back to the idea that external shocks are at the root of the process.[50] At least four types of causes are invoked and even if, to be fair, institutionalists admit that institutions are not the sole factors influencing political life, recourse to this type of explanation gives rise to a problem of coherence with institutionalist ontology, which holds that institutions are the main factors explaining political life. Explanatory models are not, however, extra-institutional to the same extent, the first two types of factors being more incoherent than the last two.

One of the most commonly used factors that explain the passage to democracy is the impact of economic crises.[51] Africa is probably the best illustration; democratization on that continent appears to be result of 'a crisis in the economic accumulation model of the post-colonial state,'[52] because in many countries such as Benin, the Congo, Mali, and Niger, liberalization was prompted by social and political organizations protesting against the social effects of economic bankruptcy. But empirically, two facts render this argument rather unsatisfactory on its own. Actually, in most parts of Africa, the economic crisis has existed since the early 1980s, and we need to ask why protest and liberalization did not occur earlier if they depend on economic crises. On the other hand, the early democratic experiments did not always occur in the poorer countries, and nothing is said about the level of crisis that has to be reached before a country initiates a shift.

A second type of factor invoked to explain the occurrence of change is the impact of military conflict. Two of the best illustrations are provided by Portugal and Argentina. The 'carnation revolution' in Portugal was triggered mainly by involvement in the colonial war, which led the Armed Forces Movement (AFM) to overthrow Caetano, Salazar's successor, and then to initiate a transition.[53] In the same way, transition in Argentina was largely due to defeat in the Falklands, which weakened military power and facilitated the advent of democracy. At this level too, although cause-and-effect relations are very clear, we can see that the explanation is even further removed from institutional factors than in the previous example.

Although the first and second transitology explanations are congruent with those given by new institutionalists, they remain extra-institutional. In this context, theorists are obviously in a better position to explain the effects of institutions once they already exist, and to show how, once established, institutions determine the direction of the democratization process, than to explain from their point of view how democratic institutions come into existence. This weakness has led some authors to provide a more institutionally based explanation of democratization processes. Valerie Bunce, for example, has provided an insightful analysis of transition in Eastern Europe by focusing on how the internal contradictions of socialist states institutions explain the process.[54]

The last two types of explanations use variables that are seen as more or less related to an institutionalist explanation of change. Both models insist on the role of interests or ideas.[55]

The 'ideas' factor reflects the insistence on the role of the cognitive and the learning and diffusion aspects of institutional models in political processes. This factor translates into an interest in explaining simultaneous democratizations: why do different countries engage in the same process at the same time? Why are identical institutional forms chosen or why do apparently identical processes subsequently diverge? This brings up the general question of change and of the origin of institutions, which is a major theoretical challenge for institutionalists and is usually dealt with through *the institutional model based on diffusion theories*. According to its proponents, causes of transition are to be sought in processes of contagion, imitation, and learning. This model is congruent with the premises of historical institutionalists who focus on cognitive processes, like Hall and Weir and Saint-Martin,[56] as well as with those of sociological institutionalists like Powell and DiMaggio, who have stressed the role of isomorphic phenomena (coercive, mimetic, or normative) which produce a homogenization of institutional forms. This model, more than the first, makes it possible to explain why transitions occur in waves. Przeworski explained that simultaneity of transitions implies a certain homogeneity, since the institutional repertory is limited and new democracies learn from the old and from each other.[57] Waves are also seen when conflict arises between the norms of the institutions in place and those of the external environment,[58] as was the case in southern Europe (Spain, Greece, Portugal, Turkey), where transition to democracy is partly linked with the creation of the European Union, its institutions, the terms of its treaties, and the requirements related to the establishment of a constitutional state.[59] This perspective also takes into account the effects of globalization, as Guy Hermet[60] and Larry Diamond[61] have done, the latter introducing the term 'global democratic revolution.'

The 'interest' factor reintroduces the actors and makes it possible to reflect on the motivations which lead them to adopt particular institutional arrangements. In transitology, this perspective then prompts a reflection on the role of actors in change, a question which can be said to be dealt with using a *strategic model*, based either on the calculative version of historical institutionalism insisting on interests but focusing on institutional settings, or on rational choice institutionalism which insists more on intentional and instrumental motivations. In the first case, we can speak of a sub-model of 'collusive transactions.'[62] Here, the emphasis is on institutional contradictions, changes in power relations and resources, and on arrangements between actors to take advantage of the opportunities provided by this political dynamic. This is the meaning of the pact model which has dominated transitology since the founding work of O'Donnell and Schmitter. These authors have focused on opposition occurring in authoritarian regimes between hard-liners and soft-liners. When soft-liners win, they negotiate with the moderate opposition in order to bring about a peaceful transition. The second sub-model does not consider these preliminaries at all, because change is seen as a cost-effective calculation made by rational actors in dominant positions. In that case, the question raised is the classic issue of preferences, while in the first, the question is what provokes internal contradictions and oppositions within authoritarian systems. To answer this second question, authors go back to prior changes in the external environment.[63]

What all the models have in common is that, in transitology, the answers to the question of causality of change largely reproduce the models given by new institutionalists who generally find the origin of change in crises and the dissemination of ideas and leadership, more than in institutionalist dynamics themselves. On this point, there is no difference between transitology and new institutionalism, and both are subject to the same criticism.

Democratization Studies between Teleology and 'Essentialism'

Explaining change leads to questioning the issue of causality, as well as the trajectories of democratization. This question, which pervades all of transitology, reflects the epistemological shift introduced by new institutionalist scholars who, according to March and Olsen, view political phenomena in terms of processes rather than results. The operationalization of this political perspective in transitology produces two types of problems: the risk of teleology found in the second precept of transitology, when authors tend to assume that any country engaged in a transition is moving towards democracy; and the risk of essentialism, with its tendency to overestimate the existence of a 'democratic process' even when the transition has clearly failed.

Insistence on processes allows a dynamic view of democratization, and makes it possible to analyse it regardless of its outcome. This option also has the advantage of offering a long-term perspective[64] and avoiding an instrumental approach which would reduce democratization to its results. However, too much insistence on process can make the latter an end in itself, and can make us forget that scientific inquiry must not leave out practical considerations. Many transitologists tend to forget that the mere existence of a democratic process says nothing about its real meaning and content, factors that were essential for the founders of transitology.[65]

Carothers showed the consequences of this omission in the case of Zaire under Mobutu, a case where the obsession with process led many transitologists to continue to consider this country to be on the path to democracy despite political chaos.[66] But transitology has progressed since then. In fact, in the first half on the 1990s, after a glorious period when a whole series of transitions occurred one after the other, the theory suffered the consequences of stagnations and setbacks seen in this process in Eastern Europe and Africa. In response, most of the authors writing in the second half of the 1990s have tended to be less process-oriented. They have paid more attention to the fact that, as O'Donnell ant Schmitter warned in their foudational work, they 'deal with transition from certain authoritarian regimes toward an uncertain "something else." That something else can be the instauration of a political democracy or the restoration of a new, and possibly more severe, form of authoritarian rule.'[67]

We now come to the risk of teleology, which was present in transitology until the middle of the 1990s. In Latin America and southern Europe, the transitions which were initiated usually led to the replacement of authoritarian governments. The successes seen in the first years of transition in Eastern Europe and in Africa reinforced two tendencies: the idea that the move towards democratization had become an unavoidable phenomenon and the idea that despite relapses or imperfections in the new systems set in place, a deeper democracy would be achieved over time. This illusion of linearity is the direct outcome of a major new institutionalist precept which holds that once they are established, democratic institutions and norms are able not only to modify the actors' world-view (creating attachment to democratic values), but also to create the conditions of their own reproduction over time.[68] This view is what leads serious transitologists like Guy Hermet to defend formal democracy on the presumption that it provides the conditions for more genuine democracy.[69] The idea that the existence of norms creates the conditions needed for a deepening of democracy is problematic because it invites a historicist approach, a tendency specifically and rigorously refuted by the institutional offensive of the 1980s.[70]

Here, a clarification can be introduced on the models of order versus models of fluid circumstances dichotomy, as well as on the question of causality, by approaching the question from the perspective of consolidology, which we are not focusing on in this chapter. Consolidology is based on different epistemological premises from transitology. Because it does not focus on the passage to, but rather the institutionalization of, a democratic regime, it is better suited for analysis in terms of order. This view sheds light on the moment when, in the process of democratization, norms outweigh actors and structural models have greater influence than contingency models. But that is another discussion altogether.

Conclusion

The preceding pages could give the impression that the use of new institutionalism in democratization studies is problematic and does not contribute to progress in the field. This is not the case. In fact, the tools of new institutionalism have contributed to make democratization studies the ground-breaking field it is today in comparative political studies. Although the literature has been enriched by other perspectives – cultural or economic – such as those of Almond and Verba on civic culture, and those of Lipset on preconditions to democracy, it was the new institutionalist approach, represented in the work by O'Donnell and Schmitter, which led to the creation of the sub-disciplines of transitology and considology. Clearly, new institutionalism played an important role at this level.

However, the sub-field of transitology entered a period of crisis after its golden age.[71] It is significant in this respect that even founding authors like O'Donnell, Schmitter, and Morlino participate in revealing the weaknesses, the unfounded concepts, and the illusions present in democratization studies in general.[72] Our objective here was to identify the relation between new institutionalism (especially historical institutionalism) and democratization studies (especially transitology) and to examine some of the problems created by this association.

We have argued that most of the models and weaknesses of transitology cannot be understood without an insight into the new institutionalist ontology and the theoretical propositions upon which transitologists build their research. Two points were examined: the impact of institutionalist ontology on transitology at the theoretical and methodological levels, and explanations of change and of the relation between democratic institutions and their environment, provided by transitologists through the use of new institutionalist tools.

First, the origin of certain theoretical problems specific to transitology, and examined in the first part of the chapter, is directly linked to new institutionalist concepts and their authors. On the one hand, transitology borrows above all from the ontological and theoretical premises of historical institutionalism, which is not only the most formal version of the new institutionalist approach, but also the one which endows institutions with the greatest structuralist influence. On the other hand, within historical institutionalism, transitologists have favoured the 'first i,' the one based on institutions, and they have simplified its usage in order to make it more formal and less contextual. This produced theoretical minimalism as well as methodological universalism. Moreover, the central place given to formal institutions created two tendencies: structuralism, inherited from the new institutionalist tendency to reify institutions,[73] and, paradoxically, a risk of teleology, the postulated ability of institutions to reproduce themselves – added to the operationalization of diffusion theories – creating the belief that once they are in place, institutions naturally impose a deepening of democracy over time. Transitologists have sometimes forgotten the warnings of institutionalist theorists themselves about the limited extent of institutional autonomy, the complexity of the concept of an institution, and the interaction between institutions and other variables.

Finally, certain unfounded concepts or weak points of transitology seem not unrelated to a new institutionalist perspective. This is particularly true of the explanations for democratic change. Therefore, it is not by chance that the models described in the second part seem incoherent in the ontological and theoretical framework of new institutionalism. In this context, we can speak of congenital flaws, because this issue relates to one of the weaknesses of the theoretical scaffolding of new institutionalism as a whole.

Notes

Some descriptive parts of this chapter were developed in an earlier review article. See Mamoudou Gazibo, 'Le néo institutionnalisme dans l'analyse comparée des processus de démocratisation,' *Politique et sociétés*, 21 (2002), 139–160.

1 Guillermo O'Donnell and Philippe C. Schmitter, *Transitions from Authoritarian Rule: Tentative Conclusions about Uncertain Democracies* (Baltimore and London: Johns Hopkins University Press, 1986).
2 Nicolas Guilhot and Philippe C. Schmitter, 'De la transition à la consolidation: une lecture rétrospective des democratization studies,' *Revue Française de Science Politique*, 50 (2000), 615.
3 Ibid., 619.
4 See the pioneering article by James G. March and Johan P. Olsen, 'The New Institutionalism: Organizational Factors in Political Life,' *American Political Science Review*, 78 (1984), 734–49.
5 See Doh Shull Shin, 'On The Third Wave of Democratization: A Synthesis and Evaluation of Recent Theory and Research,' *World Politics*, 47 (1994), 136.

6 O'Donnell and Schmitter, *Transitions*, 4.
7 For a clarification of the similarities and differences between these variables, see Peter A. Hall and Rosemary C.R. Taylor, 'Political Science and the Three New Institutionalisms,' *Political Studies*, 44 (1996), 936–57.
8 David E. Apter, 'Un regard neuf sur l'institutionnalisme,' *Revue internationale des sciences sociales*, 43 (1991), 493–513; Ove K. Pedersen, 'Nine Questions to a New Institutional Theory in Political Science,' *Scandinavian Political Studies*, 14 (1991), 125–48; Michael J. Gorges, 'New Institutionalist Explanations for Institutional Change: A Note of Caution,' *Politics*, 21 (2001), 137–45.
9 Thomas Carothers, 'The End of Transition Paradigm,' *Journal of Democracy*, 13 (2002), 5–21. See also, among many critics, Javier Santiso, 'De la condition historique des transitologues en Amérique latine, en Europe Centrale et Orientale,' *Revue Internationale de Politique Comparée*, 3 (1996) 44–5, 56ff.; and for a less pessimistic analysis, Guy Hermet, 'Une crise de la théorie démocratique?' in Corinne Gobin and Benoit Rihoux (eds.), *La démocratie dans tous ses états: Systèmes politiques entre crise et renouveau* (Louvain-la-Neuve : Academia Bruylant, 2000), 139–49.
10 Other axes are possible, and the implications of concepts borrowed from new institutionalism would be different, for instance, in the case of a connection with consolidology, which is closer to models of order.
11 Michel Dobry, *Sociologie des crises politiques: La dynamique des mobilisations multisectorielles* (Paris : FNSP, 1992).
12 O'Donnell and Schmitter, *Transitions*, 4.
13 March and Olsen, 'The New Institutionalism,' 734ff.
14 See Thomas Carothers, n9. Comparing these assumptions with certain new institutional theories clearly shows their institutionalist bias, especially in the case of the last three.
15 Hall and Taylor, 'La science politique,' 471.
16 Juan J. Linz and Alfred Stepan, *The Breakdown of Democratic Regimes* (Baltimore and London: Johns Hopkins University Press, 1978).
17 Guillermo O'Donnell, *Modernization and Bureaucratic Authoritarianism: Studies in South American Politics* (Berkeley: University of California Press, 1979).
18 Ibid.
19 On these institutional models and their methods of application, see O'Donnell and Schmitter, *Transitions*; Terry Lynn Karl and Philippe C. Schmitter, 'Les modes de transition en Amérique latine, en Europe du Sud et de l'Est,' *Revue Internationale des Sciences Sociales*, 43 (1991), 285–302. Michael Bratton and Nicolas Van de Walle, *Democratic Experiments in Africa: Regime Transi-*

tions in Comparative Perspective (Cambridge: Cambridge University Press, 1997).

20 See Denis Saint-Martin, 'Apprentissage social et changement institutionnel: La politique de 'l'investissement dans l'enfance' au Canada et en Grande Bretagne,' *Politique et sociétés*, 21 (2002), 42.

21 Peter A. Hall and Rosemary C.R. Taylor, 'Political Science and the Three New Institutionalisms,' 471.

22 Guy Hermet, 'Le temps de la démocratie?' *Revue Internationale des Sciences Sociales*, 43, (1991), 265–74.

23 Carothers, 'The End of Transition Paradigm.'

24 Guillermo O'Donnell, 'Delegative Democracy,' *Journal of Democracy*, 5, (1994), 55–69.

25 Graciela Ducantenzeiler, 'Nouvelles approches à l'étude de la consolidation démocratique,' *Revue Internationale de Politique Comparée*, 8 (2001), 191–8 ; Guillermo O'Donnell, 'Repenser la théorie démocratique: Perspectives latino américaines,' *Revue Internationale de Politique Comparée*, 8 (2001), 199–224.

26 Fareed Zakaria, 'The Rise of Illiberal Democracy,' *Foreign Affairs*, 76 (1997), 22–43.

27 For a theoretical discussion, see Paul Pierson, 'Increasing Returns, Path Dependence, and the Study of Politics,' *American Political Science Review*, 94 (2000), 251–67; Margaret Lévi, 'A Model, a Method and a Map: Rational Choice in Comparative and Historical Analysis,' in Mark I. Lichbach and Alan S. Zuckerman, *Comparative Politics: Rationality, Culture and Structure* (Cambridge: Cambridge University Press, 1997), 19–41. For application to transitology, see Michel Dobry, 'Les voies incertaines de la transitologie, choix stratégiques, séquences historiques, bifurcations et processus de path dependence,' *Revue Française de Science Politique*, 50 (2000), 593ff.

28 Karl and Schmitter, 'Les modes de transition,' 289–91.

29 Robert D. Putman, with Robert Léonardi and Rafaella Nanetti, *Making Democracy Work: Civic Traditions in Modern Italy* (Princeton, NJ: Princeton University Press, 1993), 184.

30 Bratton and Van de Walle, *Democratic Experiments in Africa*.

31 Guy Hermet, 'Un concept et son opérationnalisation: La transition démocratique en Amérique latine et dans les anciens pays communistes,' *Revue Internationale de Politique Comparée*, 1 (1994), 275–89.

32 Peter L. Berger and Thomas Luckmann, *The Social Construction of Reality* (New York: Doubleday, 1967).

33 Sven Steinmo et al., *Structuring Politics: Historical Institutionalism in Comparative Perspective* (Cambridge: Cambridge University Press, 1992).

34 O'Donnell and Schmitter, *Transitions*, 4.
35 Transitologists regard structural approaches and determinist explanations as suitable to periods of political stability. Periods of transition and of crises (regime crisis, for example) are best explained with more or less rational choice approaches, in terms of decision-making and strategic calculations. See 'Les voies incertaines de la transitologie,' 606.
36 Walter W. Powell and Paul J. DiMaggio (eds.), *The New Institutionalism in Organizational Analysis* (Chicago: University of Chicago Press, 1991).
37 Hall and Taylor, 'La science politique,' 470.
38 March and Olsen, 'The New Institutionalism,' 734–7.
39 See Shin, 'On The Third Wave of Democratization'; Hermet, 'Un concept et son opérationnalisation.'
40 Quoted by Santiso, 'De la condition historique,' 53.
41 Valerie Bunce, 'Should Transitologists Be Grounded?' *Slavic Review*, 54 (1995), 111–27.
42 Valerie Bunce, 'Comparative Democratization: Big and Bounded Generalizations,' *Comparative Political Studies*, 33 (2000), 703–34.
43 Rudolf Tökès, 'Transitology: Global Dreams and Post-Communist Realities,' *Central Europe Review*, 2 (2000), http://www.ce-review.org/00/10/tokes10.html.
44 Paul Pierson (ed.), *The New Politics of the Welfare State* (Oxford: Oxford University Press, 2001), 9.
45 One of the best illustrations of this perspective is given by Paul Pierson, who explains the limited success of the politics of dismantling the welfare state in the United States and Great Britain in the 1980s. Because of the existence of policy feedbacks such as *group interests* or *lock-in effects*, changing existing policies becomes difficult. See *Dismantling the Welfare State*, 39 and following. See also March and Olsen, who submitted that 'institutional thinking emphasizes the part played by institutional structures in imposing elements of order on a potentially inchoate world,' in 'The New Institutionalism,' 743.
46 Hall and Taylor, 'La science politique,' 476.
47 Gorges, 'New Institutionalist Explanations.'
48 Stephen Krasner, 'Approaches to the State: Alternative Conceptions and Historical Dynamics,' *Comparative Politics*, 16 (1984), 223–46.
49 Hall and Taylor, 'La science politique.'
50 Adam Przeworski, *Democracy and the Market: Political and Economic Reforms in Eastern Europe and Latin America* (Cambridge: Cambridge University Press, 1991), 98–99.
51 Bratton and Van de Walle, *Democratic Experiments*, 1.

52 Kankwenda Mbaya, 'Crise économique, ajustement et démocratie en
Afrique,' in Eshetu Shole and Jibrin Ibrahim (eds.), *Processus de démocratisation en Afrique: Problèmes et perspectives* (Paris: Karthala-Codesria, 1995).

53 Kenneth Maxwell, 'Regime Overthrow and the Prospects for Democratic
Transition,' in G. O'Donnell, P. Schmitter, and L. Whitehead (eds.), *Transitions from Authoritarian Rule: Southern Europe* (Baltimore: Johns Hopkins
University Press, 1986), 109.

54 Valerie Bunce, *Subversive Institutions: The Design and Destruction of Socialism
and the State* (Cambridge: Cambridge University Press, 1999).

55 Depending on the definition of institutions proposed by different schools of
new institutionalism, ideas, interests, and leadership can be part of the
institutionalist explanation. But this version is rejected by some, who claim
that these factors are extra-institutional. See Gorges, 'New Institutionalist
Explanations.'

56 Peter A. Hall, *The Political Power of Economic Ideas: Keynesianism across
Nations* (Princeton, NJ: Princeton University Press, 1989), and 'The Movement from Keynesianism to Monetarism: Institutional Analysis and British
Economic Policy in the 1970s,' in Sven Steinmo et al., *Structuring Politics*,
90–113; Margaret Weir, 'Ideas and the Politics of Bounded Innovation,' in
Sven Steinmo et al., *Structuring Politics*, 188–216; Denis Saint-Martin, *Building the New Managerialist State: Consultants and the Politics of Bureaucratic
Reform in Britain, Canada and France* (Oxford: Oxford University Press, 2000).

57 Przeworski, *Democracy and the Market*, 98.

58 James G. March and Johan P. Olsen, *Rediscovering Institutions* (New York:
Free Press, 1989), 167.

59 Philippe C. Schmitter, 'An Introduction to the Southern European Transitions from Authoritarian Rule,' in O'Donnell et al., *Transitions*, 4.

60 Hermet, 'Un concept et son opérationnalisation,' 289.

61 Larry Diamond, 'The Globalization of Democracy: Trends, Types, Causes,
and Prospects,' in Robert Slater, Barry M. Shutz, and Stephen R. Dorr et al.,
Global Transformation and the Third World (Boulder: Lynne Rienner, 1992),
31–69.

62 Term used by Michel Dobry to describe alliance reversals and changes
sometimes unthinkable a priori, occurring in a rapidly changing political
context. See his 'Sociologie.'

63 For example, according to Adam Przeworski, change only takes place when
an organized alternative has been set in place.

64 See the work of Santiso and Schmitter on the temporality of democratization.

65 O'Donnell and Schmitter, *Transitions*, ix and 3.

66 Carothers, 'The end of Transition Paradigm.'

67 O'Donnell and Schmitter, *Transitions*, 3.

68 An excellent analysis on the subject is provided by Crawford Young, who showed how in Africa, the institutions and practices of the colonial state crystallized into postcolonialism despite vigorous attempts by African nationalists to break with everything related to this period, after independence. See Crawford Young, *The African Colonial State in Comparative Perspective* (New Haven: Yale University Press, 1994).

69 Hermet, 'Le temps de la démocratie?' 267.

70 March and Olsen, 'The New Institutionalism,' 737.

71 See note 11.

72 O'Donnell, 'Repenser'; Leonardo Morlino, 'Consolidation démocratique: La théorie sur l'ancrage,' *Revue Internationale de Politique Comparée*, 8 (2001), 245–67. See also Michel Dobry (ed.), 'Les transitions démocratiques: Regards sur l'Etat de la transitologie,' *Revue française de Science Politique*, 50 (2000); Nicolas Guilhot and Philippe C. Schmitter, 'De la transition à la consolidation. Une lecture rétrospective des democratization studies,' *Revue française de science politique* (2000), 615–31.

73 According to March and Olsen, 'the argument that institutions can be treated as political actors is a claim of institutional coherence and autonomy. A claim of coherence is necessary if we wish to treat institutions as decision makers,' *Rediscovering Institutions*, 17.

8

Structuring Nationalism

ANDRÉ LECOURS

The impact of new institutionalism has been felt unevenly throughout the field of comparative politics. The renewed interest for institutions in political science has been clearly visible in several research areas including political parties, legislatures, and executives, particularly through rational choice institutionalism;[1] the state and sovereignty;[2] European integration;[3] social movements and interest groups;[4] development;[5] and democratic transitions.[6] One area where the impact of new institutionalism has been barely noticeable, however, is nationalism. There is a remarkable continuity in the research questions that have been central to the scholarship on nationalism, and these questions tend not to focus on the issue of structure and agency dear to new institutionalists. First and foremost is the issue of the origins of nations which is at the heart of the debate between 'modernists' and 'primordialists/perennialists'[7] that drove research on nationalism in the 1970s and 1980s, and still generates much discussion today.[8] This line of research involves assessing the theoretical importance of culture in nationalism, more specifically its connection with modern identities and political claims; consequently, it focuses on the extent to which nationalism can be viewed as a process rather than on the dynamics of structure and agency relationships per se. Second is the ethnic-civic nationalism dichotomy which dates back to the work of Hans Kohn and is still prominent in contemporary works.[9] From this angle, research consists in characterizing nationalism, that is, looking for different types with potentially distinct normative underpinnings and consequences.[10] Finally, scholarship on nationalism has always involved a concern for the political stability of 'plural' societies. In this context, the focus is on the consequence of nationalism and its management rather than on the causal factors and mechanisms behind its existence.[11]

Of course, institutions are not absent from the scholarship on nationalism, but they are often not given very much theoretical importance, although there are important exceptions.[12] Typically, when institutions are discussed, they are either the reflection of societal forces, in functionalist fashion, or instruments available for the management of diversity and competing political claims. These criticisms are not unlike those directed at the larger field of comparative politics by the early new institutionalists, and the case presented ten years ago by Sven Steinmo et al. for the 'structuring' of politics[13] can be made today in reference to the particular research subject of nationalism. Indeed, nationalism needs to be structured to account for the subjective and political importance that culture sometimes takes, to explain the specific patterns of agency featured by mobilization, and to connect macro-structural contexts to micro-level outcomes. In this context, new institutionalism, particularly its historical branch, has much to bring to the study of nationalism. By providing institutions with added theoretical importance, it shields the theorist from several problems encountered in the literature, namely, cultural essentialism, excessive voluntarism, and the formulation of explanations that are at a high level of abstraction. Moreover, the use of institutions as an analytical focal point can serve to link mass culture, elite action, and the larger socioeconomic environment.

This chapter attempts to explicitly apply historical institutionalism to the study of nationalism.[14] It is divided into three sections. The first examines the treatment given to institutions by theories of nationalism that focus on culture, economic development, elites, and state-building. The second explains why and how historical institutionalism represents a promising approach for the study of nationalism. The third uses the historical institutionalist approach to develop the case study of Belgium.

Institutions and Theories of Nationalism

Theories of nationalism have been classified in many different ways. Typically, these typologies are constructed according to the causal factor they favour. The habitual trilogy features cultural, economic, and political theories. The first two categories are straightforward and will be used here. Cultural theories focus on language, religion, or race, or use the more illusive concept of ethnicity, or ethnic origins. Economic theories link nationalism to levels or patterns of development. The political category tends to include two perspectives which will be discussed separately in the present section. The first views political elites as the motor of nationalism. The second associates it with processes of state construction.

Cultural theories were first articulated by so-called primordialist scholars such as Edward Schils, Clifford Geertz, and Harold Isaacs.[15] In this tradition, cultural explanations for nationalism are quite simple: cultural markers are the bearers of an overwhelming power to both unite and divide; they are the makers of a group identity more fundamental and more loaded with consequences than any other. Institutions are all but absent in this approach. When they are mentioned, it is in reference to the state and only to suggest that its existence in the developing world is threatened by the forces of cultural pluralism. The lack of attention paid to institutions is not surprising since this approach leaves identities unproblematized. In other words, the emergence of nations and the development of nationalism are dissociated from both the social and the political; they are not really processes but simply the natural and necessary products of cultural diversity.[16]

Institutions are barely more noticeable in the work of 'perennialist' or 'ethno-symbolist' scholars such as Anthony D. Smith and Walker Connor.[17] Their approach to nationalism has its roots in the primordialist emphasis on the power of culture, but they depart from primordialism in their effort to link nationalism to social relations and politics. From a perennialist perspective, the origins of nations may be traced to premodern cultures, and the process of their formation usually starts in the premodern era. This process is conceptualized historically insofar as social, political, ideological, and technological developments affect it, but culture remains what builds and sustains nations. In this perspective, institutions appear in the form of the centralizing and modernizing states of the seventeenth and eighteenth centuries where they represent one of these developments which shape how culture translates into national identity. Institutions, in the form of the unproblematized state, are relevant only at a particular historical period and in a secondary manner. Once the state system is consolidated, institutions lose all theoretical importance; states are still mentioned, but primarily for their failure to adequately accommodate the multinational character of the society they host.

From political theory, scholars such as Will Kymlicka and Charles

Taylor have developed culturally based frameworks to understand nationalism which are close to the primordialist/perennialist tradition.[18] Their central argument is that culture, more specifically language, has a natural subjective meaning and that it generates group identities which fulfil an individual's need to belong. These identities have natural political consequences, usually in the form of claims for recognition, autonomy, or independence, as individuals will want to take them into the public sphere. As political theorists, these scholars do not focus on politics or institutions; nevertheless, the spontaneity of the process of identity formation they depict leaves little room for institutional influence. From this perspective, institutions become important as a device for the management of diversity; they can be manipulated and reconfigured until they reflect sociocultural situations.

There is little awareness in all of these cultural theories of nationalism that political institutions play an independent role in, or simply contribute to, the constitution of nations and the development of nationalism. Treating institutions as neutral objects wrongly supposes that they are as fluid as the sociocultural 'reality' they are supposed to reflect and that they always smoothly adapt to social change. Viewing them purely in an instrumentalist perspective hides the fact that they politicize, shape, consolidate, freeze, and even create group identities. This caveat is valid not only for theories of nationalism, but also for theories of nationalist conflict management which by definition view institutions as instruments. Consociationalism, for example, shares the assumptions of the cultural approaches previously discussed about the subjective and political importance of culture. For this reason, it is sceptical about the possibility of political stability in multiethnic societies where politics attempts to transcend cultural cleavages and, consequently, advocates political-institutional arrangements that separate cultural groups and organize social and political life on their basis.[19] In doing so, however, it fails to see that institutionalizing cultural segmentation involves a reification of culture which makes it subjectively and politically important over a long period of time. Similarly, scholars who focus on federalism for managing nationalism tend to neglect the impact of the territorial division of power, and all the structures surrounding its implementation, on the construction, transformation, and politicization of identities.

Theories that favour economic factors for explaining nationalism also provide an inadequate treatment of institutions.[20] These types of theories connect nationalism with processes of economic development and, as a consequence, tend to simply ignore institutions. They suggest that nationalism is the product of uneven economic development, viewed as an unavoidable consequence of the capitalist economy. The idea is that inhabitants of both economically over- and underdeveloped areas can harbour feelings of frustration with the central state, the former because they think they are financing the rest of the country and the latter because they feel they are being neglected or exploited.[21] From this perspective, the presence of cultural distinctiveness is not absolutely necessary for the development of nationalism, although the superimposition of economic and cultural cleavages is seen as particularly combustible. In both cases, however, the crucial connection to nationalism is with macro-economic forces which operate beyond the state. One version of the economic approach to nationalism, the internal colonialism thesis, had the central state deliberately implementing exploitative policies towards regions.[22] In this context, the state was part of the theoretical explanation but, in good Marxist fashion, was made the instrument of dominant classes and therefore not granted any genuine autonomy.

Hard core economic explanations for nationalism such as the internal colonialism thesis have been on the decline for some time but the processes of globalization, and the burgeoning literature they have triggered, have served to restore the importance of macro-economic forces in theories of nationalism.[23] Scholars who bring in globalization into explanations for nationalism generally do not seek to replace social, cultural, or political factors; they suggest that globalization exacerbates whatever forces are already driving a nationalist movement. The globalization argument as it relates to nationalism holds that free trade, regional integration, and global interconnectedness through new technologies – in contributing to weakening the state – loosen the subjective ties it has with citizens and provide a new impetus, if not a necessity, for regions to take it upon themselves to protect their cultural and economic interests and to claim the political power considered necessary to act efficiently in an autonomous manner. Consequently, regions are increasingly becoming political communities rather than purely administrative arrangements, and those where a meaningful identity already has existed are likely to experience a surge in loyalty. In this context, the state in itself is not significant; its weakening is. Or, more justly, it is macro-structural factors, now of a global nature, that see their theoretical importance being bolstered.

Political elites are increasingly popular as a focus for theories of nationalism. Explaining nationalism through the behaviour of political elites entails a political conception of the phenomenon. Here, nationalism is not primarily about culture or economics but about politics and political power. These types of approaches argue that elites are instrumental in providing cultural markers with subjective meaning, politicizing identities, and defining group interests in a way that corresponds to their own or is coherent with their own objectives and ambitions. They suggest that political elites launch, sustain, and stimulate processes of identity construction and political mobilization in the context of their own power struggles.[24] Some elite-centred approaches present nationalism almost as an accidental byproduct of power struggles. In this scenario, elites feed a population's sense of identity and political aspirations without fully intending to build on it through, for example, attempts at outbidding political opponents in the hope of winning elections. Another version takes a more instrumentalist view of nationalism, squarely depicting political elites as 'ethnic entrepreneurs' who cunningly exploit fears and stereotypes to gain or maintain political power.[25]

Elite-centred approaches to nationalism have played a key role in debunking the primordialist approach and are leading the modernist camp in its debate with the perennialists. There is much to be said for conceptualizing nationalism as a form of politics. After all, nationalist claims are ultimately of a political nature and take shape in the context of the political process. Furthermore, if nationalism is a form of politics, it is not unreasonable to view it in terms of leaders and followers. The focus on elites can help explain why culture acquires subjective meaning and becomes politically relevant only in some instances, and why nationalist activity varies in intensity over time. However, theories of nationalism that focus on elites tend to marginalize political institutions. In some cases, elites would appear to be operating in an institutional vacuum.[26] This characterization runs the danger of exaggerating the voluntarist nature of the process of identity construction and the instrumentalist nature of nationalist mobilization. At a minimum, even calculating elites whose aim is to use nationalism to further their own objectives have to deal with institutional constraints and limitations. More to the point, institutional contexts shape power struggles among elites in ways that make it more or less likely that politics will become nationalist politics. In other words, the form taken by politics at a certain point in time is partly the product of the prevalent institutional environment and how it affects how elites interact among themselves and with the masses. Evacuating institutions from elite-centred theories of nationalism also presents the problem of explaining why elite power struggles lead to nationalism in some cases but not others. Indeed, theorists of nationalism who focus on elites tend not to give great theoretical importance to culture or macro-economic factors, and are therefore unlikely to call upon these factors to account for the presence of nationalism in one case and its absence in another. In this context, one explanation for the difference in outcomes would be the institutional context; whereas one set of institutions can steer politics towards nationalist politics, another can take it into the opposite direction or simply lead elites to adopt a different perspective on political issues.

Nationalism has also been explained as a consequence of modern state-building. These theories, defended by such scholars as Ernest Gellner and John Breuilly, constitute the classic modernist interpretations of nationalism.[27] For Gellner, the modern centralized state created nations through the imposition of an homogenized 'high culture.' According to this argument, modern societies need cultural uniformity and cohesion to function adequately, and the state, through national education systems and other similar tools which bring to bear its symbolic resources, can achieve such a result. From this perspective, cultural unification and national identity are a structural, functional necessity. Nationalism is therefore the byproduct of modernity. Breuilly, holding a similar type of argument, suggests that nationalism is the result of a reorganization of politics as an activity of general interest. Only with the breakdown of the system of privileges and the beginning of state intervention does the state become the focal point of politics and produce claims for legitimacy framed in nationalist terms.

These theories do feature the state and, certainly in Gellner's version, do give it theoretical importance. Indeed, nationalism is, in the orthodox modernist position as laid out by Gellner, strongly structured. Still, the state-building approach to nationalism suffers from at least four problems in its treatment of institutions. First, as was the case for the other approaches previously discussed, it speaks of the state without specifying what exactly is meant. The theoretical linkage to the state can involve several different things in various proportions: bureaucratic organization, language regimes, political party systems, legislative and executive branches, territorial division of power, military forces, and so on. Failing to flesh out the state leaves the theorist with poor analytical leverage. Second, these theories, because of the very nature of their argument, are strongly associated with a particular historical period. What they can tell about nationalism in states that have already undergone the processes they stress is unclear. Third, state-building theories focus on explaining the nationalism of the state. What does Gellner's theory tell us about sub-state nationalism? Not much, since it really is not supposed to exist, and the only way it can be explained is to see it as a reaction against the homogenizing pretenses of the state. This leaves us with a very abstract and simplistic explanation. Finally, it is legitimate to ask what is really behind nationalism in state-building theories: the state or 'modernity.' Of course, it is difficult to completely separate the two because of their historical entanglement, but could the state be removed from these theories in favour of the processes of modernity without sacrificing explanatory power? In Gellner's case, probably not. For Breuilly, however, the state and nationalism appear together; they seem to both be products of modernity rather than causally related between themselves.

Theories of nationalism could gain explanatory power by providing institutions with more theoretical importance. In this context, historical institutionalism represents an approach worth investigating. Not that historical institutionalism should be expected to explain everything about nationalism, but it can certainly help in our understanding its development as a macro-process. The following section discusses how historical institutionalism can help in structuring nationalism.

Historical Institutionalism and Nationalism

As we mentioned in the introduction, nationalism is not a research area where new institutionalism has had a major impact. This is surprising because historical institutionalism presents features that make it attractive for the study of nationalism: it provides a view on structure and agency which takes institutions seriously yet leaves room for action, conceptualized in terms of power and power relationships, and it offers a genuine historical perspective. The originality of historical institutionalism as a general approach to politics is the theoretical importance it gives to political institutions such as branches of state (executives, legislatures, courts, bureaucracies, the military); constitutions; federalism and autonomy; party systems; and language regimes. As it pertains to nationalism, this concern with the effect of institutions on sociopolitical outcomes can shed light on the processes of identity construction, transformation, and mobilization which are at the heart of nationalism. Institutions are central forces in the development and mobilization of identities in at least two ways. First, their weight is felt on political self-identification in a way that is quite independent of agency. Second, they shape agency, particularly elite struggles, behaviour, and their relationships with the masses. Nationalism involves group differentiation, that is, mechanisms of inclusion and exclusion. The delimitation of group identities, while representing an outcome that is psychological in nature, has its roots in politics and, to a great degree, in its material institutions. Indeed, political institutions contribute, independently of agency, in the creation, crystallization, and politicization of territorial identities through the boundaries they set in the subjective and political universe of citizens. For example, arrangements of territorial divisions of power, either in the form of federations or systems of autonomy, have inherent identity-generating potential. The very action of creating a 'region' with an autonomous legislature and executive, and a distinct political class, changes the dynamics of politics by creating or emphasizing a territorial dimension. In this context, the development of an identity may soon follow, even if regional politicians do not actively promote one, as the mechanisms of democratic and representative government lay the foundations for the construction of a political community. In Spain, for example, 'autonomous communities' were created after the death of Franco, partly to accommodate Basque and Catalan nationalism, and partly to act as a safeguard against authoritarianism. An unintended consequence of this regionalization was the emergence or strengthening of nationalist movements in other areas (for example, the Canary Islands, Valencia, and Galicia) and the creation of territorial identities in regions such as Madrid and Cantabria that were complete inventions.[28] Even in France, unitary state par excellence, the creation of regional governments in 1982 has generated political identification, albeit modest, with the regional political system.

Party systems also project a political context that shapes identity landscapes. For example, party systems dominated by nationalist parties generate a political discourse that favours the development of distinct territorial identities and the transformation of politics into nationalist politics. Of course, parties are representative of society, but never perfectly. Citizens may vote for a particular party for many different reasons, but they cannot control what specific part of the party's political program or agenda will be stressed following the election. Also, electoral systems rarely translate voters' preferences accurately, with majoritarian systems being the worst offenders. Even assuming that parties reflect societal tendencies fairly well, a regional political system with substantial autonomy where the executive is strong and the legislature is weak allows the party (or parties) in power to dictate the political agenda and discourse. If nationalist parties are in such a position, it is very likely that identity will permeate politics and will serve as the basis for political mobilization. Quebec offers a very strong case of party systems shaping and mobilizing identities in this manner. It has a rigid two-party system, itself the product of an institution, the electoral system, which comprises two nationalist parties, albeit with different agendas.[29] The party in power benefits from a strong executive and considerable regional powers; it therefore has all the tools to shape politics the way it wants to. As a result, politics in Quebec is, naturally, nationalist politics.

Political institutions also weigh on nationalism because they shape agency. At the centre of this relationship is power, a focal point of historical institutionalism.[30] Agency does not occur in an institutional vacuum. Who has power, and how much power one has, is greatly conditioned by the institutional context. In other words, institutions shape the patterns of the relationships political elites have among themselves and with the masses. They favour some actors at the expense of others. Some institutional situations are more conducive to conflict, and others to cooperation. Since nationalism is a form of politics, and therefore develops in the context of competition and power struggles, it is bound to be affected by the institutional environment. The Quebec case is, here again, instructive as several institutional features of Canadian and Quebec politics have shaped agency in a way that favours nationalist mobilization. The two-party system triggers nationalist outbidding, as the Quebec Liberal Party (PLQ) attempts to 'keep up' with the Parti Québécois (PQ) as a defender of Quebec's interests. Mega-constitutional politics, whose failures have been instrumental in spurring Quebec nationalism, is the product of the constitutional change of 1982 and has been made a perilous adventure by an amending formula requiring unanimity and the practice of executive federalism. Indeed, because of these institutional realities, constitutional change in Canada is an elite zero-sum game; it puts provincial leaders on the spot as they have to be seen as fighting for their province and emerging as victors, not losers, of the negotiations.

From this angle, institutions weigh on nationalism by structuring patterns of relationships between political actors in a way that makes them more or less conducive to nationalism. From a more voluntarist perspective, institutions are also important because they may offer specific opportunities to achieve certain strategic objectives. As it pertains to nationalism, the institutional context may provide nationalist leaders, or political parties, with a chance to stimulate mobilization, bolster identity, or achieve more concrete goals such as increased autonomy. In Spain, for example, the structure of the national party system is such that Basque and Catalan nationalist parties are sometimes sought to offer parliamentary support to the government. This represents an opportunity for them to obtain something in exchange, a situation they are quick to recognize and exploit as they negotiate more powers for their autonomous community.

The historical institutionalist focus on institutions does not mean that using it as an approach to nationalism would require discounting culture and socioeconomic conditions. Indeed, historical institutionalists recognize that institutions are only one ontological feature of politics; they simply suggest that great leverage can be gained from using institutions as an analytical starting point. Culture and socioeconomic conditions can be integrated to a historical institutionalist approach to nationalism in three ways. At the most general level, there is nothing in the theoretical foundations of historical institutionalism that denies the existence of cultural and socioeconomic processes which cannot be reduced to, although they are influenced by, institutions. Therefore, the linguistic make-up of a society or patterns of economic development can be factored into an explanation for nationalism, not only insofar as they are shaped by institutions, but as important contextual conditions in their own right. Second, cultural and socioeconomic situations are taken into consideration for how they are structured by institutions, thereby altering the larger context of nationalism. Finally, historical institutionalism accepts the possibility that these types of societal processes can shape institutional configurations. Indeed, this approach suggests that institutional adjustments occur when the institutional landscape becomes too severely disconnected from society, or when there are important tensions between institutions resulting from the fact that they were created at different historical periods and therefore embody incompatible social, political, cultural, economic, and ideological situations. From this perspective, the institutional context for nationalism can change if, for example, the demographic weight or relative levels of development of linguistic groups changes.

Historical institutionalism also offers a genuine historical perspective[31] that is crucial to any investigation of nationalism. Indeed, even if one accepts that the social, political, and institutional dynamic behind some contemporary nationalist movements may be very old, this does not mean that it cannot be explained and that theorists have to resort to stressing the persistence and power of culture. The historical institutionalist emphasis on exploring the process of institutional development, and its impact on agency, through time favours explanations that establish mechanisms of causality rather than ones that rely on the inherent power of given factors. Historical institutionalism is also historical in the sense that it takes sociopolitical outcomes to be contingent rather than 'givens'; indeed, as an approach, it is on the low end of the 'determinism' scale and allows the analyst to avoid cultural, economic, or other reductionisms. This is particularly important for the study of nationalism so as to avoid reifying culture or levels of economic development.

At a more specific level, a historical institutionalist approach to nationalism could be guided by the concepts of critical junctures and developmental pathways.[32] Critical junctures are used by historical institutionalists to theorize institutional construction and change. Typically, the argument is that patterns of institutional development may be diverted by an extraneous shock or as a result of inherent tensions within the institutional landscape.[33] In the latter case, it is suggested that sociopolitical processes corresponding to different institutions tend to have different historical underpinnings which lead to incongruities in the overall institutional order and create potential for change. The idea of emphasizing the incoherence between sociopolitical processes and within institutional order is the first step towards being able to conceptualize change, both institutional and sociopolitical, from a historical institutionalist perspective. However, such a conceptualization could be improved by focusing more squarely on the relationship between power relationships and/or struggles and institutions. After all, the birth of institutions has its roots, not only in certain social, political, economic, or ideological scenarios, but also, and more importantly, in specific power relationships. From this perspective, there can be two sources of change, institutional and otherwise. The first is the tensions generated by the different power logics of institutions. The second is the discrepancies that necessarily appear between institutions and society when the nature of power relationships evolves.

This perspective on critical junctures suggests that nationalism can emerge as a means of adjusting institutions to new power relationships. Political actors take aim at institutions as a target for change if they were born of, and project, a power relationship that does not favour them. If this relationship is somehow modified, these actors can apply enough pressure to trigger institutional change. For example, a national government and legislature dominated by members of a particular ethnic or linguistic group are likely to become (for the other groups) a focus of political activism. If the power relationship is altered in favour of previously disadvantaged group(s), through changes in demography, economic development or other institutions, opportunities open up to reshape these central institutions. Similarly, constitutions and federal-autonomy arrangements reflecting a specific power relationship can trigger political mobilization in the form of nationalism and go through change if the historically weaker group has been sufficiently empowered.

The notion of developmental pathways, or path dependency, is used by historical institutionalists to account for continuity through time.[34] At the broadest level, it suggests that an institutional landscape sets the parameters for agency, thereby generating patterns of action different from those occurring under other institutional conditions. In turn, these patterns of action contribute to the reproduction of existing institutions along two lines. First, actors adjust their behaviour to the institutional context. Second, they see this context shape political agendas, preferences, identities, and strategies. This last mechanism, which is less voluntaristic than the first, is central to historical institutionalism which stresses the unintended consequences of institutions. Therefore, the developmental pathways of historical institutionalists involve a linkage between agent and institutions characterized heavily by positive reinforcing feedback. Developmental pathways and critical junctures are concepts that together can be used to highlight both change and continuity. The perspective that emerges features critical junctures that trigger the creation of an institution and modify patterns of agency, that is, launching a developmental pathway, in a way that strengthens the new institutions.

Developmental pathways highlight perhaps first and foremost the impact of federal and autonomy arrangements on the processes of identity construction and nationalist mobilization. As mentioned earlier, the existence of autonomous regional institutions necessarily leads to regional politics, that is, it creates, sustains, and encourages patterns of political agency that find their logic in the regional political community. In turn, these patterns then legitimize and empower the regional institutions. This reinforcing mechanism presents great potential for the construction, strengthening, and politicization of territorial identities especially, albeit not exclusively, in the context of a distinct culture. In Spain the autonomous community of Galicia, for example, was recognized as one of three historical nationalities along with Catalonia and the Basque Country despite weak claims for such a status at the time of democratization. Galicia now boasts a more vigorous nationalist movement than other culturally distinct regions which do not enjoy such a recognition. Party systems that are fragmented along language and/or cultural lines represent another instance of an institutional structure that generates developmental pathways and affects nationalism. Nationalist parties are instrumental in nationalizing politics, an outcome which then strengthens their position.

This section attempted to discuss historical institutionalism in light of its potential to shed light on nationalism. The following section will offer a more concrete idea of a historical institutionalist approach to nationalism by developing the case of Belgium.

Nationalism in Belgium

Nationalism is a central feature of contemporary Belgian politics. Not only has the *problème communautaire* been at the centre of the country's political agenda for most of the past thirty years, but this period has seen numerous institutional reforms being implemented in the hope of accommodating Flemish nationalism and of addressing the claims of Walloons and of Brussels' French-speakers. How many nationalist movements are there in Belgium? This question is not as straightforward as it seems because of the nature of the Walloon Movement. Indeed, while the existence of a Flemish nation is widely proclaimed by Flemish political elites and resonates among Dutch-speakers in the Flemish Community and the Brussels Region, Walloon leaders speak primarily of a 'Walloon region' as opposed to a Walloon nation.[35] They do, however, speak of a Walloon culture, identity, history, society, and political community, and engage in identity construction and territorial mobilization. In this context, the Walloon Movement shares much of the same characteristics as a nationalist movement. There are also in Belgium two other instances of territorial politics, in Brussels and the German-speaking area, which are clearly not nationalist movements but do exhibit, although in embryonic form, emerging identities and patterns of territorial mobilization.[36]

Nationalism in Belgium cannot be understood independently of the structures of the early Belgian state. Indeed, the Belgian revolution of 1830 which led to the creation of that state represents the first critical juncture for the processes of identity construction and nationalist mobilization in this country. The revolution was a product of an institutional change in the Seventeen Provinces, a political entity composed of the territories of present-day Netherlands and Belgium: the adoption by William I of Orange of a new linguistic regime making Dutch the sole official language of the Kingdom. In the territories of present-day Belgium, this change threatened to marginalize a French-speaking bourgeoisie of public officials, teachers, and lawyers whose power derived greatly from a context where French was the dominant language of public life. It also angered clerics and religious conservatives, most powerful in the territories of present-day Flanders, who saw Dutch as a vehicle of Calvinism. The change of linguistic regime in the Seventeen Provinces gave new direction to politics: it spurred agency on the part of certain elites and strongly conditioned their objectives. More specifically, it created an unlikely alliance of French-speaking liberals and primarily Dutch-speaking religious conservatives whose goal was to leave the unfriendly context of the Seventeen Provinces.

The Belgian state was first and foremost the creation of the French-speaking bourgeoisie and, consequently, functioned early on almost completely in French.[37] The French language was used exclusively in parliament, the higher courts, the central administration, and the army. In Flanders, it was also dominant in courts, provincial governments, and many municipal councils. These institutions reflected their creators and were meant to anchor their power. In fact, they were intended to assimilate Dutch-speakers. The linguistic regime of the early Belgian state, as formally specified in the constitution, was one of laissez-faire, but in a society where French was associated with progress and modernity and the language of political and social elites, the relative power of the linguistic groups definitely favoured French-speakers.

The creation of the Belgian state presented the potential of leading Belgium down the path of 'political integration,' that is, the eradication of cultural differences and the construction of a strong, undifferentiated national identity. That is not to say that these things did not happen at all. Many Dutch-speakers chose to adopt French which they saw not only as the language of Belgium but also as the tongue of the future.[38] A strong Belgian identity also emerged, even among Dutch-speakers, although many of them conceptualized it in terms of bilingualism and biculturalism. Indeed, the Flemish Movement operated, until the 1870s, largely within a Belgian rather than a purely Flemish perspective.

There are two main reasons why 'political integration' did not materialize in Belgium. The first is that the Flemish Movement developed close ties with the Catholic political family, as its leaders tended to be religious conservatives. In this context, the Movement, and eventually Flemish nationalism, became a player in the struggle against secular liberals and socialists. The connection with the Catholic family gave greater political force to the Flemish Movement. The second is an institutional transformation, manhood suffrage, first plural (1893) and then single (1919). The suffrage, which was introduced in a liberal, democratic, and progressive perspective, had the unintended consequence of strengthening Flemish nationalism since it allowed Dutch-speakers to translate their demographic superiority into political power.

Suffrage and the connection of the Flemish Movement with the Catholic family altered the power relationship between language groups, making assimilation impossible. The Belgian central institutions and linguistic regime became targets of the empowered Flemish Movement, and in this context, launched Belgium into nationalist politics. As the Flemish Movement's claims for a bilingual regime for the whole of Belgium met with staunch opposition on the part of French-speaking leaders, it started to focus on the predominantly Dutch-speaking territories of the north, thereby developing the idea of a Flemish identity and nation distinct from Belgium. It also started engaging in mass mobilization to make more room for Dutch and Dutch-speakers in key societal centres such as the University of Ghent.

The rising power of the Flemish Movement led to the creation in the late nineteenth century of the Walloon Movement, whose initial objective was to oppose Flemish claims and advocate the return to a French-dominated state and society. When this objective no longer appeared attainable, in the early twentieth century, Walloon Movement leaders suggested, although with much ambiguity and hesitation, making the predominantly French-speaking region of the south the reference for political activity. This change of perspective would allow them to re-anchor their power, albeit diminished, and block off the Flemish Movement's claims for making Wallonia bilingual. It is in this context that they began looking for a distinctive Walloon culture and history, and articulating a Walloon identity.[39]

A last consequence of this sequence of events triggered by the Flemish resistance to Belgian institutions was the dissociation of Brussels from Wallonia.[40] At the very beginning of the Walloon Movement, the notion of 'Walloon' did not really have a territorial basis; it meant French-speakers, either in present-day Wallonia, Brussels, or even Flanders. When the Walloon Movement began articulating a territorially based Walloon identity defined in opposition to the Flemish one, and therefore featuring language prominently, Brussels became problematic because of its location in historically Dutch-speaking territories and its mixed sociolinguistic make-up. This 'dumping' of Brussels by the Walloon Movement planted the seed for the emergence of a distinct Brussels identity.

The structures of the early Belgian state, especially its central institutions and linguistic regime, failed to accomplish what they were designed to do, that is, create a coherent and indivisible francophone nation. In fact, Belgian political institutions had as an unintended consequence the creation of the Flemish Movement and the emergence of Flemish nationalism. These institutions gave political importance to linguistic cleavages. They became the focal point of the Flemish Movement, both in practice and symbolically, especially as it was empowered by its alliance with Catholics and manhood suffrage. As a result of these changes, the influence of the Flemish Movement on Belgian politics gradually increased after 1918, although not evenly. The collaboration of some Movement members with Germany during both world wars temporarily halted this process, as francophone elites saw in the episodes opportunities to preserve their power in Belgian politics. However, in the 1960s and 1970s, the pressure exerted by Flemish nationalism on the Belgian state became overwhelming. The Flemish Movement was now able to effectively translate the numerical superiority of Dutch-speakers into political power. In this context, Belgian political institutions, long-time targets of the Flemish Movement, were fundamentally transformed. These changes represent critical junctures for nationalism in Belgium. They did not redirect the flow that politics had taken since the late nineteenth century but rather accelerated its drive towards nationalism and other forms of territorial and identity politics.

The first of these contemporary critical junctures were the linguistic laws of 1962–1963. Belgium's initial linguistic regime had been modified twice before: in 1898 to make Dutch an official language and in the 1930s to implement territorial monolingualism. These changes were the result of Flemish nationalism, but they were accepted by francophone elites who still held political power. The formal-legal equality of languages was viewed as a provision which could defuse Flemish nationalism, although the Walloon Movement saw it as yet another sign that Flemings were robbing francophones of 'their Belgium.'[41] Territorial monolingualism satisfied the Walloon Movement which, by the 1930s, feared potential Dutch inroads into Wallonia. The linguistic legislation of the 1960s, which strengthened the monolingual status of Flanders and Wallonia[42] by freezing the linguistic border, reflected the diminishing power of French-speaking elites rather than their willingness to make strategic concessions. It favoured nationalist politics in two ways. First, it laid solid and durable foundations for the growth of Flemish and Walloon identities by strengthening and accelerating processes of linguistic homogenization which would then underpin a dichotomization of politics. This was particularly significant on the Walloon side because the Walloon identity had been only recently invented, and it lacked a historical territorial anchoring. Second, the component of these laws which specified that communes should be transferred to the 'proper' linguistic area proved to be the source of great nationalist tension. Indeed, the move of the small district of *Voeren* (*Fourons* in French) from Liège (Wallonia) to Limburg (Flanders) was decried by many Walloon activists, most importantly José Happart who became mayor of the small municipality in 1983 and then proceeded to refuse using Dutch in official proceedings, as the law prescribed. Throughout the 1970s, the Voeren issue was at the centre of violent confrontations between Flemish and Walloon activists.[43] In the 1980s, with Happart denounced as a terrorist by Flemings and seen as a hero by Walloons, nationalist conflict became so intense that it led to the downfall of a government (in 1987) and precipitated institutional reforms. Voeren was a problem created by the adjustment of the linguistic frontier which was supposed, through linguistic homogenization, to settle the *problème communautaire* for 'a generation.'

The second critical juncture was the split of political parties following linguistic lines. The immediate trigger for this change was the emergence of nationalist and regionally based parties in Flanders (*Volksunie*), Wallonia (*Rassemblement Wallon*), and Brussels (*Front Démocratique des Francophones*). This development was itself the product of heightened tensions between language groups, as demonstrated by several postwar community crises ranging from the fate of King Leopold III, who had chosen to remain in Belgium during the Second World War, to the linguistic status of the University of Leuven (*Louvain*). The new parties quickly became electoral threats to the traditional parties which were forced to take position, and become more militant, on community issues. As a result, severe tensions appeared within the Christian Democratic, Socialist, and Liberal parties which developed linguistic wings, and then split into distinct organizations. This institutional change further transformed Belgian politics into nationalist politics in two ways. First, it shrunk the political universe of Belgians to the level of linguistic communities, thereby developing the notions of distinct political communities within Belgium. This effect was reinforced and extended to the larger social arena by the fact that, as a result of the country's consociational structures, many 'civil-society' organizations also split along linguistic lines. Second, the split of the traditional parties made nationalist mobilization an attractive political and electoral strategy or, at the very least, removed incentives to behave moderately. Indeed, since francophone parties no longer had to please Dutch-speaking voters and vice versa, they could present a dichotomized view of politics and turn community issues into political-electoral assets. This outcome was clearly observable in the politics of the *Parti socialiste* (PS) which, in the early 1980s made a conscious decision to turn towards nationalist politics.[44] The peculiarity of the PS's political position in relation to the other francophone parties was that its stronghold was Wallonia, whereas the *Parti social chrétien* (PSC) and the *parti réformateur libéral* (PRL) had substantial support in Brussels, especially the PRL did. As a consequence, the PS had incentives to play 'the Walloon card,' which it did by becoming a strong supporter of federalism and of Voeren mayor José Happart whom it presented as a hero resisting Flemish power plays.

The last contemporary critical juncture which has been instrumental in accelerating nationalist politics in Belgium is the federalization process. The creation of regions (Flanders, Wallonia, Brussels) and communities (Flemish, French, German-speaking) was a response to the community tensions that the laws of 1962–1963 had failed to alleviate. In fact, transformations in the territorial division of power, implemented gradually through the reforms of 1970, 1980, 1988, 1993, and 2001, were partly the product of the potential for nationalist conflict left by these laws, as well as the consequence of the political dynamic generated by the bipolar party system. The federalization of Belgium stimulated rather than calmed nationalist politics. Similarly to the laws of 1962–1963 and the split of the traditional parties, it did so by affecting both identities and mobilization. The creation of the new institutions has given a substantial boost to the Flemish and Walloon identities. In the case of the former, the institutional change meant that the Flemish government and parliament, rather than the more amorphous Flemish Movement, would serve as the focal point of this identity. Furthermore, to eliminate any ambiguity about the legitimate representative and protector of this identity, the Flemish Region and Community have merged, and all of Flanders' resources are concentrated in a single set of institutions. In the case of Wallonia, the creation of a region has jump-started a process of identity construction, featuring the 'rediscovery' of distinctive cultural and historical elements, which had only tentatively begun under the Walloon Movement. These efforts are somewhat hampered by an institutional design featuring a French Community, distinct from Wallonia, which also commands loyalty. The federalization of Belgium also involved the creation of a Brussels Region and a German-speaking Community, both of which were set up almost by default. These entities have generated brand new, albeit it still weakly articulated, identities. In the case of Brussels, where distinctive symbols and holidays have been created, the process of identity construction really stems from institutional subtraction (French-Community minus Wallonia).[45] In the German-speaking Community, the domino effect of institutional creation and identity construction largely explains why feelings of Germanness have been considerably upgraded.[46]

The federalization of the Belgian state has also yielded situations conducive to nationalist mobilization. At the broadest level, the process of institutional change is in itself conflictual because it is viewed differently by the leaders of the two linguistic communities. On the Flemish side, federalization and decentralization are conceptualized essentially as unfinished processes. In practical terms, this means that the ultimate objective is to leave the Belgian state with not much more than power over defence. For francophone parties, the objective is to arrive at a stable point, a permanent solution, without completely stripping the central state of its powers. In this context, the very idea of further institutional reform, let alone its potential content, is acrimonious. A more specific source of nationalist tension stemming from the federalization process is the linguistic minorities. Creating sub-national entities usually involves the creation of minority language groups. That was the case in Belgium despite considerable efforts at homogenization through linguistic legislation. The issue of linguistic minorities, as Voeren demonstrated, can be particularly explosive in Belgium. It is therefore not surprising that the more than 100,000 French-speakers living just outside the Brussels Region, in Flemish territory, is an issue which has already caused friction between the two linguistic communities and carries potential for further conflict. At the heart of this problem is a difference of views concerning the nature of the bilingual facilities offered to this population and, indeed, its very future. For Flemish leaders, any arrangement is temporary and these French-speakers will eventually have to become Flemish, while for francophones, protecting these minorities is of the utmost importance.

Belgium has been on an accelerated pathway of nationalist politics since the 1960s. Language legislation, the party system, and federalization have all favoured the crystallization, if not construction of identities, and patterns of mobilization along linguistic lines. In turn, these outcomes sustain and strengthen the linguistic regime, the dichotomization of the party system, and the drive towards decentralization, following a process of re-enforcing feedback.[47] The three contemporary critical junctures and institutional transformations took place because the linguistic group with political power was also the one that sought change and, since this context still exists, it is unlikely that the nature of politics will soon change in Belgium. The country's developmental pathway seems to point to a break-up, but this scenario is unlikely considering the position of Brussels as both the capital of Europe and a primarily French-speaking city in historically Dutch-speaking territory. A more likely outcome, still coherent with Belgium's contemporary pathway, is that nationalist politics will result in the decentralization process grinding to a halt with the Belgian state being left as an empty shell.

Conclusion

Nationalism as a field of study is permeated by a few enduring research themes: the modern or ancient origins of nations; the civic or ethnic character of nationalism; the consequences of nationalist movements, primarily self-determination, secession, and violence; management strategies such as federalism, autonomy, and consociationalism.

In the context of these research avenues, the question of structure and agency is rarely raised. When scholars ask theoretical questions about the forces shaping nationalism, debates tend to revolve around the relative importance of culture, macro-economic conditions, and elite behaviour. Here, structure and agency are considered but when the former is given significant theoretical importance, it tends to take the form of economic forces. Political institutions are rarely viewed as significant structuring elements.

It is this appraisal of existing theories of nationalism that has led to the central arguments of this chapter: the necessity of structuring nationalism using political institutions and the potential presented by historical institutionalism in fulfilling this task. Historical institutionalism suggests that nationalism is deeply contingent upon institutional forms and their evolution and that institutional configurations are central in determining whether politics becomes nationalist politics. The Belgian case highlights this relationship. More specifically, it has suggested a two-step process as a possible scenario for the emergence and development of nationalism. Initially, identity construction and nationalist mobilization are launched as the power relationship between linguistic groups evolves in a way that makes it no longer congruent with the institutional context. Then, institutional changes that were made to adjust the situation, or simply occurred as a result of nationalist tensions, sustained, reproduced, and stimulated nationalism. This last outcome suggests a caveat to decision-makers looking to manage nationalist movements: institutional 'solutions' to nationalism may very well lead to unforeseen, unintended consequences that will aggravate rather than lessen tensions and conflict.

Notes

1 Kenneth Shepsle and Barry Weingast, *Positive Theories of Congressional Institutions* (Ann Arbor: University of Michigan Press, 1995); Michael Laver and Kenneth Shepsle, 'Coalitions and Cabinet Government,' *American Political Science Review*, 84 (1990), 843–90; Arash Abizadeh, 'Informational Constraints and Focal Point Convergence: Theoretical Implications of Plurality-Rule Elections for the New Institutionalism,' *Rationality and Society*, 13 (2000), 99–136; James Lindsay, 'Congress, Foreign Policy, and the New Institutionalists,' *International Studies Quarterly*, 38 (1994), 281–304.
2 Stephen Krasner, 'Sovereignty: An Institutional Perspective,' *Comparative Political Studies*, 21 (1988), 66–94.

3 Paul Pierson, 'The Path to European Integration: A Historical Institutional-ist Approach,' *Comparative Political Studies*, 29 (1996), 123–63; Joseph Jupille and James A. Caporaso, 'Institutionalism and the European Union: Beyond International Relations and Comparative Politics,' *Annual Review of Political Science*, 2 (1999), 429–44.

4 Marco Giugni, 'Ancien et nouvel institutionnalisme dans l'étude de la poli-tique contestataire,'*Politique et sociétés*, 21 (2002), 69–90; Eric Montpetit, 'Pour en finir avec le lobbying: Comment les institutions canadiennes défi-nissent l'action des groupes d'intérêt,' *Politique et sociétés*, 21 (2002), 91–112.

5 Einar Braathen, 'New Institutionalism in Development Studies: Weberian Contributions,' *Forum for Development Studies*, (1996), 215–41.

6 Voir Mamoudou Gazibo, 'Néo-institutionalisme et démocratisations com-parées,' *Politique et sociétés*, 21 (2002), 139–60. See also, Emis Cavaduas, 'El nuevo institucionalismo en América Latina,' *Ciencas de Gobierno*, 5 (2001), 11–25.

7 Scholars such as Clifford Geertz, Harold Isaacs, and Pierre van den Berghe, who made rigid connections between nationalism and cultural and/or bio-logical markers, were labelled primordialists in the 1970s and 1980s. Oth-ers, such as Anthony D. Smith, who also oppose the notion of the modernity or novelty of nations and who give central importance to culture in their explanations for nationalism but reject, in principle, determinism, have opted for the term 'perennialist' or 'ethno-symbolist.'

8 In a recent book commissioned by the Association for the Study of Ethnic-ity and Nationalism 'to provide cutting-edge discussions of the major issues in important sub-fields of nationalism' (p. 1), several contributions deal in one way or another with the question of the modernity of nations and nationalism. Montserrat Guibernau and John Hutchinson (eds.), *Understanding Nationalism* (Cambridge: Polity Press, 2001). See the chapters by Anthony Smith, 'Nations and History,' 9–31; John Breuilly, 'The State and Nationalism,' 32–52; and John Hutchinson, 'Nations and Culture,' 74–96.

9 Hans Kohn, *The Idea of Nationalism: A Study in Its Origins and Background* (New York: Macmillan, 1944); Raymond Breton, 'From Ethnic to Civic Nationalism: English Canada and Quebec,' *Ethnic and Racial Studies*, 11 (1998), 85–102.

10 David Brown, 'Are There Good and Bad Nationalisms?' *Nations and Nation-alism*, (5) 1999, 281–303.

11 Arendt Lijphart, *Democracy in Plural Societies* (New Haven: Yale University Press, 1977); Alain-G. Gagnon and James Tully (eds.), *Multinational Democ-racies* (Cambridge: Cambridge University Press, 2001).

12 For example, the work of Michael Keating and Donald Horowitz. See respectively, *State and Regional Nationalism: Terrritorial Politics and the European State* (London: Harvester Wheatsheaf, 1988) and *Ethnic Groups in Conflict* (Berkeley: University of California Press, 1985).

13 Sven Steinmo et al., *Structuring Politics: Historical Institutionalism in Comparative Perspective* (Cambridge: Cambridge University Press, 1992).

14 To my knowledge, one of the only pieces on nationalism that explicitly seeks to bring insight from new institutionalism is Siobhan Harty, 'The Institutional Foundations of Sub-State National Movements,' *Comparative Politics*, 33 (2001), 191–210.

15 Edward Shils, 'Primordial, Personal, Sacred and Civil Ties,' *British Journal of Sociology*, 8 (1957), 130–45; Clifford Geertz (ed.), *Old Societies, New States: The Quest for Modernity in Asia and Africa* (London: Free Press, 1963); Harold Isaacs, *Idols of the Tribe: Group Identity and Political Change* (Cambridge, Mass.: Harvard University Press, 1975).

16 Jack Eller and Reed Coughlan, 'The Poverty of Primordialism: The Demystification of Ethnic Attachments,' *Ethnic and Racial Studies*, 16 (1993), 183–202.

17 Anthony D. Smith, *The Ethnic Origins of Nations* (New York: Blackwell, 1986); Walker Connor, *Ethnonationalism: The Quest for Understanding* (Princeton: Princeton University Press, 1994).

18 Will Kymlicka, *Multicultural Citizenship: A Liberal Theory of Minority Rights* (Oxford: Oxford University Press, 1995); Charles Taylor, *Rapprocher les solitudes: Écrits sur le fédéralisme et le nationalisme au Canada* (Ste-Foy: Les Presses de l'Université Laval).

19 Arendt Lijphart, *Power-Sharing in South Africa* (Berkeley: University of California, 1985).

20 An exception is Juan Díez Medrano, *Divided Nations: Class, Politics and Nationalism in the Basque Country and Catalonia* (Ithaca: Cornell University Press, 1995).

21 See Joseph R. Rudolph Jr and Robert J. Thompson, 'The Ebb and Flow of Ethnoterritorial Politics in the Western World,' in *Ethnoterritorial Politics, Policy and the Western World* (Boulder: Lynne Rienner, 1989), 4–5.

22 Michael Hechter, *Internal Colonialism: The Celtic Fringe in British National Development, 1536–1966* (Berkeley: University of California Press, 1975).

23 See the discussion in Montserrat Guibernau, 'Globalization and the Nation-State,' in Guibernau and Hutchinson, *Understanding Nationalism*, 242–68.

24 Paul Brass, *Ethnicity and Nationalism. Theory and Comparison* (London: Sage, 1991).

25 Joseph Rothschild, *Ethnopolitics: A Conceptual Framework* (New York: Columbia University Press, 1981).

26 Brass, *Ethnicity and Nationalism*.
27 Ernest Gellner, *Nations and Nationalism* (London: Blackwell, 1983); John Breuilly, *Nationalism and the State* (New York: St Martin's Press, 1982).
28 Luis Moreno, *La federalización de España. Poder político y teritorio* (Madrid: Siglo Veintiuno de España, 1997), 123–40.
29 This party system also features a smaller third party, the Action démocratique du Québec (ADQ).
30 Ellen M. Immergut, 'The Theoretical Core of the New Institutionalism,' *Politics and Society*, 26, (1998), 16.
31 Ibid., 20.
32 For a good discussion of these two concepts, see Kathleen Thelen, 'Historical Institutionalism in Comparative Politics,' *Annual Review of Political Science*, 1999, 369–404.
33 Or, as suggested by Lieberman, between institutional and ideational realms. See Robert C. Lieberman, 'Ideas, Institutions, and Political Order: Explaining Political Change,' *American Political Science Review*, 96 (2002), 697–712.
34 Pierson, Paul, 'Increasing Returns, Path Dependence and the Study of Politics,'*American Political Science Review*, 94 (2000), 251–68.
35 See Philippe Destatte, 'Present-day Wallonia: The Search for an Identity without Nationalist Mania,' in Kaz Deprez and Louis Vos (eds.), *Nationalism in Belgium: Shifting Identities, 1780–1995* (New York: St Martin's Press, 1998), 219–28.
36 Serge Govaert, 'A Brussels Identity? A Speculative Interpretation,' and Hubert Jenniges, 'Germans, German Belgians, German-Speaking Belgians,' in *Nationalism in Belgium*, 229–39 and 240–8.
37 Louis Vos, 'The Flemish National Question,' in *Nationalism in Belgium*, 83–4.
38 Jan Moruanx, *Lettres sur le mouvement flamand: Adressées aux populations wallonnes en vue de prévenir la division ethnique de notre nationalité* (Bruxelles: J. Lebègue, 1894), 18.
39 Chantal Kesteloot, *Mouvement wallon et identité nationale* (Brussels: Courrier hebdomadaire du CRISP, no. 1392, 1992).
40 Vincent Vagman, *Le mouvement wallon et la question bruxelloise* (Brussels: Courrier hebdomadaire du CRISP, no. 1,434–5, 1994).
41 Jules Destrée, 'Open Letter to the King, Concerning the Separation of Flanders and Wallonia (1912),' in Theo Hermans, Louis Vos, and Lode Wils (eds.), *The Flemish Movement. A Documentary History, 1780–1990* (London: Athlone Press, 1992), 206–15. Translated by Lesley Gilbert.
42 Brussels kept its status as a bilingual area.

43 Kenneth D. McRae, *Conflict and Compromise in Multilingual Societies: Belgium* (Waterloo: Wilfrid Laurier University Press, 1986), 290.

44 Liesbet Hooghe, *A Leap in the Dark: Nationalist Conflict and Federal Reform in Belgium* (Ithaca: Cornell University Press, 1991).

45 Govaert, 'A Brussels Identity?' 231.

46 Jenniges, 'Germans, German Belgians, German-Speaking Belgians,' 240–8.

47 Paul Pierson, 'When Effect Becomes Cause: Policy Feedback and Political Change,' *World Politics* 45 (1993), 595–628.

9

Institutional Change and Its Consequences: The Rational Foundations of Party System Change in India

CSABA NIKOLENYI

The general election of 1989 ushered in a new era in the history of India's national party system. The previous four decades, since the country gained its independence in 1947 and held its first competitive multiparty elections in 1952, had been characterized by a recurring pattern whereby national elections would result in single-party major-ity victories leading to the formation of single-party majority govern-ments. This pattern, however, came to a definite end with the 1989 election, which resulted in a sudden increase in the fragmentation of the party system. A central characteristic of the new era is the inability of any single political party to win a legislative majority in the Lok Sabha (the lower house of India's national parliament), which also pre-cludes the possibility of the formation of single-party majority govern-ments. Since 1989, government by coalition has become the norm in India.

This transformation of the party system has been one of the central concerns of scholars interested in Indian politics. However, until the recent publication of Pradeep Chhibber's work[1] on this subject, com-parative political scientists have by and large ignored this very impor-tant case. This is not a trivial shortcoming, for, as this chapter will argue, the Indian case provides a valuable lesson both for the broader comparative understanding of party system change and the apprecia-tion of the role that institutions play in the process.

The chapter will begin with an overview of the evolution of the national party system of independent India. It will show that the post-1989 fragmentation has been the result of a sudden decline in party aggregation, that is, the linkage of candidates and would-be legislators across electoral districts under a common party label. The next section will point out that existing explanations that stress the role of the executive selection process[2] or economic centralization[3] in providing incentives for aggregation cannot convincingly account for the Indian story. Therefore, an alternative theory is proposed that predicts party aggregation, specifically the willingness of would-be legislators to form a majority party, to be a function of the credibility of the majority party's commitment to adopting the ideal point of the median legislator, the optimal social choice, as government policy. The last section will show that in India it was the passage of a constitutional amendment in 1985, imposing a high penalty on party defectors, that generated this predicted effect. The new law strengthened the leadership of parliamentary parties, which rendered a commitment to the socially optimal equilibrium, the ideal point of the median legislator, by the majority party non-credible.

The Dependent Variable: Party System Change

The conventional wisdom in the Indologist literature has identified the following six stages in the evolution of the Indian party system: (1) The period from 1947 to 1967 was the era of one-party dominance by the Congress Party; it is also referred to as the Congress system. (2) The next four years comprised the first coalitional period. (3) From 1971 to 1977, for the second time, the Congress was dominant. (4) This was followed by the second coalitional period (1977–1980). (5) Throughout the 1980s the Congress party dominated again, for the third time. (6) From 1989 onwards it has been uninterrupted multipartism.[4]

The first period was characterized by the dominance of one party, the Indian National Congress Party, which won legislative majorities in both the national and subnational elections, as shown in Figure 9.1. The Congress never received a majority of India's popular vote. Nevertheless, it benefited from the seat bonus that India's single-member simple plurality electoral system conferred on it as a large political party with a solid nationwide following.[5]

The election of 1967 marked the beginning of the first coalition period. That year, the Congress not only failed to win majorities in a number of state elections, which were held concurrently with the national election, but it also managed to secure only a bare majority in the Lok Sabha (the lower house). Although the 1971 election brought

Figure 9.1. The Congress Party in the Indian party system, 1952–1996.

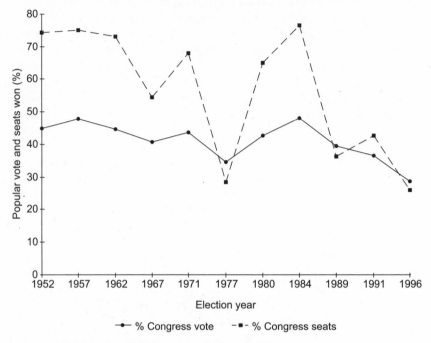

Source: David Butler, Ashok Lahiri, and Prannoy Roy, *India Decides: Elections 1952–1995* (New Delhi: Books and Things, 1995), 67

the Congress back to dominance, it gave way to a fragile and unstable two-party system. In 1977, the Janata Party formed an alternative non-Congress majority government for the first time since Independence at the national level. Once again, however, the Congress, this time named the Congress(I),[6] reasserted its dominance in the 1980 election. This third period of Congress dominance lasted until 1989. The general election of that year produced the first in the current series of hung parliaments. Thus, as of 1989 the Indian party system has been acknowledged to have moved to the stage of genuine multipartism.

This conventional periodization of the history of the Indian party system revolves around the fluctuating fortunes of the Congress Party, the historically dominant unit of the political system in India. As such, it offers more of a description of the history and the evolution of the competitive position of that party than a genuine tracking of changes

Figure 9.2. The percentage share of seats won by the largest party, 1952–1996.

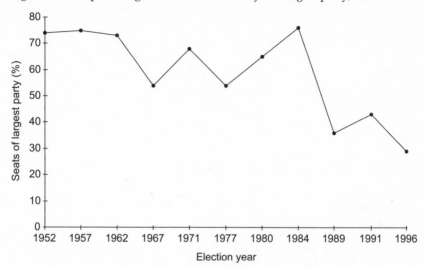

in the structural attributes of the party system itself. As a result, it has also exaggerated the number of genuinely critical changes that the party system went through. A good contrast to this conventional six-stage chronology is offered by Chhibber, who distinguishes two stages instead: First, the pre-1989 period characterized by the presence of *catch-all* parties, and second, the more recent post-1989 period marked by the rise of *cleavage-based* parties each representing a different social and political constituency.[7] This transition from a catch-all to a fragmented cleavage-based party system is indicated, among others, by the disappearance of majority parties (see Figure 9.2) and the overall increase in the number of viable parties in the system (see Figure 9.3). Both Figures 9.2 and 9.3 clearly show that the party system of India went through a genuine transformation only as of 1989 – but not earlier. Therefore, although the electoral fortunes of particular political parties, especially those of the Congress(I), may have fluctuated over time, these changes did not fundamentally alter the system before 1989.

Chhibber has further noted that the fragmentation of the Indian party system in the 1990s is the result of a decline in party aggregation across the electoral districts. At the same time, the format of party competition at the level of the electoral districts has remained noticeably

Figure 9.3. The fragmentation and the effective number of parties in the Indian party system, 1952–1996.

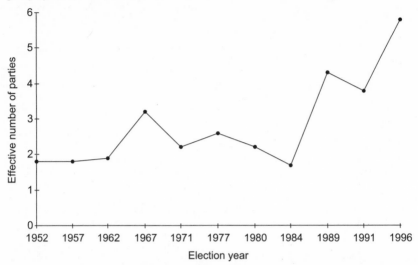

Note: For a definition of the effective number of parties, see the text. The values are based on parties' share of parliamentary seats. The scores are based on the author's calculations.

stable throughout the entire post-Independence period. Party aggregation refers to the extent to which political parties link across electoral districts to form larger entities. Suppose, for example, that there were D number of districts in a polity and that there were k parties, or candidates, competing against one another in each of these districts. If so, then it is theoretically possible that there will be a total of Dk parties in the system. Of course, this would be the case of extreme non-aggregation as there would be no two districts with the same two parties competing therein. At the other extreme of a hypothetical continuum of party aggregation, one may conceive of a system where the k parties are the same in every district.[8]

Operationally, the degree of party aggregation is calculated as the difference between the fragmentation of the party system at district level and the fragmentation of the party system at the national level. Party system fragmentation at either level is computed according to the Laakso-Taagepera index of the effective number of parties.[9] The effective number of parties at the district level D is defined as follows:

$$D = \Sigma \, (1/ \, \Sigma^{t=1} \, p_{n,d}{}^2) \, / \, d$$

where p represents the percentage of the vote polled by party n in district d in a given election, with $t = 1$. Thus, D gives the mean of the effective number of parties in all districts.[10] The effective number of parties at the national level N is computed as follows:

$$N = 1/ \, \Sigma^{t=1} \, P_n{}^2$$

where P is the percentage of the total national vote polled by party n in a given election, $t = 1$. Therefore, the degree of party aggregation, which is the absolute value of the difference between D and N is given by the following formula:

$$|D - N| = |[\Sigma \, (1/ \, \Sigma^{t=1} \, p_{n,d}{}^2) \, / \, d] - [1/ \, \Sigma^{t=1} \, P_n{}^2]|$$

Chhibber has shown that throughout the post-Independence period, D (the mean of the effective number of parties) has remained at or near 2, while N, (the effective number of parties at the national level, as shown in Figure 9.3) has increased considerably as of late. This finding is significant for two reasons. First, it demonstrates that Duverger's famous law on the impact of electoral rules on the number of viable parties works in India very well.[11] This law predicts that the single-member simple plurality (SMSP) electoral rule, which is what India has used consistently since 1962, will foster a two-candidate, or two-party, competition at the district level, just as Chhibber shows to be the case.[12] Second, the finding also suggests that the fragmentation of the system is not rooted in deep-seated electoral alignments among the *mass* electorate at the district level, because D has remained constant throughout the entire post-Independence period. Instead, the source of fragmentation of the party system must be located in variables that affect the calculation of party *elites*, the candidates and would-be legislators, to link across the district and aggregate their efforts under a common party label.

A Theory of Party Aggregation

Existing accounts of party aggregation emphasize the importance of political institutions. They assume that the prevailing rules of the political game create incentives according to which office-seeking political actors, candidates and would-be legislators, decide whether it is in their interest to link across electoral districts and aggregate into larger political parties. It is assumed that office-seeking candidates form linkages and establish large organizations if by so doing they can increase the probability of capturing the political office that they covet. In a presidential system, for example, the office of the institutionally strong chief executive, elected concurrently with the legislature under strong pluralitylike electoral rules, may be a strong motivating source of party aggregation because 'presidential ambition may ... lead to the organisation of legislators from each district into two nation-wide electoral alliances, or parties.'[13]

Because India is a Westminster-type parliamentary democracy, presidential ambition per se is an unlikely source of party aggregation.[14] However, as in presidential systems, the desire to capture and control the most important executive office, the premiership, may very well be such a source. Since legislative and executive elections are linked in parliamentary systems, the extent to which the pursuit of the premiership encourages party aggregation depends on the powers of the prime minister and the incentives of the electoral system through which control of the premiership is decided. Cox noted that, on both counts, parliamentary democracies of the Westminster type provide greater incentives for party aggregation than those that subscribe to the consensus model of democracy.[15] In the former, the prime minister is a very powerful head of government, whereas in the latter the prime minister is genuinely *primus inter pares* alongside ministerial colleagues in the cabinet. With regard to the electoral process, Westminster systems are characterized by plurality elections, while consensus systems employ proportional election rules. Nonetheless, this office-oriented explanation cannot alone account for the observed variation that has taken place in the degree of party aggregation in India since 1989. The institutions of the Westminster model that India adopted upon Independence have remained essentially the same ever since. Therefore, party aggregation should also have remained more or less at the same level since the office-seeking incentives provided by the Westminster-type of institutional arrangement have also remained unaltered.

In an attempt to account for party aggregation in India and the United States specifically, Chhibber and Kollmann have emphasized the central role of economic centralization, that is, the concentration of economic power in the hands of the central as opposed to local governments.[16] They claim that greater degrees of economic centralization in the hands of the national government increase the incentives for elites to concentrate their efforts on attaining power nationally. Conversely, economic decentralization should encourage elites to focus on winning office at the sub-national level, which will be reflected in a decline in party aggregation. While this explanation offers a robust account for inter-temporal change in party aggregation in both India and the United States for much of the time frame that they examined, Chhibber and Kollman also observed that the party aggregation scores for India in the late 1980s, precisely the period that this chapter is trying to explain, are anomalous. Acknowledging that some factors other than economic centralization may have been at work to produce the decline in party aggregation in the late 1980s, for example, the leadership technique used by the late Prime Minister Rajiv Gandhi, they offer no systematic effort to uncover what these factors may be.[17]

It appears that purely office-seeking perspectives cannot adequately account for the gradual disaggregation of the Indian party system. Therefore, it may be worthwhile to approach the problem with an explicitly policy-oriented view which assumes that political actors – candidates and would-be legislators – are also motivated by the pursuit of their ideal policies. This, of course, does not make the assumption of office-seeking behavioural motivation redundant. Quite the contrary, the two complement one another. On the one hand, office-seeking remains very important because only by being in office can political actors pursue their ideal policies. On the other hand, rational candidates cannot and will not pursue office in a policy-blind fashion. Instead, they will want to seek out and appeal to the ideal policy preferences of the core members of the electoral constituency that the candidate expects will bring him or her to victory and/or return to office.

In a significant way, such strategies are shaped by political institutions, specifically the electoral system. Downs's classic study has shown that in a two-candidate race under a single-member simple plurality electoral rule, the electorally rewarding strategy for both candidates is to appeal to the district's median voter.[18] This strategy, when employed by all actors, produces a centripetal (or centre-seeking) equilibrium that leads to ideologically moderate and consensual party politics in that district. As a consequence, the more such districts that there are across the entire system, the more moderate and consensual party politics will be in the overall polity. Different electoral rules, however, yield different results. In particular, proportional electoral rules tend to encourage candidates to disperse widely within the ideological space and develop their policy niche. The precise extent of this centrifugal (or centre-fleeing) equilibrium depends on important features of the electoral system, such as the size of the district, which directly constrains the number of viable contenders, the number of votes that each voter can cast, and the specific manner in which voters can cast their votes.[19] India has used the SMSP electoral rule for most of its post-Independence history, and therefore, the following paragraphs will specifically highlight the theoretical consequences that can be derived from this particular institutional variable.

As mentioned, the SMSP electoral rule compels viable candidates to campaign for the support of the median voter in each district. The winning candidate will thereby enter the legislature with the incentive to support adoption of policies that approximate the ideal position of the district's median voter as closely as possible. It is highly unlikely that the median voters of any two districts would have an identical ideological location. Therefore, it is safe to further assume that for each and every legislator there is a *unique* location – or ideal point – in the ideological space within the legislature. Let the ideal point of legislator i be represented by x_i, and note that x_i is defined by the ideal point of the median voter in the district that i represents. During the life cycle of the legislature, each legislator i will be interested in ensuring that the public policies adopted by legislative majority, and in consequence by the government, denoted x_g, will be the closest possible to x_i. The smaller the difference between the two, the greater the likelihood that legislator i will be re-elected, because the smallest difference most closely approximates the ideal position of the constituency's median voter.

A central finding of social choice theory is that under majority rule, which is the normal decision-making rule of parliamentary chambers, the ideal position of the median legislator of the chamber x_c will be adopted and maintained as the equilibrium policy.[20] Thus, the median legislator has a unique ideal position x_c, with exactly as many ideal points to the left as to the right. When the median legislator's policy is adopted, that is, when $x_g = x_c$, the value of $(x_g - x_i)$ summed for all i will be at its minimum. Therefore, policy-seeking legislators will be interested in ensuring that, under majority rule x_c, the social optimum, will always be adopted as x_g. The definition of the median legislator also implies that the majority party will always include the median legislator within its contingent. In turn, this should enable the majority party to produce the socially efficient policies at the median legislator's position, which will ensure the re-election of its legislators and maintain the dominant position of the party in the system.

The ability to determine the social optimum makes the median legislator a very powerful player not only in the chamber in general but also within the legislator's own majority party. Although the majority party can derive significant benefits from having the median legislator among its ranks, it could also suffer considerable intra-party tension as a result. This tension is the function of the ideological distance between two key players: the median legislator of the chamber and the median legislator of the majority party. In the same way as the median legislator's ideal point defines the socially efficient policy point for the entire chamber, the median legislator of the majority party itself x_m defines the ideal position of the majority or governing party. The latter (x_m) represents the ideological consensus within the party, whereas the former (x_c) determines the consensus within the entire legislature. The value of the difference between the two $(x_c - x_m)$ defines the magnitude of the internal ideological and policy-related tension within the majority party. The policy that the majority party will eventually settle on and pursue depends on the outcome of a bargaining game between these two players.

With regard to the structure and the outcome of this bargaining, two scenarios may be distinguished:

(1) $x_c = x_m$

In this scenario, the median legislator of the chamber is identical to the median legislator of the majority party. There is no conflict between the two. Therefore, the value of intra-party tension is zero and the median legislator of the party, who is also the median legislator of the chamber, will determine policy. The identity $x_c = x_m$ guarantees that the social optimum x_c will be adopted as government policy (x_g). It is important to note that such an occurrence is highly circumscribed, for it hinges on an extremely well-balanced configuration of parties in the legislature. To be precise, if the median position of the majority party occupies the median position of the legislature, then, following from the definition of the median, there are exactly as many legislators to the left of the left-most legislator of the party as there are to the right of its right-most legislator. For this reason, in a two-party legislature, this scenario is impossible. In a multiparty legislature, this means that the legislative weight of the left and the right must be identical.

(2) $x_c \neq x_m$

In all other cases the two actors are not identical, and the value of intra-party tension will then be greater than zero. Nonetheless, as discussed above, the median legislator's pivotal position can effectively decide the game. This would generate a socially efficient outcome for the legislature, at x_c, for the majority of legislators within the majority party. But it is inferior to x_m and, therefore, generates a conflict. On the one hand, the majority of legislators within the majority party, more precisely those with ideal points closer to x_m than to x_c, have an incentive to compel the median legislator to accept x_m as government policy. On the other hand, the median legislator of the chamber, together with all other legislators in the majority party – with ideal points lying closer to x_c than to x_m – are interested in getting the majority in the party to accept x_c as government policy.

Location enables the median legislator of the chamber to present a credible threat to the majority within that legislator's political party, with the ever-present possibility for the median legislator to switch sides and form an alternative majority with the other 'half' of the legislature – that will implement x_c as government policy. The credibility of such a threat, however, declines with the value of the penalty p that the existing rules impose on intra-party rebellion. If $0 = p < (x_c \leq x_m)$, then the power of the median legislator of the chamber is unconstrained, and that legislator will be able to get the majority party's support in implementing x_c. If, however, $p > (x_c - x_m)$, then the median legislator and that legislator's faction within the party will be deterred from rebelling because the price for accepting x_m is less than is the price of the penalty.

A high penalty on intra-party rebellion has a direct consequence for party aggregation. Would-be legislators with ideological and policy positions at or near the median of the chamber, as well as all other candidates with ideological positions closer to this median than to the median of the majority party that they might otherwise form, will not be interested in linking and forming a majority party. They anticipate that because $p > (x_c - x_m)$, the median of the majority party will rule and the socially efficient outcome x_c cannot be implemented. Therefore, the only way in which they can circumvent this problem and restore the social optimum is by ensuring that the median legislator of the chamber is not subject to the penalty of rebellion. This can be done by limiting party aggregation and thus denying even the possibility that there is a majority party median in the legislature. Should there be a majority party median in the legislature, under sufficiently high values of p, it could rein in the median legislator of the chamber and produce a socially inefficient policy output.

In sum, this policy-seeking perspective sheds slight on an important limitation of the extent to which the Westminster rule of executive formation may encourage would-be legislators to link across districts. If the rules of the game impose a sufficiently high penalty on intra-party rebellion, the median legislator of the majority party will have the credibility to impose and implement government policy that is different from the social optimum, which would be defined by the median of the chamber. The anticipation of this discourages would-be legislators from pursing party aggregation who know that their re-election requires the adoption of that social optimum. In contrast, the autonomy and freedom of individual legislators is guaranteed under $0 \leq p < (x_c - x_m)$. In such cases, the office-seeking motivation generated by the Westminster rule of executive formation will be unhindered in motivating would-be candidates to aggregate across districts and form a majority party that will allow the preferences of the median legislator of the chamber to drive the policy and legislative processes.

Party Aggregation and Fragmentation in India

Political life in India received a terrible shock in 1984 when Prime Minister Indira Gandhi was assassinated by her two Sikh body guards. To get maximum benefit from the electorate's sympathy vote in the ensuing general election, the inner circle of the Congress(I) Party's leadership selected the late prime minister's son Rajiv Gandhi, a young man with no political experience, as her successor and the party's candidate for prime minister. This choice produced the desired effect, indeed, as in 1984 the Congress(I) Party won its largest ever electoral victory (as Figure 9.2 shows). However, with the benefit of hindsight, it must be said that this huge electoral success also marked the end of an entire period in the party system – because it was also the last time that any party would win a majority of seats in the Lok Sabha.

The new prime minister was confronted with an ambiguous situation. On the one hand, he had at his disposal a large legislative majority that allowed him to exercise effective control over the legislative business and agenda, as well as to adopt and pursue government policies as he deemed appropriate. On the other hand, he would also have to cope with the problem of intra-party rebellion and defections. This was certainly not a novel problem or phenomenon in Indian politics; however, it was one that would be of particular concern for a novice political leader, who was as yet untrained in the art of securing alliances and intra-party support. With regard to defections, Hardgrave and Kochanek have noted that prior to 1989 there had been 'more than 2,700 recorded cases since 1967, most within the state assemblies. Congress had been the principal beneficiary, with as many as 1,900 defections to Congress ... Between March 1967 and June 1968, the high days of defection, 16 state governments were brought down by defections. Of the 438 legislators who changed parties during this period, 210 were rewarded with ministerships.'[21]

In an attempt to render his leadership credible, Rajiv Gandhi's new government quickly secured the passage of an amendment to the Indian constitution that would impose harsh penalties on legislative defectors. The passage of the Anti-Defection Law in January 1985 changed fundamentally the institutional environment in which political actors make their calculations and estimations with regard to the utility of party aggregation. The law, which was proposed as the 52nd Constitutional Amendment Bill, stipulates that

> a member of a legislature, state or national, belonging to any political party shall be disqualified for being a member
>
> (1b) if he votes or abstains from voting in such House contrary to any direction issued by the political party to which he belongs or by any person or authority authorized by it in this behalf, without obtaining, in either case, the prior permission of such political party, person or authority and such voting or abstention has not been condoned by such political party, person or authority within fifteen days from the date of such voting or abstention;
>
> (2) An elected member of a House who has been elected as such otherwise than as a candidate set up by any political party shall be disqualified for being a member of the House if he joins any political party after such election [par. 2].

> Where a member of a House makes a claim that he and any other members of his legislature party constitute the group representing a faction which has arisen as a result of a split in his original political party and such a group consists of not less than one-third of the members of such legislature party,

(a) he shall not be disqualified under sub-paragraph (1) of paragraph 2 ...

(b) from the time of such split, such faction shall be deemed to be the political party to which he belongs for the purposes of sub-paragraph (1) of paragraph 2 and to be his original political party for the purposes of this paragraph [par. 3].

(1) a member of a House shall not be disqualified under subparagraph (1) of paragraph 2 where his original political party merges with another political party and he claims that he and any other members of his original political party

(a) have become members of such other political party or, as the case may be, of a new political party formed by such merger; or

(b) have not accepted the merger and opted to function as a separate group ...

(2) For the purposes of sub-paragraph (1) of this paragraph, the merger of the original political party of a member of a House shall be deemed to have taken place if, and only if, not less than two-thirds of the members of the legislature party concerned have agreed to such merger [par. 4].

The amendment enjoyed general all-party support in both houses of parliament, which was not surprising for several reasons. First, the amendment sought to strengthen the leadership of each and every party, not just that of the Congress (I), vis-à-vis their recalcitrant legislators. Therefore, the leadership of all main parties had a vested interest to ensure that the amendment was passed. Second, since defections could be construed to be a major source of political instability in the country, it was also electorally and politically risky to vote against a constitutional amendment that sought to restrict it. Although individual legislators would see their autonomy to express and represent their views compromised, especially when in conflict with their party's line, they would not want to be seen to vote against a proposed piece of legislation that was seemingly aimed at making political life more orderly in the nation.

This institutional change has fundamentally transformed the incentive structure that political actors face with regard to party aggregation. In particular, since the Anti-Defection amendment was aimed at strengthening the leadership of political parties at the expense of the autonomy of individual legislators, it also made the generation of socially optimal policies non-credible. Since individual legislators

Table 9.1   The performance of the Congress Party in the 1985 state elections in India (percentage of votes)

State	1984 (National election)	1985 (State elections)
Andhra Pradesh	41.8	37.5
Bihar	51.8	39.3
Gujarat	53.2	55.5
Himachal Pradesh	67.6	55.5
Karnataka	51.6	41.1
Madhya Pradesh	57.1	48.9
Maharashtra	51.2	43.5
Orissa	57.5	51.1
Punjab	37.6	45.2
Rajasthan	52.7	46.6
Sikkim	25.8	24.2
Uttar Pradesh	51.0	39.3
Pondicherry	58.9	32.7
Mean change	−7.49	

depend on their re-election for retaining the support of the median voter in their district, they also have a vested interest in ensuring that the policies preferred by the median legislator would prevail, as explained in the previous section. However, the Anti-Defection Law metes out a harsh penalty on all those who rebel against the leadership of their party. In the case of the majority party, this clearly means that x_m would be adopted and not x_c. Rational policy-seeking candidates would, therefore, not want to join forces and form a new majority party because there is no credible mechanism to compel the leadership to agree to implement the social optimum.

Indeed, the dismantling of the majority party, the Congress(I), began immediately after the passage of the Anti-Defection Law. In March 1985, only three months after the passage of the bill by both houses of parliament, eleven states and the Union Territory of Pondicherry were to hold their local elections. It has been reported that an unprecedented number of incumbent Congress(I) legislators changed party labels before this round of elections, and that this resulted in a significant reversal in the electoral fortunes of the Congress(I).[22] On average, the Congress(I) Party mustered 7.5 per cent fewer votes than it had in the same states in the preceding (1984) national election (as shown in Table 9.1).

The magnitude of this reversal is not surprising. The historical average difference between the national governing party's vote share in a national election in a state and its vote share in a subsequent sub-national election in the same state between 1971 and 1991 was –6.6 per cent. Clearly, the negative swing that the Congress(I) suffered in the 1985 state elections was more than the normal electoral penalty that governing parties in India face.

The de-aggregation of the majority party steadily continued throughout the term of the 1984 Lok Sabha as evidenced by by-election results. In the five years between 1984 and 1989, twenty-six by-elections were held; of these, nine were because of the resignation of the incumbent legislator and the rest because of the death of the representative of the district. On average, there was an 11.83 per cent vote swing against the Congress(I) in these polls; however, the party was still able to win fifteen of the twenty-six contested seats. Apart from the period 1971 to 1977, this was the only time that the Congress(I), as a national governing party, experienced a negative swing in its share of the by-election vote compared with the percentage of votes it had polled in the previous national election. Most importantly, however, of the six by-elections necessitated by the resignation of the incumbent Congress (I) representative, the Congress(I) managed to win only three. This was in stark contrast to the success rate of the Congress (I) in defending its seats in by-elections held in the previous legislative cycle. Between 1977 and 1980, incumbent Congress(I) legislators resigned in nine districts, and the party managed to field a winning candidate in all but one of them.

In the successive national legislatures elected since the adoption of the Ant-Defection Law in 1985, no party has managed to win a majority of the seats, just as the policy-oriented model predicts. It is worth noting, nonetheless, that because of its central ideological position, the median legislator's party has not ceased playing a pivotal role in the government formation and policymaking process. As Table 9.2 shows (see Abbreviations at end of this chapter), of the six governments formed in India since 1989, the median Congress (I) Party has been either an active member or an outside supporter of four of them.

In 1990, the tiny Samajwadi Janata Party (SJP), with a mere fifty-four members of parliament, formed a government only because of the external support it was offered by the Congress(I) Party. In 1991, the Congress(I) led a single-party minority government, which proved able to form the only stable cabinets in the entire post-1989 period. In the Lok Sabha elected in 1996, the United Front coalition of parties survived in office as long as it did because of the support of the Con-

Table 9.2   Governments elected in India since 1989

Year	Governing party (parties)
1989–90	Janata Dal, TDP, AGP, DMK, ICS (supported from outside by Left Front and BJP)
1990	Samajwadi Janata Party (supported from outside by Congress(I))
1991–96	Indian National Congress(I)
1996–97	United Front (supported from outside by Congress(I))
1997–98	United Front (supported from outside by Congress(I))
1998–99	BJP and allies

gress(I). When the Congress(I) withdrew its support, in the spring of 1997, the United Front was only able to form a new cabinet after it had agreed to fulfil the conditions that the Congress(I) had set as a precondition for renewing its support.

The Congress(I) has played a pivotal role in the life of the other two cabinets as well, but in those cases its role was that of a destabilizer. The coalition minority government formed by the Janata Dal and its allies after the 1989 election attempted to bypass the median party by consulting with the right-wing BJP. Similarly, the BJP-led minority government of 1998 made attempts to bring smaller left-of-centre parties into the coalition. However, on both occasions, the median party could intervene and disrupt the formation of these informal ends-against-the-centre coalitions in the legislature. In the first case, the Congress(I) exploited factional competition within the Janata Dal and offered to support in office that faction which eventually seceded and formed the Samajwadi Janata Party. In 1998, the Congress(I) lured the AIADMK, a regional party concentrated in the southern state of Tamil Nadu, away from the BJP-led coalition by offering to form a coalition government in which the AIADMK would have a greater role in policymaking than it had had to that point.

Conclusion

The twin processes of fragmentation and the disappearance of legislative majorities in the Indian party system since 1989 can be understood to be the result of the rational choices that political actors made under the new incentives provided by the Anti-Defection Law of 1985. By strengthening party cohesion at the expense of the freedom of individual legislators, the new law removed the advantage inherent in the spatial position of the median legislator vis-à-vis the leadership of the majority party. Under the terms of the law, the median of the majority party can rein in the median legislator of the chamber and produce socially sub-optimal policies away from the latter's position. To prevent the generation of such policies, and advance their own re-election, rational actors will want to deny, and in fact have denied, the emergence of a majority party median by refraining from cross-district linkage on a large enough scale to create a majority party in the legislature.

This chapter has stressed the important role that institutional change has played in bringing about the fragmentation of the Indian national party system. Although the explanation singles out a unique and idio-syncratic piece of Indian legislation, the Anti-Defection amendment to the constitution, its applicability is by no means limited to this single case. The theoretical section has suggested that any rule and regulation that imposes a sufficiently large penalty on internal dissent will deter party aggregation, particularly the formation of majority parties. Therefore, it would be important to examine whether party aggrega-tion in other Westminster systems, such as Canada or Great Britain, where the office-seeking incentive for cross-district linkage is as strong as it is in India, varies with the absence or presence of such rules. It is important, however, not to confuse such rules with internal party mechanisms that may be used by party leaders to enforce disciplined voting in the legislature by members of their caucuses. According to the theory advanced in this chapter, such instruments may not credibly and necessarily prevent the median legislator from determining the legislative and policy output of the chamber. When they do, the theory leads us to expect party aggregation to decline. Otherwise, sustained periods of majority party government attest to the ability and the cred-ibility of the legislature to produce socially optimal policies at the median.

Abbreviations

AGP   Asom Gona Parishad
BJP   Bharatiya Janata Party
DMK   Dravida Munnetra Kazagham
ICS   Indian Congress (Socialist)
TDP   Telugu Desam Party

Notes

1 Pradeep Chhibber, *Democracy without Associations: Transformation of the Party System and Social Cleavages in India* (Ann Arbor: University of Michigan Press, 1999).

2 See, for example, Gary Cox, *Making Votes Count: Strategic Coordination in the World's Electoral Systems* (Cambridge: Cambridge University Press, 1997), 186–93.

3 Pradeep Chhibber and Kenneth Kollmann, 'Party Aggregation and the Number of Parties in India and the United States,' *American Political Science Review*, 92 (1998), 329–42.

4 This periodization was suggested by Ram Joshi and Kirtidev Desai, 'Towards a More Competitive Party System in India,' *Asian Survey*, 18 (1978), 1091–1116. It has been brought up to date in M.P. Singh, 'From Centrist Predominance to Polarized Pluralism: The Post-1989 Party System in India,' in M.P. Singh and Rekha Saxena (eds.), *India's Political Agenda: Perspectives on the Party System* (Delhi: Kalinga Publications, 1996), 35; and Rekha Saxena, 'Party System in Transition,' in *India's Political Agenda*, 49–81.

5 The single member simple plurality system (SMSP) tends to reward disproportionately large parties with solid support all across the country and regionally concentrated small parties. The logic of this is quite simple. According to this electoral formula, in each electoral district the candidate with the largest number of votes wins the single seat that is being contested. Since a candidate does not need to have a majority support in the district in order to win, a party whose candidates may win in a majority of the districts may thus end up securing less than a majority of the popular vote across all those districts. In this situation, the party will receive a seat bonus, that is, its share of the parliamentary seats will exceed its proportional share of the vote. For more on the effects of electoral laws, see the classic work by Douglas Rae, *The Political Consequences of Electoral Laws* (New Haven: Yale University Press, 1971).

6 The (I) stands for the party's leader at the time, Indira Gandhi. Because of frequent splits and changes in their organizational identity, Indian political parties often resort to using their leader's initial to distinguish themselves from other factions or splinter groups originating from the same parent party.

7 Chhibber, *Democracy without Associations*.

8 Cox, *Making Votes Count*, 184; Chhibber and Kollmann, 'Party Aggregation,' 330.

9 Marku Laakso and Rein Taagapera. 'Effective Number of Parties: A Mea-

sure with Application to West Europe,' *Comparative Political Studies*, 12 (1979), 3–27.

10 Differences in notation aside, this formula is borrowed from Chhibber and Kollmann, 'Party Aggregation,' 331.

11 Maurice Duverger, *Political Parties* (New York: Wiley, 1954). For a contrary view, see Yogendar Yadav, 'Reconfiguration in Indian Politics: State Assembly Elections, 1993–95,' *Economic and Political Weekly*, 20 (1996), 95–104.

12 Chhibber, *Democracy without Associations*, 56. In the first elections, some electoral districts returned two or three candidates.

13 Cox, *Making Votes Count*, 190.

14 The Indian presidency is a largely ceremonial office, although the head of state enjoys considerable discretionary authority in deciding whom to invite to attempt to form a government in a hung parliament. The chief executive is elected for a five-year term by an electoral college, rather than by popular vote, consisting of the two houses of the national parliament and the subnational legislatures. The electoral formula used is the single transferable vote. The national and subnational legislatures are elected non-concurrently, and the upper chamber of the national parliament, the Rayja Sabha, is filled by delegates of the subnational legislatures. Thus, the process of selecting the Indian president is a far cry from the requirements that Cox posits to be necessary for parties to have an incentive to aggregate.

15 Cox, *Making Votes Count*, 192.

16 Chhibber and Kollmann, 'Party Aggregation.'

17 Ibid., 338.

18 Anthony Downs, *An Economic Theory of Democracy* (New York: Harper and Row, 1957). Note that the rest of the theoretical and analytical discussion will be based on the assumption of a one-dimensional ideological space.

19 Gary Cox, 'Centripetal and Centrifugal Incentives in Electoral Systems,' *American Journal of Political Science*, 34 (1990), 903–35.

20 Duncan Black, *The Theory of Committees and Elections* (Cambridge: Cambridge University Press, 1958). This result also holds in more complex two- or *n*-dimensional spaces. In such cases, the social optimum is at the location of the generalized median of the space, the yolk. See Nicholas Miller, Bernard Grofman, and Scott Feld, 'The Geometry of Majority Rule,' *Journal of Theoretical Politics*, 1 (1989), 379–406.

21 Robert L. Hardgrave and Stanley A. Kochanek, *India: Government and Politics in a Developing Nation* (Fort Worth: Harcourt College Publishers, 2000), 273.

22 Ibid., 272–5.

Part 4

New Institutionalism and Public Policy Analysis

This fourth part looks at the contribution of new institutionalism to the study of public policy. At the broadest level, these chapters analyse the impact of institutions as intermediate-level variables on micro-level behaviour and policy outcomes. They focus on how institutions shape policymaking, including the mobilization of actors and the structuring of policy networks and interest groups. Two chapters argue that institutions have far-reaching consequences not strictly for policy outcomes but also for the organization of civil society and the role played by groups in the political process. The other articulates a critique of new institutionalism's reliance on path dependency to explain policy outcomes and proposes an alternative approach.

Eric Montpetit's chapter examines the influence of institutional structures on policymaking, with particular emphasis on the behaviour of groups in Canada. Montpetit suggests that the architecture of the Canadian state generates policy networks that are structured differently, and follow a different logic, from their American counterparts. He argues that Westminster parliamentarism, with its concentration of power in the hands of the prime minister, works to form closed policy networks, where actors are tightly connected because groups always have to fear the unilateral imposition of a decision by the prime minister and his cabinet. In the United States, where power is more fragmented, these types of policy networks are less likely. Montpetit then examines the relationship between the structure of policy networks and the behaviour of groups. He argues that actors involved in closed and cohesive networks with a high level of interconnectedness, such as those found in Canada, develop a sense of trust towards each other. Therefore, this type of network compounds the cooperation-inducive effect of Westminster parliamentarism because the attitudes they create tend to foster deliberative as opposed to strategic behaviour.

In the next chapter, Denis Saint-Martin and Alexandra Dobrowolsky question the relevance of the retrenchment approach to the welfare state for explaining the recent policy focus on children in both Britain and Canada. The authors argue that the retrenchment-expansion dichotomy leads to a purely quantitative conceptualization of change (growth or reduction) and that, consequently, qualitative change involving values, goals, and policy designs is ignored. They suggest that between this dichotomy there is room for policy experimentation and redesign and that, in this context, ideas, social learning, and agency play a more important role in policymaking than the retrenchment position typically assumes. Retrenchment, the authors argue, involves strictly a politics of interests, or powering, while current policy experiments are driven by social knowledge and ideational forces and, therefore, correspond more to a logic of puzzling.

In his chapter, Luc Juillet takes a continental perspective and explains the failure by the Canadian and American governments to amend the Migratory Birds Convention in a way that accommodates aboriginal and indigenous subsistence hunters. The question Juillet raises is the following: why were associations and non-governmental organizations successful in maintaining the status quo when the two governments pushed for a liberalization of the regime? Juillet suggests that the answer lies in the institutional structure of the American political system. He shows how forces opposed to changing the Convention, both American and Canadian, focused their activities on the United States Senate because it represents an effective 'veto point,' that is, an actor whose support is needed to alter the status quo. Also crucial is the fact that there was no equivalent veto point in Canada because treaty-making is an executive prerogative and because, for this case, provincial approval was not required. In this context, the dynamic of group interest politics was strongly shaped by the institutional environment, as the potential yielded by the American legislative branch for mounting an effective opposition led the U.S. Senate to be strategically targeted by such actors as the Canadian Wildlife Federation.

10

Westminster Parliamentarism, Policy Networks, and the Behaviour of Political Actors

ÉRIC MONTPETIT

Nowadays, policy studies can hardly produce convincing explanations without accounting for the role of institutions.[1] Assessing the precise impact of institutions on policy choices, however, remains a difficult task. Institutional effects, Fritz Scharpf has argued, are contingent on several additional factors. He discussed two of them: the nature of policy challenges and the constellation of the normative preferences of policy actors. Adding to the complexity, he contended, actors' preferences are themselves influenced by institutions.[2] This idea has been further pursued by Pierson and Skocpol, who have emphasized that there are intense interactions among these variables. The interactions are so intense that they appear to be bundled together, but they are often treated as independent by rational choice theorists in their explanations of policy decisions.[3] Despite these difficulties, I propose in this chapter a non-deterministic account of the influence of Canadian institutions, occasionally bundled with other factors, on policymaking.

In doing this, I attempt to take advantage of one acknowledged strength of historical institutionalism, namely, its capacity to bridge the macro, meso, and micro levels of analysis. Rational choice, even when it attempts to account for institutional effects, displays a bias for micro-level analysis that does not serve public policy studies well. As Pierson and Skocpol argued, the micro-level games to which rational choice analysts are attached lead them to study institutions that often have only a partial policymaking role.[4] Rational choice studies, for example, have revealed the nature of the political games occurring within the U.S. Congress, but it is not Congress alone that makes American policies. Likewise, rational choice analysis, more than any other theoretical tradition, has shed light on political games within local communities.[5]

Insights emanating from these studies, however, suffer serious deficiency when it comes to understanding policymaking at the level of an entire country and beyond.

Inspired by historical institutionalism, I propose in this chapter a comprehensive perspective on policymaking in Canada. Specifically, I argue that the architecture of the Canadian state tends to shape Canadian policy networks in a manner that is distinctive from networks commonly found in the United States. Canadian Westminster parliamentarism casts a shadow that encourages the formation of closed networks of actors which establish tight interconnections between state agencies and civil society. In turn, the distinctive Canadian networks, I further argue, incite actors to behave in a less-strategic manner than their American counterparts. The network structures commonly observed in Canada foster communicative action to a greater extent than the network structures usually associated with the American institutional environment.

The chapter is divided into three sections. I begin with a discussion of macro-level institutions. I then move on to discuss their influence on meso-level institutions, or policy networks. I end the chapter with a discussion of the influence of networks on political behaviour. The reader should note that the chapter is organized in this manner for the sake of clarity; this organization is not to deny that political behaviour can also shape networks and networks macro-political institutions.

The Architecture of the Canadian State

In this section, I discuss two aspects of the architecture of the Canadian state: federalism and Westminster parliamentarism.

Federalism

Scholars of federations have found it useful to distinguish between functional federations and jurisdictional federations.[6] Functions and jurisdictions refer to the methods of sharing competencies between the federal and the sub-federal governments. When competencies are shared along functions, the central government is generally responsible for policy formulation, while sub-federal states handle policy implementation. Germany and the European Union come closest to this ideal type. When competencies are shared along jurisdictions, the central government and federated governments are responsible for both policy formulation and implementation, but in a limited number of policy domains. For example, sub-federal states may be fully responsible for health care while the federal government is fully responsible for defence. Canada comes closer to this latter ideal type, jurisdictional federalism.

Specialists distinguish between these two types of federation because they have noticed more intergovernmental cooperation in functional federations than in jurisdictional federations.[7] As Scharpf argued, functional federations are multi-actor systems that require cooperation.[8] On the one hand, if sub-federal governments want policy change, they need the cooperation of the federal government. On the other hand, it would be unwise for the federal government to formulate public policies without the cooperation of federated governments that will eventually have the capacity, through their discretion about the implementation of such policy, to distort policy objectives. Conversely, jurisdictional federations are multi-actor systems where intergovernmental conflicts and competition are frequent because policy change is possible through unilateral action. Assuming that the federal government of a hypothetical jurisdictional federation possesses all the responsibilities relevant to environmental management, say, it can devise environmental policies alone and exercise a tight control over its own bureaucracy during policy implementation. In real life, jurisdictional duplications and overlaps may justify the organization of frequent intergovernmental meetings,[9] but in the end governments of jurisdictional federations normally possess the capacity to decide policy change alone in the sectors where they have jurisdiction. In fact, scholars of Canadian federalism have argued that political payoffs are often higher when governments, in a competitive manner, decide to act unilaterally rather than cooperatively.[10]

Westminster

In Westminster systems, the principle of ministerial responsibility makes parliament the supreme instance of authority but, in a paradoxical manner, it also encourages the concentration of power in the hands of the executive. In Canada, parliament is supreme because the government must preserve parliamentary confidence to govern.[11] A simple motion carried, or a defeat in a vote regarding an important legislative project, is generally sufficient to require the government to step down and to ask the Governor General to launch the electoral process. In comparison, the U.S. Congress has very few means at its disposal to dismiss the president. The latter can be dismissed from office only in accordance with a very strict procedure and only in exceptional circumstances. Congress cannot dismiss a president simply by disapproving of his legislative projects.

This parliamentary supremacy in Canada – and here the paradox takes hold – has encouraged ever greater concentrations of executive power. More precisely, to ensure relative political stability, a large degree of control over legislative activity has been conferred on the prime minister and cabinet. This control serves to limit defeats of the government in parliament and hence to regulate the frequency of elections. This control is exercised in part by virtue of the prerogative enjoyed by the prime minister to appoint members of parliament to key posts, a prerogative which enables the prime minister to enforce strict party discipline. In contrast to their U.S. counterparts, Canadian legislators are obliged to vote, virtually without fail, according to the party line; if they do not do so, they become vulnerable to weighty sanctions, which can be as serious as exclusion from caucus.

This concentration of power in Canada is not limited to control over votes cast by members of parliament because the prime minister plays a key role in defining what the party line will be. Donald Savoie has shown that, by virtue of the bureaucratic resources at the prime minister's disposal, notably the Privy Council Office, the prime minister and a few of his senior ministers exercise strict control over the governmental agenda. Caucus meetings may have been intended for backbenchers to participate in the development of their ruling party's agenda, but Savoie concluded that, instead, they provide the prime minister with the opportunity to justify his or her own priorities to the party, and to legitimate the decisions that he or she has already made.[12] To put it succinctly, the margin for manœuvre among parliamentarians is slim, not only at the level of deciding what the party line should be, but also at the level of what initiatives to back in the House of Commons. These institutional attributes of the architecture of the Canadian state are not without consequences for policymaking activities that occur outside its strict boundaries. In the next section, I turn to these consequences.

Policy Networks

As opposed to parliament and federalism, policy networks are informal meso-level structures. They are normally treated as structures that shape the relationship between interest groups and the administrative agencies of the state for the purpose of policy development.[13] Policy networks are not simply an aggregation of individual actors.[14] They are clusters of actors who interact in distinctive rule-guided manners. Networks can vary along at least four interrelated dimensions:

1 Networks can be either open to a large number of actors or be closed. Openness and closeness are tacit rules which are often the most distinctive feature of policy networks.
2 Networks can closely or loosely interconnect state and civil society actors. The degree of interconnection, or of actors' autonomy, is also an implicit rule that regulates the interactions between actors.
3 Resources or policy capacities may be evenly or unevenly distributed between state and civil society actors within networks. While policy capacities are attributes of individual actors, the quality of their distribution has an undeniable effect on the interaction between state and civil society actors. When capacities are skewed in favour of state actors, for example, they can attain objectives of their own by manipulating civil society actors.
4 Networks can be more or less cohesive depending on the extent to which actors adhere to similar ideas. Ideas, just like rules, regulate actors' interactions.

From these structural characteristics, political scientists have produced several typologies of policy networks.[15] For the sake of simplicity, I retain only four types of policy networks, those most often encountered in empirical analyses pertaining to industrialized countries. They are presented in Table 10.1. Naturally, the four characteristics presented above enable the construction of a much longer typology.

Networks are constructed over time, and therefore particular networks are associated with particular historical contexts. Pierson, for instance, claimed that policy networks in the historical context of the welfare state differ markedly from those of the previous political context.[16] The emergence of the welfare state, he has contended, is the result of pressures from powerful trade unions in what may appear as issue networks. Erecting the welfare state, however, necessitated building bureaucratic organizations capable of developing and administering complex public policy. The welfare state also served to establish interest groups which, similar to the civil service machinery, made sig-

Table 10.1   Typology of policy networks

	Openness	Interconnection	Policy capacities	Cohesion
Issue network	Very high	Very low	Unevenly distributed in favour of civil society	Very low
Pluralist network	High	Low	Even	Low
Corporatist network	Low	High	Even	High
Clientelist network	Low	High	Unevenly distributed in favour of civil society	High

nificant commitments. They committed themselves to various ends such as data collection for policy development, building expertise to support policymakers, and building administrative capacity to help the state implement policies.[17] Therefore, in comparison with the pre-welfare state context, pluralist and even corporatist and clientelist networks are far more common in the contemporary context, and they give shape to what Pierson called the new politics of the welfare state. This new politics of the welfare state offers powerful resistance to policy change.[18]

Where most policy network analyses depart from Pierson's new politics of the welfare state is in the importance they give, to not only historical contexts, but also to sector and country differences. Policy analyses have revealed significant network differences between sectors within a single country or between countries in a single sector, showing that the new politics of the welfare state does not offer equal resistance, across sectors and countries, to policy change.[19] Between sectors and countries, networks vary along the four interconnected dimensions presented in Table 10.1.

Crucial to several of these dimensions is the quality of the mobilization of civil society within a sector. The openness of networks, for example, is often a matter of whether the associational system is integrated or fragmented. When the interest groups in a sector are integrated within one or a limited number of peak associations, the openness of the network is more easily limited to these actors. Likewise, the degree of interconnection between state actors and civil society can be limited by the availability of groups that can legitimately claim to represent the sector. When civil society is fragmented, a close interconnection between state actors and a few groups is likely to be highly contested by political opponents. Lastly, cohesion should also be a matter of group integration within a sector. Peak associations will typically resolve conflicts over policy ideas internally, while a mobilized but fragmented civil society within a sector will hold policy debates out in the open.

But how to explain sectoral and country differences in the quality of mobilization of civil society? Following Schmitter and Streeck, Coleman and Montpetit emphasized two mobilization logics, which at times conflict and at times reinforce each other.[20] Mobilization within a sector can first depend upon a logic of membership. In industrial sectors, mobilization can be restricted, for example, by a structure favourable to small and diverse businesses at the expense of concentration around national champions. To this diverse economic base yet more cleavages can be added, such as regional and linguistic splits, which are common in Canada. Within such a context, where members have so little in common, mobilization is likely to suffer. The best for which one can hope under such conditions is an associational system that is profoundly fragmented. When the logic of membership discourages mobilization, the development of corporatist or clientelist policy networks appears unlikely.

This logic of membership can be either reinforced or contradicted by a second logic, namely, that of influence. Because an associational system jibing with state structure is an influential system, civil society is likely to organize along state structures. A jurisdictional federation, organized in such a way as to allow the expression of regional differences, encourages a territorial differentiation of interest groups consistent with the jurisdictional division of competencies between the federal and sub-federal governments. And where the territorial divisions of a federation correspond with identity cleavages, the logic of influence and the logic of membership work together to promote, not only territorial differentiation, but even the fragmentation of the associational system. At this point in my analysis, the relationship between the macro institutions and meso structures should become clear.

In Canada, the logic of membership and the logic of influence reinforce each other to fragment civil society into distinctive federal and provincial associational systems that function independently.[21] The logic of influence in Canada insulates provincial and federal associational systems from each other, so much so that each can function in a manner not too distant from the associational systems of unitary states. Coleman and Montpetit observed that territorial differentiations in the organization of interest groups is less pronounced in jurisdictional federations, such as Canada, than in functional federations, such as Germany, where intergovernmental cooperation on most policy issues can hardly be avoided.[22] As explained above, the governments of a jurisdictional federation can act unilaterally in the sectors upon which they have exclusive jurisdiction, thereby reducing the necessity for interest groups to organize with a view to influencing federal and sub-federal governments simultaneously, because both work cooperatively. It is enough for a group in a jurisdictional federation to possess the capacity to influence the government constitutionally empowered to act unilaterally in the sector of interest.

Since Canadian jurisdictional federalism segregates associational systems along federal and provincial lines, the influence of these associational systems should largely depend on the cohesion between their structures and their respective parliamentary institutions. In other words, the quality of group mobilization in Canada is relatively contingent upon the logic of influence associated with Westminster parliamentarism.[23] As explained above, the political hierarchy in Canada is heavily burdened by the concentration of power in the hands of the prime minister. Savoie suggested that the prime minister of Canada is placed at the summit of a hierarchy that he controls almost perfectly.[24]

However, Savoie neglected the possibility that this hierarchy, far from being coercive, does little more than cast a shadow over policy networks. To effectively avoid what Scharpf called the problem of motivations, whereby office holders use their power to serve their own objectives, the hierarchies in the public sector are generally subjected to accountability structures.[25] Such accountability structures are often fraught with dysfunctions, which is often distressing for all except the supposedly accountable office holders.[26] Nevertheless, these dysfunctions in the formal apparatus do not mean that elected members are exempt from all forms of accountability, or that they can disregard the policy preferences emanating from civil society, especially in the Canadian context where governments are formed by 'brokerage' political parties.[27] Electoral victories in Canada are rarely due to parties actually having a cohesive agenda on the ideological front; rather, they are a function of the ability of parties to broker and maintain a coalition of heterogeneous supporters. Consequently, a prime minister who owes his victory to brokerage will likely prefer endorsing decisions made on a consensual basis within horizontal networks of disparate interest groups and ministries over his discretionary power.[28] Succinctly put, more often than not, the hierarchical nature of power in Canada merely casts a shadow over the true locus of decisions.

The idea here is not to minimize the importance of the concentration of power in the Canadian parliamentary system, but rather the opposite, since I argue that it can encourage more cooperation within associational systems and policy networks. Scharpf suggested that achieving cooperation among actors who are divided, whether at the level of their identity or at the level of their interests, is generally problematic.[29] Uncertain of the motivations of their peers, interest groups that have neither a shared identity nor any shared interest often choose not to cooperate; in such a case, there is a risk of paralysis for any government attached to brokerage politics. Groups can be prompted to cooperate, however, when placed under the shadow of hierarchy. That is, the situation is considerably different when the actors situated in the horizontal structure know that the prime minister and the cabinet can impose upon them a decision entirely detached from the logic of brokerage.[30] It is for the sake of avoiding the imposition of such decisions upon them that groups, which are otherwise distant from each other, will sometimes choose to set aside their mutual distrust, if not their particular grievances. Over time, such close relationships may be formalized to give rise to peak associations. Under the shadow of hierarchy, the logic of influence likely encourages, if not greater integration of interest groups, at least greater interconnection between network actors. In short, in sharp contrast to the portrait as drawn by Savoie, the consequence of the concentration of power in the hands of the prime minister, more often than not, would consist in the facilitation of horizontal collaboration, which is otherwise problematic, within public policy networks.[31]

My intention is not to claim that policy networks in Canada are corporatist and clientelist rather than pluralist or issue-oriented simply because of parliamentary institutions. The quality of mobilization of civil society will vary according to the logic of membership within any particular sector as well as according to the logic of influence that may arise from the necessity of intergovernmental cooperation in sectors where overlaps are significant. Nevertheless, hierarchical parliamentary systems in Canada should contribute to make corporatist and clientelist policy networks more prevalent than in countries where the parliamentary system is not as hierarchical, such as in the United States.

Strategizing and Deliberating

I have thus far claimed that networks closed to a limited number of tightly interconnected actors, who hold cohesive policy ideas, are more common in Canada than in the United States, thanks to parliamentary institutions. Does this mean that Canadian and American political actors will adopt political behaviours belonging to two clearly distinctive categories? This is the question to which I now turn, a question which incidentally bridges the meso and micro levels of analysis. David Marsh and Martin Smith may have hinted at an answer when affirming that networks 'involve the institutionalization of beliefs, values, cultures and particular forms of behaviour.'[32] I have myself already hinted at the answer when I suggested above that Canadian political actors may be more inclined to cooperation than American actors are. But I want to advance here that behavioural differences are even more significant than this when networks are fundamentally different.

Rule guidance is the type of behaviour commonly associated with historical institutionalism. The origin of this behavioural category can be traced back to the idea of bounded rationality,[33] whereby actors are viewed as satisfiers instead of optimizers. Given the difficulty of computing all possible alternatives and deciding which one most optimally matches one's interest, actors stop analysing once they are satisfied with the knowledge that a solution serves their interest.[34] Historical institutionalists go slightly further in advancing that actors' analysis of alternatives consists in verifying whether they match the prevailing norms in their institutional environment. Socialized in particular institutional environments, actors tend to be satisfied when they see a good fit between proposed solutions and the institutional norms to which they are accustomed. In other words, rule guidance functions according to a logic of appropriateness that is largely defined by institutions. This conception of actors' behaviour departs from dominant rational choice analysis, which conceives individuals as making decisions based on careful assessments of the consequences of the various alternatives offered to them.

Risse argued that the logic of appropriateness commonly associated with historical institutionalism does not have to be treated in a mutually exclusive fashion from rational choice's logic of consequentialism.[35] In fact, rule guidance may appear as a rather elastic notion. Schneider and Ingram, for example, argued that the U.S. institutional context teaches politicians to be self-regarding in making decisions.

American politicians, Schneider and Ingram suggested, are taught to carefully analyse the alternatives presented to them and assess them for their electoral consequences.[36] In other words, what appears appropriate in the American institutional context is to abide by a logic of consequentialism. Rule guidance and strategic action cannot be treated as two mutually exclusive behavioural categories if the rule is to act strategically.

In this sense, one should not see historical institutionalism as a direct challenge to the central rational choice contention that actors act strategically. While strategic behaviour is a possibility, several other possibilities exist, hence the importance of subjecting political behaviour to empirical analysis. For the purposes of this chapter, I contrast strategic action with communicative action, which extends what Scharpf has called problem-solving. Strategic action and communicative action constitute two distinctive categories of behaviours that analysts may encounter in their empirical research.

Typically, actors are said to act strategically when they assess the consequences of various policy alternatives as functions of their own self-interest. This notion of self-interest has been largely criticized for being too easily imputed to several kinds of motivation.[37] The focus has consequently changed, even in the rational choice literature, from interests to preferences. Actors act strategically when they attempt to obtain the translation of their preferences into public policy. Strategic action can typically take three forms: loyalty, voice, or exit.[38] Actors are loyal when their preferences closely match those of actors in positions of authority. When the difference in preferences is manageable, actors will negotiate and consider compromise or use rhetoric to attempt changing the preferences of their opponents. When negotiations and rhetoric fail, exiting becomes an alternative which may perpetuate the status quo if it comes from actors in veto positions.[39]

Of German origin, the ideas of communicative action and problem-solving are far less common in the largely American public policy literature. Building on the work of Habermas, Risse suggested that communicative action is the mode of social interaction that enables policy learning or changes in policy preferences outside strategic considerations.[40] Communicative action follows a process of argumentative rationality or dialogue wherein actors become willing to relax their commitment to their policy preference 'to challenge and to justify the validity claims inherent in them – and they are prepared to change their view of the world or even their interests in light of the better argument.'[41] In other words, under communicative action, actors are prepared to put their preferences on the back burner for the sake of truth-seeking. Their prime motivation is identification of the best possible policy solution for the problem at issue. This means that actors, in contrast to when they act strategically, are willing to abandon control over the eventual outcome of the dialogue, even if it may lead far away from their initial preferences. Deliberation and dialogue quality become the central concerns of actors under communicative action. Political interactions here are not strategic, but opportunities to argue in pursuit of unforeseen ideas to resolve policy problems.

Given the particular network environment that characterizes Canada, should actors be more inclined to adopt strategic or deliberative behaviours? Again, behaviours should be analysed empirically, and generalizations are hazardous. Institutions can send different signals to different actors when they do not squarely send conflicting signals. Consequently, from time to time, institutions may fail to create any particular behavioural inclination. Nevertheless, policy researchers, I argue, can reasonably expect to observe deliberative behaviours more frequently in Canada than in systems where political power is more fragmented, such as in the United States.

Trust among actors appears to be the central condition favourable to communicative action. Actors are more likely to accept challenges to their preferences if they trust that other network actors will also, at least from time to time, accept challenges to their own preferences. Offe argued that trust within a very large constellation of actors tends to be problematic and will necessarily involve verticality in a critical manner. Not everyone can be involved in the making of collective decisions when the collective is very large. In issue and pluralist policy networks, for example, decisions have to be made authoritatively by brokerage or arbitration among the vast range of ideas and interests involved.[42] And naturally, the legitimacy of arbitration will depend on the extent to which the participants trust the arbiters. In other words, vertical trust is central within pluralist and issue networks.

According to Offe, such vertical trust arises from institutions that embody four values: truth-telling, contract honouring, fairness, and solidarity.[43] Failure on any of these values should raise suspicions and endanger the legitimacy of arbitration among the preferences of participants. Offe observed that 'any evidence of institutions permitting (or failing to detect) lies, of being unable to make actors keep contracts and honour promises, of being biased and permitting unfair advantages, and of failing to compensate at least some major kinds of social inequalities appear to be the only legitimate reasons for "systemic" distrust and eventually cynicism. Such failures are taken as evidence that institutions have failed to inculcate their meaning and mission to agents and make them loyal.'[44] The importance of cynicism in modern society[45] may attest to the difficulty of designing institutions that embody all of these values.[46] For pluralist and issue networks, the problem is particularly consequential as participants, suspicious of each other, will be inclined to resort to strategies aimed at satisfying their preferences first instead of communicative action.

Naturally, vertical distrust, generated by poorly designed political institutions, will also be problematic for corporatist and clientelist networks, as it should encourage cynicism, among outsiders, directed at network participants. However, corporatist and clientelist networks possess the advantage over pluralist and issue networks to render possible what Offe called trust from experience within networks.[47] Trust from experience develops out of personal relationships. When networks sufficiently limit participation to permit personal contacts, actors can make up their own minds about each other's trustworthiness without having to rely on the values embodied in institutions. In addition, when the number of actors is sufficiently limited to allow personal relationships, more often than not trust becomes the norm rather than the exception. Offe argued that 'the easiest case is building trust through continued interaction with concrete persons whom we typically know for a considerable period of time.'[48] According to Offe, experimental trust has two reinforcing aspects: moral obligation and self-interest. The numerous reasons given by the trustee to justify receiving trust and the risk attached to trusting that the truster has accepted create powerful moral obligations when the roles are reversed. Over time, actors acquire 'a sense of moral obligation to honor trust.'[49]

In addition to this sense of moral obligation, actors may realize that trusting, because it constitutes a favour normally returned, is in their self-interest. Offe put it thus: 'Within organizations, being trusted can be used to buffer deviation from routine – be it in the sense of experimentation and innovation, be it in the sense of partial failure and malperformance that will be, if only up to a point, more easily ignored or forgiven and less severely sanctioned if the person who commits it is being trusted. In either sense, being trusted enhances the autonomy and the size of the feasible set of the agent.'[50] Offe insisted that self-interest is insufficient: If an actor utilizes trust only for strategic purposes and fails to abide by moral obligations, personal relationship will be insufficient to prevent a deterioration of trust. Suffice it to insist, however, that is the form of trust most easily achieved.

It should be obvious that trust requires policy networks to be restricted to a limited number of actors. If they are wide open, networks will constantly allow the entry of new actors with whom no one has previously shared an experience and therefore who inspire suspicion that incites actors to retrench behind strategic action. In contrast, actors in closed policy networks should, over time, benefit from sufficient experience to allow the development of a sense of obligation to honour trust. Once trust is developed in this manner, interactions are more likely to correspond to communicative action. Offe suggested that trust enhances actors' autonomy, allowing experimentation and innovation. This can be taken to mean that in situations of trust actors will not hesitate to challenge each other's ideas and preferences. In turn, unforeseen solutions to problems might emerge out of such deliberations and such challenges to taken-for-granted ideas and preferences. This may run against common wisdom, but innovation and problem-solving may be more easily attained when networks are restricted to a limited number of actors. Closeness encourages trust and trust enables communicative action and discourages narrowly conceived strategic actions.[51]

Corporatist and clientelist networks, two closed types of networks, do not equally encourage communicative action and problem-solving. Clientelist networks rarely involve more than one well-defined group in civil society and comprise state agencies that are poor in policy capacity. As I have said above, actors challenge the preferences of others when others can trust that the challengers are equally capable of accepting challenges; and it is out of such communicative actions that unforeseen solutions emerge. This assumes a symmetrical relationship in terms of actors' capacity not only to be challenged, but also to challenge. As Table 10.1 suggests, such symmetry is absent from clientelist networks because only civil society can challenge the state. Under these circumstances, challenges are not for the sake of truth-seeking, but are more strategically conceived to place state actors in subservient positions. State agencies' preferences will be challenged when they deviate too much from those of the civil society actor. In short, communicative action requires not only trust, it also requires a relative symmetry in the policy capacities of the participants in the network.

Such symmetry normally characterizes corporatist networks (see

Table 10.1). With equal capacity to accept challenge, but also to challenge, actors in corporatist networks should more frequently than those in other network types prefer communicative action over strategic action. However, distinctions should be established among corporatist networks: Some corporatist networks are bipartite or sectoral, while others are multipartite or intersectoral.[52] Going against common wisdom again, state and civil society actors, I suggest, do challenge each other in sectoral or bipartite corporatist networks. The state actor in a bipartite corporatist network, even when closely interconnected to a single sectoral civil society group, can propose significant challenges to the group's preferences, if only because it belongs to a system of government required to adopt a wider perspective on policy problems. It is also fair to argue that the span of challenges, and therefore the capacity for problem-solving, is higher in multipartite or intersectoral corporatist networks. With a variety of perspectives coming from groups belonging to different sectors and also from state agencies with diverse responsibilities, the most innovative ideas should be produced in multipartite corporatist networks. Incidentally, because of the appearance of horizontal issues such as the environment and the multiplication of issue overlaps, bipartite or purely sectoral policy networks are increasingly unsustainable and are slowly replaced with multipartite or intersectoral networks.[53]

To return to the main question, political actors will in fact less frequently act strategically and will more often choose communicative action or deliberative behaviours when policy networks nurture trust among actors who possess comparable policy capacities. I have argued that such networks are more common in political systems where hierarchy casts a shadow over networks, such as in Canada, than in systems of fragmentation of power such as that in the United States. This is not to say that American actors will never opt for communicative action and that Canadian actors will never opt for strategic action, but only that the former behaviour should be at least slightly more common in Canada and the latter behaviour more common in the United States.

Conclusion

That Canadian political actors, in comparison with American political actors, deliberate more before making policy decisions – a behaviour apparently nobler than strategic action – is a bold argument to make. It may appear to be an idealization of Canada, which is not my purpose here; several examples can be invoked to prove the argument wrong. But empirical analyses may never be exhaustive enough to prove the argument entirely wrong or entirely right, and here may rest a weakness, so to speak, of historical institutionalism.

As Pierson and Skocpol have argued, case studies are the foundation of historical institutionalism, and case studies often tell conflicting stories because institutions send conflicting signals.[54] For example, some actors in positions of authority will take the view that greater capacity to realize bold policy objectives can be achieved quickly in Westminster parliamentarism. Other actors may see in the parliamentary system a clear line of accountability, and therefore, they will act carefully, if not incrementally, to avoid being held responsible for a significant mistake. Which one of these is dominant in Westminster-type parliamentarism will only be known after a critical mass of case studies have been produced. Because producing a critical mass of such empirical studies takes time, while institutions and the signals that they send continue to evolve within historical contexts, the powerful answers sought by positivist thinkers are likely to remain wishful thinking. Meanwhile, we are left with thoughtful speculations such as the one that I propose in this chapter. It should be kept in mind, however, that this thoughtful speculation possesses a significant advantage over rational choice theory: It presents a comprehensive set of propositions on policymaking in Canada, propositions that bridge the macro, meso, and micro levels of analysis.

Notes

The author acknowledges the support of the Social Sciences and Humanities Research Council of Canada (grant no. 410–2001–0338) and Fonds Québecois de la Recherche sur la Société et la Culture (FQRSC) (grant no. 72634).

1 Peter Hall and Rosemary Taylor, 'Political Science and the Three New Institutionalisms,' *Political Studies*, 44 (1996), 936–57.
2 Fritz W. Scharpf, 'Institutions in Comparative Policy Research,' *Comparative Political Studies*, 33 (2000), 771.
3 Paul Pierson and Theda Skocpol, 'Historical Institutionalism in Contemporary Political Science,' in Ira Katznelson and Helen V. Milner (eds.), *Political Science: State of the Discipline* (New York: W.W. Norton, 2002), 693.
4 Ibid., 696.

5 Elinor Ostrom, Roy Gardner, and James Walker, *Rules, Games and Common-Pool Resources* (Ann Arbor: University of Michigan Press, 1994).

6 William D. Coleman and Éric Montpetit, 'Multitiered Systems and the Organization of Business Interests,' in Justin Greenwood and Henry Jacek (eds.), *Organized Business and the New Global Order* (London: Macmillan Press Ltd. in collaboration with the International Political Science Association, 2000); Dietmar Braun (eds.), *Public Policy and Federalism* (Aldershot: Ashgate, 2000).

7 Herman Bakvis and William M. Chandler (eds.), *Federalism and the Role of the State* (Toronto: University of Toronto Press, 1987).

8 Scharpf, 'Institutions,' 782.

9 Donald V. Smiley, *The Federal Condition in Canada* (Toronto: McGraw-Hill Ryerson, 1987).

10 Alan C. Cairns, 'The Other Crisis of Canadian Federalism,' *Canadian Public Administration*, 22 (1979), 175–95; Garth Stevenson, 'Federalism and Intergovernmental Relations,' in Michael S. Whittington and Glen Williams (eds.), *Canadian Politics in the 1990s* (Toronto: Nelson Canada, 1995); Kathryn Harrison, *Federalism and Canadian Environmental Policy* (Vancouver: UBC Press, 1996).

11 The same is true at the provincial level.

12 Donald J. Savoie, *Governing from the Centre: The Concentration of Political Power in Canada* (Toronto: University of Toronto Press, 1999).

13 Éric Montpetit, 'Policy Networks, Federal Arrangements, and the Development of Environmental Regulations: A Comparison of the Canadian and American Agricultural Sectors,' *Governance: An International Journal of Policy, Administration and Institutions*, 15 (2002), 6.

14 On this point, see Keith Dowding, 'Model or Metaphor? A Critical Review of the Policy Network Approach,' *Political Studies*, 43 (1995), 136–58.

15 Michael M. Atkinson and William D. Coleman, 'Strong States and Weak States: Sectoral Policy Networks in Advanced Capitalist Economies,' *British Journal of Political Science*, 19 (1989), 47–67; Franz Van Waarden, 'Dimensions and Types of Policy Networks,' *European Journal of Political Research*, 21 (1992), 29–52; Rod A.W. Rhodes, 'Policy Networks: A British Perspective,' *Journal of Theoretical Politics*, 2 (1990), 293–317; Hans T.A. Bressers and Laurence J. O'Toole Jr, 'The Selection of Policy Instruments: A Network-based Perspective,' *Journal of Public Policy*, (18) 1998, 213–39.

16 Paul Pierson, *Dismantling the Welfare State? Reagan, Thatcher, and the Politics of Retrenchment* (Cambridge: Cambridge University Press, 1994).

17 Wolfgang Streeck and Philippe C. Schmitter, 'Community, Market, State – and Associations? The Prospective Contribution of Interest Governance to

Social Order,' in Wolfgang Streeck and Philippe C. Schmitter (eds.), *Private Interest Government* (London: Sage, 1985), 1–29.

18 Paul Pierson, 'The New Politics of the Welfare State,' *World Politics*, 48 (1996), 143–79.

19 William D. Coleman, Michael M. Atkinson, and Éric Montpetit, 'Against the Odds: Retrenchment in Agriculture in France and in the United States,' *World Politics*, 49 (1997), 453–81; David Marsh and Martin Smith, 'Understanding Policy Networks: Towards a Dialectical Approach,' *Political Studies*, 48 (2000), 4–21.

20 Philippe C. Schmitter and Wolfgang Streeck, 'The Organization of Business Interests: A Research Design to Study the Associative Action of Business in the Advanced Industrial Societies of Western Europe,' discussion paper of the International Institute of Management – Labour Market Policies Division, IIM/LMP 1981/13, Wissenshaftszentrum, Berlin, 1981; Coleman and Montpetit, 'Multitiered Systems,' 160.

21 William D. Coleman, 'Le nationalisme, les intermédiaires et l'intégration politique canadienne,' *Politique et sociétés*, 28 (1995), 31–52.

22 Coleman and Montpetit, 'Multitiered Systems.'

23 Rodney Haddow, 'Interest Representation and the Canadian State: From Group Politics to Policy Communities and Beyond,' in Alain-G. Gagnon and James Bickerton (eds.), *Canadian Politics*, 3rd ed. (Peterborough: Broadview Press, 1999), 512.

24 Savoie, *Governing from the Centre.*

25 Fritz W. Scharpf, *Games Real Actors Play: Actor-Centered Institutionalism in Policy Research* (Boulder: Westview Press, 1997), 178–83.

26 Sharone L. Sutherland, 'The Al-Mashat Affair: Administrative Accountability in Parliamentary Institutions,' *Canadian Public Administration*, 34 (1991), 573–604.

27 Harold D. Clarke, Jane J. Jenson, Laurence LeDuc, and Jon H. Pammett, *Absent Mandate: Canadian Electoral Politics in an Era of Restructuring*, 3rd ed. (Vancouver: Gage, 1996).

28 A study by Mark McDonald illustrates this perfectly. He has shown that the government preferred a network of organized actors over the pressure exerted by Monsanto, an agricultural biotechnology firm that tried to have a controversial product rbST approved in the 1990s. Mark R. MacDonald, 'Socioeconomic versus Science-Based Regulation: Informal Influences on the Formal Regulation of rbST in Canada,' in G. Bruce Doern and Ted Reed (eds.), *Risky Business: Canada's Changing Science-Based Policy and Regulatory Regime* (Toronto: University of Toronto Press, 2000), 156–81.

29 Fritz W. Scharpf, 'Games Real Actors Could Play: Positive and Negative

Coordination in Embedded Negotiations,' *Journal of Theoretical Politics*, 6 (1994), 27–53.

30 This occurs very rarely, but it does occur just the same, making it a credible threat. Municipal amalgamation in Quebec, something for which the Parti québécois government seems to be paying a high electoral price, constitutes one example.

31 Scharpf, 'Games Real Actors Could Play.'

32 Marsh and Smith, 'Understanding Policy Networks,' 6.

33 Herbert Simon, *Administrative Behavior*, 2nd ed. (New York: Free Press, 1957).

34 Charles Lindblom, 'The Science of "Muddling Through,"' *Public Administration Review*, 19 (1959), 79–88.

35 Thomas Risse, '"Let's Argue!": Communicative Action in World Politics,' *International Organization*, 45 (2000), 1–39.

36 Anne Larason Schnieder and Helen Ingram, *Policy Design for Democracy* (Lawrence: University Press of Kansas, 1997).

37 Susan D. Phillips, 'Of Public Interest Groups and Sceptics: a Realist's Reply to Professor Stanbury,' *Canadian Public Administration*, 36 (1993), 606–16.

38 Albert O. Hirschman, *Exit, Voice and Loyalty: Responses to Decline in Firms, Organizations and States* (Cambridge, Mass.: Harvard University Press, 1970).

39 George Tseblis, 'Decision Making in Political Systems: Veto Players in Presidentialism, Parliamentalism, Multiculturalism and Multipartism,' *British Journal of Political Science*, 25 (1995), 289–325.

40 Risse, 'Let's Argue!'

41 Ibid., 7.

42 Paul A. Sabatier, 'Policy Change over a Decade or More,' in Paul A. Sabatier and Hank C. Jenkins-Smith (eds.), *Policy Change and Learning: An Advocacy Coalition Approach* (Boulder: Westview, 1993), 27.

43 Claus Offe, 'How Can We Trust Our Fellow Citizens?' in Mark Warren (ed.), *Democracy and Trust* (Cambridge: Cambridge University Press, 1999), 73–5.

44 Offe, 'How Can we Trust?' 75.

45 Ronald Inglehart, *Modernization and Postmodernization: Cultural, Economic, and Political Change in 43 Societies* (Princeton, NJ: Princeton University Press, 1997); Susan J. Pharr and Robert D. Putnam (eds.), *Disaffected Democracies: What's Troubling the Trilateral Countries?* (Princeton, NJ: Princeton University Press, 2000).

46 Fritz W. Scharpf, *Governing in Europe: Effective and Democratic?* (Oxford: Oxford University Press, 1999).

47 Perola Öberg, 'Does Administrative Corporatism Promote Trust and Delib-

244 Éric Montpetit

eration?' *Governance: An International Journal of Policy, Administration and Institutions*, 15 (2002), 455–75.

48 Offe, 'How Can We Trust?' 50.

49 Ibid.

50 Ibid., 51.

51 This is not to say that strategic action never yields positive results. Scharpf, in Chapter 6 of *Games Real Actors Play*, showed how positive results may be obtained through strategic interactions. However, communicative action involves fewer risks.

52 Van Warden, 'Dimensions and Types'; Montpetit, 'Can Québec Neo-corporatist Networks Withstand Canadian Federalism and International-ization?' in Alain-G. Gagnon (ed.), *Québec: State and Society*, 3rd ed. (Peter-borough: Broadview Press, 2004), 165–81.

53 Montpetit, 'Les réseaux néo-corporatistes.'

54 Pierson and Skocpol, 'Historical Institutionalism.'

11

Social Learning, Third Way Politics, and Welfare State Redesign

DENIS SAINT-MARTIN and ALEXANDRA DOBROWOLSKY

I would like to make yet one more appeal for a strong family and child-centred strategy for welfare state reconstruction. A revised social model requires a future-oriented perspective, and must therefore focus on those who will become tomorrow's adults. When goals for the future are defined in terms of maximizing Europe's competitive position in the world economy, the need to invest in today's children becomes obvious.

> Gøsta Esping-Andersen, 2000, *A Welfare State for the 21st Century*, 31. Report to the Portuguese presidency of the European Union, prepared for the Lisbon Summit, March.[1]

[Today] socially minded liberals tend to presume that expensive and inclusive new social programs are impossible. Many try, instead, to appeal to public sympathy by arguing that children should be helped as a separate category. Advocacy groups ... believe that upper-middle class and corporate support is most likely to be forthcoming for social programs framed as 'saving children' or 'investing in America's future'... But child-focused liberalism is not a bold position.

> Theda Skocpol (2000), *The Missing Middle*, 16–17

Early policy efforts at promoting the welfare of children and mothers in the nineteenth century played a key role in the formation of the modern welfare state.[2] Now, as we are entering the twenty-first century, children are once again at the top of the political agenda. As a result of social changes and new knowledge, child-related issues have taken on greater significance across a broad range of policy sectors.[3] Increasingly, decision-makers in industrialized nations are recognizing the importance of the 'early years' as a new policy space worthy of government intervention and new 'social investments.'[4]

The factors driving the current policy focus on children are not the same as the ones in the nineteenth century. Infant mortality rates have radically declined and child labour is no longer a pressing social or political issue, in western countries at least. Today, the challenge is defined as being more closely linked to changes in the labour market, family structure, life-cycle patterns, and gender relations. These changes are creating new risks and new needs. In the postwar era, the risk of poverty was largely concentrated in the elderly population.[5] But nowadays, it has shifted to young people and particularly children living in families headed by single mothers or those headed by two adults with limited job skills.[6]

Both New Labour in Britain and the Liberal Party of Canada have made reducing child poverty one of their central objectives. A plethora of policy initiatives, review documents, and new spending measures show the priority that both the British and Canadian governments now give to reforming social policy in general and to tackling child poverty in particular. Underlying most of these changes is the emergence of what Gøsta Esping-Andersen has called a 'child-centred strategy for welfare state reconstruction.' In this vision children are investments with potentially important subsequent payoffs both in terms of human capital formation and as a way to combat family poverty by facilitating the entry of women into the labour market – enabling women to *de-commodify* themselves, to use Ann Orloff's term.[7]

Whether the current policy interest in children is comparable to what happened in the nineteenth century when the adoption of measures to promote the welfare of children created a policy space that eventually led to a more progressive or generous form of social policy is still moot.[8] Only time will tell. What is becoming apparent, however, is that the various policy transformations that we discuss in the next section, as well as recent empirical evidence showing that social expenditures on children increased in most of the member countries of the Organization for Economic Cooperation and Development (OECD) in the last half of the 1990s, would appear to contradict certain key assumptions that are part of the retrenchment approach to welfare state reform. Following Paul Pierson's path-breaking work, social policy analysts have often described the 1990s as a decade of dismantlement and cutback, or as a period of policy paralysis in the face of powerful and deeply entrenched interests.[10]

But how useful is the retrenchment approach to help us understand the rise of what has been described as the 'investing in children paradigm'[11] or what Theda Skocpol has called 'child-focused liberalism?'[12] This is the key question we are asking in this chapter. Our analytical strategy is to bring ideas and political agency back into the analysis of welfare state restructuring to demonstrate that the social policy landscape is not as 'frozen' as path-dependency arguments have tended to suggest.[13] To do so, we use a policy or social learning approach to examine recent social policy changes in Britain and Canada – two countries that belong to the 'liberal' family of welfare regimes. Between the expansion-retrenchment dichotomy, we argue that there is a space for policy experimentation and redesign, where social learning processes are crucial and much more important than they so far have been deemed to be by the proponents of the retrenchment approach. When restructuring is conceived of within the strict confines of the expansion-retrenchment dichotomy, the only changes that matter are those of a *quantitative* nature measured in terms of either growth or reduction. However, between expansion and retrenchment, there is also a wide range of *qualitative* changes that involve the values, goals, and design of policy that an ideas-based approach can help to illuminate. In other words, if retrenchment has essentially been driven by a politics of interests – by *powering*, to use Heclo's terms,[14] we hypothesize that much of the policy experiments currently undertaken under the 'investing in children' banner are also driven by ideas and social knowledge – by *puzzling*.

The chapter is organized as follows. In the first section we briefly describe the emergence of the 'social investment' model as a new design for reforming the welfare state and provide a sustained critique of the retrenchment approach, highlighting its limitations in accounting for recent changes in social policy. These limitations, we argue, are the product of path dependency and the retrenchment thesis's reification of policy. In contrast, we develop a more actor-based interpretation that underlines the dynamics of social learning. To highlight the centrality of learning processes in the politics of 'investing in children,' the second section looks at the role of various social actors and institutions in producing the knowledge and ideas that gave rise to the recent policy changes where the notion of investing in children figures prominently. The third section compares and contrasts the British and Canadian cases, while the fourth offers some concluding comments.

The Social Investment State and the Retrenchment Approach

In the past few years, terms like the 'social investment model'[15] or the 'social investment state'[16] have emerged in policy circles as a new design for transforming the postwar welfare state. The term 'social investment state' was first coined by Anthony Giddens in his book entitled *The Third Way*, which calls for a 'new partnership' in the assignment of welfare function to families, markets, and states. According to the OECD, the 'social investment approach' requires that social expenditures be focused on areas where returns are maximised in the form of social cohesion and active participation in society and in the labour market. 'As with all investment, this implies taking a long-term view of the costs and benefits ... Such an approach implies greater investment in children ... as well as the maintenance of human capital over the life course.'[17] Since the results that investments are expected to produce are located in the future – children, as future workers – are crucial in this type of scenario.[18] As John Myles and Jill Quadagno have argued, 'if the Third Way has a soft spot it is for children.'[19] Children matter because human capital formation matters. Or as Esping-Andersen has put it, in 'a knowledge intensive society there is one clear guideline for social policy: Give absolute highest priority to ensuring the welfare of children.'[20]

In Great Britain, Prime Minister Tony Blair promised to pursue this priority after releasing a policy document entitled *Children First*, in which he argued that 'the welfare of all our children is central to our reform of the welfare state ... Providing children with a good start in life is the best investment the Government can make.'[21] In Britain the issue of child poverty has been one of the main drivers of social policy reform in the past few years. In his March 1999 Beveridge lecture, Blair set out an 'historic mission' to end child poverty by 2020. During his first term, numerous policy initiatives were put into place by the government to support this new commitment.[22]

As in Britain, reducing child poverty and changes in social policy have almost become synonymous in Canada. The National Children Agenda (NCA) is at the heart of the process of social policy reform. The NCA is an intergovernmental collaborative effort (with the exception of Quebec) led by the Ministerial Council on Social Policy Renewal. This council was created in 1996 at the First Ministers' Meeting, when the prime minister and premiers made tackling child poverty a common priority.[23]

'Powering' and Retrenchment Politics

How useful is the retrenchment approach (RA) to explain recent social policy changes that focus on the notion of investing in children? This is the key question we address in the following pages. But before doing so, we briefly describe the retrenchment approach, as well as its assumptions and methods.

In his classic study of social policy in Britain and Sweden, Hugh Heclo argued that policy development was not only a matter of *powering* – of power struggles among competing interests.[24] Policymaking in his view was also about *puzzling* – learning what to do in a complex social environment. In the past few years, this view of the policy process has produced a significant literature on policy or 'social learning,' which Peter Hall has defined as 'a deliberate attempt to adjust the goals or techniques of policy in the light of the consequences of past policy and new information so as to better obtain the ultimate objects of governance.'[25] The learning approach to policy focuses on ideas and how major changes in policy are the result of a 'paradigm shift.'[26] When a change in paradigm occurs in a given policy sector – such as the shift from Keynesianism to monetarism in the case of economic policy – this is considered to be a fundamental change, not just an incremental adjustment.

Thus, in the early 1990s, while scholars like Hall were describing changes in economic policy in terms of a paradigm shift, students of social policy like Paul Pierson and others were demonstrating that leaders of the new right had failed to achieve their goals of significantly reducing the size of the welfare state.[27] This was mainly due to institutional constraints and the power of the pluralist interests attached to various social programs. Pierson's work very much focused on the sources of *resistance to change,* as he discovered that little reform had occurred in Britain and the United States in spite of the political will of Prime Minister Margaret Thatcher and President Ronald Reagan. As a result of Pierson's work, the resilience of the welfare state and the focus on continuities in social policy across time emerged in the 1990s as a major theme in the scholarly literature.

The politics of retrenchment, as studied by Pierson and others, is very much a product of the time on which it focuses: the 1980s when the new right emerged forcefully in politics with its radical agenda of reducing the size of the state as a way to create more breathing space for the dynamic forces of the market. Students of retrenchment politics took the political goals of the new right seriously: Thatcher and Reagan said they would cut social programs, and students of the welfare state convincingly showed why welfare reform fell short of what these leaders' rhetoric had promised. Even if the analysis was rich in historical and institutional contexts, the key indicators used to measure success or failure were mainly quantitative in nature and focused on social expenditures, since new right leaders had themselves framed their objectives in the quantitative language of reduction. And since the cuts they made in social programs proved to be relatively modest or non-existent, students of retrenchment politics concluded that radical restructuring was not politically feasible because past policy choices conferred upon opponents of retrenchment power and resources that they could mobilize to block or slow down the reform process. As a consequence, the issue of welfare state restructuring has been defined for the past few years as one of 'permanent austerity,'[28] involving either the status quo or small incremental changes.

When Do Small, Successive, Incremental Adjustments Add Up to a 'Big' Change?

The retrenchment approach to the study of the welfare state, then, has been influenced by the politics of the new right of the 1980s, but how does it fare in the current context where the Third Way, rather than the new right, seems to be the dominant political flavour of the day? Third Way leaders in Europe, such as Blair and German Chancellor Gerhard Schroeder – and even the prime minister of Canada – were elected not on a platform of welfare state cutback and retrenchment. They pledged to renew or redesign the welfare state, not to dismantle it. Of course, these kinds of election promises are met with a lot of scepticism by observers, especially in more left-leaning circles. Yet, there is no reason why students of the welfare state should not take such claims seriously: after all, students of retrenchment politics did not question the honesty of Reagan and Thatcher when they both promised to cut social programs. Nobody doubted their motivations. Why should things be different now? Third Way leaders say that they want to modernize and redesign social policy. Their stated objective is not about either *retrenching* or *expanding* the welfare state. Whether this goal is realized or not in the future remains an open question. Nonetheless, it is an objective that seems to raise problems for the retrenchment approach, which sees the history of the modern welfare state through the lenses of a dichotomy opposing a postwar politics of expansion versus a post-1980s politics of retrenchment. Where does redesign of social policy fit in this picture? How can we account for *qualitative* changes to policy in a model equipped to describe change in terms of growth or reduction?

In terms of the retrenchment approach, the evolution of social policy in the past twenty years is marked by incrementalism. But this 'raises the thorny question of how to distinguish radical change from incremental adjustments?'[29] Policy changes are almost always incremental. In public policy, the term 'radical' is politically loaded and always needs to be looked at critically. Only historical perspective can tell if a given change or transformation was radical or not. When looked at from the present, most changes – at least in the world of public policy – appear small and incremental. In other words, students of retrenchment politics are too close to the reality that they are studying – they lack historical distance – to establish a convincing distinction between radical and incremental changes in policy. Their only yardstick for historical comparison is the post–Second World War period of welfare state expansion. But, as Fiona Ross has rightly argued, 'welfare state expansion was also incremental ... Welfare states were not built over a decade or two, so why would we expect them to be dismantled over a decade or two?'[30]

The point here is not to argue that the retrenchment approach is ahistorical. On the contrary, it is often historically overdetermined, placing too much stress on the power of path-dependent institutions in shaping present and future policy possibilities. Rather, the intent is to highlight what Richard Clayton and Jonas Pontusson have called the 'presentist concerns of the retrenchment literature.'[31] Of course, it would be unfair to criticize scholars for not having been able to foresee what happened *after* the period on which they focus much of their analysis (that is, the Reaganite and Thatcherite 1980s). But unlike a good bottle of wine, the retrenchment approach might not be able to age very well. What happens if welfare state politics move into an era where retrenchment does not seem to be the primary goal? Or are we fated to live in an era of retrenchment forever, in what Pierson has called 'permanent austerity?'[32] To put it differently, is it plausible to think that – when taken as a whole – the kind of marginal and incremental adjustments that are said to represent the only type of change possible in the era of retrenchment, might eventually end up looking a lot like a fundamental policy change? In retrospect – and after more than twenty years of small, successive, changes in welfare state restructuring – is it possible that a paradigm shift is taking place in social policy? These are the type of questions that the retrenchment literature is not well equipped to address for at least two reasons. First, as already mentioned, is its 'presentist' concern. Second, is its neglect of the role of ideas and learning processes in policy development, to which we will now turn.

When Policy Becomes Structure

In the retrenchment approach, policy development is primarily a matter of *powering* and not *puzzling*. According to Pierson, 'in retrenchment politics, policy-learning arguments appear to be less applicable. Whatever relevance policy learning may have in other contexts, its role in the formation of the agendas of retrenchment advocates has been minimal.'[33] It is not precisely clear why Pierson has contended that policy learning is not applicable to retrenchment politics. One reason seems to be linked to the ideological vigour or conviction of the new right's agenda. Reagan and Thatcher were so ideologically committed to 'radical retrenchment that lessons learned from the specific features of past policies played very little part.'[34]

A second reason why students of retrenchment have not shown much interest in *puzzling* is that they tend to see policy learning as a technocratic activity that deals primarily with complex policy issues, whose analysis and study often 'remains insulated from broader political conflicts.'[35] Apparently, the details involved in the politics of retrenchment were not sufficiently important for policy learning to matter. Or, alternatively – and this goes back to the first reason mentioned above – everything was so politicized and driven by new right ideology that there was no space for policy learning to matter. In other words, when ideology is strong, policy learning is not as relevant. Yet, somewhat contradictorily, according to Peter Hall, learning processes played a crucial role in driving the shift from Keynesianism to monetarism in British economic policy – a policy sector, which like social policy, was also placed under the command of the same ideologically committed Prime Minister Thatcher.

For Pierson, policy is clearly an independent variable. As he has argued, 'policies themselves must be seen as *politically consequential structures*' (our emphasis).[36] In this view, policies are structures that cause social actors to act in certain ways. While we would agree that policies can affect social action, their meaning is never completely given nor predetermined.[37] As more than thirty years of implementation research shows, the same policy may mean very different things to different actors because policy choices invariably occur in conditions of uncertainty. Cognitive limitations also undermine assumptions of rationality.[38] By not taking into account the processes by which actors give meaning to policies, the retrenchment approach ends up giving greater causal power to policy as structure than agency. Retrenchment fails to take into consideration the 'two-sidedness of the social world,' a world where we are both the creators and the creatures.[39] In other words, the retrenchment approach fails to see policy changes in terms of a relationship between structural possibilities and political agency.

Social Learning and Welfare State Redesign

Our central hypothesis is that policy-learning processes matter more now than they may have under the politics of retrenchment because the current situation cannot be accurately described as one of either cutback or expansion. But before going further, it is important to address the basic question of whether the changes that we associate with the politics of 'investing in children' represent mere incremental adjustments or a significant policy shift. First, as we already have argued, most policy changes are incremental in nature. The other option, of radical change, is not an empirical category. It is a *straw person*, an unrealistic yardstick that students of retrenchment have used to reinforce their thesis about the frozen character of the welfare state. Since no one can show that radical changes have indeed been implemented, the retrenchment thesis looks valid because it is not falsified. But how far can the retrenchment elastic be stretched? Is everything retrenchment? At which point does the cumulative impact of small, successive, incremental change add up to produce a more substantial transformation? Basically, the answer is when the whole becomes more than the sum of the parts. In other words, when something like a more or less coherent paradigm starts to take shape. Of course, the apparent coherence of the paradigm is largely a political construction. By definition, incrementalism is incoherent, it is 'disjointed.'[40] Incrementalism is about muddling through and putting out fires. There is no long-term view. Thus, building coherence in what at first glance may appear to be a long series of isolated and unrelated changes requires, first, historical distance. Coherence can only be built retrospectively. Now, more than twenty years after the rise of the new right, this historical distance exists. Second, it also requires political interests, of the sort found in the dynamics of partisan realignment when parties of the centre (the Liberals in Canada) or the centre-left (Labour in Britain) find themselves largely in agreement with the politics of fiscal conservatism, but are still under strong internal pressures to project a socially caring posture. As we discuss below, however, such historical and political possibilities are strongly shaped by a third variable: the design of the institutions of the welfare state.

Child Poverty in Liberal Regimes

One striking feature that emerges constantly from international comparative studies on child poverty is that the group of countries that Esping-Andersen qualified as belonging to a 'liberal regime' (Britain, Canada, and the United States) all have much higher levels of child poverty than the conservative (France and Germany) and the social democratic regimes (the Nordic countries).[41] In this sense, neo-institutionalists are absolutely right in saying that 'policy shapes politics': liberal social policy does not, by itself, create the problem of child poverty, but it certainly provides the institutional and political conditions to make this a potentially significant public policy issue – to make this a 'focusing event.'[42] The problem of child poverty is more severe in liberal regimes where social benefits are comparatively low and where the degree of *de-commodification* is weak. The problem of child poverty is global and caused by multiple factors. But nowhere has it become a top political issue as it has in the Anglo-Saxon liberal countries.[43] One major study on child poverty in industrialized nations concluded: 'As might be expected, there is an association between welfare effort and low rates of child poverty. Countries with a higher share of national income devoted to welfare transfers and services also tend to have lower child poverty rates.'[44] Of course, market incomes – the revenues derived from paid work – are also crucial in shaping poverty levels. But as Esping-Andersen showed, market incomes and the extent of *de-commodification* generally go hand in hand. Child poverty is thus also a product of 'market failures,' but again, such failures are stronger in liberal regimes.[45]

Although it has become a top policy priority only in recent years, the issue of child poverty in Britain and Canada is not new and has long been the focus of organizations or movements in civil society that are preoccupied with children's welfare. In the two countries, children's aid societies as well as maternalist and pro-natalist movements have long been active in advocating on behalf of children's health and well-being.[46] But throughout the twentieth century, and especially with the 'golden age' of welfare sate expansion that followed the Second World War, child poverty rates declined in most industrialized nations.[47] Child poverty did not disappear altogether, but after the war, children's aid societies and other similar organizations that had been involved in fighting poverty at home began to turn their attention to the global scene, as when the United Nations created the U.N. Children's Emergency Fund (UNICEF) in 1946 to promote children's concerns.[48]

The Canadian Scene

UNICEF has acted as a global catalyst for children's issues both at the international and national levels. In Canada, much of the debate on child poverty was inspired by initiatives taken at the global level, such as the 1979 International Year of the Child and the 1989 U.N. Convention on the Rights of the Child.[49] In response to the passage of the Convention, the Canadian House of Commons unanimously passed in November 1989 a resolution affirming that members of Parliament would seek to eliminate child poverty by the year 2000. Canada is one among many countries that signed the U.N. Convention, which promised certain protections to children's economic and physical well-being. These U.N. activities placed pressure on the Canadian government to promote children's rights and resolve child poverty. Additional pressures came when a number of international studies, especially those using the Luxembourg Income Study database, indicated that Canada in the mid-1980s had one of the highest rates of child poverty.[50] These statistics were subsequently revealed in public hearings before several parliamentary committees and released by the Canadian Council for Social Development (CCSD) in *The Canadian Fact Book on Poverty*, a series of publications produced by the CCSD since the late 1970s.[51]

CCSD is a non-profit organization created in the 1920s. It produces research on security, employment, poverty, child welfare, and social policies.[52] Since the 1980s, data drawn from CCSD studies have been widely used by anti-poverty groups, such as the National Anti-Poverty Organization (NAPO) and the Child Poverty Action Group (CPAG). NAPO is an advocacy organization created in 1971, while CPAG was established in 1986 in Toronto. The Canadian version of CPAG was based on the British model (discussed below) and created to bring public awareness of the poverty experienced by children. Network building has been a key activity of CPAG. In 1988, it initiated the formation of the Child Poverty Coalition. This included several organizations from civil society like the CCSD, the Canadian Council on Children and Youth, the Vanier Institute of the Family, and the Canadian Institute on Child Health.[53] The coalition produced a series of fact sheets and has developed an active lobbying strategy directed at parliamentarians. Advocacy, political lobbying, and a favourable international context created by the 1989 U.N. Convention on the Rights of the Child led the House of Commons to adopt its unanimous resolution of 'eliminating poverty among Canadian children by the year 2000.' This commitment became the organizing focus of the Child Poverty Coalition. In 1991, the Coalition transformed itself into Campaign 2000, a cross-national coalition of organizations and community groups committed to promoting and securing the full implementation of the federal parliament's resolution. Campaign 2000 has grown to a membership of more than eighty-five groups.[54] Campaign 2000 conducts political lobbying and public education activities to keep the issue of child poverty on the policy agenda.[55]

In spite of all this social mobilization, not much was done after 1989 by the Conservative government in terms of implementing policies to fulfil the goal of eradicating child poverty by 2000. But, unlike their counterparts in the House of Commons, who are subjected to strong party discipline, members of the appointed Senate have shown a much greater openness to the ideas advocated by the groups involved in the coalition against child poverty. Following the 1989 resolution, Canadian Senate committees produced a number of reports on child poverty.[56] The Senate's openness to child-related issues was subsequently consolidated with the appointment of Landon Pearson. Pearson, a children rights activist and former head of the Canadian Council on Children and Youth, was a founding member of the coalition that gave birth to Campaign 2000.[57] In May 1996, she was named Advisor on Children's Rights to the Minister of Foreign Affairs to provide advice to the minister concerning children's issues in the foreign policy context.

Throughout the late 1980s and early 1990s, as long as the deficit remained the number one preoccupation of governments, the child poverty movement made little headway. By the late 1990s, however, the federal and many provincial governments managed to get the deficit under control. While some in the ruling Liberal party argued for tax cuts rather than new expenditures, 'the child poverty activists were more in line with majority thinking.'[58]

As mentioned in the first section of the chapter, the prime minister and the provincial premiers agreed in 1996 to make the reduction of child poverty, a collective priority, and subsequently they initiated the National Children's Agenda. The NCA process began in 1997. According to the federal government, the need for a common children's agenda was justified by 'strong evidence, including scientific research, that what happens to children when they are very young shapes their health and well-being throughout their lifetime. Science has proven what we have intrinsically known all along – healthy children grow into healthy, successful adults, who will shape our future.'[59]

The 'science' to which the federal government refers in describing the NCA and which is now finding its way into policy, is derived from neurobiology, developmental psychology, and population health research.[60] As one Canadian observer recently noted, 'the rediscovery, in the policy world, of the role of early childhood as a lifelong determinant of health, well-being and competence ... has occurred because issues of early childhood development began to be expressed in a credible vocabulary for modern society – the vocabulary of science.'[61] In Canada, much of the knowledge focusing on the importance of the early years has been produced and disseminated by the Canadian Institute for Advanced Research.[62] CIAR is a prestigious think tank founded in 1982 by a group of academics and business people as a private sector initiative. Fraser Mustard, CIAR's founding president and a medical scientist, has been described as an 'intellectual activist' who has long been involved in neuroscience and children's health research.[63] As head of the CIAR, Mustard has acted as a 'policy entrepreneur' and established various channels of communication with federal and provincial policymakers to disseminate knowledge about the importance of investing in the early years. In 1995, Mustard made a presentation to the Ontario Conservative caucus a few months before that party was elected to form a majority government. After becoming premier of Ontario, the Conservative leader appointed Mustard on the Premier's Council on Economic Renewal (an advisory body) and asked Mustard to review the research on the lifelong impact of childhood development.[64] Issued in 1999, and entitled the *Early Years Study*, the report by Mustard and his co-author recommended a comprehensive child development strategy. The report called on all levels of government to invest in children and cited research evidence showing that spending produced higher returns in early childhood than at later stages in the life cycle.[65]

The *Early Years Study* involved several researchers from across Canada, as well as community-based organizations and government agencies, such as Human Resources and Development Canada and Statistics Canada. The study used data from the Longitudinal Survey of Children and Youth. Begun in 1994 and funded by the federal government, the LSCY is the most comprehensive survey ever undertaken in Canada.[66] It is conducted by the federal Department of Human Resources and Development, which is responsible for 'ensuring that the data and research results are used to advise policy.'[67] The survey seeks to establish a national database on the life experiences of children and youth and has been tracking more than 22,000 children from birth to age eleven years. The findings from the first cycle of the LSCY were presented at a conference called Investing in Children: A National Research Conference, which was held in Ottawa in late 1998. 'This is an opportunity to turn research into concrete action, an opportunity to apply the research and translate it into action in real life settings,' said the Minister for Human Resources and Development in the opening speech of the conference. 'With the LSCY,' he added, 'we can set out more options. We can make more informed choices ... because we know that solid policies depend on solid information ... [We also] understand that we can learn from international, as well as national and local research ... Our intent is to use knowledge from facts and experiences to guide our choices.'[68]

A few months later, as part of the National Children's Agenda process, federal and provincial ministers of social services agreed to work with their health colleagues to move forward quickly on early childhood development. In February 2000, the federal government tabled what was presented as its 'children's budget.'[69] The Finance Minister announced a $2.5 billion increase per year on the Canada Child Tax Benefit. The budget also outlined the government's strategy for 'investing in Canada's children' and referred to 'current evidence suggesting that the early years of childhood are especially vital to a child's future ability to develop and to learn.'[70]

Within the ranks of the ruling Liberal party, the 'children's budget' set those who wanted tax cuts to help families against those wanting more social spending on children.[71] Among the latter, John Godfrey, a member of Parliament from Toronto, has been described as being 'passionate about the politics of giving children a good start in life.'[72] Godfrey has chaired the Liberal caucus committee on the Children's Agenda and was a former research partner of Fraser Mustard at CIAR. In Ottawa, Godfrey has been said to be 'one of the most outspoken proponents for an activist Children's Agenda – one that is shaped by science.'[73] In 1999, he travelled with the Finance Minister to early childhood education centres so that the Finance Minister could see what Godfrey was talking about. Subsequently presenting his 'children's budget,' the Finance Minister called on 'all governments to work together and reach agreement on a national action plan to support early childhood development.'[74] By September 2000, an intergovernmental agreement on early childhood development was reached between all levels of government. As indicated earlier, Ottawa made a $2.5 billion commitment over five years to early childhood initiatives. In the press release announcing the agreement, First Ministers outlined their vision of early childhood development as an investment in the country's future: 'Canada's future social vitality and economic prosperity depend on the opportunities that are provided to children today. The early years of life are critical in the development and future well-being of the child, establishing the foundation for competence and coping skills that will affect learning, behaviour and health ... New evidence has shown that development from the prenatal period to age six is rapid and dramatic and shapes long-term outcomes ... Intervening early to promote child development during this critical period can have long-term benefits that can extend throughout children's lives ... First Ministers therefore agree to work together so that young children can fulfill their potential to be healthy, safe and secure, ready to learn, and socially engaged and responsible.'[75]

The British Scene

Third Way ideas such as the ones developed by Giddens, and articulated into policy prescriptions by influential think tanks like Demos and the Institute for Public Policy Research, clearly had some impact on New Labour's approach to welfare state reform.[76] As is well known, when Tony Blair became Labour leader in 1994 he sought to change the party's position on economic and social policies, looking for a more market-oriented approach. This change was shaped by domestic and electoral factors. But as Desmond King and his colleague found, 'an important feature of Blair's leadership has been Labour's desire to learn from experience elsewhere. Since 1994 the party has been influenced by developments in the United States.[77] Following President Bill Clinton's election in 1992, Labour 'modernisers' like Blair and Gordon Brown established close links with the new Democratic administration in Washington. And Blair's close personal relationship with Clinton continued to flourish after Labour's election victory in May 1997.[78]

In his articulation of the Third Way, Blair has regularly emphasized that European economies must learn from the achievements of the United States, especially the flexibility of its labour market. Of course, processes of policy learning and 'policy transfer' between Britain and the United States are not new. But they have increasingly been intensified over the past years, especially since the 1980s.[79] Ideological affinities between Thatcher and Reagan provided a rationale for the Conservatives to imitate U.S. policy practices. The Blair administration re-affirmed this connection, and with the advent of Third Way politics, New Labour has been increasingly inclined to look towards American policies in the development of British equivalents.[80] This is reflected in a parliamentary report by the Social Security Committee entitled *Lessons Learned from the United States of America*.[81] This can also be seen in a book by Laurence Mead entitled *From Welfare to Work: Lessons from America*, which was published in 1997 by the Institute of Economic Affairs, a British-based, free market think tank.[82] Labour's strategy for social policy reform 'owes much to ministers' perceptions of developments in the United States.'[83] In a commentary, Frank Field, the Labour Minister for Welfare Reform from 1997 to 1999, gave qualified support to the type of 'workfare' policy outlined by Mead.[84] Field then launched the Green Paper on Welfare Reform, which introduced Labour's new welfare-to-work program and promised, among other things, to tackle 'the scourge of child poverty.'[85] In the 1970s, Field was head of the Child Poverty Action Group (CPAG), an advocacy and research organization that lobbies government on issues related to family poverty.[86]

In Britain, the issue of poverty has been defined as a 'children's issue,' in some quarters at least, since the 1960s, when CPAG was created as a result of research conducted by Titmuss and his colleagues at the London School of Economics.[87] LSE has always been a key site for the production of social knowledge and ideas, especially in relation to the policy agenda of the Labour party, with which the institution has had, since its founding, a 'special connection.'[88] In December 1997,

Blair created the Social Exclusion Unit and located it at the heart of the Whitehall policymaking machinery as a sign of his commitment to foster greater social cohesion in British society. At almost the same time, the Centre for Analysis of Social Exclusion (CASE) was established at LSE to study the processes and institutions that prevent exclusion. Since 1997, various workshops and meetings (focusing mostly on poverty issues) have been organized between CASE researchers and policymakers. A few days after Blair declared his intentions to eradicate child poverty, the Treasury released, in March 1999, *Tackling Poverty and Extending Opportunity*, promising to tackle poverty 'at source.'[89] As the report claimed, 'the seeds of poverty and lack of opportunity are sown in childhood. Children who grow up in poverty are much less likely to succeed as adults.'[90]

The analysis and research evidence on which the report develops its policy prescriptions came from a workshop organized jointly by the Treasury and CASE.[91] The workshop brought together policymakers from various government departments and academics to review the evidence on persistent poverty and lifetime inequality. Much of the data presented at the workshop came from longitudinal studies, such as the National Child Development Study (NCDS). The NCDS is a birth-cohort survey that has been following the lives of a group of people born in Britain in March 1958 (about 17,000 individuals). The aim of the study is to improve understanding of the factors affecting human development over the whole life span.[92] Various datasets (both old and new) drawn from the NCDS have provided an increasing amount of evidence about the effects of child poverty on later life chances. As the Treasury report on *Tackling Poverty* recognized, with the advent of new panel datasets 'we now have the potential to gain new and important insights into the causes of inequality of opportunity' and 'use this as a focus for policy action.'[93]

CASE subsequently released a document entitled *Investing in Children*, which reviews the recent brain research evidence that emphasizes the importance of the early years.[94] The document called on policymakers to raise public investments in children and approvingly cited a 1997 U.S. report of the Council of Economic Advisors to the President (*The First Three Years: Investments That Pay*), in which it is stated that 'scientists and educators have identified the first three years of life as a time when children have "fertile minds." Efforts to help children during these years are especially fruitful. Because of the long-lasting effects, early investments can have big payoffs. They avert the need for more costly interventions later in life, and so contribute to happier, healthier, and more productive children, adolescents, and adults.'[95]

Activists and social organizations concerned with early childhood have also been exercising pressures on government since at least the early 1990s. For example, the Early Childhood Education Forum was created in 1992 to 'raise public awareness and influence public policy in the field of early years care and education.'[96] The Forum is a coalition of third sector organizations, professional associations, and local authority officers. It is organizationally part of the National Children's Bureau. NCB was originally created as an academic research institution. In 1963, NCB transformed itself into a think tank promoting the interests and well-being of children across every aspect of their lives. NCB has a well-established research department, and it was one of the leading actors in the development of the National Child Development Study in the late 1950s. NCB's research department carries out consultancy and policy evaluation studies on matters related to children. It 'works closely with a range of central and local government departments.'[97] NBC also ensures a process of knowledge dissemination to policymakers through publications, special seminars, and conferences. In addition, NCB provides regular advice and briefings to the All Parliamentary Group for Children, a cross-party group of about 140 members of Parliament and Peers that meets approximately once a month to discuss child-related issues. NCB is a founding member of the End Child Poverty Action Group, a broadly based coalition of groups and citizens created in 2001 to build awareness and support for programs and policies to end child poverty in Britain. The End Child Poverty coalition also involves the British Association for Early Childhood Education (BAECE). Wendy Scott, BAECE's chief executive, was appointed in 1999 as a policy adviser on early childhood in the Department of Education.[98]

Over recent years, the Blair government has encouraged a greater role for outside expertise in the policy process.[99] In 1999, the Cabinet Office released its *White Paper on Modernizing Government*, outlining a program of reform of policymaking within Whitehall.[100] Particular emphasis was laid on the need for policymaking to work in 'partnership,' to involve more 'outside experts' and become more outward-looking, 'learning lessons from other countries, and integrating the EU and international dimension into our policymaking.'[101] Attention was also drawn to the problem of ensuring that policies are developed and delivered across institutional boundaries to address issues that cannot be tackled on a departmental basis – the need for what has come to be called 'joined up' governance.[102] 'Joined up' thinking is at the heart of structures like the Social Exclusion Unit and the Children and Young People's Unit. The White Paper also emphasizes drawing lessons from experience, treating policymaking as a continuous learning process involving research, testing, evaluation, and feedback.[103] As part of the White Paper's recommendations, the government has established a new Centre for Management and Policy Studies within the Cabinet Office. The centre is headed by Ron Amman, former chief executive of the Economics and Social Research Council. At the ESRC, Amman was a leading advocate of 'evidence-based policy-making,' which is about using research evidence to underpin policy and practice.[104] His job at the Centre is defined as providing 'a window at the heart of government for the best new thinking from the academic community.'[105]

Discussion and Comparisons

Policy-learning processes are difficult to ignore when studying social policy in the current period because the Third Way is in itself an exercise in ideological experimentation. 'Ideological pragmatism' aptly describes the Third Way. Ruth Lister has suggested that the Labour government's key characteristic is pragmatism, epitomized by the slogan 'what matters is what works.'[106] This might be interpreted to be pure rhetoric and political marketing by 'spin' doctors. But it can also be seen as indicating a certain openness or willingness to learn from others. If we reverse the logic of Pierson's argument that ideological conviction under the new right made policy learning marginal in retrenchment, should we not expect policy *puzzling* to play a greater role in the context of the Third Way, where decisions are to be made by non-ideological, pragmatic governments? Of course, in politics, arguments about pragmatism or about defining oneself as being non-ideological are profoundly political gestures. But the point here is that policymakers in appealing to the virtues of pragmatism are seeking to project a more de-politicized view of the policy process, based on 'what works' – which, as mentioned above, is now referred to in Whitehall as 'evidence-based policy-making.'[107]

Another reason for taking *puzzling* more seriously is the nature of the actors who are the object of this growing policy attention: children. Children are not politically controversial. Here the need to *power*, to make political compromise between competing interests is not as strong, because nobody wants to be 'against' children. As Paul Pierson

himself recognized, policy learning is generally more important in relation to issues that remain 'insulated from broader political conflicts.'[108]
In Canada, what came to be known as the 'Children's Agenda' has
indeed been above partisan politics. It was an all-party unanimous
motion in the House of Commons that officially recognized child poverty as a top policy priority in Canada. And as we have seen, the Senate
– which is intended to be a non-partisan chamber of 'sober second
thought' – either through bi-partisan committees or through the work
of individual senators, like Landon Pearson who calls herself the 'Sen-
ator for Children' – played a key role in channelling the ideas of civil
society organizations within state institutions. In Britain, the establishment of the All Parliamentary Group on Children also provides some
indication that child-centred policies can cross party lines.

Exogenous Learning as Social Learning

One important aspect highlighted by the brief account, in the second
section, describing how the politics of 'investing in children' developed in Britain and Canada, is the increasingly global character of
policy-learning processes. This is something that students of retrenchment like Pierson have failed to take into consideration when arguing
that *powering* is more important than *puzzling* in restructuring the welfare state. The problem is that Pierson used a very narrow conception
of policy learning, which is seen as the same thing as policy or program evaluation, the 'last' stage in the policy cycle where policymakers
gather data to learn about the performance and impact of government
programs. Policy evaluation is, of course, a learning exercise. The point
is that this is just one among many other types of learning exercises
involved in the policy process. In the past, policy evaluation was
largely conducted inside government, by bureaucrats. In countries
where government has a parliamentary form, policy evaluation studies have usually been produced by government itself, rather than by
think tanks and independent research institutes, as this is more the
case in the United States.[109] In addition, government ministers in both
Britain and Canada are not forced by law (only by politics) to disclose
the results of evaluations done internally by their department. When
government is the main producer of knowledge about the performance
of programs, state officials have somewhat greater control over policy-
learning processes.

But the increasing involvement of outside organizations reduces the ability of ministers to direct policymaking in ways possible within traditional hierarchical structures. In the case of child poverty, a large proportion of the research that sparked the debate in Canada and Britain came from outside government, from domestic social organizations often using data produced at the global level.[111] Policymakers in liberal regimes learned about the effects of social policies as a result of external pressures coming from civil society, by groups like CPAG in Britain or the CCSD in Canada. They did not simply learn about child poverty through their own, internal, social policy evaluation studies. Using a narrow conception of policy learning as policy evaluation would also lead us to conclude that policy-learning processes are irrelevant to explain why the notion of 'investing in children,' has become a rallying point for social policy reform. But things look very different if we use a broader conception of policy learning that also includes the knowledge generated by organizations in civil society. In other words, the idea of 'investing in children,' which has its roots in the 1980s debate about child poverty, is very much a product of *exogenous* – rather than strictly *endogenous* – policy-learning processes. Policy learning can occur endogenously or exogenously. As we have just explained, it can be a process more or less imposed on policymakers from outside government, from the broader social environment. Or it can originate within government, as policymakers attempt to refine and adapt their policies in the light of their past actions.[111] The type of learning, which Pierson argued played no role in retrenchment, is *endogenous* learning; but the type we describe here is more *exogenous*. Of course, the two are not totally separated, but it is analytically useful to make the distinction between them. *Endogenous* learning is somewhat more technical and closer to what Richard Rose has called 'lesson-drawing,'[112] whereas the second type is much closer to what Hugh Heclo and Peter Hall called 'social learning' – which originates outside the policy process and affects the broad goals of policy. Here learning is not restricted to senior politicians and bureaucrats. It extends to a more general social process involving civil society actors.

Exogenous policy learning is very similar to the practice of 'learning from others,'[113] or what has been described in the literature as 'policy transfer.' Throughout the 1980s, and as a result of the new public management, most governments spent their energy and resources focusing on improving managerial efficiency and effectiveness.[114] One key goal was to cut 'red tape' and make government 'leaner.' But twenty years of downsizing and cutback management have affected not only the size of government, but also government's research and policy think-ing capacities.[115] As a result, governments increasingly rely on outside sources of knowledge and expertise for policy development. This is also part of the 'new governance' approach which no longer sees the policymaking process in a top-down, hierarchical manner, but rather as a more open, fluid, pluralist process involving interdependent pol-icy networks.[116] Under such arrangements, policy-learning processes become more *exogenous* than they were in the past.

Policy transfer is not new.[117] But the rapid growth in communica-tions of all types, combined with the dramatic increase in the number of international organizations over the past fifty years, has accelerated the process. Nowadays, organizations like the OECD or the EU have strong research and knowledge dissemination capacities. For example, the OECD's notion of 'active society' has played an influential role in shaping social policy reform in a number of countries.[118] International research projects like the Luxembourg Income Study, which includes twenty-five countries on four continents, greatly contributed to mak-ing child poverty a pressing public policy issue through its research and diffusion activities.[119] In the past twenty years, LIS has enhanced the possibilities for states to 'learn from others' because of its well-accepted method for measuring and comparing poverty across nations.[120] Recently, agencies like the World Bank, the European Coun-cil, as well as U.S. think tanks with global connections such as the Brookings Institution and the Rand Corporation, are all actively advo-cating more 'investments in children.'[121]

But even if the politics of investing in children originates in learning processes that were, at least initially, exogenous, this does not mean that it necessarily represents a society-centric form of politics. On the contrary, children have long been seen as a public or national resource that the state has a responsibility to protect – somewhat like territorial sovereignty, for example. And as all politicians know, children do pro-vide good election material. In Canada, for example, the issue of child poverty became important in the 1980s, when the country was gov-erned by a new right government, elected on a platform of welfare state dismantlement. As we have seen, this issue was to a large extent imposed upon Conservative politicians by external social forces. But Prime Minister Brian Mulroney did not feel compelled to respond to these pressures by putting forward a child-centred project of social policy renewal. Such a project only emerged later, in the mid-1990s, when the Liberals in Canada and then New Labour in Britain, came to power and eventually began to talk about investing in children as a way to distinguish themselves from their Conservative predecessors and as a sign of their commitment to social justice. In the context of the Third Way, the idea of investing in children provides the political 'glue' or strategy to build new social coalitions in favour of what is presented to the public as a more 'activist' version of the liberal approach to social policy.

Conclusion

The notion of 'investing in children' is partly drawn from all the *puzzling*, researching, and thinking in which experts from a wide variety of disciplines have been engaged over the years as a result of changes in the labour market, the structure of the family, and life cycle patterns. New knowledge has been produced using datasets recently made available from longitudinal studies on child development. Of course, data 'never speak by themselves' – not in the policy world at least – and the experts, scientists, and others involved in social policy *puzzling* have all interpreted the recently made available evidence in different ways. But in spite of all these differences, views increasingly tend to converge and underscore the need for a children-centred strategy of social policy renewal.[122] For experts in the health sector, economists in the field of human capital, education specialists seeking to improve the ability for lifelong learning, labour market analysts looking for ways to increase women's participation in the market, and even for demographers and pro-natalists preoccupied with declining rates of fertility and the future fiscal sustainability of the welfare state, the focus on the early years appears to constitute an optimal policy strategy for the post-industrial welfare state.

But, of course, even if in the *puzzling* process experts may have come up with what seems to be a technically efficient idea or theoretical construct for addressing a range of social policy problems, ideas – even when they are good – do not always become policies. Experts have often developed interesting theories and concepts that have had little or no impact on policy. 'To become policy, ideas must link up with politics – the mobilization of consent for policy.'[123] And politics involves power. It is here that the *puzzling* of experts meets the *powering* of politicians. When this 'link up' process is successful, significant policy shifts are likely to emerge. In short, the notion of investing in children triumphed in Britain and Canada in part because of the increasing scientific credibility of early childhood development issues,[124] and because of its attraction as a political strategy to forge a new social coalition – of the sort looked for by *Third Way* leaders.

In terms of the overall argument made in this chapter, this conclusion leads to at least two observations. First, although we have emphasized the importance of policy learning throughout the chapter, it is important to recognize that politics – *powering* – is not absent from current attempts at constructing a child-centred approach to social policy renewal. Rather, the point is to highlight how students of retrenchment have, in their own words, 'downplayed the independent role of ideas and learning processes in ... the politics of programmatic retrenchment.'[125] In this chapter, we have tried to avoid using a strategy of either/or: *puzzling* or *powering*. Even if we have put more emphasis on the role of learning processes, we are well aware that without politics, the notion of investing in children would have had no impact on policy. In short, we have followed Heclo's advice: the policy process is both a matter of *puzzling* and *powering*. This is something that students of retrenchment seem to have forgotten along the way.

The second and last point has to do with the label most adequate to describe the current era. We have argued throughout the chapter that the retrenchment label is not useful to describe the type of social policy experimentation that is now occurring in Britain and Canada in the name of 'investing in children.' Students of retrenchment may not entirely disagree with this analysis and are likely to argue that we may now have entered a new expansionary era – the other side in their favoured retrenchment–expansion dichotomy. If this argument is correct, it is, accordingly, not inappropriate to bring policy-learning arguments back, since *puzzling* was indeed a crucial element in the postwar politics of welfare state expansion. In other words, if we really are in an era of expansion, as students of retrenchment would call it, then it is only 'normal' to expect ideas to play a more important role in policy development. We would strongly disagree with such a view. If the current period cannot be adequately described as merely one of retrenchment or dismantlement, as we have argued, it is far from certain that it can be represented as a period of welfare state expansion. Expansion is indeed taking place in some sectors, such as spending on children and families. But growth in one sector often comes at the price of reduction in other sectors, such as unemployment insurance, for example. It is much too soon to know if the politics of investing in children will lead to expansion. It is much more fruitful to go beyond the expansion-retrenchment dichotomy and see the current period as one of policy experimentation. This dichotomy may work when looking at the welfare state at the macro-level of aggregate social expenditures. But the welfare state is not a unified entity. Thus, it is more useful to consider a disaggregated view of the welfare state that allows for far greater variations and possibilities across different sectors of social policy.

Notes

An earlier version of this chapter was published as 'Apprentissage social et changement institutionnel: La politique de "l'investissement dans l'enfance" au Canada et en Grande-Bretagne,' *Politique et Sociétés*, 21 (2002), 41–67.

1 http://www.nnn.se/seminar/pdf/report.pdf.
2 Julia S. O'Connor, Ann S. Orloff, and Sheila Shaver, *States, Markets, Families: Gender, Liberalism and Social Policy in Australia, Canada, Great Britain and the United States* (Melbourne: Cambridge University Press, 1999). Susan Pedersen, *Family, Dependence and the Origins of the Welfare State* (Cambridge: Cambridge University Press, 1993).
3 Sheila B. Kamerman, 'The New Politics of Child and Family Policies,' *Social Work*, 41 (1996), 111–28.
4 Council of Economic Advisors, *The First Three Years: Investments That Pay* (Washington, DC: author, 1997).
5 John Myles, *Old Age in the Welfare State* (Lawrence: University Press of Kansas, 1989).
6 Robert Sykes, Bruno Palier, and Pauline M. Prior (eds.), *Globalization and European Welfare States* (New York: Palgrave, 2001).
7 Ann S. Orloff, 'Gender and the Social Rights of Citizenship,' *American Sociological Review*, 58 (1993), 303–28.
8 Ibid.
9 Sheila B. Kamerman and Alfred J. Kahn, 'Investing in Children: Government Expenditure for Children and Their Families in Western Industrialized Countries,' in Giovanni A. Cornia and Sheldon Danziger (eds.), *Child Poverty and Deprivation in the Industrialized Countries, 1945–1995* (Oxford: Oxford University Press, 1997), 91–121. Sheila B. Kamerman and Alfred J. Kahn, 'Child and Family Policies in an Era of Social Policy Retrenchment and Restructuring,' in Koen Vleminckx and Timothy S. Smeeding (eds.), *Child Well-Being, Child Poverty and Child Policy in Modern Nations* (Bristol: Policy Press, 2001), 501–26. Rebecca L. Clark, Rosalind Berkowitz King, Christopher Spiro, and C. Eugene Steuerle, *Federal Expenditures on Children,*

1960–1997 (Toronto: Urban Institute, 2001). http://newfederalism.urban. org/html/op45/occa45.html.

10 Colin Hay, 'Globalization, Welfare Retrenchment and the Logic of No Alternative,' *Journal of Social Policy,* 27 (1998), 525–32. Alain Noël, 'Permanent Austerity? Deliberating the Post-Industrial Welfare State,' paper prepared for the XVIIIth World Congress of the International Political Science Association, Quebec, 1 Aug. 2000; Fiona Ross, 'Interest and Choice in the "Not Quite so New" Politics of Welfare,' *West European Politics*, 23 (2000), 11–34.

11 Jane Jenson, 'Canada's Shifting Citizenship Regime: Investing in Children,' in Michael Keating and Trevor C. Salmon (eds.), *The Dynamics of Decentralization* (Montreal and Kingston: McGill-Queen's University Press, 2001), 107–24.

12 Theda Skocpol, *The Missing Middle* (New York: W.W. Norton, 2000), 17.

13 Gøsta Esping-Andersen, 'After the Golden Age? Welfare State Dilemmas in a Global Economy,' in Gøsta Esping-Andersen (ed.), *Welfare States in Transition: National Adaptations in Global Economies* (London: Sage, 1996), 24.

14 Hugh Heclo, *Social Policy in Britain and Sweden* (New Haven: Yale University Press, 1974).

15 John Midgley, 'Growth, Redistribution and Welfare: Toward Social Investment,' *Social Service Review,* 74 (1999), 3–21; John Myles and Deborah Street, *Should the Economic Life Course Be Redesigned?* (Working Paper Series, Pepper Institute on Aging and Public Policy, Florida State University, 1994).

16 Anthony Giddens, *The Third Way: The Renewal of Social Democracy* (Cambridge: Polity Press, 1998).

17 www.oecd.org//publications/letter/0601.html. See also Ruth Lister, 'Investing in the Citizen-Workers of the Future: Transformations in Citizenship under New Labour,' *Social Policy and Administration*, 37 (2003) 427–43.

18 Denis Saint-Martin, 'De l'État-providence à l'État d'investissement social?' in Leslie Pal (ed.), *How Ottawa Spends 2000–2001: Past Imperfect, Future Tense* (Toronto: Oxford University Press, 2000), 33–58.

19 John Myles and Jill Quadagno, 'Envisioning a Third Way: The Welfare State in the 21st Century,' *Contemporary Sociology,* 29 (2000), 27.

20 Gøsta Esping-Andersen, *A Welfare State for the 21st Century.* Report to the Portugese Presidency of the European Union, prepared for the Lisbon Summit, 2000, 3. http://www.nnn.se/seminar/pdf/report.pdf.

21 http://www.dss.gov.uk/publications/dss/1998/csgp/main/foreword.htm.

22 Alexandra Dobrowolsky, 'Rhetoric versus Reality: The Figure of the Child and New Labour's Strategic "Social Investment State,"' *Studies in Political Economy*, 69 (2002), 43–73.

23 http://socialunion.gc.ca/news/96nov27e.html.
24 Heclo, *Social Policy.*
25 Peter Hall, 'Policy Paradigms, Social Learning and the State,' *Comparative Politics,* 25 (1993), 278.
26 Jane Jenson, 'Paradigms and Political Discourse: Protective Legislation in France and the U.S. before 1914,' *Canadian Journal of Political Science,* 22 (1989), 235–58.
27 Paul Pierson, *Dismantling the Welfare State?* (Cambridge: Cambridge University Press. 1994).
28 Paul Pierson, 'Irresistible Forces, Immovable Objects: Post-Industrial Welfare States Confront Permanent Austerity,' *Journal of European Public Policy,* 5 (1998), 539–60.
29 Richard Clayton and Jonas Pontusson, 'Welfare State Retrenchment Revisited: Entitlement Cuts, Public Sector Restructuring, and Inegalitarian Trends in Advanced Capitalist Countries,' *World Politics,* 51 (1998), 67–98.
30 Ross, 'Interest and Choice,' 6.
31 Clayton and Pontusson, 'Welfare State Retrenchment Revisited,' 69.
32 Pierson, 'Irresistible Forces.'
33 Pierson, *Dismantling the Welfare State?* 48.
34 Ibid., 49.
35 Ibid., 42.
36 Ibid., 46.
37 John W. Kingdon, *Agendas, Alternatives and Public Policies,* 2nd ed. (New York: HarperCollins, 1995).
38 Frank Fischer and John Forrester (eds.), *The Argumentative Turn in Policy Analysis* (Durham: Duke University Press, 1993).
39 Philip Abrams, *Historical Sociology* (Ithaca: Cornell University Press, 1982).
40 Charles Lindblom, *The Policy Making Process* (Englewood Cliffs, NJ: Prentice-Hall, 1968).
41 Gøsta Esping-Andersen, *The Three Worlds of Welfare Capitalism* (Princeton, NJ: Princeton University Press, 1990).
42 Thomas A. Birkland, *After Disaster: Agenda Setting, Public Policy and Focusing Events* (Washington, DC: Georgetown University Press, 1997).
43 Koen Vleminckx and Timothy S. Smeeding (eds.), *Child Well-Being, Child Poverty and Child Policy in Modern Nations* (Bristol: Policy Press, 2001).
44 Bruce Bradbury and Markus Jäntti, *Child Poverty across Industrializing Nations* (Innocenti Occasional Papers, Economic and Social Policy Series no. 71, UNICEF International Child Development Centre, Florence, 1999), 55.
45 John Myles, *When Markets Fail: Social Welfare in Canada and the United States*

(Working Paper Series, Pepper Institute on Aging and Public Policy, Florida State University, 1995).

46 Lisa A. Merkel-Holguin and Eve P. Smith (eds.), *A History of Child Welfare* (New Brunswick, NJ: Transaction Books, 1996).

47 Giovanni A. Cornia and Sheldon Danziger, *Child Poverty and Deprivation in the Industrialized Countries, 1945–1995* (Oxford: Oxford University Press, 1997).

48 Maggie Black, *Children First: The Story of the UNICEF, Past and Present* (New York: Oxford University Press, 1996).

49 Rianne Mahon, *School-aged Children across Canada: A Patchwork of Public Policies* (Ottawa: Canadian Policy Research Networks, CPRN Study no. F/10), 2001.

50 Maureen Baker, *Canadian Family Policies: Cross-National Comparisons* (Toronto: University of Toronto Press), 1995.

51 Richard Splane, *75 Years of Community Service to Canada: The Canadian Council on Social Development, 1920–1995* (Ottawa: CCSD, 1996).

52 http://www.ccsd.ca.

53 Susan McGrath, 'Child Poverty Advocacy and the Politics of Influence,' in Jane Pulkingham and Gordon Ternowetsky (eds.), *Child and Family Policies: Struggles, Strategies and Options* (Halifax: Fernwood Publishing, 1997), 183.

54 http://www.campaign2000.ca.

55 David Hay, 'Campaign 2000: Family and Child Poverty in Canada,' in Pulkingham and Ternowetsky, *Child and Family Policies*, 116–33.

56 See, for example, Senate Committee on Social Affairs: *Child Poverty and Adult Social Problems*, Dec. 1989, and *Children in Poverty: Toward a Better Future*, Jan. 1991.

57 http://sen.parl.gc.ca/lpearson.

58 Mahon, *School-aged Children*, 10.

59 http://socialunion.gc.ca/nca/nca1_e.html.

60 Daniel Keating and Clyde Hertzman (eds.), *Developmental Health and the Wealth of Nations* (New York: Guilford Press, 1999).

61 Clyde Hertzman, 'The Case for an Early Childhood Development Strategy,' *Isuma: Canadian Journal of Policy Research*, 1 (2000), 16.

62 http://www.ciar.ca/.

63 Edward Greenspon, 'A Year in the Life of the Canadian Family,' *Globe and Mail*, 11 September 1999.

64 Fraser Mustard, Margaret N. McCain, and Jane Bertrand, 'Changing Beliefs to Change Policy: The Early Years Study,' *Isuma: Canadian Journal of Policy Research*, 1 (2000), 76.

65 http://www.childsec.gov.on.ca/3_resources/early_years_study/early _years_study.pdf.

66 http://www.hrdc-drhc.gc.ca/arb/conferences/nlscyconf/flyer-e.shtml.

67 Satya Brink and Susan McKellar, 'NLSCY: A Unique Canadian Survey,' *Isuma: Canadian Journal of Policy Research*, 1 (2000), 111.

68 *http://www.hrdc-drhc.gc.ca/arb/nlscy-elnej/Pettigrew.pdf.*

69 Alanna Mitchell, 'The Children's Budget: Faith and Disbelief,' *Globe and Mail*, 21 January 2000.

70 http://www.fin.gc.ca/budget00/bp/bpch6_2e.htm#Children.

71 Leslie Pal (ed.), *How Ottawa Spends 2000–2001: Past Imperfect, Future Tense* (Toronto: Oxford University Press, 2000).

72 Anne McIlroy, 'An MP's Passion for Families,' *Globe and Mail*, 18 September 1999.

73 McIlroy, 'An MP's Passion.'

74 http://www.fin.gc.ca/budget00/features/bud_child_e.html.

75 http://socialunion.gc.ca/news/110900_e.html.

76 Alan Finlayson, 'Third Way Theory,' *Political Quarterly*, 70 (1999), 271–80.

77 Desmond King and Mark Wickham-Jones, 'From Clinton to Blair: The Democratic Party Origins of Welfare to Work,' *Political Quarterly*, 70 (1999), 63.

78 Alan Deacon, 'Learning from the U.S.: The influence of American Ideas upon New Labour thinking on Welfare Reform,' *Policy and Politics*, 28 (2000), 5–18; Robert Walker, 'The Americanization of British Welfare: A Case-Study of Policy Transfer,' *Focus*, 19 (1998), 32–40.

79 Harold Wolman, 'Understanding Cross-National Policy Transfers: The Case of Britain and the U.S.,' *Governance*, 5 (1992), 27–45. David P. Dolowitz, *Learning from America: Policy Transfer and the Development of the British Workfare State* (Sussex: Sussex Academic Press 1998).

80 Alan Deacon, 'Learning from the U.S.' 5–18.

81 http://www.publications.parliament.uk/pa/cm199798/cmselect/ cmsocsec/552ii/ss0202.htm.

82 In the United States, academics like Mead provided much of the theoretical underpinnings for the New Democrats' policy on welfare (see King and Wickham-Jones, 'From Clinton to Blair,' 64).

83 Laurence Mead, in Alan Deacon (ed.), *From Welfare to Work: Lessons from America* (London: Institute of Economic Affairs, 1997), xiii.

84 Frank Field, 'Re-inventing Welfare: A Response to Laurence Mead,' in Alan Deacon (ed.), *From Welfare to Work: Lessons from America* (London: Institute of Economic Affairs, 1997).

85 *http://www.dss.gov.uk/publications/dss/1998/pip/index.htm.*

86 Frank Field, *Poverty and Politics: The Inside Story of the Child Poverty Action Group Campaigns of the 1970s* (London: Heinemann, 1982).

87 Rodney Lowe and Paul Nicholson, 'The Formation of the Child Poverty Action Group,' *Contemporary Record*, 9 (1995), 612–37; Keith Banting, *Poverty, Politics and Policy: Britain in the 1960s* (London: Macmillan, 1979), 72–3.

88 Ralf Dahrendorf, *LSE: A History of the London School of Economics and Political Science, 1895–1995* (New York : Oxford University Press, 1995).

89 *http://www.hm-treasury.gov.uk/pdf/1999/povertyall.pdf.*

90 http://www.hm-treasury.gov.uk/pdf/1999/povertyall.pdf, 3.

91 http://www.hm-treasury.gov.uk/pdf/1999/perspov2.pdf.

92 http://www.mimas.ac.uk/surveys/ncds/.

93 http://www.hm-treasury.gov.uk/pdf/1999/povertyall.pdf, 3–5.

94 Sheldon Danziger and Jane Waldfogel, *Investing in Children: What Do We Know? What Should We Do?* CASE Paper no. 34 (Centre for Analysis of Social Exclusion, London School of Economics, 2000).

95 Council of Economic Advisors, *The First Three Years*, 22.

96 http://www.ncb.org.uk/.

97 http://www.ncb.org.uk/.

98 http://www.early-education.org.uk/.

99 Neil Williams, 'Modernising Government: Policy-Making within Whitehall,' *Political Quarterly*, 70 (1999), 452–60.

100 http://www.cabinet-office.gov.uk/moderngov/download/modgov.pdf.

101 http://www.cabinet-office.gov.uk/moderngov/download/modgov.pdf, 16.

102 Rod A.W. Rhodes, 'New Labour's Civil Service: Summing-up 'Joining-up,' *Political Quarterly*, 71 (2000), 151–67.

103 http://www.cabinet-office.gov.uk/moderngov/download/modgov.pdf, 17.

104 http://www.bl.uk/information/news/h-t156–2.html.

105 http://www.cmps.gov.uk/.

106 Ruth Lister, 'Doing Good by Stealth: The Politics of Poverty and Inequality under New Labour,' *New Economy*, 8 (2001), 67.

107 http://www.bl.uk/information/news/h-t156–2.html.

108 Pierson, *Dismantling the Welfare State?* 42.

109 James A. Smith, *The Ideas Brokers: Think Tanks and the Rise of the New Policy Elite* (New York: Free Press, 1991).

110 Keith Pringle, *Children and Social Welfare in Europe* (Philadelphia: Open University Press, 1998); Jane Pulkingham and Gordon Ternowetsky (eds.), *Child and Family Policies: Struggles, Strategies and Options* (Halifax: Fernwood Publishing. 1997).

111 Colin J. Bennett and Michael Howlett, 'The Lessons of Learning: Reconciling Theories of Policy Learning and Policy Change,' *Policy Sciences*, 25
(1992), 275–94.

112 Richard Rose, *Lesson-Drawing in Public Policy* (Chatham: Chatham House,
1993).

113 James I. Gow, *Learning from Others: Administrative Innovations among Canadian Governments* (Ottawa: Canadian Centre for Management Development, 1994).

114 Denis Saint-Martin, *Building the New Managerialist State: Consultants and
the Politics of Public Sector Reform in Comparative Perspective* (Oxford:
Oxford University Press, 2000).

115 Herman Bakvis, 'Rebuilding Policy Capacity in the Era of the Fiscal Divi-
dend,' *Governance*, 13 (2000), 71–104.

116 Rod A.W. Rhodes, *Understanding Governance* (Buckingham: Open University Press, 1997).

117 David P. Dolowitz and David Marsh, 'Learning from Abroad: The Role of
Policy Transfer in Contemporary Policy-Making,' *Governance*, 13 (2000),
5–24.

118 William Walters, 'The Active Society: New Designs for Social Policy,'
Policy and Politics, 25 (1997), 221–32.

119 Cornia and Danziger, *Child Poverty*.

120 Scott Groginsky, Steve Christian, and Laurie McConnell, 'Early Childhood
Initiatives in the States: Translating Research into Policy,' *State Legislative
Report*, 23 (1998), 14 June.

121 See, for example, Mary E. Young, *Early Child Development: Investing in the
Future* (Washington, DC: World Bank, 2000). See also the 2000 report
Investing in Children by the Children's Roundtable at the Brookings Institu-
tion, and the study by Lynn A. Karoly et al., *Investing in Our Children*
(Rand Corporation, 1998).

122 Groginsky, Christian, and McConnell, 'Early Childhood Initiatives.'

123 Peter Gourevitch, 'Keynesian Politics,' in Peter A. Hall (ed.), *The Political
Power of Economic Ideas* (Princeton: Princeton University Press, 1989), 87.

124 Hertzman, 'The Case for an Early Childhood Development Strategy,' 16.

125 Pierson, *Dismantling the Welfare State?* 177.

12

National Institutional Veto Points and Continental Policy Change: Failing to Amend the U.S.–Canada Migratory Birds Convention

LUC JUILLET

The growth in popularity of new institutionalism has renewed attention to the influence of the institutional context of political relations on policy development and change. With few exceptions, the impact of domestic political institutions has not been extensively explored in the field of international policy. Using some of the theoretical tools developed by new institutionalism, especially the concept of veto point, this chapter is a contribution towards our understanding of international policy change. Through analysis of a case drawn from U.S.-Canada environmental policy, it is argued that domestic political institutions, as well as transnational political activism, should be considered important variables for understanding the political dynamics of continental policy change.

In the late 1970s, the American and Canadian governments attempted to amend the U.S.–Canada Migratory Birds Convention in order to modify some provisions causing prejudice to aboriginal communities living in northern Canada and Alaska. The Migratory Birds Convention underpins the North American regime for protecting birds that migrate between the two countries, including waterfowl species that are the object of an important annual harvest. Ratified in 1916 amidst concerns for declining bird populations, the Convention imposed a ban on killing waterfowl during the reproductive season. Unfortunately, because of migration patterns, the ban had the effect of rendering illegal the subsistence harvest of these birds by aboriginal communities living in the north. In 1979, both national governments signed an agreement to amend the Convention to rectify this situation.

However, despite several years of efforts, the parties were unable to ensure ratification of the protocol of amendment.

This chapter examines and explains this failure. Ratification of the 1979 protocol of amendment was blocked in the United States by opposition from environmental groups, recreational hunters, and state wildlife agencies, who feared that its implementation, particularly in Canada, would lead to sharply increased and uncontrolled kills by aboriginal peoples and endanger the sustainability of bird populations. However, it was the institutional requirements for treaty ratification both in the United States and Canada that played the key role in structuring the politics leading to abandoning the amendment. The constitutional requirement for Senate approval of any international treaty to which the United States is a party provided opponents an institutional veto point which they could exploit to delay the amendment's ratification – which eventually sealed its fate – even though both national governments were for ratification.

Institutional Vetoes, Treaty-Making, and Continental Policy Change

Veto points and institutional configurations occupy a significant place in new institutionalism.[1] Veto points or veto players can be defined as the set of actors whose formal approval for the adoption of public policy is made necessary by the institutional context.[2] Veto points are generally determined by the constitution or other structural features of the political system, such as the party system.

Different political systems generate different sets of veto players in their policy and legislative processes, and, as a result, their institutional configurations for policy change are not identical. Particular institutional configurations offer correspondingly particular sets of opportunities and incentives to interest groups and state actors seeking to influence policy decisions.[3] In some cases, veto players have the institutional capacity to set the agenda; theirs is an enviable position. These veto players formulate proposals for policy change which will subsequently require the approval of all veto players in that particular institutional environment. Other veto players may have the institutionally sanctioned power to kill or amend a policy proposal but not to set the agenda.

In any case, veto players occupy key points in the policymaking process, and their institutional prerogatives force all policy actors to pay special attention to them. To effect a change in policy, actors must seek to ensure that their policy proposals are acceptable to the veto players. By structuring the process around the approval of key institutional players, the institutional configuration itself contributes significantly to determining the political dynamics concerning particular policy issues. The requirement that actors must gain the approval of veto players means that institutional veto points have an enormous influence on the strategic behaviour of policy actors and on policy outcomes.[4] To change policy, or even preserve the status quo, policy actors must formulate their positions, adapt their political rhetoric, and generally develop their strategy in ways that will win veto players to their side. The impact of veto points on the policymaking process and on the politics of policy change extends far beyond the actual imposition of vetoes by veto players. The very existence of veto players influences the overall politics associated with any policy at issue.

The characteristics of an institutional configuration also contribute to making policy change a more or a less difficult process. Generally speaking, the greater the number of veto points, the less likely the success and the lower the frequency, of change. The size and nature of the winning coalition of actors that is required to effect a change in policy is, at least in part, determined by the institutional parameters of the policy process. Given actors with similar political preferences and resources, differences in political institutions will determine variations in their influence on the policy process and outcome. The more fragmented and open the political institutions, the less likely the success of policy change.[5]

Based on these general propositions, new institutionalists generally argue that for achieving policy change the more open institutions of the U.S. Congress require broader winning coalitions of political actors than would be the case in Canada with its more centralized political institutions of cabinet government. More veto points mean that interest groups and state actors have more possibilities to block undesired changes in policy. In the case of Canada, policy change is to a great extent determined by the preferences of executive state actors who, through their control of a majority of the seats in parliament, are better able to isolate themselves from societal pressures because of the relative scarcity of veto points.

The traditional distinction between American Congressional government and Canadian cabinet government takes on a new dimension in the context of drawing up a treaty between Canada and the United

States. The two countries have different constitutional provisions for the making and ratification of international agreements, and these differences are represented by different institutional configurations for enacting policy change at the international level. The negotiation of international agreements is a prerogative of the executive in the United States. But treaties signed by the executive must obtain the approval of two-thirds of the Senate in order to be ratified by the United States. Once international ratification is secured, treaties become the 'law of the land' and can be implemented domestically by the federal government even when the subject matter falls under state jurisdiction.[6]

In Canada, the institutional context is significantly different. Treaty-making is also an executive prerogative, but the executive alone has the authority to both negotiate and sign binding international agreements. Although an informal practice of consultation has developed, the federal government is not constitutionally obligated to obtain parliamentary approval for the ratification of treaties. The implementation of treaties nevertheless requires domestic legislation to translate international commitments into domestic law. However, given the traditional control of a parliamentary majority and the strength of party discipline in the Canadian parliament, the federal executive generally remains firmly in control of its treaty obligations.[7]

The point of weakness for Canadian institutions lies in the division of powers. The Supreme Court of Canada has found that the federal government cannot domestically enforce its international obligations when these require the adoption of legislative measures that fall within provincial jurisdictions. Then the federal government must secure implementing legislation from each province. As a result, while the federal executive is firmly in control of making treaties, the implementation of treaties opens up a large number of veto points, embodied by provincial governments. The exact number of these veto points is difficult to determine as it depends on the number of provinces whose collaboration is required for effective implementation of the particular obligations of a particular treaty.

History has provided an exception to this institutional reality in the case of Canada. Under Canadian constitutional law, treaties ratified by the British government at the time when it was still conducting Canada's foreign relations, designated as 'Empire treaties' under section 132 of the Constitution Act, 1867, can be implemented unilaterally by the Canadian parliament, even when their subject matter would otherwise fall within provincial jurisdiction. This provision was enacted at the time to ensure that commitments made by the British Crown on behalf of the Commonwealth could be effectively implemented in Canada despite the new division of powers. This historical exception proves crucial for the case under discussion here because the Migratory Birds Convention (MBC), ratified in 1916, is an Empire treaty.

In sum, the constitutional provisions for the making and the ratification of treaties in the United States and Canada offer distinct institutional configurations in both countries. In Canada, institutions provide veto points at the provincial government level when provincial co-operation is required for effective implementation of federal treaties. When the federal government does not have to rely on provincial legislation for implementation because the treaty has Empire status, the single veto point is the federal cabinet. In the United States, although state governments do not have the benefit of a veto on implementation, the requirement for Senate approval provides a decisive veto point. As a result, the federal executive and the Senate floor (and the Senate Foreign Relations Committee) all represent veto opportunities. As such, U.S. institutions provide more opportunities to prevent policy change at the international level.

Using this heuristic framework, this study attempts to shed some light on the political dynamics and the substantive outcome of the failed attempt to amend the Migratory Birds Convention in the late 1970s and early 1980s. It is argued that the opponents of changes to the Convention did not have much success in influencing policy in Canada, in large part because of the lack of accessible veto points. In contrast, these same opponents succeeded in influencing continental policy by focusing their pressures on the U.S. veto point, the U.S. Senate.

Northern Aboriginal Communities and the Migratory Birds Convention

The U.S.–Canada Migratory Birds Convention, ratified in 1916, is one of the oldest international agreements that addresses environmental governance in North America. Negotiated at a time of heightened concerns about over-harvesting and species extinction, the main purpose of the treaty is to provide a framework for the management of bird populations migrating across the two countries in order to prevent excessive depletion of the resource.[8] This objective is pursued mainly through regulations that ban the killing of non-game birds and strictly regulate the harvest of game birds, such as waterfowl. In particular, the Convention imposes a closed season on the harvest of waterfowl, from 1 February to 1 September, in order to limit pressures on bird populations during their reproductive period.

In crafting the Migratory Birds Convention, both national governments paid little attention to the interests and needs of northern aboriginal populations, which represented a relatively minor political constituency at the time. Furthermore, because of the migratory patterns of waterfowl, the closed season effectively resulted in a complete harvest ban in the northern regions, where the main species arrive and depart mostly during this seven-month period. Relatively small populations inhabit these regions, but the value of waterfowl hunting is significant in these communities because many of these individuals still depend on the subsistence harvest for food and clothing and because the aboriginal harvest also embodies special cultural and spiritual value.[9] As a result, the treaty's ban on a spring subsistence harvest was considered as especially egregious by northern aboriginal peoples, indeed, a denial of their way of life.

In the 1970s, the realization of large-scale natural resource development projects, mainly oil extraction in Alaska and hydroelectricity production in Canada, made it imperative to establish more peaceful relationships with northern aboriginal communities and to clarify the right of access to northern natural resources. These imperatives led to new legislation and the signing of landmark agreements, such as the Alaska Native Claims Settlement Act in 1971 and the James Bay and Northern Quebec Agreement in 1975. They also provided aboriginal leaders with a new bargaining chip, which they used to gain promises about the protection of the subsistence lifestyle of their communities, including the recognition of their right to hunt waterfowl for subsistence throughout the year.[10]

As a result, in July 1978, the Canadian and American governments met for the first time to negotiate an amendment to the Migratory Birds Convention of 1916 to accommodate indigenous subsistence hunters living in the north. The negotiations were expedited and a protocol of amendment was signed the following January. The text of the amendment was somewhat disconcerting in its simplicity and brevity: It amended article 2 to grant to both national governments the authority to set the seasons during which aboriginal peoples could harvest migratory birds for their own nutritional and other essential needs. In sum, the amendment would not have provided a blanket exemption from hunting regulations to indigenous communities as a matter of right, but it would have provided both national governments the possibility of allowing a more extensive, but still limited and regulated, spring harvest by northern aboriginal communities.

Following the signing of the treaty, both countries needed to meet the constitutionally required conditions for ratification. In Canada, the necessary steps were taken quickly: within a few days, the federal cabinet granted permission to the Minister of the Environment to proceed with the ratification of the protocol of amendment through an exchange of instruments.[11] In the United States, however, the Constitution made the process more onerous and it opened the door to a coalition of actors opposing the protocol. In the end, the Administration failed to obtain the required approval of the Senate.

That the protocol of amendment was negotiated and signed without difficulty in a mere six months would suggest a great deal of control by national governments over the conditions of policy change at the international level. However, the subsequent failure to obtain ratification demonstrates the importance of the influence of sub-national state actors, non-state actors, and domestic institutions in shaping such continental policy change. As the following historical analysis will show, by using the veto points open to them, a transnational coalition of opponents to the amendment to the Migratory Birds Convention succeeded in blocking its ratification, despite the clearly expressed position of both national governments in favour of ratification.

The Use of Veto Points: Blocking the Amendment to the Migratory Birds Convention

After the protocol was signed in 1979, the American and Canadian governments were faced with a barrage of opposition from domestic actors.[12] Provincial and state wildlife authorities, environmentalists, and recreational hunters in both countries voiced concern that a poorly controlled aboriginal harvest during the reproductive season would have deleterious effects on the sustainability of several species. Recreational hunting associations also feared that a decline in waterfowl populations would result in a sharp reduction in the quotas for hunters throughout Canada and in the lower 48 states. Some organizations in both countries also argued that permitting an aboriginal harvest during the spring season would be fundamentally inequitable, creating two classes of citizens. Thus, the amendment was opposed because of concerns for the environment, the interests of users living to the south, and differing conceptions of justice.

Opposition in Canada manifested itself soon after it became known that an amendment to the Convention had been negotiated by the Canadian and American governments. Provincial authorities were the first to voice their concerns. Despite assurances by the federal government that the provinces would be consulted on drafting the ensuing regulations, most provinces complained that the federal government had negotiated the amendment without their input.[13] Several federal-provincial meetings were held to reassure provinces; nevertheless, disagreement persisted, and some western provinces even began to threaten to challenge the constitutionality of the amendment in court.[14]

Two prominent conservation groups, the Canadian Wildlife Federation and its American counterpart, the National Wildlife Federation, then joined the provinces in their opposition. They feared that the terms of the amendment, coupled with excessive discretion for both national governments for setting the associated regulations, would lead to an extensive and poorly controlled spring harvest in the north. The two organizations launched a joint campaign to oppose the protocol in the United States, mainly by lobbying against Senate approval.[15]

In hopes of winning them over, the Canadian Environment Minister had his officials meet with the wildlife federations 'to try to convince them that their interests were not pushed aside.'[16] The attempt was a failure. On 6 March 1980, intensifying its efforts at home, the Canadian Wildlife Federation wrote to all provincial ministers responsible for wildlife resources to advise them that CWF had taken a strong stance against the 1979 protocol and that CWF favoured its renegotiation on the basis of consultations with the provinces.

The federal government was not moved. The next month, the Minister of the Environment announced that he wanted to go ahead with ratification and implementation of the protocol notwithstanding the growing opposition. Ratification of the treaty was clearly within the jurisdiction of the federal government and, given the Empire treaty status of the Migratory Birds Convention, implementation of the amendment would not require provincial approval. It was thought that, if needed, the collaboration of provincial wildlife authorities in implementing the as-yet-to-be-drafted regulations could always be gained later.

This resolve on the part of the Canadian executive was soon over-run, however, by the success of lobbying efforts in the United States.

Soon after the Canadian government's decision to go ahead with the amendment despite opposition, the U.S. Department of the Interior notified the Canadian government that the protocol would not get through the U.S. Congress because of the intense lobbying against it by various interest groups. Opposition by American and Canadian environmentalists, as well as by recreational hunters, made it seem very unlikely that the amendment would be approved by the required two-thirds of the U.S. Senate. Thus, international ratification of the agreement was stalled. The Department of the Interior indicated that several U.S. senators had become sufficiently alarmed by the prospect of a poorly controlled aboriginal harvest in the Canadian north that they would withhold their support. The inability to push the protocol of amendment in its original form through the American Senate essentially forced the Canadian government to attempt to accommodate some of its domestic opponents.

Seeking to Overcome the Senatorial Veto

In light of these developments, in 1980 the protocol was further discussed at the annual meeting of the Canadian Council of Resources and Environment Ministers, the main federal-provincial forum on environmental issues. The federal government agreed to explore the possibility of renegotiating some aspects of the protocol. However, during consultations, a senior official of the U.S. Fish and Wildlife Service warned that amending the protocol might, in fact, make it harder to achieve ratification. U.S. Senators were already concerned that the amendment, as it stood, would threaten the sustainability of some bird populations and that declining populations would mean a smaller harvest for U.S. recreational hunters. In this context, demands from Canada's provinces to extend the new spring harvest to additional provincial and territorial residents would not be well-received.

In an attempt to break this impasse, the deputy minister of Environment Canada wrote to his provincial and territorial counterparts in July 1981. He attached a copy of the draft regulations that would be adopted to implement the protocol upon ratification by the United States. The draft regulations made it clear that the new provisions would provide aboriginal peoples only with limited and tightly controlled access to waterfowl in the springtime. The federal government hoped that the draft regulations would serve as a focal point for provincial and territorial input and that this would be sufficient to get their support for the amendment. But the provinces and the territories declined any invitation to engage in discussions over implementation unless they could be associated with the negotiation of the actual agreement. Stuck between wildlife federations advocating the status quo or a new agreement and the provinces seeking both more stringent language on regulations and some exemption for their non-aboriginal citizens, the Canadian government was again at a deadlock.

The outlook for the protocol was not improving in the United States, either. Contemplating mounting political opposition abroad and at home, as well as a potential defeat in the Senate, on 24 January 1981 the U.S. Department of the Interior asked the Senate Foreign Relations Committee to delay further action on the protocol until it had had an opportunity to deal with the growing objections to its ratification.[17] In the preceding months, the most severe blow had come from the International Association of Fish and Wildlife Agencies (IAFWA), which, despite its name, is an association of American state wildlife agencies formed to lobby the federal administration. To firmly express the states' opposition, IAFWA adopted a resolution putting on record 'its opposition to ratification of the protocol by either the United States or Canada until it is clarified which peoples will qualify for subsistence taking of waterfowl and their eggs, what this utilization is estimated to be by species, and how regulations are to be enforced.'[18] By withdrawing its support, IAFWA, which embodied the states' opposition for many U.S. senators, added a powerful voice to the lobby against the protocol.

Recognizing that much of the opposition derived from concerns about the regulation of the spring harvest in Canada,[19] the U.S. government proposed a new strategy to its Canadian counterpart in November 1981: The two countries would negotiate an 'implementation report' with key opposing stakeholders, detailing how the amended convention would be implemented. The implementation report would then be annexed to the protocol of amendment at the time of ratification and would be considered binding on both countries.[20]

In this context, the Canadian government was forced, once again, to try to address domestic concerns in order to overcome institutional barriers originating in the United States. Ottawa's underlying motivations for yielding to this more conciliatory approach are evident in a letter written by the deputy minister of the Department of the Environment to his American counterpart in January 1982: 'While ratification of the Protocol in Canada is not at issue, the delay since the Protocol was signed and the knowledge that ratification in the United States is not assured have encouraged opposition to the Protocol from various sources in Canada. ... [We] have concluded that we should move to have the existing Protocol ratified along with an adequate negotiation [implementation] report.'[21]

The IAFWA assumed a key role in this last effort to avoid the Senate's veto. It organized a meeting in February 1982 of Canadian and American officials, as well as conservation and hunting organizations, including the Wildlife Legislative Fund of America, the Canadian Wildlife Federation, the National Wildlife Federation, the National Rifle Association, Ducks Unlimited, and the Waterfowl Habitat Owners Alliance. At this meeting, the representative of the U.S. Senate Foreign Relations Committee made it clear that the Senate might be willing to tie its approval of the protocol closely to the content of such an implementation report. However, several non-governmental participants in attendance expressed doubts about whether such a procedure would be legally binding. In the end, most hunting and conservation organizations rejected the idea of an implementation report, preferring that the protocol be completely renegotiated.[22] Nevertheless, encouraged by the modest support of some American states, most notably California, the U.S. and the Canadian governments decided to pursue the negotiation of an implementation report.

The Constitution Act of 1982 and the Migratory Birds Convention

It is impossible to know whether the implementation report strategy would have worked. Soon after the meeting, broader political developments in Canada rendered the approach of the 1979 amendment unacceptable for aboriginal peoples in Canada. In the early 1980s, Canadians were in the midst of repatriating and fundamentally amending their constitution. There were bitter debates between Ottawa and the provinces. Besides the adoption of a new Charter of Rights and Freedoms, the 1982 constitutional reform had also provided protection to existing aboriginal and treaty rights. This change had a great impact on the future of the Migratory Birds Convention and the political dynamics underlying its amendment.

The implications for aboriginal rights of the Constitution Act, 1982 were not evident at the time of its adoption. Section 35, on aboriginal rights, was formulated in very broad terms, leaving the details to be worked out later. To define the new constitutional rights of aboriginal peoples more precisely, a series of constitutional conferences were scheduled, with the first to be held in March 1983. However, it was clear that *some* aboriginal rights had been granted constitutional status and that their meaning for subsistence hunting might have serious consequences for the Migratory Birds Convention. This situation created problems of both timing and approach for the proposed amendment to the Convention.

First, the timing of the federal-provincial-aboriginal conferences created problems for the negotiation of an implementation agreement for the protocol. The federal cabinet, at the insistence of the Department of Indian and Northern Affairs (DIAND) and later of the Federal-Provincial Relations Office, expressed the concern that the development of an implementation report defining the rights of northern aboriginal hunters prior to the conclusion of constitutional talks with the provinces and aboriginal associations would hinder these discussions. Moving ahead on the amendment to the Migratory Birds Convention could be interpreted as a sign that the federal government had already made up its mind on a crucial aspect of these rights and was ready to proceed without negotiations with aboriginal peoples. This situation would leave Ottawa vulnerable to severe criticism by aboriginal leaders. Since the definition of aboriginal hunting rights was now a constitutional exercise, it could no longer be dealt with separately from the main constitutional process, especially if the alternative process was heavily influenced by U.S. interests, environmentalists, and recreational hunters. As a result, the negotiation of the implementation report would need to be postponed.

Second, and more importantly, there were now strong concerns about the position of the Canadian Wildlife Service, which held that the new aboriginal spring harvest provisions should only apply to the territory north of 60° and to the area covered by the James Bay and Northern Quebec Agreement. If the aboriginal rights recognized by the Constitution were found to include a right to the yearlong subsistence harvesting of waterfowl on ancestral lands, the approach of the 1979 protocol of amendment to the Migratory Birds Convention, with its emphasis on the assignment of broad administrative discretion for Canadian authorities to define the scope and nature of the subsistence harvest, with the declared intention to limit the harvest to northern communities as opposed to all aboriginal peoples, would likely prove to be unconstitutional. The institutional environment of Canadian politics was shifting, and the resulting institutional configurations might very well render the approach of the 1979 protocol untenable.

At the time, the Canadian Wildlife Service clearly understood how the constitutional changes of 1982 were fundamentally altering the political and legal context of the MBC amendment debate. An internal briefing note written at the time is worth quoting at length:

> The Department of Indian and Northern Affairs and southern Indian organizations have the view that *all* Indians and Inuit throughout Canada, even southern Indians living an urban lifestyle, should benefit under the Protocol *as a matter of aboriginal right*. The Canadian Wildlife Service, the U.S. Fish and Wildlife Service, all provinces and territories and conservation and hunter organizations believe that the *existing* waterfowl hunting seasons can accommodate the needs of *southern* Indians because birds are then available. The Protocol is needed to allow legal access to northern people for subsistence use of birds which are generally only available in the spring and summer ... If the Protocol were to apply to all native Canadians as a matter of aboriginal right, it would be unacceptable to conservation organizations in Canada and the United States and *to the United States Senate*. Without an American agreement, there will be no Protocol amending the 1916 Convention (emphases added).[23]

In other words, the constitutional changes in Canada placed the federal governments of both Canada and the United States in a difficult position with regard to the amendment to the Migratory Birds Convention. The extension of the spring harvest exemption to southern aboriginal communities (at least those with demonstrable aboriginal and treaty rights) increasingly seemed to be required by the Canadian constitutional environment. However, such an expansion of harvesting opportunities would be seen by most people (including those within the Canadian Wildlife Service) as detrimental to conservation and would only diminish the chances for U.S. ratification of the protocol. Thus it happened that the amendment negotiated in 1979 was, for all practical purposes, left to die on the agenda of the Foreign Relations Committee of the U.S. Senate.

Lessons for Understanding Continental Policy Change

What lessons can we draw from this examination of an attempt to amend the U.S.–Canada Migratory Birds Convention in terms of continental policy change in North America and the role of domestic institutions in any such change?

First, this analysis provides a strong indication that transnational lobbying by non-state and sub-national state actors is an important variable for understanding policy change at the international level. The outcome of the case would be impossible to explain by focusing our analysis exclusively on national state actors. The federal governments of both Canada and the United States were able to rapidly conclude an agreement on policy change. This would tend to support the contention that national executive actors in these countries retain the capacity to isolate themselves effectively from societal pressures and exercise firm control of continental bargaining. This case as a whole, however, reveals the significant influence of non-state and sub-national state actors on continental policy change in North America. In the end, the amendment to the Migratory Birds Convention was defeated by the opposition of a transnational coalition of these actors, despite the clear preferences of and substantial efforts deployed by the federal executives in both countries. In a time when the density of transnational networks seems to be expanding, and when Canada and the United States are undergoing increasing continental integration, the importance of recognizing such potential influence should only become more necessary in providing an adequate understanding of continental policy change.

Second, this case study offers strong support for taking into account the intervening role of domestic institutions in realizing or defeating continental policy change. The key role of the U.S. Senate's veto, established by American constitutional requirements for the approval of international treaties, in structuring the politics around the ratification process is particularly revealing. In contrast to the institutional configuration prevailing in the United States, the more centralized Canadian institutions offer fewer opportunities for influence by domestic opponents of policy change at the international level. In spite of clear and widespread opposition from environmentalists, recreational hunters, and provincial authorities, the Canadian executive was quite prepared and capable to push ahead with ratification.

Only after opponents to the protocol succeeded in translating their vocal opposition into a likely defeat of the amendment by the Senate Foreign Relations Committee did the government of Canada show more openness and greater determination to accommodate opponents of the amendment. Indeed, Ottawa was pushed into modifying its policy position by the need to preclude the U.S. Senate's anticipated veto. Canada's more conciliatory proposals, such as the tabling of draft regulations in advance of ratification and its agreement to negotiate a 'binding implementation report,' were both intended as answers to concerns that were deemed to be impeding Senate approval.

In sum, in the context of more open and fragmented institutions, the U.S. Senate became the focal point for opponents of the amendment – on both sides of the border. This veto point was used to great effect by opponents to delay the approval of the protocol, eventually leading to its abandonment. Given the clear preferences of both national executives and their efforts to achieve ratification, the U.S. Senate veto is an indispensable factor in accounting for the fate of the 1979 protocol on the U.S.–Canada Migratory Birds Convention. Moreover, its importance in the continental policy process helps to account for the events and political dynamics that led to the protocol's demise, including the roles and strategies of non-state and sub-national state actors. For example, the development of an informal transnational coalition of opponents allowed, in this case, groups such as the Canadian Wildlife Federation to influence the outcome of the policy process to an extent that would not have been possible within the confines of the Canadian parliamentary system alone.

This case study suggests that transnational strategies may bear some important potential for Canadian non-state actors attempting to influence continental policy changes. Continental integration, as far as it suggests a growth in transnational activism and a more prevalent role for continental treaties, could, in some cases, empower some non-state actors by providing them with broader access to institutional veto points located in other countries, whose approval is required for continental policy change. Provided that they can defend their positions in a language that resonates with these foreign veto players, they could do abroad, because of the fragmented institutions of the U.S. political system, what they are not able to do at home because of the more centralized nature of Canadian institutions.

Third, while this case study should certainly encourage us to extend the use of the veto point theoretical framework to the study of continental governance, it also illustrates the necessity to proceed cautiously. Under other circumstances, provincial governments could have constituted de facto veto points for ratifying continental treaties. If provincial cooperation had proven absolutely essential for effectively implementing the agreement in Canada, there is no doubt that the political dynamics would have been very different. But the Migratory Birds Convention was a special case. Since it was ratified before 1931, its

Empire treaty status effectively closed off any provincial veto points by providing the federal government with the constitutional authority to implement its provisions unilaterally.

This constitutional particularity underscores the importance of grounding new institutionalist analyses in a detailed and contextualized examination of the cases at hand and of being careful in generalizing findings. This is especially important because such institutional complexities and particularities are not rare. For example, the evolving boundaries of the division of powers in Canada and the changing constitutional practices in the United States, such as the growing use of Congressional-Executive Agreements in lieu of international treaties, will matter a great deal in the creation of veto points. We must be careful not to let the desire to increase the import of theoretical propositions lead us into an oversimplification of the institutional environment of contemporary politics. In particular, the tendency of the literature to consider the Canadian political system as a centralized system with very few veto points and the U.S. regime as being more fragmented may prove questionable when accounting for the role of provincial governments in many policy fields.

Finally, the importance of the Constitution Act, 1982 in indirectly deciding the fate of the 1979 protocol on the Migratory Birds Convention serves to illustrate the evolving nature of political institutions and the potential impact of domestic institutional changes on continental policymaking. In essence, changes in domestic institutions can have the consequence of modifying the institutional configuration of the policy process, thereby modifying the relative influence of policy actors and transforming the strategic environment. Depending on the nature of the change and the context in which it is occurring, such change in institutional configurations could increase or diminish the capacity for policy change.

In the case of the 1979 protocol, the recognition of aboriginal rights in the Canadian Constitution Act, 1982, generated significant institutional uncertainty and raised the possibility of providing a new veto to the Canadian courts in charge of upholding a stronger version of aboriginal hunting rights than the one contemplated in the 1979 protocol. Of course, the courts did not have to actually invalidate the measures proposed by the protocol (impose their veto) because the amendment was deliberately abandoned by the national governments many years before greater clarity about the meaning of aboriginal rights was attained through case law. As it turned out, this institutional uncertainty, the possibility of a future adverse court ruling, and the general political shift in favour of a more expansive interpretation of aboriginal rights were enough to prevent the policy change proposed by national wildlife authorities by rendering its terms politically unacceptable.

Although this story goes beyond the historical period examined in this chapter, it should also be noted that the 1982 institutional change eventually contributed to policy change. The recognition of the constitutional rights of aboriginal peoples had the longer term effect of undermining the Migratory Birds Convention itself, which appeared to have become incompatible with Canadian constitutional law because of its restrictions on the aboriginal waterfowl harvest. In the 1990s, the courts' interpretation of aboriginal constitutional rights as they apply to hunting obliged the Canadian and U.S. governments to negotiate a second protocol of amendment to the Convention, one that granted more extensive rights to aboriginal hunters than the 1979 protocol had. The Supreme Court's *Sparrow* decision of 1990, in particular, had the effect of severely weakening the political influence of environmentalists and recreational hunters opposing an aboriginal hunting amendment. By threatening to undermine the Migratory Birds Convention itself, *Sparrow* significantly helped to overcome the U.S. Senate's decision to veto.[24] The more recent developments concerning the Convention could also serve to illustrate how, in some circumstances, institutional changes can be formidable drivers of policy change.

Conclusion

In the preceding analysis, we have shown that the particular institutional configurations provided by the American and Canadian constitutions regarding international treaty-making played an important role in structuring the politics associated with the Migratory Birds Convention throughout the late 1970s and early 1980s. The bilateral efforts of both national executives throughout this period were frustrated by an informal coalition of non-state and sub-national state actors opposed to an aboriginal exception to the continental rules, in force since the late 1910s, protecting migratory birds. While the strength of the opposition mounted by recreational hunters, environmentalists, and sub-national state wildlife authorities undoubtedly accounts for this policy outcome, the institutional veto provided to the U.S. Senate by the American Constitution with regard to the ratification of international treaties is also essential to an explanation of the amendment's failure. It is by enlisting the support of the Senate Foreign Relations Committee that opponents forced both national executives to seek a compromise that would answer their concerns and ultimately block the proposed policy change.

More generally, this case study demonstrates the importance of domestic institutional variables in explaining the outcome and the dynamics of continental policy change. Because of constitutional constraints on international treaty-making, the national institutional configurations of the countries involved, with regard to the processes of treaty-making and ratification, identify specific veto players that acquire disproportionate importance in the policymaking process and affect the domestic and transnational political dynamics surrounding specific attempts at continental policy change. To better ascertain the nature of these veto players and their impact on continental politics and policymaking, further research is necessary. As we have shown, the institutional rules dealing with treaty ratification and implementation in both countries can vary based on the case under consideration; thus, empirical investigation of a broader array of divergent cases would be an appropriate next step.

Notes

1 See, in particular, George Tsebelis, *Veto Players: How Political Institutions Work* (Princeton, NJ: Princeton University Press, 2002), and 'Decision-Making in Political Systems: Veto Players in Presidentialism, Parliamentarism, Multicameralism and Multipartyism,' *British Journal of Political Science*, 25 (1995), 289–325. Ellen Immergut, *Health Politics: Interests and Institutions in Western Europe* (Cambridge: Cambridge University Press, 1992); and Kent Weaver and Bert Rockman (eds.), *Do Institutions Matter?* (Washington, DC: Brookings Institution, 1993).

2 Tsebelis, 'Decision-Making in Political Systems,' 293.

3 Immergut, *Health Politics*, 25–8.

4 It should be emphasized here that, in the perspective adopted in this study, institutions are considered to be intervening variables for explaining political phenomena. They are not replacing such variables as interest groups or class as important units of analysis, but rather they are strengthening interest-based explanations by revealing the impact of the institutional context on group preferences, strategies, and interactions with other actors.

5 Tsebelis, 'Decision-Making in Political Systems,' 313.

6 See Luzius Wildhaber, *Treaty-Making Power and Constitution* (Stuttgart:

Helbing and Litchtenham, 1971), 322–34; and Jeffrey Friesen, 'The Distribution of Treaty-Implementing Powers in Constitutional Federations: Thoughts on the American and Canadian Models,' *Columbia Law Review*, 94 (1994), 1415–50.

7 See Allan E. Gotlieb, *Canadian Treaty-Making* (Toronto: Butterworth, 1968); Friesen, 'The Distribution of Treaty-Implementing Powers'; Ronald J. Delisle, 'Treaty-Making Power in Canada,' in Ontario Advisory Committee on Confederation, *Background Papers and Reports* (Toronto: Queen's Printer of Ontario, 1967), 115–48.

8 For an exploration of the historical context, see Kurkpatrick Dorsey, *The Dawn of Conservation Diplomacy: U.S.–Canadian Wildlife Protection Treaties in the Progressive Era* (Seattle and London: University of Washington Press, 1998).

9 See, for example, C.H. Scott, 'The Socioeconomic Significance of Waterfowl among Canada's Aboriginal Cree: Indigenous Use and Local Management,' *ICBP Technical Publication*, no. 6, 1987; and H. Loon, 'Sharing: You Are Never Alone in a Village,' *Journal of Indigenous Studies*, 3 (1989), 1–12.

10 In the case of the James Bay and Northern Quebec Agreement, this commitment was explicitly inscribed in the agreement itself, see article 24.14.2.

11 The order-in-council authorized the Secretary of State 'to take the action necessary to bring the Protocol into force for Canada.' See Marie-Josée Nadeau, Legal Counsel, Department of the Environment, 'Memorandum to File Entitled Migratory Birds Protocol – Binding Effect of a Negotiation Report,' dated 1 March 1982.

12 Unless indicated otherwise, much of the material of this section was obtained through a series of personal interviews conducted with J. Anthony Keith, a former director of the migratory birds section at the Canadian Wildlife Service, as well as from his personal files dating from the mid-1970s to the mid-1980s, which are kept at the offices of the National Wildlife Research Centre.

13 Letter from John Fraser, Minister of the Environment, to Jack Epp, Minister of Indian and Northern Affairs, dated 6 Feb. 1980; and Canadian Wildlife Service, internal briefing note entitled 'Protocol: Chronological Summary of Significant Developments,' personal files of J. Anthony Keith, undated, 3.

14 The argument was that the amendment was incompatible with the Natural Resources Transfer Agreement. The Canadian Wildlife Service, and the Minister of the Environment, rejected this argument on the basis of a legal opinion from the Department of Justice, which it held since Nov. 1978. See letter from P. M. Ollivier, Associate Deputy Minister, Department of Justice,

to Jim P. Bruce, Assistant Deputy Minister, Department of the Environment, dated 28 Nov. 1978.

15 Letter from Jack Epp, Minister of Indian and Northern Affairs, to John Fraser, Minister of the Environment, dated 12 Dec. 1979, 1.

16 A.G. Loughrey, Director General, Canadian Wildlife Service, Memorandum entitled 'Amendment of Migratory Birds Convention Act – Revised Report,' dated 23 July 1979, 3.

17 Migratory Birds Management Office, U.S. Department of the Interior, *Issue Paper on the U.S./Canada Protocol on Subsistence Hunting of Migratory Birds*, Washington, 18 Aug. 1981, 1.

18 International Association of Fish and Wildlife Agencies (IAFWA), *Resolution No. 17 – Protocol on Migratory Bird Treaty* (Washington, DC: 1980).

19 For example, in Nov. 1981, the National Wildlife Federation wrote again to the Department of the Interior to reiterate its continued opposition to Senate approval. In its letter, the NWF complained that it was frustrated by the refusal of the Department of Interior to come to grips with the fact that the real problem with the protocol was that it endangered the conservation of waterfowl in Canada. Letter from Jay Hair, Executive Vice-President, National Wildlife Federation, to Ray Arnett, Assistant Secretary for Fish, Wildlife and Parks, Department of the Interior, dated 4 Nov. 1981, 1.

20 This option was presented in the following document: Migratory Birds Management Office, U.S. Department of the Interior, *Issue Paper on The U.S./Canada Protocol on Subsistence Hunting of Migratory Birds*. See also, Bert Tétreault, Director General, Canadian Wildlife Service, Memorandum entitled Proposals by U.S. Fish and Wildlife Service on Implementing the Protocol to the Migratory Birds Convention, addressed to M.A. Prahdu, Director of Legal Services, Department of the Environment, dated November 27, 1981.

21 Letter from Blair Seaborn, Deputy Minister, Department of the Environment to Ray Arnett, Assistant Secretary for Fish, Wildlife and Parks, U.S. Department of the Interior, dated 8 Jan. 1982.

22 J. Anthony Keith, Acting Director of Migratory Birds Branch, Canadian Wildlife Service, to Dr William B. Mountain, Assistant Deputy Minister, Environmental Conservation, Department of the Environment, Memorandum entitled 'Discussion on the Protocol to Amend the Migratory Birds Convention,' Washington, dated 10 Feb. 1982, 1.

23 Canadian Wildlife Service, internal briefing note entitled 'Briefing Note: Protocol to Amend the *Migratory Birds Convention*,' personal files of J. Anthony Keith, undated, 2. This political conundrum would eventually be ended by the 1990 *Sparrow* decision, which, for all practical purposes, led

the federal government to work on the assumption of existing constitutional protection for all aboriginal subsistence hunting.

24 For an in-depth examination of these events and negotiation of a second
protocol of amendment to the MBC in the 1990s, see Luc Juillet, *Aboriginal
Rights and the Migratory Birds Convention: Domestic Institutions, Non-State
Actors and International Environmental Governance*, (doctoral dissertation,
Carleton University, Ottawa, 2000).

Part 5

New Institutionalism and International Relations

The last part of this book assesses the impact of new institutionalism on the field of international relations. International relations has its own institutionalist tradition, but this literature rarely comes into contact with the new institutionalism in comparative politics despite the fact that institutionalist analyses in both fields tend to share similar dilemmas. In this context, cross-disciplinary dialogue can only enhance our theoretical understanding of institutions. In this spirit, the contributions in this part show how new institutionalism can be used to gain insight into three issues central to international relations: sovereignty, war and peace, and diplomatic recognition.

This part looks at questions of institutional creation and transformation as well as at the impact of institutions on political processes. The first chapter adopts a design for institutionalist analysis that is often featured in comparative politics, namely, a focus on national political institutions for explaining political outcomes, and uses it in examining war and peace in the international system. This new institutionalist research strategy for international relations presents the advantage of offering more specific causal links than macro-structural approaches such as neo-realism. The two other chapters ask the question of how institutions of a more amorphous nature, sovereignty and international personality, come to emerge and sometimes to disappear. To address these issues, the chapters make use of new institutionalist concepts such as isomorphism in conjunction with insight from constructivist international relations theory.

In his chapter, Norrin Ripsman suggests that new institutionalism can serve to refine 'democratic peace theory,' the idea that democratic states do not wage war against one another. He explains how this theory's foremost weakness is its reliance on the vague concept of 'regime type' which wrongly suggests that all democratic regimes are institutionally alike. Ripsman argues that a focus on intermediate-level institutions can provide not only a linkage between democracy and peace, but also explain why some democratic regimes are more likely to engage in warfare than are others. He identifies elements of institutional differentiation between democratic states which are relevant for explaining war and peace: general political structures such as systems of government and party systems, foreign policy structures, decision-making procedures, and political norms. Ripsman then suggests that democratic states are likely to go to war when these elements form contextual conditions where the political executive is highly autonomous from other branches of the state as well as society.

Deryuan Wu's chapter brings new institutionalism to international relations to examine what he calls the global diffusion of 'One China,' that is, the process by which the People's Republic of China (PRC) has become the sole legitimate political representative of China to the exclusion of Taiwan's Republic of China (ROC). For Wu, the puzzle is the political and diplomatic institutionalization of the 'One China' perspective despite the reality of two different governments controlling the territories across the Taiwan Strait. To explain this seemingly surprising situation, he draws from both historical and sociological institutionalism. From sociological institutionalism, Wu takes the concept of institutional isomorphism. He suggests that the diffusion of the 'One China' perspective followed such a process of isomorphism: the 'Canadian formula' which 'took note' of the PRC's position on Taiwan as an inalienable part of its territory was taken up by most other states. He also shows, using historical institutionalist logic, how the early policy choice of the ROC to speak of 'One China,' internationally represented by Taipei, had the unintended consequence of making it 'hostage' to this position when it became associated with the Beijing diplomacy. Wu then argues that this reproduction process represents a significant constraint on Taiwan, which has come to be treated as a pariah state, and how it empowers Beijing's international leverage on Taipei.

Finally, Jeremy Paltiel's chapter focuses on the traditional reference point of new institutionalism, the state, and on the closely related concept of sovereignty. Paltiel views sovereignty as a historical construct and, drawing from both new institutionalism and institutionalist theories of international relations, looks at how the universalization of the

European conception of statehood has reconstructed East Asian politics along the lines of the western model. He argues that the forcible introduction of the western notion of sovereignty through imperialism profoundly shaped politics in East Asia and, more specifically, the relations of East Asian states with the West. Western norms, Paltiel suggests, were taken and copied by these states for the purpose of becoming legitimate actors in the international system. The chapter considers the cases of Japan, Korea, and Taiwan, although it focuses primarily on China. It includes a discussion of how an international structure, the World Trade Organization, presents Chinese leaders with rules and norms that can be exploited for domestic politics purposes.

13

Moving beyond (or beneath) the Democratic Peace Theory: Intermediate-Level Institutions and Foreign Security Policy

NORRIN M. RIPSMAN

The foreign economic policy literature and the foreign policy literature more broadly have adapted well to new institutionalism. One subfield, however, has remained relatively impervious to its more powerful insights. The foreign security policy literature, dominated as it has been by realists and traditional scholars, has largely ignored the influence of political institutions. To the extent that security theorists have included institutions in their analyses, their focus has been on the role of macrolevel institutions, such as regime type. Indeed, the most popular institutional theory in the security studies area is the widely accepted, but poorly specified 'democratic peace theory' (DPT) which posits that democratic regimes are unlikely to wage war with one another because of their normative and structural constraints. In particular, DPT assumes that public and legislative involvement in the foreign policy processes of democratic states will compel leaders to reject coercion as a means of securing the consent of other free peoples and will slow down the process of mobilization for war, thereby creating time for mediation and negotiations.

In this chapter, I criticize the democratic peace theory from a liberal institutionalist perspective. My argument is that, in their focus on macrolevel institutions, democratic peace theorists have ignored intermediate-level institutions, and this undermines the utility of the theory. Specifically, there are important institutional, procedural, and normative differences between democratic states that affect the foreign policy autonomy of different democratic leaders and, consequently, their ability to make decisions independently of domestic opinion. Domestic political institutions that grant high levels of autonomy reduce the impact of the public and the legislature, thereby eliminating the constraints that democratic peace theorists assume are common to all democracies.

The chapter has three sections. The first introduces democratic peace theory; discusses its structural, normative, and commercial logic; and considers theoretical and empirical challenges made by critics of the theory. The second section criticizes the theory from an institutionalist perspective and discusses the importance of intermediate-level institutions for differentiating between democracies. In the final section, I will consider the importance of new institutionalism for the broader study of foreign security policy.

Democratic Peace Theory and Its Critics

Over the past two centuries, democratic states have been about as war prone as other regimes,[1] but they have rarely, if ever, waged war against each other. Quantitative analyses have so consistently shown that the incidence of war between democracies is near zero that Jack S. Levy has concluded that 'the absence of war between democracies comes as close as anything we have to an empirical law of international relations.'[2] Democratic peace theorists seek to explain this powerful relationship between regime type and conflict by positing that the particular characteristics of democracies prevent them from using force against each other to settle disputes.[3]

Two different, but complementary, mechanisms have been used to explain the dearth of wars between democracies. The normative explanation assumes that these states share certain normative predispositions which embrace the right of all people to self-government and reject coercion as a legitimate means of securing consent from free peoples. Consequently, they prefer to resolve disputes – both internal and external – without resorting to the use of force.[4] Since all democracies are expected to share these norms, they do not feel threatened by other democratic states, and in turn, they are not compelled to threaten or behave aggressively. To borrow from the realist lexicon, the security dilemma between democratic states is almost non-existent. The security dilemma between democratic and non-democratic regimes, however, is intense, because the latter are based on coercion and not consent, with regard to both domestic and international politics. Moreover, democracies do not feel constrained from using force against regimes that do not respect the will of their own population. Thus, democracies tend to remain at peace with other democracies, but frequently find themselves embroiled in conflicts with non-democratic states.

Second, democratic political institutions which require leaders to mobilize public support for policy changes slow down the process of mobilization for war considerably. This is particularly the case because the public, which directly bears the costs of war, and its representatives in the legislature, who depend on public support, will be reluctant to go to war without good reason. Leaders must, therefore, take the time to persuade the country that war is in the national interest. Therefore, the domestic political structures of democratic states create time for peaceful resolution of conflicts. Other democracies are apt to seize upon this time to attempt to resolve disputes without violence, while non-democratic states are likely to exploit this perceived weakness of democracies. Thus, democratic regimes are prone to remain at peace with each other, but hostile towards non-democratic states.[5]

Michael Doyle has identified a third potential explanation for the democratic peace. Because democratic states tend to be free-traders and are hospitable to foreign commerce, a 'spirit of commerce' develops among them which increases the incentives to maintain peace in order to continue reaping the benefits of economic interaction.[6] This 'commercial liberal' argument implies that the economic ties that bind trading states provide them with heavy opportunity costs, in terms of trade and investment, of using force to resolve disputes, as well as an economic means of extracting resources from territory that is more efficient than military force.[7]

There is some disagreement among the theory's proponents about the definition of 'democracy' or, more precisely, the group of states to which the logic of democratic peace theory is supposed to apply. Doyle, drawing upon Immanuel Kant, referred to both 'republican' states – those that have constitutions enshrining the separation of powers, representative government, and the rule of law – and 'liberal' states – those that have 'market and private property economies; polities that are externally sovereign; citizens who possess juridical rights' [and] 'republican' (whether republican or monarchical) representative government.'[8] John Owen's basic unit was the 'liberal democracy,' a state 'that instantiates liberal ideals, one where liberalism is the dominant ideology and citizens have leverage over war decisions.'[9] Bruce Russett used a more standard definition of 'democracy,' incorporating 'a voting franchise for a substantial fraction of citizens, a government brought to power in contested elections, and an executive either popularly elected or responsible to an elected legislature, often with requirements for civil liberties such as free speech.' To these criteria, he added the requirement of 'stability,' namely, that representative government must be in place for three years before a state can earn the designation 'democracy.'[10] Moreover, Russett applied a lower threshold to states of the nineteenth century, because most 'democracies' in that era had more restricted franchises that denied the vote to women, non-propertied men, and other groups. This disagreement provides some confusion about the scope of democratic peace theory. Nonetheless, it has not undermined the theory's widespread popularity.

Critics have attacked democratic peace theory on several grounds. Some challenge the 'fact' of democratic peace. After all, although none of the states that Doyle or Russett defined as democratic waged war against each other while they merited the designation 'democracy,' there are a number of potentially problematic classifications that could lead us to underestimate the incidence of wars between democratic states. The cases most frequently identified as potential wars between democracies include, inter alia: the War of 1812 between the United States and Great Britain; the American Civil War; the Spanish-American War of 1898; Finnish involvement against the Allies in the Second World War; and wars between Israel and Lebanon in 1948 and 1967. In addition, a number of near misses – cases of low-level hostilities, unconventional warfare, and proxy wars between democracies that do not meet the definition of war, yet still represent the use of force – suggest that common democracy may not restrain states from using violence to resolve conflicts with other democratic states. Notable among these are the American covert action against the democratically elected Salvador Allende government in Chile in the 1970s, British support for the invading autocratic Arab states against democratic Israel in 1948–1949, the French reoccupation of the Rhineland in 1923, and several American covert operations against democratically elected governments in the Third World during the Cold War.[11]

Moreover, some critics such as John J. Mearsheimer, contend that the absence of wars between democracies in the past cannot be interpreted as evidence of a democratic peace, because democracies were few and far between for most of this period and, therefore, had few opportunities to come into conflict with each other.[12] Since war is a rare event in international politics, David E. Spiro demonstrated that the absence of war between democracies – even if the questionable cases are correctly classified as not wars between democracies – is not statistically significant and may, therefore, simply reflect random selection.[13] If some or all of the questionable cases are incorrectly classified and do represent wars between democracies, then the empirical record may actually indicate that democratic states wage war with each other as frequently as, or, perhaps, even more frequently than, do other states.

Still others have argued that the absence of war between democracies over the past two centuries can be better understood through a variety of alternative explanations. Realists, such as Christopher Layne, have maintained that balance of power considerations in the twentieth century required the democratic states to align against common, threats, including Imperial Germany, Nazi Germany, and the Soviet Union.[14] Therefore, balance of power or balance of threat theory might provide more appropriate explanations of the national security decisions of democratic states than democratic peace theory does.[15] In addition, during the post–Second World War era the United States was by far the dominant actor in the western alliance and, therefore, used its preponderance of power to maintain order among the many democratic regimes that comprised the West. In the Cold War era, as the United States became a truly global hegemon, it continued to stabilize relations not only among democratic states, but in many cases, among non-democratic regimes as well. Thus, it is possible that hegemonic stability theory can explain the absence of wars between democracies in precisely the periods when democracies became more numerous on the international stage.[16]

Liberal alternative explanations also abound for the postwar period – the most significant period of 'democratic peace.' Indeed, for David R. Davis, John R. Oneal, and Bruce Russett, democratic peace theory has represented only one leg of the 'Kantian tripod for peace.' The high levels of economic interdependence engendered between the states of the western world and the proliferation of cooperative international institutions also served to dampen conflict in precisely the part of the world where democracies abounded.[17] Although these complementary liberal theories of commercial liberalism and liberal institutionalism both have their critics,[18] they do offer plausible competing explanations for democratic peace theory. For how could we conclude with certainty that, absent the proliferation of democratic regimes, economic interdependence and international institutions would not maintain peace and stability? Thus, peace is overdetermined in the most important postwar era by both liberal and realist factors, making it extremely difficult to find conclusive empirical support for the democratic peace proposition.

One could also challenge the theoretical foundation of the theory. An implicit and essential assumption of the structural DPT is that, in all polities, the public is more peaceful than are its leaders. After all, the people bear the costs of war, both economic and physical; leaders typically do not risk their persons in war, and they can compensate themselves for economic losses through increased taxation.[19] This must hold true even in non-democratic states since the theory assumes that changing the structure of all polities to democracy will restrain them from using force because of structural constraints that empower the people and their representatives in the legislature. In many instances, however, this assumption is empirically false.

One need only consider the two long-running contemporary 'peace processes' – between Israel and the Palestinians and between the Unionists and the Republicans in Northern Ireland – to observe that both are top-down, rather than bottom-up processes. Over the years, leaders of both sides of both of these negotiations have made unpopular compromises in the name of peace that they subsequently had to sell to their reluctant constituents. Indeed, Israeli Prime Minister Yitzhak Rabin paid the ultimate price for moving too far ahead of his population in the name of a settlement. For their parts, Kings Hussein and Abdullah of Jordan, President Hosni Mubarak of Egypt, and Chairman Yasser Arafat of the Palestinian Authority have all faced constant domestic pressure and the threat of insurrection as a result of their peace agreements with Israel.

That the public can be more bellicose than its leaders also has a strong theoretical foundation. Two contending theories of international relations – the traditional realist theory of foreign policy and the diversionary war theory – both make this assumption. Traditional realists, such as Walter Lippmann, Reinhold Neibuhr, and others, argued that democratic states have a difficult time reaching conciliatory, stable postwar peace settlements with their former enemies because public hostility interferes with moderation on the part of national leaders.[20] In addition, the diversionary theory of war asserts that a leader facing domestic political difficulties may engage in a foreign war to bolster her or his position with a rally-around-the-flag effect.[21] In other words, leaders may capitalize on the public's willingness to wage war. There are, therefore, equally strong theoretical and empirical reasons to doubt the democratic peace theorists' claim that the public is more peaceful than are its leaders and is willing to restrain bellicose leaders.

Finally, some have also taken issue with the policy recommendation that flows from democratic peace theory: namely, that spreading democracy spreads peace and stability.[22] Instead, Edward D. Mansfield and Jack Snyder have demonstrated that democratizing states are actually far more war prone than are other types of states.[23] Therefore, not only might spreading democracy actually increase conflict in unstable regions if the transition is not complete, but the theory itself is underspecified, because only stable democracies are likely to be subject to its logic.[24]

In the next section, I will complement these more traditional challenges to democratic peace theory with a critique stemming from an institutionalist perspective.

Democratic Peace Theory and New Institutionalism

New institutionalism attempts to provide a richer understanding of social and political phenomena by analysing the degree to which actors' behaviour and political outcomes are shaped by the social and political institutions within which they operate. As Kathleen Thelen and Sven Steinmo have emphasized, macrolevel institutions – such as class and regime type – are useful institutions to consider in political analysis, because they are certain to have an effect on political choices; however, the real value-added of institutionalist theory is its focus on intermediate-level institutions – such as the particular institutions, conventional practices, and political norms of particular states – which allows analysts to explain differences within categories or 'variations on a theme.'[25]

From an institutionalist perspective, democratic peace theory represents an advance on structural realist – or neo-realist – theories of foreign security policy. Kenneth Waltz, the founder of the structural realist school, argued that domestic political regimes have no meaningful impact on foreign security policy. Instead, in the anarchical international system, where they must prize their security and survival above all other goals, states must formulate their policies consistently with the dictates of the balance of power or they risk extinction. In other words, international anarchy – the absence of a central authority in the international system to coerce states and regulate their behaviour – socializes all states, regardless of their regime type.[26]

Democratic peace theory, with its emphasis on regime type, a macrolevel institution, as a determinant of foreign security policy within the anarchical international environment represents a step forward for the foreign policy literature. DPT acknowledges that systemic pressures must be filtered through and interpreted by domestic institutions prior to affecting policy choices. Including these institutions as variables in the analysis, thus, accommodates greater complexity and allows researchers to focus on different policy responses to common international stimuli.

Nonetheless, democratic peace theory is still remarkably unsophisticated because it explains different policy choices only in terms of regime type, while it ignores the considerable variety of intermediate-level institutions that can exist within each regime type. DPT assumes that 'democracy' is a homogeneous category of states, which allow the public and their representatives in the legislature a comparable degree of power to influence foreign policy decisions and scrutinize the executive. In other words, it assumes that policy decisions on matters of war and peace are 'bottom up' decisions instead of 'top down' ones, and that all democratic executives lack decision-making autonomy in the foreign security policy area. In a democracy, according to DPT, if the public and its leaders disagree on whether to wage war, the public must win out or the theory – which assumes that the pacific public restrains aggressive leaders – fails.

In ignoring the intermediate-level institutions that differentiate among democratic states, the theory paints a caricature of democracy, rather than an accurate picture. Democracies – regimes characterized by popular sovereignty, where the ultimate source of authority resides within the people as a whole[27] – vary in several important respects. Popular sovereignty is exercised differently in different states that would be classed as democratic, according to the institutional structures, decision-making procedures, and procedural norms that comprise the state's domestic decision-making environment.[28] As the domestic decision-making environments differ, so does the degree of autonomy that their executives have to construct foreign security policy.[29] Let us consider each of these differences in turn.

The first element of differentiation between democratic states is the formal institutional structure of each state, which is composed of the intermediate-level institutions that define the rules for the exercise of authority within the state. These structures typically include constitutional provisions, which delimit procedures, responsibilities, and patterns of institutional growth over time.[30] Two broad categories of institutional structures affect the conduct of foreign security policy. First, there are the structural features that determine the way in which democracy is practised in a particular state, including, inter alia, the nature of democratic governance (presidential, parliamentary, or mixed), the extent of concentration or separation of executive power, the electoral procedure (single-member constituencies, proportional representation, or mixed), the number of political parties that participate meaningfully in the electoral and policy processes, and the frequency of elections.[31] Each of these features can have a significant effect on the autonomy of the government to make unpopular decisions. For example, a Westminster-style parliamentary system, such as Great Britain, with a single-party majority government should afford its executive greater autonomy to conduct policy independently of the legislature than would a multiparty parliamentary system, such as Israel, in which the executive is dependent on a multiplicity of parties. Alternatively, a presidential system with an executive from one party and a legislature dominated by another should afford its executive less autonomy than a parliamentary regime, whose cabinet necessarily commands a majority of support in the legislature.

In addition, there are structural features which pertain exclusively to the foreign policy apparatus, including the number of institutions and actors that contribute meaningfully to policy determination, the extent and frequency to which they must report to the legislature or the public, whether the foreign minister is a member of the legislature or an executive appointee, and whether the executive or the legislature appoints other key foreign policy officials. These institutional features can also have a marked impact on the executive's autonomy to make decisions of war and peace. For example, all things being equal, a constitution, such as the British one, which privileges the executive in matters of foreign affairs grants it greater autonomy than a constitution, such as the American one, that divides power between the executive and the legislature.[32] When the foreign minister and other foreign policy officials are political appointees responsible to the executive, with only nominal parliamentary scrutiny – as in the United States – they can conduct foreign policy with greater independence than if they were drawn from the legislature and responsible to the public in direct parliamentary elections, as in Canada.

In addition to these formal institutional structures, another two, less formal, intermediate-level institutions condition the executive's freedom of action in different democratic contexts. First, each polity has its own unique decision-making procedures that regulate the process of policymaking. These are routinized patterns of behaviour and informal rules that govern actors' conduct, but they do not necessarily stem from the structure of the institutions themselves. Such procedures can constrain or enable policymakers just like formal institutional structures or, more precisely, they can modify the scope of action that institutional structures allow leaders. Thus, conventions, such as party discipline in Canada and Great Britain, which routinize support for the government, grant it greater autonomy to make policy choices. Alternatively, the recent American practice of executive consultation with Congress before dispatching troops can constrain leaders and prevent them from exercising the full degree of their institutional authority.

The second group of less formal institutions are the prevailing procedural norms of the polity. These are widely accepted standards that provide a broad consensus on the way politics ought to be conducted in terms of the rights and obligations of political actors and institutions.[33] Of particular importance in this regard are the legislative norms that affect the legislature's usage of whatever structural rights it has to scrutinize the foreign policy process.[34] These norms can affect autonomy in two ways. First, they may work within particular institutional structures by inspiring decision-making procedures consistent with those norms. Non-partisanship and Congressional restraint in the conduct of American foreign relations after the Second World War, for example, stemmed from a norm that required both parties to curtail bickering over the direction of national security policy because of its paramount importance in a hostile international environment. As a result, decisions on foreign security policy were largely left in the hands of the executive despite the formidable constitutional powers that Congress possessed. Paradoxically, the French Fourth Republic held the parallel, but reverse, norm that foreign security policy was far too important to leave to the executive. Thus, French norms encouraged legislative interference and reduced executive autonomy over foreign affairs. In this manner, different norms resulted in different national practices.

Alternatively, when norms are powerful enough they can occasionally shape the way in which institutions are interpreted and operate. Changes in prevailing norms regarding the conduct of foreign affairs, for example, can affect the judicial interpretation of constitutional provisions that define and delimit institutional structures; hence, they alter the way the institutions operate. Indeed, important U.S. Supreme Court rulings on the division of foreign relations powers just prior to the Second World War reflected changing American attitudes on the importance of foreign policy and, thus, construed the president's authority over international affairs to be quite broad despite the constitutional division of powers between the President and the Congress. Consequently, they greatly enhanced the autonomy of the U.S. national security executive.[35] Norms, then, can affect not only the practices or procedures that actors follow, but also the institutional setting itself.

These structural, procedural, and normative institutional differences among democracies grant democratic executives widely varying degrees of autonomy to pursue policies independently of the legislature and the public at large. Thus, as I have demonstrated elsewhere, the three great power western democracies in the early post-war era – Great Britain, France, and the United States – varied considerably in their ability to pursue independent policies. On the one hand, the French Fourth Republic had a remarkably constrained national security executive that had no autonomy to take unpopular decisions because of a constitution that enshrined the principle of parliamentary sovereignty, the multiplicity of undisciplined political parties (which, due to proportional representation, led to fragmented, unstable cabinets) and its procedural norms of obstruction in matters of foreign affairs because of their importance. On the other hand, the British and American national security executives were extremely autonomous. The British cabinet benefited from single-party majority governments with party discipline, constitutional conventions that favoured the cabinet in matters of foreign affairs, and procedural norms that discouraged members of parliament from interfering in foreign policy because of its importance. The U.S. foreign security executive was also highly autonomous because of the Supreme Court's decisions that privileged the executive over the legislature in matters of foreign affairs; the National Security Act of 1947, which constructed the powerful and well-insulated institutions of the 'national security state'; and procedural norms that, especially in the context of the emerging Cold War, national security required the president to conduct foreign policy with minimal interference. As a result, the Anglo-Saxon governments during this period enjoyed levels of autonomy that many non-democratic leaders would have coveted. Consequently, these governments were able to pursue unpopular policies towards defeated Germany after the Second World War (such as German economic rehabilitation and Ger-

man re-armament) with impunity when they believed they were necessary, while the French government did so only with great difficulty
and was punished for it.[36]

The implications for democratic peace theory are profound. If
democracies exhibit significant differences in their degree of foreign
security policy autonomy from public and parliamentary opinion, then
structural democratic peace theory, which assumes that all democratic
executives are equally constrained, is incorrect.[37] Furthermore, since
democracies partake of different norms, the normative explanation is
equally suspect. Thus, an institutionalist approach that considers the
impact of intermediate-level institutions reveals the folly of treating
democracy as a homogeneous category of states.

Instead, it would be useful for researchers to examine the conditions
under which democracies will be more peaceful and those under
which they will not. This implies three steps. First, it would be useful
to examine the circumstances under which public attitudes are likely
to be conciliatory and those under which they are likely to be bellicose.[38] Second, we will need to examine the international political circumstances that could encourage political leaders to be more
conciliatory and those under which they will be more bellicose. Finally,
an analysis – like the one above – of the state's democratic institutions
that assesses its relative level of autonomy will then determine
whether the executive or the public and its legislative representatives
will have more control over policymaking. Building such a comprehensive theory of democratic foreign security policy, however, is
beyond the scope of this chapter.

Conclusion: Institutionalism and the Study of Foreign Security Policy

This chapter has demonstrated that the democratic peace theory is
flawed because of its failure to capitalize on the insights of new institutionalism. Specifically, although its incorporation of the macrolevel
institution of regime-type represents progress from the influential
realist and neo-realist schools of foreign security policy that privilege
the international system over the states themselves, it sacrifices richness and accuracy by ignoring the intermediate-level institutions that
determine the shape and style of decision-making in states with similar regimes. As a result, it overestimates the similarities between
democracies.

Beyond democratic peace theory, the security studies literature, as a whole, would benefit if it incorporated the insights of institutionalist theory. While the foreign policy literature, more broadly speaking; international political economy research; and the subdiscipline of international organization have been more heavily influenced by institutionalism, the security studies literature has remained largely impervious to its insights. This is somewhat natural given the traditional consignment of national security to the realist paradigm because of its high stakes and the immense costs that states incur if their national security policies diverge from the requirements of the international balance of power. Nonetheless, as we have seen in this chapter, domestic political institutions affect even the way states construct their foreign security policies. Hence, to explain and predict the security choices of different states more accurately, it behooves us to build sophisticated second-image theories, that incorporate institutional differences among states beyond simply regime type.

Notes

I thank Ara Karaboghossian for his excellent research assistance in the preparation of this manuscript.

1 See Zeev Maoz and Nasrin Abdolai, 'Regime Types and International Conflict,' *Journal of Conflict Resolution*, 33 (1989), 3–35; and Stuart A. Bremer, 'Democracy and Militarized Interstate Conflict, 1816–1965,' *International Interactions*, 18 (1993), 231–50. John R. Oneal and Bruce M. Russett, however, contend that democracies are, in fact, less conflict prone in aggregate than other states, in 'The Classical Liberals Were Right: Democracy, Interdependence, and Conflict, 1950–1985,' *International Studies Quarterly*, 41 (1997), 267–94.

2 Jack S. Levy, 'Domestic Politics and War,' *Journal of Interdisciplinary History*, 18 (1988), 662. For a sampling of quantitative analyses confirming the low incidence of wars between democratic states, see Melvin Small and J. David Singer, 'The War-proneness of Democratic Regimes, 1816–1965,' *Jerusalem Journal of International Relations*, 1 (1976), 50–69; Maoz and Abdolai, 'Regime Types'; Bremer, Democracy and Militarized Interstate Conflict,' and Bruce M. Russett, *Grasping the Democratic Peace* (Princeton, NJ: Princeton, University Press, 1993).

3 The democratic peace literature is quite extensive. Key theoretical treatises include Michael Doyle: 'Kant, Liberal Legacies, and Foreign Affairs, part 1,'

Philosophy and Public Affairs, 12 (1983), 205–35; 'Kant, Liberal Legacies, and Foreign Affairs, part 2,' *Philosophy and Public Affairs*, 12 (1983), 323–53; 'Liberalism and World Politics,' *American Political Science Review*, 80 (1986), 1151–61; Russett, *Grasping the Democratic Peace*; John M. Owen, 'How Liberalism Produces the Democratic Peace,' *International Security*, 19 (1994), 87–125; and James Lee Ray, *Democracy and International Conflict: An Evaluation of the Democratic Peace Proposition* (Columbia: University of South Carolina Press, 1995).

4 William J. Dixon referred to this as 'the norm of bounded competition.' See his 'Democracy and the Peaceful Settlement of International Conflict,' *American Political Science Review*, 88 (1994), 15–16. See also Owen, 'How liberalism Produces the Democratic Peace.' Bruce Russett and Zeev Maoz have found the normative explanation to be the most powerful explanation of the democratic peace; see his 'Normative and Structural Causes of Democratic Peace,' *American Political Science Review*, 87 (1993), 624–38.

5 See Margaret G. Hermann and Charles W. Kegley, Jr, 'Rethinking Democracy and International Peace: Perspectives from Political Psychology,' *International Studies Quarterly*, 39 (1995), 514; and Russett, *Grasping the Democratic Peace*, 38–40.

6 Doyle, 'Kant, part 2,' 350–1.

7 Robert Keohane, 'International Liberalism Reconsidered,' in John Dunn (ed.), *The Economic Limits to Modern Politics* (Cambridge: Cambridge University Press, 1990), 165–94. Empirical support for commercial liberalism, see John R. Oneal and Bruce N. Russett, 'The Kantian Peace: The Pacific Benefits of Democracy, Interdependence, and International Organizations, 1885–1992,' *World Politics*, 52 (1999), 1–37. Barry Buzan criticized this position in 'Economic Structure and International Security: The Limits of the Liberal Case,' *International Organization*, 38 (1984), 597–624. For recent empirical challenges to the commercial liberal argument, see Norrin M. Ripsman and Jean-Marc F. Blanchard, 'Commercial Liberalism under Fire: Evidence from 1914 and 1936,' *Security Studies*, 6 (1996–97), 4–50; and Katherine Barbieri, 'Economic Interdependence,' *Journal of Peace Research*, 33 (1996), 29–49.

8 Doyle, 'Kant, part 1.'

9 Owen, 'How Liberalism Produces the Democratic Peace.'

10 Russett, *Grasping the Democratic Peace*, 14–16.

11 On the Chilean coup and British arms shipments to the Arab states, see Raymond Cohen, 'Pacific Unions: A Reappraisal of the Theory that "Democracies Do Not Go to War with Each Other,"' *Review of International Studies*, 20 (1994), 210–20. On the re-occupation of the Rhineland, see Chris-

topher Layne, 'Kant or Cant: The Myth of the Democratic Peace,' *International Security*, 19 (1994), 33–8. On American covert action against a number of democratically elected governments, see David P. Forsythe, 'Democracy, War, and Covert Action,' *Journal of Peace Research*, 29 (1992), 385–95. For an excellent book that examines both near misses and potential misclassifications, see Miriam Fendius Elman (ed.), *Paths to Peace: Is Democracy the Answer?* (Cambridge: MIT Press, 1997).

12 John J. Mearsheimer, 'Back to the Future: Instability in Europe after the Cold War,' *International Security*, 15 (1990), 50.

13 David Spiro, 'The Insignificance of the Liberal Peace,' *International Security*, 19 (1994), 50–86. See also, Raymond Cohen, 'Needed: A Disaggregate Approach to the Democratic-Peace Theory,' *Review of International Studies*, 21 (1995), 324.

14 Layne, 'Kant or Cant,' 39–45; Mearsheimer, 'Back to the Future,' 50–1.

15 See Miriam Fendius Elman, 'The Need for a Qualitative Test of the Democratic Peace Theory,' 1–57, in Elman, *Paths to Peace*; and Henry S. Farber and Joanne Gowa, 'Polities and Peace,' *International Security*, 20 (1995), 123–46. On balance of power theory, see Hans J. Morgenthau (with Kenneth W. Thompson), *Politics among Nations*, 6th ed. (New York: McGraw-Hill, 1985); and Kenneth N. Waltz, *Theory of International Politics* (New York: McGraw-Hill, 1979). On balance of threat theory, see Stephen M. Walt, *The Origins of Alliances* (Ithaca: Cornell University Press, 1987).

16 On hegemonic stability theory, see Robert Gilpin, *War and Change in World Politics* (Cambridge: Cambridge University, 1981); Stephen D. Krasner, 'State Power and the Structure of International Trade,' *World Politics*, 28 (1976), 317–47; Charles P. Kindleberger, *The World in Depression, 1929–1939* (Berkeley: University of California Press, 1973), chap. 14; and A.F.K. Organski and Jacek Kugler, *The War Ledger* (Chicago: University of Chicago Press, 1980).

17 David R. Davis, John R. Oneal, and Bruce Russett, 'The Third Leg of the Kantian Tripod for Peace: International Organizations and Militarized Disputes, 1950–85,' *International Organization*, 52 (1998), 441–67. See also, Bruce Russett and John Oneal, *Triangulating Peace: Democracy, Interdependence and International Organizations* (New York: W.W. Norton, 2001).

18 For theoretical and empirical challenges to commercial liberalism, see note 9. Although Doyle considered economic interdependence to be one of the contributors to the democratic peace, most theorists view democratic peace theories and commercial liberalism as separate theories with different causal mechanisms. For a theoretical critique of liberal institutionalism, see John J. Mearsheimer, 'The False Promise of International Institutions,' *International Security*, 19 (1994–95), 5–49.

19 Immanuel Kant, *Perpetual Peace: A Philosophical Essay,* translated by M. Campbell Smith (New York: Garland, 1972), 122–3.

20 Walter Lippmann, *Essays in the Public Philosophy* (Boston: Little, Brown, 1955), 18–21; and Reinhold Niebuhr, *The Structure of Nations and Empires* (New York: Scribner's, 1959), 197.

21 See Jack S. Levy, 'The Diversionary Theory of War,' 259–88, in Manus I. Midlarsky (ed.), *The Handbook of War Studies* (Boston: Unwin Hyman, 1989).

22 This policy implication of democratic peace theory is discussed at length in Joshua Muravchik, *Exporting Democracy: Fulfilling America's Destiny* (Washington: AEI Press, 1991); Larry Diamond, 'Promoting Democracy,' *Foreign Policy,* 87 (1992), 25–46. See also, Russett, *Grasping the Democratic Peace,* 124–38.

23 Edward D. Mansfield and Jack Snyder, 'Democratization and the Danger of War,' *International Security,* 20 (1995), 5–38; 'Democratic Transitions, Institutional Strength, and War,' *International Organization,* 56 (2002); Jack Snyder, *From Voting to Violence: Democratization and Nationalist Conflict* (New York: W.W. Norton, 2000).

24 Russett, in fact, made a similar point. He argued that only stable democracies – those that have undergone a peaceful change of power – can truly be considered democracies and, therefore, part of the zone of democratic peace. *Grasping the Democratic Peace,* 16.

25 Kathleen Thelen and Sven Steinmo, 'Historical Institutionalism in Comparative Politics,' in Sven Steinmo, Kathleen Thelen, and Frank Longstreth (eds.), *Structuring Politics: Historical Institutionalism in Comparative Analysis* (Cambridge: Cambridge University Press, 1992), 10–11. See also, G. John Ikenberry, 'Conclusion: An Institutional Approach to American Foreign Economic Policy,' in G. John Ikenberry, David A. Lake, and Michael Mastanduno (eds.), *The State and American Foreign Economic Policy* (Ithaca: Cornell University Press, 1988), 219–43; Peter Hall, *Governing the Economy: The Politics of State Intervention in Britain and France* (New York: Oxford University Press, 1986); Peter J. Katzenstein, 'Conclusion: Domestic Structures and Strategies of Foreign Economic Policy,' in Peter J. Katzenstein (ed.), *Between Power and Plenty: Foreign Economic Policies in Advanced Industrial States* (Madison: University of Wisconsin Press, 1978), 295–336.

26 Kenneth Waltz: *Foreign Policy and Democratic Politics: The American and British Experience* (Boston: Little, Brown, 1967), 306–11, and *Theory of International Politics* (New York: McGraw-Hill, 1979). Defensive structural realists are somewhat more sophisticated in assuming that all states typically behave consistently with the dictates of the international system; however, imperialistic cartel regimes and those with militaristic general staffs

occasionally make suboptimal decisions. See Jack Snyder, *Myths of Empire* (Ithaca: Cornell University Press, 1991); and Fareed Zakaria, 'Realism and Domestic Politics: a Review Essay,' *International Security*, 17 (1992), 177–98.

27 V.O. Key, *Public Opinion and American Democracy* (New York: Knopf, 1961), 97; Daniel Deudney, 'The Philadelphia System: Sovereignty, Arms Control, and Balance of Power in the American States-Union, Circa 1787–1861,' *International Organization*, 49 (1995), 197–99.

28 The following discussion draws upon Norrin M. Ripsman, *Peacemaking by Democracies: The Effect of State Autonomy on the Post–World War Settlements* (University Park: Penn State University Press, 2002), chap. 2.

29 That even democratic executives vary in decision-making autonomy is demonstrated by Eric A. Nordlinger, *On the Autonomy of the Democratic State* (Cambridge: Harvard University Press, 1981); Peter J. Katzenstein (ed.), *Between Power and Plenty: Foreign Economic Policies in Advanced Industrial States* (Madison: University of Wisconsin Press, 1978); and Hugh Heclo, *Social Policy in Britain and Sweden* (New Haven: Yale University Press, 1974).

30 For an excellent study that explains U.S. policy adaptation to the oil shocks of the 1970s in terms of the structure and growth of the American state, see G. John Ikenberry, *Reasons of State: Oil Politics and the Capacities of American Government* (Ithaca: Cornell University Press, 1988).

31 See Arend Lijphart, *Democracies: Patterns of Majoritarian and Consensus Government in Twenty-One Countries* (New Haven: Yale, 1984); Matthew Soberg Shugart and John M. Carey, *Presidents and Assemblies* (Cambridge: Cambridge University, 1992); and Helen V. Milner, *Interests, Institutions, and Information* (Princeton, NJ: Princeton University Press, 1997), chap. 4.

32 In Great Britain, by long-standing constitutional convention, the conduct of foreign affairs is considered to be a royal prerogative, exercised by cabinet, which was initially known as 'the committee for foreign affairs.' Charles Carstairs and Richard Ware, 'Introduction,' in Charles Carstairs and Richard Ware (eds.), *Parliament and International Relations* (Buckingham: Open University Press, 1991), 1–7. In contrast, Edward S. Corwin has described the U.S. constitution as 'an invitation to struggle for the privilege of directing American foreign policy' in the *The President: Office and Powers, 1787–1957* (New York: University Press, 1957), 171.

33 See Robin M. Williams, Jr, 'The Concept of Norms,' in David L. Sills (ed.), *International Encyclopedia of the Social Sciences* (New York: Macmillan, 1968), vol. 11, 204–8; Stephen D. Krasner, 'Structural Causes and Regime Consequences: Regimes as Intervening Variables,' in Stephen D. Krasner (ed.), *International Regimes* (Ithaca: Cornell University Press, 1983), 2; Friedrich V.

Kratochwil, *Rules, Norms and Decisions* (Cambridge: Cambridge University, 1989), chaps. 2 and 3.

34 See, for example, Barbara Sinclair, *The Transformation of the U.S. Senate* (Baltimore: Johns Hopkins University Press, 1989), 14.

35 Ripsman, *Democracies and Peacemaking*, chap. 3.

36 Ibid.; and Norrin M. Ripsman, 'The Curious Case of German Rearmament: Democracy and Foreign Security Policy,' *Security Studies*, 10 (2001), 1–47. Thomas Risse-Kappen similarly has demonstrated that western executives responded differently to their domestic antinuclear movements in the 1980s because of their different domestic institutional structures in his 'Public Opinion, Domestic Structure, and Foreign Policy in Liberal Democracies,' *World Politics*, 43 (1991), 479–512.

37 In this regard, see also Miriam Fendius Elman, 'Unpacking Democracy: Presidentialism, Parliamentarism, and Theories of Democratic Peace,' *Security Studies*, 9 (2000), 91–126; and Susan Peterson, 'How Democracies Differ: Public Opinion, State Structure, and the Lessons of the Fashoda Crisis,' *Security Studies*, 5 (1995), 3–37.

38 I thank an anonymous reviewer for suggesting this. My initial instinct is that countries embroiled in bitter enduring rivalries that have already produced interstate wars are more likely to be characterized by bellicose public attitudes, whereas publics that do not have a recent history or warfare or a long-standing grievance with an adversary will be more conciliatory. This, however, needs to be investigated carefully.

14

Canada and the Global Diffusion of 'One China'

DER-YUAN MAXWELL WU

As new institutionalism began to surge in popularity in political science,[1] the question of its empirical relevance became a subject of concern. In international relations, new institutionalism is mostly associated with regime theory, which aims to explain the formation of multilateral clusters of shared rules, expectations, procedures, or principles that result from and facilitate cooperative behaviour within typically 'low politics' issue areas.[2] However, there are several versions of new institutionalism that can be applied in this context. Working from a broader institutionalist perspective, but in a way divergent from mainstream international relations regime theory, this chapter examines a case of 'high politics' conflict: the ongoing 'one China' sovereignty dispute between the People's Republic of China (PRC) and the Republic of China (ROC) on Taiwan, which has often been ignored by international relations theorists.

The problem essentially boils down to the dual issues of which government, Beijing or Taipei, represents 'China' in the world, and whether Taiwan deserves a separate representation. Although the former issue was largely settled with Beijing being recognized as the government of China, the latter issue remains contentious. The recent decade of Taiwanese democratization and self-assertiveness in foreign policy have already put into serious question the 'one China' complex. Beijing's conduct of missile tests around Taiwan in March 1996 revealed its 'time bomb' nature.

For more than three decades, the existing 'one China' arrangement has not only boosted Beijing's global profile as the government of China, but it has also squeezed Taipei's diplomatic space. How was the 'one China' complex institutionalized on a global scale despite the evident existence of two governments controlling distinct territorial units across the Taiwan Strait? What role did Canada play in this global process? This chapter seeks to address both issues through the lenses of historical as well as sociological-organizational institutionalism. I first identify some defining features of the perspectives. Then, I sketch the genesis of the problem in its international setting, and explore the formation and consolidation of a 'one China' institution through an examination of Canada's and other countries' practices in establishing diplomatic ties with the PRC. Finally, the impact and meaning of 'one China' around the world will be recast in new institutionalist terms.

Laying the New Institutionalist Framework

In many ways, the new institutionalist perspective is epitomized by W. Richard Scott, one of the leading scholars in the sociological branch of new institutionalism. Scott identified 'institution' as entailing 'regulative,' 'normative,' and 'cultural-cognitive' pillars. The regulative element refers to enforceable rules and laws that are usually backed by sanctioning power and monitoring mechanisms. The normative element includes norms, values, and roles, or involves the creation of moral beliefs as well as prescriptive and obligatory systems that, overall, create social expectations. The cultural-cognitive element serves to define, constitute, and legitimize actors' capacities, rights, interests, and identities, and their corresponding, relevant activities.[3] In this vein, 'institution' can be defined to be a human-constructed arrangement, formally or informally organized, which consists of cultural-cognitive, normative, and regulative elements that serve to stabilize interactions or provide meaning to human actions.

As this chapter assumes that the development of international relations new institutionalism can benefit from the insights provided by historical as well as sociological institutionalism,[4] it is necessary to synthesize some of their defining features. From those approaches, six sets of propositions regarding the formation and impact of institution can be identified. First, the development of institutions often entails historical contingency. This is manifested in the existence of contending ideas and broader institutional possibilities at an early stage; the occurrence of unintended consequences of policy decisions; and the emergence of actors, or policy entrepreneurs, who capitalize on the new windows of opportunity. Second, the rise of a given institution means that a set of ideas in defining 'reality' have prevailed to then be embodied as over-arching principles in authoritative texts and represented through hege-monic interpretations for social interactions thereafter. Other sets of ideas or interpretations are correspondingly marginalized.

Third, the institutionalization of an arrangement is manifested in the transformation of the guiding principles into workable rules and pro-cedures in concrete policy areas, as well as in institutional isomor-phism at the levels of both fundamental and elaborated rules. Here, 'institutionalization' refers to the process by which some actors pro-duce and reproduce, given arrangements with the latter constraining and constituting the actors' interest, identity, and behaviour. 'Institu-tional isomorphism' can be defined as the process by which a given actor learns and incorporates successful institutional arrangements adopted by other agencies to the effect that the organizations con-cerned become, over time, more and more homogeneous in their struc-ture and practices. Fourth, the impact of institutionalization can be epitomized by 'path dependency': a derived arrangement limits the range of policy or institutional options that used to be available before institutionalization.[5]

Fifth, institutional development often proceeds through the mutual constitution of actors and institutional structure. On the one hand, given entities are embedded in broader systems of meaning. The inter-ests and identities of given actors are shaped or entrenched by the institution, whereas other actors' interests are marginalized. On the other hand, the persistence of that institution requires constant prac-tices by the actors concerned.[6] Finally, the strength of institutional development can be measured by the organizing coherence of Scott's three pillars. Most importantly, the ultimate success of an institution hinges upon the degree to which its cultural-cognitive element prevails so that the whole institution becomes taken for granted as the only conceivable arrangement.

Let us now turn to the case of the development of the 'one China' institution.

Years of Contending Ideas

The contemporary 'one China' issue involving Taiwan[7] did not emerge on the world stage until the 1940s when a series of contingent events contributed to its development. In the context of an eventual victory of the Allies in the Second World War, the Cairo Declaration of 1943 stated that 'Formosa (Taiwan) and the Pescadores (Penghu Islands) ... shall be restored to (the ROC).'[8] Less than five years after it fell to Nationalist (Kuomintang or KMT) control, the island became an international cynosure as the Chinese Communists' victory over the KMT on the mainland was imminent. After 1949, the issue of Taiwan was intertwined with that of China's representation internationally, given that the KMT-state on Taiwan continued to claim to be the sole legal government of China.

The abrupt outbreak of the Korean War fundamentally changed the course of history for Taiwan. Many countries, including Canada, were forced to postpone their plans of recognizing Beijing.[9] The Truman Administration intervened to fend off Communist advances in the region. Thus, the war reinforced the demarcation between the mainland and Taiwan.

Moreover, the timing and form of the legal termination of the state of war with Japan not only contributed to the separation, but pointed to a possible trajectory for Taiwan in the future. As neither Chinese party participated in the San Francisco Peace Conference of September 1951, Tokyo concluded a separate peace treaty with the KMT government in Taipei the following April, formally relinquishing its sovereignty over Taiwan while making no reference to country to which the island belonged. This implied a de jure 'frozen' status for Taiwan, thereby complicating the 'one China' issue.

Later on, Beijing initiated the first offshore islands crisis. Washington responded by signing the Mutual Defense Treaty with Taipei in December 1954. Similar crises erupted three years later. The boundary across the strait was thus further solidified.[10]

These crises had far-reaching consequences, since they tilted the balance of representation politics against Taipei, and led to a situation where the existence of the Communist China could no longer be ignored. The persistent demarcation further discredited Taipei's international mandate of 'one China (ROC),' in view of its failure to recapture the mainland. As a result, in the wake of the Sino-Soviet split, the western divergence on the China representation issue became increasingly important. Several alternative arrangements for tackling the Beijing-Taipei logjam surfaced. Among these were the French recognition of Beijing and Canada's proposal with respect to China's representation in the United Nations.[11]

In many ways, the French case itself presented a mixture of innovative ideas and experiments in the context of a new leadership and political environment. After General Charles de Gaulle came to office in 1958, the pursuit of a more independent French foreign policy outside the framework of NATO gradually emerged. The end of the Algerian War in 1962, at a time when Communist China was disengaging from the Soviet bloc, opened a window for an eventual normalization.[12]

In the first encounter in late 1963, while being faced with Beijing's demand to sever ties with Taipei first, the French delegation proposed that the precondition be dropped, since the KMT would almost inevitably take the initiative thereby meeting the requirement. Beijing appeared to acquiesce.[13] This bred new policy experiments in Washington and Taipei.[14] Even after Paris and Beijing agreed, on 27 January 1964, in a joint communiqué to 'establish diplomatic relations and to appoint their ambassadors within three months' but made no reference to the issue of Taiwan,[15] Taipei did not withdraw its diplomatic mission as had been anticipated. At the time, there was speculation that Paris was pursuing a 'two China' policy and that Beijing had dropped its steadfast objection to it. The PRC Foreign Ministry nonetheless set out its stance the next day: 'recognition of new government [means] the representatives of the old ruling group can no longer be ... present side by side with [those] of the new government ... It was with this understanding that [we] reached agreement ... on the establishment of diplomatic relations ... The Chinese government deems it necessary to reaffirm that Taiwan is part of China's territory and that any attempt ... to create "two Chinas" is absolutely unacceptable.'[16]

The ROC kept its representative in Paris for two weeks. Only after having received an oral demarche from the French chargé d'affaires, did Taipei ultimately announce its decision to cut ties with Paris, to avoid being humiliated by its representative being forced out.[17] Notwithstanding the outcome, the French approach had created ambiguous room for development of 'two Chinas.'

Canada, for its part, in 1963–4 began translating its 'one China, one Taiwan' ideas into a proposal aiming at multilateral institutionalization while expanding unofficial contacts with Beijing through wheat sales and a program of exchange of correspondents.[18] This approach was presented as a declaratory resolution in the United Nations to the effect that both Beijing and Taipei could coexist in the General Assembly, that Beijing should succeed Taipei in the Security Council, and that eventual settlement of competing territorial claims of both parties should be left for further investigation. However, this move failed to garner adequate support, and a similar venture in 1966 also failed.[19] So did an Italian alternative proposal to set up a 'study committee.' During the period, moreover, the sporadic American and British claims that the legal status of Taiwan was undetermined were never actualized in a concrete institutional form. The idea of 'one China' in favour of Beijing, by contrast, started to take shape as Ottawa took new initiatives on the bilateral front.

The Formation of the 'One China' Institution and Its Diffusion

The mainland–Taiwan boundary was reinforced as a result of the Korean War, the peace treaty with Japan, and the Taiwan Strait crises of the 1950s, but not institutionalized decisively because of other contingent forces. Among them were the Sino-Soviet split, the loosening of the Cold War system, and the rise of independent-minded or rapprochement-oriented leaders, namely, de Gaulle, Pierre Trudeau, and Richard Nixon. These contingent factors became even more evident in the late 1960s. It was under these circumstances that the contemporary 'one China' institution emerged. The Canadian initiative contributed to its formation, although the outcome of Taiwan's marginalization was hardly intended.

The Stockholm Negotiations and the Canadian Formula

Pierre Trudeau's rise to leadership marked a new era for Canadian diplomacy. On China, he notably promulgated the objective 'to recognize the [PRC] government as soon as possible ... taking into account that there is a separate government in Taiwan.'[20] This goal was further elaborated by his foreign minister, Mitchell Sharp, in a press conference: 'We intend to have negotiations with the PRC designed to bring about recognition of that government. We also have to recognize that there is a government on Formosa. [But] we wouldn't be recognizing the government of Formosa as government of China.'[21] Accordingly, a far-reaching China policy review was conducted by the Department of External Affairs (DEA), albeit in a much cautious tone. A major reason for the DEA's reluctance to embrace an outright 'one China, one Taiwan' policy rested in Canada's own sensitivities and vulnerability in regard to Quebec.[22]

In the end, DEA recommended that a feasible objective be to establish formal official relations with Beijing while maintaining full non-diplomatic ties with Taipei, and that the option of reciprocal exchange of non-official trade offices with Taiwan be left open.[23] The cabinet approved in late January 1969 the proposal and authorized negotiations with the PRC's delegates in Stockholm. Up to this stage, although the cabinet decision did not go as far as to propose a simultaneous recognition of both 'one China' and 'one Taiwan,' the realization of 'one Taiwan' in some foreseeable future remained open.

Then came the twenty-month, eighteen-session Stockholm negotiations, which could roughly be divided into three main phases: (1) preliminary talks, (2) substantive discussions on principles, and (3) give-and-take on the content of an agreement text.[24] In the first encounter in February 1969, the Chinese side put forward three 'constant principles' making it clear that Canada must recognize Beijing as the sole and lawful government of the Chinese people, Taiwan as an inalienable part of Chinese territory, and support Beijing's legitimate rights in the United Nations.[25]

As substantive talks began in the spring and summer, the main focus centred upon the Taiwan issue. The Chinese side strenuously demanded that Canada recognize its sovereignty over the island, and requested Ottawa's explanation of its previous policy statements full of 'one China, one Taiwan.' In response, the Canadian side not only stressed their 'neither challenge nor endorse' (NCNE) position on Beijing's claim, but eventually managed to have Secretary of State for External Affairs Mitchell Sharp publicly state the stance in July.[26] Ottawa's pledge not to promote 'one China, one Taiwan' or 'two Chinas' in the statement thus signalled the beginning of its 'one China' policy, with 'one Taiwan' in parentheses.

The remaining sessions of the Stockholm negotiations then essentially revolved around whether a statement on Taiwan should be incorporated in texts, as well as searches for an acceptable formula to phrase both sides' positions on Taiwan. In the beginning, the Canadian side argued for the French formula of a short joint communiqué without reference to Taiwan, which was rejected by Beijing negotiators.[27] Thereafter, the Canadians took pains in searching for a concise formula substituting for NCNE to register their 'non-position' on Taiwan, whereas the Chinese were preoccupied with trying to show the existence of mutual consensus on the issue.[28]

Ultimately, both sides settled on a four-paragraph text. In it, paragraphs 2 and 3, which codified the 'one China' statement read:

2 The Chinese Government reaffirms that Taiwan is an inalienable part of

the territory of the PRC. The Canadian Government takes note of this position of the Chinese ...

3 The Canadian Government recognizes the PRC Government as the sole legal government of China.[29]

The 'take-note-of' (TNO) expression on Taiwan was thereafter often referred as the 'Canadian formula.' In the negotiators' words, the phrase meant 'we have understood it without necessarily agreeing with it and would certainly take Chinese government's strong views into account ... in Canadian decisions relating to Taiwan.'[30] On 13 October 1970, Mitchell Sharp made a statement in the House of Commons announcing the accomplishment and elaborating Ottawa's position on Taiwan.[31]

The Canadian practice was unprecedented: Canada was the first western country formally asked to both take a stand on the Taiwan issue and embody it in a formal diplomatic text. As mentioned above, the Sino-Franco Joint Communiqué did not refer to the issue. Moreover, the official and ex post facto statement to address it came through Beijing's unilateral clarification.

'One China' Institutional Isomorphism

In the context of the Canadian practice, we can witness a globalizing process characterized by 'institutional isomorphism.' Overall, this took three major forms: the direct incorporation of the exact Canadian phraseology into joint communiqués with the PRC; the reproduction of the Canadian 'one China' formula, albeit in different words; and the explicit recognition, mostly witnessed in the 1990s, of Beijing's claim on Taiwan or the pledge of no official relations with Taiwan.

direct incorporation
So far, fifteen countries have used 'take note of' to record their position on Taiwan in texts announcing the establishment of diplomatic relations with the PRC. In chronological sequence, these countries are: Italy (6 November 1970), Chile (15 December 1970), Belgium (25 October 1971), Peru (2 November 1971), Lebanon (9 November 1971), Iceland (8 December 1971), Malta (31 January 1972), Argentina (16 February 1972), Greece (5 June 1972), Venezuela (28 June 1974), Brazil (15 August 1974), Ecuador (24 December 1979), Columbia (7 February 1980), Côte d'Ivoire (1 March 1983), and Uruguay (3 February 1988).[32] Overall, the ramifications of the Canadian formula could be seen in

both spatial and temporal dimensions: It spread to South America, Africa, Europe, and the Middle East, while its diffusion lasted for a span of nearly eighteen years.

similar construction
Many other countries similarly participated in the construction of the 'one China' institution as they moved to recognize Beijing. In these instances, there was a common acknowledgement that the PRC had a vital say in the eventual resolution of the Taiwan issue.

Acknowledgment

To date, nine countries have acknowledged Beijing's position on Taiwan. The first and foremost example was the Shanghai Communiqué concluded when Nixon visited the PRC in February 1972:

> The Chinese side reaffirmed: The [PRC] government is the sole legal government of China; Taiwan is a province of China. [It] firmly opposes any activities which aim at the creation of 'one China one Taiwan,' 'one China two governments,' 'two Chinas,' and 'independent Taiwan.' The U.S. side declared: The United States acknowledges that all Chinese on either side of the Taiwan Strait maintain there is but one China and that Taiwan is a part of China. The U.S. government does not challenge that position.[33]

The statement marked a formal end to the American 'two Chinas' exercise and the beginning of the public endorsement of 'one China' policy, although Beijing-Washington normalization was not completely realized until seven years later. Nonetheless, the announcement of Nixon's trip in July 1971 and the publication of the Shanghai Communiqué drew a series of moves by numbers of countries in the same trajectory.

Among these, the United Kingdom first joined the bandwagon and concluded an agreement with the PRC on the exchange of ambassadors on 13 March 1972, in which the British similarly 'acknowledged' the Chinese position on Taiwan and decided to remove their official representation there. Then, seven countries followed suit. In chronological order, they were: Australia (21 December 1972), New Zealand (21 December 1972), Spain (3 March 1973), Malaysia (31 May 1974), Thailand (1 July 1975), Fiji (5 November 1975), and West Samoa (6 November 1975).[34] Noteworthy is that there are evidences of institutional learning from the Canadian experience.[35]

Other Equivocal Formulas

The 'one China' globalizing process went beyond simple adoptions of the Canadian and American formulas by other countries. To begin with, Tokyo reproduced the 'one China' statement to the effect that it 'fully understands and respects' the Chinese stand on Taiwan in the Sino-Japanese Joint Communiqué of 29 September 1972. This phraseology was later incorporated into the Sino-Philippino Joint Communiqué of 9 June 1975.[36]

Likewise, in the Dutch case, the announcement of exchange of ambassadors on 16 May 1972, was coupled with the statement that the Netherlands 'respect' the Chinese position on Taiwan. South Korea followed suit on 24 August 1992.[37] Other countries, such as San Marino, Sierra Leone, and South Africa, had made public their positions on Taiwan with the phrases of 'pay attention to,' 'hold,' and 'view,' respectively.[38]

Formula with Explicit Recognition

As many countries opted for a 'flexible' formula to enshrine their positions on Taiwan in diplomatic texts, others either made no statements on the issue or explicitly recognized that Taiwan was part of China. In the latter case, prior to 1990 there were ten countries taking such a clear position.[39] In the post–Cold War era, while fewer and fewer countries were free to keep silent on the issue, there was a growing tendency for countries that otherwise might be spared from the demand to take sides. These include virtually all of the republics of the former Soviet Union, as well as Bosnia and Hercegovina, Croatia, Macedonia, and Slovenia, and the 'mini-state' of the Cook Islands.

Meanwhile, some countries that did not take positions on Taiwan while establishing diplomatic ties with the PRC were now requested to make the 'one China' statement during state visits. For example, when President Boris Yeltsin visited Beijing in April 1996, he 'reiterated that Taiwan is an inalienable part of the Chinese territory' and pledged that 'Russia will not establish official relations nor enter into official contacts with Taiwan.'[40] Later, joint communiqués were phrased in a similar vein during state visits of the Polish and Yugoslav presidents. Moreover, the French, although they had not referred to the issue in the 1964 text, formally recognized Beijing's claim over Taiwan in January 1994.[41] Finally, during his state visit to mainland China in the summer of 1998, President Bill Clinton proclaimed the 'three nos' policy: that Washington would not support 'one China, one Taiwan' or 'two Chinas,' Taiwan's independence, or separate Taiwanese membership in international organizations that require sovereign statehood.[42]

In brief, the 'one China' institutionalization could be traced to the practices of Canada and a few other countries, which commonly codified in joint communiqués a 'no challenge' on Beijing's position on Taiwan, albeit in varying words.[43] Nonetheless, coupled with this horizontal spread of the 'one China' codification was a vertical elaboration of the rule in concrete issues.

Institutional Elaboration in Policy Realms

The global codification of the 'one China' principle in bilateral texts generally did not go so far as to define the extent to which Taiwan's external relations with other countries should be regulated. This governance issue emerged with respect to how the admission and nomenclature of Taiwanese delegations or contact with officials from Taiwan should be tackled. In this regard, international sporting competitions provide abundant opportunities for host countries to elucidate the 'one China' principle, although they are not the only ones. In the Canadian case, an obvious occasion was the 1976 Montreal Olympics, although similar Canadian practices on these issues were evident prior to the event.

In the aftermath of the Canadian recognition of the PRC, a series of episodes broke out over the display of symbols and titles of the 'ROC' by some Taiwanese delegates on Canadian soil, which led to Beijing's protests and DEA's intervention.[44] Moreover, some Taiwanese attempting to attend international conferences held in Canada were denied entry because they intended to represent the 'ROC.'[45]

In the area of sports, with traces of institutional learning from New Zealand,[46] Canadian policy prior to the 1976 Olympics was already made. In effect, Taiwanese teams would not be allowed in if they claimed to represent the 'ROC' and if a no-political-activity assurance could not be obtained from them. As a result, a Taiwanese amateur boxing team finally decided not to participate in an international tournament held in Montreal in late 1975.[47]

In the case of the 1976 Olympics, similar issues arose, although Mitchell Sharp assured the International Olympic Committee (IOC) that all teams 'will be free to enter Canada pursuant to the normal regulation.'[48] Ottawa had hoped that the IOC would have resolved the longstanding China and Taiwan membership problem before the issue burst to the fore.

As the IOC failed to achieve this during the Winter Olympics of February 1976, Ottawa decided to take a middle course in late May: 'Taiwanese will be able to enter Canada to take part in the games provided they do not proclaim themselves while in Canada as representatives of the "Republic of China," use the flag, anthem or any other symbol of the "Republic of China," or use a team designation that includes the word "China."'[49]

The issue triggered a crisis in early July after negotiations between Canada and the IOC failed. On the eve of the opening ceremony, Prime Minister Trudeau finally offered a compromise that would have allowed Taiwan to fly its flag and play its anthem, but not to call itself 'ROC.'[50] While Taipei turned down the offer, other alternative arrangements proposed by the IOC and Taiwan were declined by Ottawa.[51] Eventually, Taiwan withdrew from the 1976 games.

Canada attempted on various occasions to elucidate the 'one China' principle laid down in 1970. This policy elaboration was made with reference to some countries' practices. There was abundant evidence indicating that prior to the 1976 Montreal Olympics, Canada had consulted with Australia, Austria, Belgium, West Germany, Italy, New Zealand, and Sweden, over their handlings of non-official relations with Taiwan.[52] Thus, the Canadian practice constituted part of global institutional isomorphism.

The Impact and Meaning of the Institutionalization of 'One China'

As demonstrated above, the 'one China' institutional development since 1970 involved a dual process. The first was the embodiment of the 'one China' idea in bilateral texts. This began with the successful Canadian arrangement of 1970 that was mimicked and reproduced on a global scale. The second entailed a concrete elaboration of the basic 'one China' principle in various policy realms, which similarly betrayed traces of institutional isomorphism.

Notwithstanding the neat fashion in which the formation of the 'one China' institution was represented above, the whole process did not result from a grand institutional design unfolding in a linear or predetermined way. Historical processes often developed in a contingent way. Two short notes might suffice to illustrate the logic of historical institutionalism. First, the Nationalist insistence on a 'one China (ROC)' solution at an early stage had the unintended consequence of putting Taiwan itself into a hostage position later on. It might be fair to assume that had Chiang Kai-shek foreseen the current condition in which Taiwan finds itself, he might not have made such a choice. Second, there is no evidence that, at the time of the negotiations with the Canadians, the Chinese, by laying out their 'three constant principles,' were confident of a success that would pave the way for Sino-American normalization later.

The unpredictable development that led to the trajectory of institutionalization in this case points to the relevance of both historical and sociological institutionalism. The Canadian institutional choice as well as subsequent developments limited the range of future possibilities and foreclosed once-available options. In the Canadian case, as soon as Ottawa committed itself not to challenge the Beijing position that Taiwan was a part of China, it was no longer feasible to publicly express sympathy with the cause of Taiwanese self-determination as Canada had in the early to mid-1960s.

Obviously, the repercussions of the 'one China' institutional development are far-reaching. It constrains Taiwan's freedom of policy action and choices, while favouring the mobilization of the PRC's interests.

The ROC state continued to survive on Taiwan, which could partly be attributed to some adaptive measures taken to strengthen its domestic legitimacy in reaction to its loss of international mandate.[53] Nonetheless, Taipei's incessant pursuit of a broader diplomatic space reveals the power of the tenacious 'one China' institution.

From the late 1980s onwards, the KMT began attempting to escape from the 'one China' straitjacket by stretching its own 'one China (ROC)' principle.[54] However, the power of the institutionalized 'one China' meant that many countries were reluctant to break earlier rules and practices when the issue of Taiwan was invoked. The consequence of this global process is a continuing marginalization of Taiwan in diplomatic communities, despite its extensive ties to the world trade system.

By 1990, Taiwan was labelled as a 'pariah' or 'outcast' state, comparable to the historical exclusion of Israel and South Africa.[55] In the late 1990s, the condition did not improve much. In one study, it was observed that while recent international practices had become flexible enough as to create some functional substitutes for normal consular institutions to govern the increasingly extensive non-official relations between Taiwan and countries around the world, the status of Taiwan as a 'non-state' entity ironically has also been institutionalized in this process.[56]

Taiwan's diplomatic marginalization is also empirically evident. In 1949, there were forty-six countries recognizing the ROC, compared with sixteen for the PRC. In 1973, the number fell to thirty-nine, whereas Beijing garnered eighty-five recognitions. As of January 2005, there were only twenty-five countries maintaining diplomatic ties with Taipei.[57]

Moreover, there is a universal trend of treating Taiwan differently when issues of Taiwanese entry and nomenclature arise. As mentioned above, the Canadian elaboration of the 'one China' principle came in a form that virtually prohibited Taiwan from calling itself the 'ROC' in international events, such as the 1976 Montreal Olympics, held in Canada.

Furthermore, the constraining effect of the 'one China' institution affects not only Taiwan but also other countries concerned. There are restrictions upon visits or stays in many countries by the Taiwanese president, vice-president, premier, vice-premier, or foreign minister. Lee Teng-hui's trip to Cornell University for an alumni reunion in summer 1995 was considered by Beijing to be a 'serious transgression' of the rule, which partly led to the Missile Test Crisis in March 1996.

Finally, the hegemonic 'one China' arrangement evidently prevails over any interpretations initiated by Taiwan. Although theoretically Taiwanese leaders can freely explain their policies, the actual exercise often turns out to be ineffective, or even to backfire. The failure of the KMT's redefinition of the mainland-Taiwan ontology as 'one country, two governments,' 'one country, two political entities,' or its policy representation as 'one-China-oriented-transitional-two-China'[58] in the early 1990s illustrates the dominant effect of the 'one China' institution. So does the fruitless release of the Taiwanese 'One Divided China' policy document in early 1997. Two years later, Lee Teng-hui's statement depicting the cross-strait ties as 'special state to state relations' in July 1999[59] also backfired and incited conflict with Beijing and Washington. More recently, in his effort to highlight and reassert the sovereign status of the island state, President Chen Shui-bian said, on 3 August 2002, that while 'Taiwan and China [are] standing on opposite sides of the strait, there is one country on each side.' The statement 'provoked heated discussion,' which forced Taipei to send an envoy to reassure Washington, and necessitated that the government make official statements to further clarify its position.[60]

In addition to limiting Taiwan's freedom of action, the 'one China' institution enables the PRC to intervene in Taiwan's international activities. Not surprisingly, Beijing has taken numerous opportunities to reiterate the 'one China' principle in order to entrench its interests.

Since the mid-1980s, as more and more states began to expand their non-governmental ties with Taiwan and the island's democratization as well as 'pragmatic diplomacy' were set in motion, the PRC increasingly found it necessary to specify domains that Taiwan and other countries should not transgress. This is exemplified by Beijing's release of two major documents in August 1993 and February 2000.[61]

In both cases, Beijing explicitly warned countries which have established diplomatic relations with Taiwan and reaffirmed its opposition to Taiwan's lobbying for 'one country, two seats' in international organizations that require sovereign statehood. The question of Taiwan's participation, Beijing maintained, can be considered only under the 'one China' premise and in light of the nature or statutes of the international organizations concerned. Thus, for the PRC, Taiwan is ineligible for membership in any intergovernmental organizations (IGOs). Likewise, the case of the Asian Development Bank (ADB) and APEC 'cannot constitute a "model" applicable to other [IGOs].' As well, in both documents, Beijing reiterated its objection to arms sales and technology transfers to Taiwan 'in any form or under any pretext.'

At this juncture, it should be stressed that the relations between the PRC and the 'one China' structure are mutually constitutive. The former is embedded in the latter to the extent that Beijing's interests are legitimated by the 'one China' institution, and the latter's persistence ultimately depends upon the continuing practices of the PRC and other countries. Beijing's requests for joint communiqués on the occasions of formal state visits as well as its own policy elaborations thus testify to both dimensions of the agent-structure relations.

The issue of continuing practices begets an interesting question: Why is the existing 'one China' institution more tenacious and influential than its predecessor, the preliminary 'one China (ROC)' arrangement that allowed Taipei to represent China in the 1950s and 1960s? Here, Scott's three pillars of institution are relevant. It is suggested that institutions which are characterized by a high degree of convergence and coherence among the three pillars and controlled by the party whose interest is primarily at stake would be more influential than those lacking such traits of organization.

To be sure, the existing arrangement before 1970 was transitory, and the mainland-Taiwan boundary was assumed to be tentative. Neither the demarcation nor the KMT's unilateral claim that Taipei was the capital of all of China were institutionalized with the cohesive organization of regulative, normative, and cultural-cognitive elements. The ad hoc arrangement for Taipei to represent China at the time was not so much a symbol of support for the KMT's 'one China (ROC)' crusade as an expedient instrument for strategic maneuvering in the heyday of the Cold War. In many ways, the cultural-cognitive, normative, and especially regulative power of the arrangement was not controlled by the ROC. Rather, Taipei's representation was essentially bolstered by American sanctioning power. Meanwhile, Western countries were prepared cognitively and normatively to accept Beijing as the major, if not exclusive, government of China.[62] However, as long as they continued to maintain diplomatic ties with Taipei, their cognitive belief that the Communists effectively controlled the mainland and the normative expectation that diplomatic recognition should thus extend to Beijing were not actualized, let alone institutionalized with the aid of legal power. Thus, the 'one China (ROC)' arrangement at the time not only tended to be loosely organized and uncohesive, but also often split in divergent directions.

The historical context has changed profoundly since the Sino-Canadian normalization of October 1970. Thereafter, common practices developed through numerous bilateral, face-to-face negotiations resulting in the codification of the 'one China' idea in joint texts. These have strengthened both the normative and the regulative elements of the new institution in Beijing's favour. The legal and moral implications were that previous western support for the cause of self-determination for the residents on Taiwan had been replaced by at best a formal urge for a peaceful resolution of the dispute. The PRC now has legitimate grounds to interfere in the nature and scope of foreign states' relations with Taiwan. Moreover, as Beijing was recognized by more and more countries in the world, the PRC's missions abroad were expanding accordingly. This helped extend its surveillance networks to monitor the position of other states on the Taiwan issue. The regulative power of the 'one China' institution has been further magnified since the late 1970s when Deng Xiaoping reformed the economy and began to open the (mainland) Chinese market to the outside world. Beijing's global monitoring system was then equipped with a growing capacity to deliver rewards and penalties. Thus, in sharp contrast to the pre-1970 situation, the three institutional elements were organized in a much more cohesive way and consolidated in the hands of the PRC.

Moreover, the strength of institutionalization can be demonstrated by the degree of prevalence of the cultural-cognitive pillar. The most influential form of institutionalization is to make the operation of an institution as spontaneous as possible, so as to have the institution taken for granted as the only conceivable way of organizing life and order. Thus, for Mary Douglas, 'the high triumph of institutional thinking is to make the institutions completely invisible.'[63] Likewise, Michel Foucault highlighted this dimension of power: In contrast to previous modes of power and control, in the modern or post-modern era it is those who are subject to punishment who are visible, whereas those who wield the power of discipline cease to be visible.[64] Interestingly, this line of argument can also be found in pre-modern Chinese literature. For example, the Taoist notion of 'governing by not acting' and the Confucian conception that 'weed bends while wind blows' similarly testify to the ultimate importance of the cultural-cognitive element of institutions.

In the case of the 'one China' institution, and given the interests at stake, Beijing will closely monitor the process and set in motion regulative force if required. As long as Beijing finds it necessary to use coercion, the highest stage of the 'one China' institutionalization has not yet been achieved. After all, 'additional control mechanisms are required only insofar as the process of institutionalization is less than completely successful.'[65]

To sum up, using historical and sociological institutionalism this chapter explored the 'one China' phenomenon, the time that the issue first appeared on the world stage through a period of contingency and contending ideas. It highlighted the role played by Ottawa in the formation of that institution: in initiating the Stockholm negotiations, which eventually led to the embodiment of the 'one China' idea based on the Canadian formula used in diplomatic texts, and as a result of institutional isomorphism. The 'one China' principle in concrete policy realms was demonstrated by examining Ottawa's admission and designation policies towards Taiwan in the area of sports, as exemplified by the 1976 Montreal Olympics.

The chapter recast the meaning and impact of the 'one China' institutionalization in the context of new institutionalism. It was argued that institutions function as filters that foreclose other possibilities of historical development which had been relatively open in the past. In the case of Taiwan, freedom of policy action and diplomatic space was marginalized, and the PRC's action in interfering with Taiwan's international relations was legitimized. Meanwhile, Beijing's interests are embedded and entrenched in the development of the 'one China' institution. Finally, the state of the 'one China' institutional development was to be more influential than its predecessor in light of the coherence of its cultural-cognitive, normative, and regulative elements and their consolidation within the hands of the PRC. The chapter also pointed out what remains to be done for the institution to operate in a more successful way.

Notes

Parts of this chapter were presented to the 1998 Canadian Political Science Association and the 2000 International Political Science Association conferences. Comments from the following scholars on earlier drafts are gratefully acknowledged: Scott Bennett, Dan Cohn, Norman Hillmer, André Lecours, Kim Richard Nossal, Daniel Osabu-kle, Jeremy Paltiel, Fiona Robinson, Rob Shields, Sharon Sutherland, and anonymous reviewers. Its major revision was undertaken with the support of the Chiang Ching-kuo Foundation and the Canadian Asian Studies Association through the CCK Post Doctoral Fellowships. Host institutions and professors that offered favourable settings or advice include the Department of Political Science, University of Ottawa; University of Toronto – York University Joint Centre for Asia Pacific Studies; B. Michael Frolic; André Laliberté; and Claire Turenne Sjolander.

1 The development of institutionalism was particularly evident in economics, political science, and sociology. In each of these disciplines, boundaries are typically drawn between 'old' and 'new' species. However, not all institutionalists accepted this distinction. For example, see Philip Selznick, 'Institutionalism "Old" and "New,"' *Administrative Science Quarterly*, 41 (1996), 270–7.

2 See Stephen Krasner (ed.), *International Regimes* (Ithaca: Cornell University Press, 1983); Volker Rittberger (ed.), *Regime Theory and International Relations* (Oxford: Clarendon, 1993); O.R. Young, *International Cooperation* (Ithaca: Cornell University Press, 1989).

3 W. Richard Scott, *Institutions and Organizations*, 2nd ed. (Thousand Oaks: Sage, 2001), 41–70. In Scott's typology, each school of new institutionalism

tends to highlight the importance of one of the three pillars: economics focuses on the 'regulative,' political science on the 'normative,' and sociology on the 'cultural-cognitive.' Paul Hirsch, however, criticized Scott's 'cognitive' pillar as becoming a stand-alone theory. See 'Sociology without Social Structure: Neoinstitutionalist Theory Meets Brave New World,' *American Journal of Sociology*, 102 (1997), 1704–20.

4 Some of their similarities deserve a brief note. For example, both commonly see institutions as filters that favour given sets of interpretation of political life; they emphasize the importance of reflexive learning, ex post facto rationalization, and the role of 'ideas' in the policymaking process. Both stress the embeddedness of organizational entities in a broader context, although the sociological stream of new institutionalism highlights the role of symbolic meaning systems in the process of legitimization and the mechanism of 'institutional isomorphism' in the process of institutionalization. Historical institutionalism stresses 'historical contingency' and 'path dependency.'

5 B. Guy Peters, *Institutional Theory in Political Science: The 'New Institutionalism'* (London: Continuum, 1999), 63–5.

6 In this sense, sociological institutionalism converges with Anthony Giddens's 'structuration theory' and social constructivism in international relations. See Der-yuan Wu: 'On the Linkage between Social Constructivism in International Relations and New Institutionalism in Sociological and Organizational Analysis,' *Taiwanese Political Science Review*, 7 (2003), 3–37, and 'Institutional Development and Adaptability: Canada, Taiwan and the Social Construction of "One China"' doctoral dissertation, Department of Political Science, Carleton University, 2000, 50–60.

7 Taiwan was first embroiled in the 'unification-vs-dividedness' debate in the late seventeenth century as a bastion of the Min loyalist Koxinga attempted to recover the mainland. This crusade failed. Only after it began being effectively controlled by Manchu China, Taiwan was ceded to Japan in the 1895 Treaty of Shimonoseki.

8 It has been argued that (for both the Nationalists and the Communists) 'when it comes to explicit claims to sovereignty over Taiwan, there is a deafening silence between 1911 and ... the Second World War.' See Christopher Hughes, *Taiwan and Chinese Nationalism* (London: Routledge, 1997), 5–6, 12–13.

9 On the Canadian case, see Stephen Beecroft, 'Canadian Policy towards China, 1949–57,' in Paul Evans and B. Michael Frolic (eds.), *Reluctant Adversaries* (Toronto: University of Toronto Press, 1991), 49–52; Chester Ronning, *A Memoir of China in Revolution* (New York: Pantheon, 1974), 171–5.

10 An observer highlighted the American role and 'comparable' political identity crises faced by Chiang Kai-shek and Mao Zedong that contributed to the demarcation. See Shiping Zheng, 'Making Sense of the Conflict between Mainland China and Taiwan,' in Vendulka Kubalkova (ed.), *Foreign Policy in a Constructed World* (Armonk: M.E. Sharpe, 2001), 208–11.

11 At the time, there were also Saudi Arabian and Belgian 'one China, one Taiwan' proposals to resolve the 'one China' dispute.

12 Francois Fejto, 'France and China: The Intersection of Two Grand Designs,' in A.M. Halpern (ed.), *Policies toward China* (New York: McGraw-Hill, 1965), 42–6; 52–8.

13 Department of External Affairs (DEA) file 20-1-2-PRC, Pt. 1, vol. 8874, Paris telegram (tel.) to Ottawa (OTW), 28 Nov. 1963.

14 *The Foreign Relations of the United States (FRUS)*, 1964–68, vol. 30, 5–8, 12.

15 Stephen Erasmus, 'General de Gaulle's Recognition of Peking,' *China Quarterly*, 18 (1964), 195–200.

16 *Survey of China Mainland Press*, Jan. 1964, 23.

17 DEA file 20-Taiwan-1-3, Pt. 1, vol. 8882, Washington tel. to OTW, 13 Feb. 1964.

18 See DEA file 20-1-2- PRC, Pts. 1–3, vol. 10056.

19 Don Page, 'The Representation of China in the United Nations: Canadian Perspective and Initiatives, 1949–71,' in Evans and Frolic, *Reluctant Adversaries*, 89–97.

20 DEA file 20-1-2-China-1, Pt. 1.2, vol. 10088, PMO Press Release, 29 May 1968.

21 Ibid., OTW tel. to Washington (WST), 30 May 1968.

22 Ibid., Memorandum (Memo) for Minister (Min), 3 July 1968.

23 Ibid., Pt. 4, vol. 10089, Memo for Min, 31 Oct. 1968.

24 Robert Edmonds, 'Canada's Recognition of the People's Republic of China,' *Canadian Foreign Policy*, 5 (1998), 201–17; B. Michael Frolic, 'The Trudeau Initiative,' in Evans and Frolic, *Reluctant Adversaries*, 189–216. For a round-by-round narrative in the context of Canada-U.S. relations, see Der-yuan Wu, 'Engaged Independence: A Case of the Sino-Canadian Stockholm Negotiations, 1969–70,' paper presented at the 2001 CPSA Conference, Laval University, Quebec City, 27–9 May 2001.

25 DEA file 20-1-2-China-1, Pt. 7, vol. 8814, Stockholm tel. to OTW, 21 Feb. 1969.

26 See ibid., Pts. 10–11, vols. 8814–8815.

27 See ibid., Pts. 12–13, vol. 8815.

28 See ibid., Pts. 14–18, vols. 8815–8816.

29 Ibid., Pt. 19, vol. 8816, Stockholm tel. to OTW, 3 Oct. 1970.

30 Ibid., Pt. 14, vol. 8815, Stockholm tel. to OTW, 26 Jan. 1970.

31 *External Affairs*, Nov. 1970, 378–9.

32 *Peking Review (PR)*, vols. 14, 15, 17; *Beijing Review (BR)*, vols. 23, 26.

33 John H. Holdridge, *Crossing the Divide* (Lanham: Rowman and Littlefield, 1997), 266.

34 See *PR*, vols. 15–18.

35 For example, the Australians requested a Canadian provision of information on the Stockholm talks. Ottawa then produced a ten-page summary account of the negotiations and made it available to Canberra. DEA file 20-1-2-PRC, Pt. 14, vol. 8773, OTW tel. to Canberra, 1 June; Summary Note, 4 June 1971.

36 *PR*, vol. 15, no. 40, 12–13; vol. 18, no. 24, 7–8.

37 *PR*, vol. 15, no. 21, 20; *Foreign Broadcasting Information Service (FBIS)*, CHI-92-164, 24 Aug., 1992, 16.

38 *FBIS* CHI-91-089, 8 May 1991, 9; *PR*, vol. 14, no. 32, 22–4; *BR*, vol. 41, no. 3, 4.

39 In chronological sequence, these were: Maldives, Guinea-Bissau, Niger, Botswana, Jordan, Antiqua and Barbuda, Angola, Lesotho, Bolivia, and Nicaragua.

40 *BR*, vol. 39, no. 20, 6.

41 *BR*, vol. 40, no. 49, 6–7; vol. 37, no. 4, 4.

42 In the Shanghai Communiqué of 1972 and the Joint Communiqué of 17 August 1982, Washington linked its adherence to the 'one China' policy or gradual reduction of arms sales to Taiwan with the PRC's commitment to a peaceful resolution of the issue. See Der-yuan Wu, '"New" Track of Institutionalization?' paper presented at the American Association for Chinese Studies Conference, New York City, 30 Oct. to 1 Nov. 1998, 16.

43 This, however, does not mean that the emergence of the Canadian formula was the only determinant for the policy actions of other countries.

44 These took place at the British Columbia International Trade Fair of 1971 as various Taiwanese acrobatic groups were touring. See DEA files 20-1-2-PRC, Pt. 19, vol. 8773; Pts. 22, 25; vol. 8774; file 20-1-2-Taiwan, Pts. 7–8, vol. 8789.

45 See ibid., Pt. 20; files 20-1-2-Taiwan, Pts. 6–7, vol. 8789.

46 DEA file 68, vol. 3060, letter to USSEA, 23 April 1975.

47 DEA file 55-26-OLYMP-1976-3-TAIWAN, Pt. 1, vol. 10926, Memo for Min, 13 Nov. 1975.

48 See DEA file 36 Pt. 2, vol. 3056.

49 Ibid., Pt. 1, Sharp letter to Killanin, 28 May 1976.

50 B. Michael Frolic, 'Logical and Unsatisfactory: Canada's China Policy and

the Exclusion of Taiwan from the 1976 Montreal Olympics,' unpublished paper, 19 May 1996, 18.

51 See DEA file 55-26-OLYMP-1976-3-TAIWAN, Pt. 2.1, vol. 10926; Ming-che Yang, 'Fiasco at the Olympics,' *Free China Review*, 26 (1976), 9–14.

52 See DEA file 20-1-2-Taiwan, Pt. 8, vol. 8789.

53 See Der-yuan Wu, 'Institutional Development and Adaptability,' chapt. 8. See also, Robert Madsen, 'The Struggle for Sovereignty between China and Taiwan,' in Stephen D. Krasner (ed.), *Problematic Sovereignty* (New York: Columbia University Press, 2001), 169–83.

54 Christopher Hughes, *Taiwan and Chinese Nationalism* (London: Routledge, 1997), 46–69.

55 Deon Geldenhuys, *Isolated States* (Cambridge: Cambridge University Press, 1991); Efraim Inbar, *Outcast Countries in the World Community* (Denver: University of Denver Press, 1985).

56 Francoise Mengin, 'Taiwan's Non-Official Diplomacy,' *Diplomacy and State-craft*, 8 (1997), 244–6.

57 See ROC Ministry of Foreign Affairs (MOFA) Web site: www.mofa.gov.tw/newmofa/index.htm

58 As stated by then-Economic Minister P.K Chiang at the 1993 APEC meeting.

59 Government Information Office (GIO), 'Looking beneath the Surface of the "One China" Question' (1997); *Getting Real* (1999).

60 See *China Times*, 4 and 6 Aug. 2002. For the clarifying statement, see *Taipei Journal*, 23 Aug. 2002. http://publish.gio.gov.tw/FCJ/past/02082323.html

61 *BR*, vol. 36, no. 36, 1–8; vol. 43, no. 10, 16–24.

62 Madsen, 'Struggle for Sovereignty,' 158–9.

63 Mary Douglas, *How Institutions Think* (Syracuse: Syracuse University Press, 1986), 98.

64 Michel Foucault, *Discipline and Punish: The Birth of the Prison*, translated by A. Sheridan (New York: Vintage Books, 1995).

65 Peter L. Berger and Thomas Luckmann, *The Social Construction of Reality* (New York: Doubleday, 1967), 55.

15

Constructing the State: Sovereignty in Comparative and International Perspectives – The View from East Asia

JEREMY PALTIEL

This chapter provides a synthesis of neo-institutional analysis with social constructivism in examining the impact of the institution of state sovereignty as imposed on and adapted in East Asia. This institution was imposed on East Asia by the western powers, and in the process East Asian institutions were reshaped and adapted to those of the principal states of the international system. Where the international system does not directly regulate the internal structure of states, it does so indirectly, for example, through access to resources, trade privileges, and private and public capital flows, and thus consolidates state elites and anchors the state's institutions within its domestic society.

The social constructivist approach to international relations focuses on how the international system, or international society constructs the state. Realists and particularly neo-realist theorists put considerable intellectual capital into the proposition that the existence of sovereign states is what organizes an international system and that this system is the result of and dependent on the existence of sovereign states in determining international relations behaviour. Social constructivists, in a manner highly reminiscent of new institutionalist arguments about the state, counter the realists' argument with the contention that the international system not only determines international relations behaviour, it is also explicitly determines what is the state and what is state sovereignty.

James Rosenau defined the state as 'the norms governing relationships, the habits of voluntary and coerced compliance, and the practices of cooperation through which large numbers of people form a collectivity that possesses sovereign authority over them.'[1] Norms and sovereignty form a central axis of what defines a state.

This renewed attention to the norms and laws of political science that prevailed before the Second World War is ironic. Of course, this is not a true repetition of the mode of legal formalist research. Instead, both historical sociologists and rational choice institutionalists are examining the conditions that give rise to the constraining power of institutions and, by implication, the state. This approach informs, and is much informed by, the sociology of law. Thus, the shift to new institutionalism marks a broad return to the central concerns articulated in the work of Max Weber. Using this approach,

> The sociologist seeks to describe how the behavior of individuals is causally influenced by their own normative commitments to the law and their beliefs concerning the commitments of others ... In short, even though the sociology of law does not itself seek to establish judgments of a normative sort, it is centrally concerned with what may be called *the phenomenon of normativity* – the fact that human beings are influenced in their behavior by their commitment to evaluative standards, including those contained in the legal order.[2]

Behaviorists also have traced their intellectual parentage to Weber (and Emil Durkheim), but their research has tended to focus on individual beliefs to the exclusion of the *organization* of beliefs in institutions that carry sanctioning power. Focusing on individual beliefs, without considering the intervention of organized structures, effectively ignores this essential characteristic of the phenomenon of law.

Ideas matter. This is not simply because they animate the behaviour of individuals – this is the false premise behind 'political culture' theory – but because ideas are embodied in institutions. These institutions constrain actors by selecting leaders who conform to an approved agenda of views and who devise decision-making rules to restrict choice within a limited range of recognized options. Institutionalists like James March and Johan Olsen situated their research program in the phenomenon of 'bounded rationality.' Herbert Simon, March's mentor, recognized that decision-makers cannot possibly rationally evaluate all possible options. Organizations both create and channel information flows. 'Bounded rationality' for rational-choice institutionalists is determined by the opportunity costs of the information associated with rational decision-making models.

For historical sociologists, 'path dependent' models of constrained choice are associated with the imposed range of choices that have been predetermined by previous patterns of choice in accordance with the limited information and norms that are learned in particular organizational settings. 'Hegemony,' is the term preferred by Marxist sociologists, influenced by the thought of Antonio Gramsci. Hegemony refers to the constraints imposed on information processing and choice by ideology dominant within the state apparatus. As used by Cox in international political economy, Gramscian hegemony is not very different from what John Ruggie has called the 'imbedded liberalism' of international regimes.[3] In different terms, they refer to political behaviour and how it is conditioned by institutionalized norms.

The paradigmatic shift represented by new institutionalism represents a reaffirmation, implicit or explicit, of the contribution of Max Weber to the epistemology of the social sciences. This outlook recognizes that constraints on human behaviour are no less 'real' for being ideal or socially constructed. Human beings must manoeuvre in a world where other persons' commitments and intentions, organized by ideologies, norms, conventions, and laws, form a latticework of imposed choices. That this matrix is formed socially, through the cumulative intentions of human beings, imposes a no less real or 'objective' constraint on individual behaviour than do those characteristics of the physical environment on which human beings have no influence whatsoever. The central nexus of organized social thinking is the state, backed up by the power and means to coerce. Organized coercive violence exemplifies the state as a social construction, because coercion is only as effective as the social nexus that supports it. Recognizing the coercive and exclusive character of the state's recurrent reliance on violence is the context for the discussion of *sovereignty*, the foundation of coercive authority in modern western thought.

The East Asian Encounter as a Clash of Institutions

Stephen Krasner pointed out that states may fail when faced with challenges outside the range of the policy options that they have been designed to meet.[4] The encounter between the trading powers of the West and the East Asian polities in the mid-nineteenth century was a true clash of normative systems, of civilizations. Faced with the technological and military power of the states of the capitalist West, the institutions of the East Asian polities failed. The Opium Wars that began in 1839 ushered in a process of societal reconstruction and reformation of the international state system that has not been fully played out more than a century and a half later. States and state systems collapsed when they were forced to meet the terms of normative engagement that were imposed on them by the powerful western states. Subsequently, East Asian states *accumulated* power through adaptation to external norms. By deploying external resources, they transformed selective engagement with external agencies into institutional mechanisms for shaping societal outcomes.

The elements that combined in the reconstitution of national polities and international relations in East Asia involved the organization and purpose of the state, the relationship of the state to the economy, and the interactions of states under capitalism.

The failure of China to mount an effective defence against Great Britain in 1839–42 and later, led to the collapse of the normative order in East Asia, triggering the process that encouraged Japanese to literally 'leave Asia and enter Europe' (*datsu A nyu Ô*) and propelled generations of Chinese to seek *jiuguo zhenli* – 'the truth that will save China' – an ideological construct capable of restoring China's innate greatness. The East Asian examples convey a complex process of internal and external legitimation. Once domestic authority collapsed, new domestic institutional arrangements were legitimated by reference to external international norms. These may or may not have conformed to domestic political interests and ideals. As a result, new identities had to be negotiated both internally and externally.

One of the founding texts of new institutionalism, Theda Skocpol's *States and Social Revolutions*, is premised on the relationship of the state as an internal organization to its survival within the international system. In the three cases she studied, the failure of the state to stand up to international competition precipitated revolutions that reorganized power. Revolutions reconfigured authority in a manner that enabled the state to focus its coercive power more effectively on challenges emanating from the outside. But the reconstitution of state power in the great revolutions that Skocpol examined is only half the story. The French, Russian, and Chinese revolutions had an impact on the organization of the interstate system at least as profound as the relationship of the state to domestic society. The principle of *cuius regio, eius religio*, enshrined in the treaty of Westphalia of 1648, did not usher in an age of tolerance and pluralism in the recognition of internal state forms. Not only was the non-European and non-Christian world subjected to continued imperial expansion, but within Europe itself, the French Revolution ushered in an age of national wars. Revolutionary France was opposed in the first instance by a 'Holy Alliance' of states that had participated in the Peace of Westphalia. An international community did not reach truly universal dimensions until the conjunction of decolonization and the coexistence of opposing social systems within the confines of a single United Nations. The fact this system never achieved full legitimacy was played out in the politics of the Cold War.

The idea that the state system consists of heterogeneous units of like function has never been more than an ideal or a myth. The states of East Asia were introduced to the institution of the sovereign nation-state by having their sovereignty denied or infringed upon.[5]

Unlike the experience of colonial Africa and much of the rest of colonial Asia, in the historic polities of East Asia (China, Japan, and Korea) a dominant ethnocultural identity had consolidated political power over territorial space long before the modern impingement by the West. Political authority did not take the form of Westphalian sovereignty, but a recognizable 'state' exercised political power over a definable territory and entertained neighbourly relations within cultural norms.

In East Asia, the boundaries of the historic polity and the modern nation-state largely coincide, yet the meaning that attaches to the territory and frontier was imported from Europe only by the agency of western imperialist intervention.

The historic 'states' of East Asia, represented the contours of a historic identity that formed the vessel of an emergent nationhood. The nation was an 'imagined' community (as described by Benedict Anderson) that traced a narrative relationship to a historic identity disrupted but not eliminated by western intervention. The West was experienced as the power that denied the nation its political expression at the same time that it furnished the norms that underpinned the institutions of the nation-state. The sovereignty that was contradicted by western privilege became the ideal of national revival. For this reason, institutions gained legitimacy through the perception of successful *competition* with rather than *conformity* to western norms and values.[6]

Dimensions of Sovereignty

Over the past half century the realist school has dominated international relations theory.[7] This paradigm takes state sovereignty as the axiomatic basis of the international system and attempts to create a positivistic science of international relations based upon it This school arose in direct opposition to normative approaches to the relations among states that were criticized as being 'idealist.'[8] Sovereignty is not an axiom of the state, but a legal concept connected to specific European legal institutions. The intrinsic relationship between the state, sovereignty, and the law was well understood in the European context but would have been a complete mystery in Asia.[9] Sovereignty is a legal institution, connected with other legal institutions of unmistakably western pedigree, and not an axiom of international relations theory, as imagined by realist scholars of international relations theory.[10]

The traditional Chinese state was a formal hierarchy centred on the Emperor, but it was also a network of networks built around loyalty to the ruling house. Positive law in this structure had the quality of compulsory communication within the hierarchy of the state but did not extend to private obligations. There was no private law in traditional China. While the Emperor's role was to be the linchpin joining heaven and earth, the Emperor's sovereignty comprised nothing more than loyalty to his person. The state was the administrative domain within which this loyalty prevailed. It consisted of both an inner realm where the civil bureaucrats were dispatched, taxes were collected, and regular communications were maintained with the capital, and an outer realm where loyalty did not entail administrative command and control. The western zero-sum division of territory into exclusive zones of sovereignty simply did not apply, because the Westphalian notion of sovereignty that presupposes the coexistence of sovereign states is a notion foreign to Chinese thinking. Historically, when the inner realm of the Chinese cultural sphere became divided among contending states, the situation was regarded as abnormal, and a matter of contending sovereigns – not as international relations among commensurable units.[11]

Stephen Krasner recognized sovereignty as an institution with embedded norms and tried to reconcile this concept with the central tenet of realism – that international relations is a self-help system where power is ultimately decisive and norms are ineffective. He called this outcome 'organized hypocrisy.' Michel Oksenberg, who applied Krasner's approach in surveying sovereignty in East Asian history, ultimately concluded that the concept of sovereignty effectively constrains the range of choices available to resolve such problems as Taiwan and Tibet.[12]

Sovereignty and East Asia

The problem of international relations that emerged from the impingement of the western powers on Chinese administration from the

Opium Wars onward has been about establishing the terms of commensurability of states in the absence of norms to support this: 'It took
China over 150 years to understand, analyse and adapt itself to that
system – originating from the Treaty of Westphalia in 1648 – a system,
which, ironically is culturally alien and morally deplorable to the Chinese and which had inflicted enormous pain on them since the Opium
War.'[13] When the Chinese state was forced into regular dealings with
western powers, each side of the relationship approached the other
through incommensurable frameworks. Although westerners confronted a social structure that appeared to have the familiar outlines of
a state – that is, a regular territorial administration headed by a 'sovereign' emperor, that this political unit was 'objectively' commensurate
with European powers was irrelevant. The cognitive framework, the
deep understanding of commensurability, had to be learned – *by both
sides* – and it is still being learned today.

From the very beginning, western powers focused on the incompatibility and incommensurability of Chinese legal institutions with their
own. One of the prime elements included in the so-called unequal treaties was the principle of *extraterritoriality*, that is, the removal of western persons from the jurisdiction of Chinese courts and legal officials.[14]

The general insouciance with which the Chinese have treated the
law finds no parallel in international law and sovereignty. Even before
the Opium War, Commissioner Lin, whose 'war on drugs' initiated the
fateful clash of China and the West, had commissioned a partial translation of Vattel's *Le loi des gens* to buttress his admonition of the British
opium merchants. And not long after the Treaty of Nanking was
signed, one of the first acts of the Zongli Yamen (China's first foreign
affairs department) was to commission a translation of Wheaton's *Elements of International Law*. This translation contains the first use of the
term 'rights' in any East Asian language.[15]

China sought to restore its sovereign rights almost as soon as it was
capable of diplomatic negotiations. The linkage between the reform of
China's judicial system and the abolition of extraterritoriality was
established not long after this had been accomplished in Japan. This
linkage was imbedded in the commercial treaty China signed with
Great Britain as early as September 1902.[16] China again strenuously
pressed its case for the restoration of its sovereign rights at the Versailles Conference of 1919 and refused to sign the treaty when it was
rebuffed. Later, at the Washington Conference in 1921, the Chief Justice
of the Supreme Court of China stressed that extraterritoriality 'is a der-

ogation of China's sovereign rights and is regarded by the Chinese people as a national humiliation.'[17] Although the resolution on China adopted by the conference called for a fact-finding mission to be dispatched within three months, it did not arrive until 1926, in the wake of further demands for 'treaty revision' that followed the nationalist upsurge of the 25 May incident of 1925.[18] China once again protested the derogations from Chinese sovereignty, but the mission concluded that China's legal reform and judicial administration 'had yet to achieve a sufficient degree' to warrant the abolition of extraterritorial rights.[19]

The newly established Nationalist Government in Nanjing redoubled the effort to abolish extraterritoriality and restore tariff autonomy from 1928 onwards, and pressed ahead with legal reform, culminating in the completion of the so-called Six Codes in the early 1930s. Chinese legal codes were largely based on Japanese models, not only because so many Chinese had received a modern education in Japan and because Japanese had pioneered the adaptation of western (largely German) legal forms and their translation into Chinese characters: 'The choice of Japan as a model for legal reform was no accident. Japan's success in reversing extra-territoriality and in becoming a mighty power in the Asian area was seen to be the result of it having a constitution and a legal system based on Western models.'[20]

The turmoil occasioned by growing Japanese encroachment following the Manchurian Incident in 1931 and civil war hampered further progress towards treaty revision. Japanese occupation of the Treaty Ports eventually rendered western privileges moot, but it was China's status as an ally in the war against the Axis powers that permitted the revision of treaties with Great Britain and the United States in January 1943.[21] The historical record indicates a persistent and irrevocable wish of every Chinese regime to restore China's sovereignty and to reverse the derogations imposed on China in the nineteenth century. China's stance on the sovereignty question demonstrated the following: First, China was put in a relatively passive situation, dependent on shifts in international relations in terms of its ability to press its claims. Second, its capacity and status as a sovereign entity were severely restricted both in domestic policy and in international relations. China had no real independent foreign policy decision-making capacity, and even after its achievement of tariff autonomy, its economic independence was severely constrained. Third, China's approach to sovereignty was purely defensive, calculated on restoring or regaining lost rights, and often dependent on foreign actors for assistance in restoring rights from others. China was thus never able to put forward its own views of sovereignty, and as a result fell short of the status of a great power. Fourth, although China lacked the power to assert its own views of sovereignty, China stood in solidarity with weak and small states.[22]

The determination to restore and enhance China's sovereignty and prestige was the core mission in the foundation of the Peoples's Republic of China. Mao Zedong's declaration on founding the People's Republic that 'henceforth the Chinese People has stood up' is symbolic evidence, while the use of force in Korea and Tibet in 1950 was its active proof. The new regime was determined to exercise untrammeled jurisdiction within its frontiers, and it was prepared to back its determination with coercive force. This was done successively in Tibet, Korea, the Taiwan Strait, the Indian border, the Russian border, and on the border with Vietnam. Only after sealing its borders and defining the limits of its jurisdiction did the Chinese state seriously begin to promote movements across the frontier.

The Chinese state finds its claims of territorial extension and cultural-ideological differences sustained by the norms of Westphalian sovereignty. International law is the justification of Chinese claims that are then projected back onto the reluctant West. The West, especially since its victory in the Cold War, appears to have fallen back on natural law notions of the common normative purposes of states, reading into sovereignty norms the values of democracy and human rights.[23]

The 'normative' approach favoured by Chinese theorists, however, finds in sovereignty a bedrock guarantee of normative *difference* and a consistent basis for assuring cultural relativism. Sovereignty became for China and Chinese people an unfulfilled ideal, a violated norm, and an institution from which they were illegitimately excluded. State institutions gained legitimacy only through the perception of successful competition to rather than conformity with western norms and values. As Alastair Iain Johnston has put it, 'sovereignty values are still a central driver of Chinese foreign policy ... A realpolitik strategic culture still colours the world-views of many security policy decision-makers, [a] world view in which military force is still a potentially useful tool.'[24] China has become even more committed to the norms of sovereignty than other contemporary states. The full expression of national sovereignty and a complete recovery from the 'century of humiliation' inflicted on China beginning with the Opium Wars is the core value behind Beijing's claim to Taiwan. Indeed the Chinese approach to international law is essentially as a means to safeguard and promote national sovereignty: 'Sovereignty had always been and still was the most basic principle of international law and the most valuable characteristic of the state. There could not be any power superior to the sovereign state. Any attempts to subvert, dilute or transform sovereignty through such devices as "world law" or "transnational law" were contrary to international law. The problem of modern states was how to maintain, not how to relinquish or diminish, sovereignty.'[25]

This rigid and uncompromising stance on sovereignty is justified in terms of China's historical treatment, but ironic in that the concept owes nothing to Chinese tradition and is a purely western invention. Sovereignty as an institution, as a social construction, was copied instrumentally precisely in order to participate in the state system dominated by the West. The examples of Korea and Japan shed particular light on this process.

Japan

The modernization of Japan is virtually synonymous with the restoration of Japanese sovereignty. While a retrospective view of the Meiji period commonly regards the Meiji Oligarchs as single-mindedly devoted to socio-economic transformation, in fact, the overriding objective of the Meiji oligarchs was the achievement of full and equal sovereign status with the western powers, symbolized in treaty revision. They were particularly interested in gaining tariff autonomy and expunging the extraterritorial privileges of resident foreigners. It is to this end they undertook to establish a western-style constitutional system, promulgate a western legal code, establish western political institutions including a court system, and build a modern army and navy on western lines.

It would be difficult to point to a group of political leaders more clearsighted about their objectives. Ito Hirobumi, the principal architect of the Meiji Constitution, repeatedly traversed Europe in search of an appropriate script for political institutions. He and his contemporaries held no illusions concerning the necessity to conform to a new and alien model. Fukuzawa Yukichi's famous slogan *Datsu A Nyu Ô* – leave Asia, Join Europe – was a dramatic illustration of a well-understood imperative. Ito and his contemporaries understood full well that they did not have the option of writing their own script. The choice was not mimesis or creative originality, nor was it a dichotomous juxtaposition of instrumental reason versus conformity to external norms. They were following western scripts and not 'adapting' a western model.

The Japanese leaders were interested in content as well as form, but they felt utterly constrained by the range of forms already offered by western powers. They used instrumental reason to minimize the consequences they hoped to avoid – for example, minimizing the effects of the adoption of a western legal system by deliberately establishing a court system that was capable of handling only a very small volume of cases. But they could not foresee, nor could they avoid, the forms influencing the outcomes – as in the emergence of parliamentary government. While there was no mistaking the determination to achieve substantive equality with the West on the basis of national military power, there can be no mistaking the acute sensitivity with respect to the formal requirements of international recognition. The promulgation of a constitution and a western-style legal code, that is, the outward institutions of a western 'civilized' state were directly stimulated by the wish to abolish the privilege of extraterritoriality that western powers enjoyed pursuant to the treaties that had opened Japan to western trade.[26]

To further buttress their claim to join the Euro-American powers, Japan embarked on the enterprise of imperial expansion and colonization. As Peter Duus has argued, 'a world dominated by western imperialism provides both context and model for agents of Meiji modernization. ... In much the same way that they imported, assimilated, and transformed other cultural and institutional structures from the Western world, they adopted imperialist practices as well. Given the successful example given by Western nations, it was natural that the acquisition of foreign possessions alongside building a modern army and navy was essential to establishing Japan's bona fides as a "civilized" state and society.'[27]

Japan's accession to full sovereignty within the international system can be confidently dated from the signing of the Anglo-Japanese Naval Treaty in 1902. This treaty also marked the culmination of the process of treaty revision. It should be admitted that this achievement was not based solely or even primarily on the basis of mimesis alone – clearly Japan's victory in the first Sino-Japanese War played a determinative role, further consolidated with Japan's stunning victory over Russia in 1905. Both the exhibition and demonstration of power and the adoption of an institutional structure that conformed to western norms were the basis of Japan's acceptance as a sovereign state. The failure of the western Allies to agree to Japan's proposal to include a clause on racial equality in the Versailles Peace Treaty at the conclusion of the First World War, as well as failure to achieve parity with the United States and Britain in Washington Naval Disarmament conferences suggested that full equality was still beyond reach.

Contrary to Krasner's claim that power is decisive and mimesis or copying is a distinctly minor theme of international relations, Japan's modernization was indeed a case of 'copying' for the express instrumental purpose of gaining entry to the society of sovereign states. Norms did not substitute for power, but the normative conformity meant a great deal about how power was deployed.

Korea

Korean foreign policy disastrously eschewed western norms of recognition until it was too late. The Korean Court vacillated between reliance on the Chinese tributary system as a form of clientelism (the traditional policy of *Sadaejuyi* or 'serving the Great')[28] and paying lip-service to sovereignty through the Treaty of Kanghwa, which implied, in fact, a dominant and privileged role for Japan. As Bruce Cumings put it, 'the Sino-Korean tributary system was one of inconsequential hierarchy and real independence, if not equality. The Western system that Korea encounters however was one of fictive equality and real subordination.'[29] When the Japanese Empire forced the Korean Court to sign the Treaty of Kanghwa in 1876, this was for Japan one of its first acts as a modern sovereign state, and while article 1 of the treaty recognized Korea as an 'autonomous' state with sovereign rights, the intent was to impose on Korea the same type of subordination that western states had earlier imposed on China. 'Concluded in the name of sovereign equality and against the putative hierarchy of the Chinese world order, the real effect of the treaty was to erase the centuries of essential equality between Japan and Korea.'[30] The successive defeats of China in the war of 1894–95 and Russia in 1904–05 allowed Japan finally to annex Korea and rule it as a colony until Japan in turn was defeated in 1945.

During the colonial period Korean elites engaged in a most striking instance of seeking western recognition to gain sovereignty. Korea, which had never sought to be a sovereign state in western terms, now sought sovereignty on the basis of self-determination. Korean elites responded to Woodrow Wilson's Fourteen Points and the declaration on the principle of the self-determination of nations by sending a delegation to the Versailles Peace Conference, in the hope of restoring Korea's lost sovereignty as part of the general peace settlement that followed the First World War. Coinciding with the Korean delegation's overture to the conference, peaceful demonstrations were coordinated in the Korean capital, Seoul, and throughout Korea on 1 March 1919.[31] These demonstrations were ultimately put down, and the Korean delegation failed to secure a place at the peace table. China's own attempt to restore her sovereignty over former German possessions using the same argument was equally unsuccessful at Versailles and sparked the better known demonstrations of 4 May 1919.

In the wake of the tragic bisection of the Korean peninsula in 1945, the two Korean states have pursued sovereignty in competitive but highly asymmetrical fashion. The South (Republic of Korea, ROK) adopted a fairly consistent strategy based on external recognition, symbolized in the early years by a policy of full conformity with the United States and the United Nations. The ROK has acquiesced in the division of the country and has been willing since the 1970s to concede sovereignty only on its own soil. By contrast, the Democratic People's Republic of Korea (DPRK) in the North refuses to acknowledge the legitimacy of the other Korean state and predicates domestic sovereignty on the promise of national unification and the exclusion of foreign powers. Only once the tide had decisively swung against the North, following the Seoul Olympics of 1988 and the eventual end of the Cold War and Soviet support, did the North reluctantly agree to dual entry to the United Nations and parallel recognition. Nevertheless, the North obstinately clings to a notion of sovereignty that virtually isolates it from engagement with other states.

The foreign policy of the DPRK is a particularly interesting case of the dynamics of power and recognition. With an economy based on autarky and self-reliance, and a totalitarian organization of society, it represents an extreme case of a state virtually outside international society. And yet, North Korea demonstrates both the desire and an active strategy of seeking recognition through the use of military power, namely, through brandishing nuclear and missile threats against its neighbours. Without normal channels of economic interdependence, North Korea is forced to manipulate the security dilemma in a desperate game of international engagement. Operating on the frontier of the security dilemma, North Korea oscillates between demonstrative threats as a ploy to gain recognition and a weakened economy – induced by its self-imposed isolation.

Taiwan

Perhaps the most interesting example of an attempt by any state to secure sovereignty through a strategy of recognition is that of Taiwan (formally known as the Republic of China). The progress of democracy on Taiwan appears as an active refutation of the 'Asian exceptionalism' to democracy and human rights currently fashionable in certain countries, most notably Singapore and Malaysia. Instead, the theme President Lee Teng-hui constantly reiterated in his inaugural address following the presidential elections of 1996, which were held under the threat of missiles from the Mainland, was *Zhuquan zai min* – 'Sovereignty lies with the People.'

We may contrast this situation with the legitimation discourse which was adopted by the communists on the mainland, and even, also the legitimation discourse of the KMT Republican government in Nanjing. These regimes employed revolutionary discourse that altered and to an extent obviated the idea of the 'sovereignty of the people' that both regimes rhetorically espoused. Both regimes based their legitimacy primarily on the process of revolution carried out in the name of the people. The communists in particular defined 'the people' in exclusionary terms. The primary focus of national sovereignty for the communists was external, aimed at China's place in the world at large and the goal of 'saving China' through socialism and the revolution. To this very day the Mainland regime continues to declare its legitimacy by touting the progress of the Chinese state and the emergence of China as a powerful actor on the world stage. It justifies its opposition to 'bourgeois liberalization' and the demands of human rights activists inside and outside China on the grounds that this would fatally weaken the Chinese state.

The process which culminated with the direct election of Lee Teng-hui in March 1996 can be said to have begun with the ROC's loss of the Chinese seat at the United Nations in 1971. The 28 February uprising of 1947 reinforced the KMT's pan-Chinese but effectively exclusionary view of sovereignty and legitimacy following its retreat to the island in 1949. The loss of prestige and international legitimacy implied by its loss of the Chinese seat at the United Nations meant that the KMT could no longer base its sovereignty and legitimacy exclusively in terms of the Chinese state and nation in relation to the outside world. The effort to gain domestic legitimacy involved the KMT, and led to its acquiescence to the formation of the Democratic Progressive Party in 1986 and the abolition of martial law just over a year later. The process of indigenization was completed by Lee Teng-hui following the death of Chiang Ching-kuo in 1988.

The expansion of participation in politics to gain greater internal legitimacy had a direct bearing on the regime's ability to gain legitimacy and respect for its sovereignty internationally. In Taiwan's case the dilemma was twofold – the KMT had to gain the support of the people on Taiwan in order to counter the claims for sovereignty over the island from the communists on the Mainland, whose capacity to speak for the 'Chinese nation' could not be gainsaid unless the 'Chinese nation' could directly voice its dissent, and second, international support for ROC status as a sovereign state would only be forthcoming from the liberal West (and especially the United States) if there were demonstrable evidence that this stance had popular support.

In significant respects, these elements are also present in the democratization process in the Republic of (South) Korea. There too, the opposition could only be co-opted if the military abandoned its authoritarian control, and there too, there was a rival claimant for sovereignty and a critical requirement for international support in an era when the division of the world into two opposing blocs was coming to a close. The end of the Cold War was the context for the emergence of the debate over Asian values and the so-called end of history with the triumph of liberal values.[32] The 'Asian values' debate[33] emerged as a political response to the economic rise of Asian countries and as an explicit attempt to challenge the cultural hegemony of the West as expressed in human rights diplomacy. The importance of this debate is generally expressed through its symbolic purposes (the cultural hegemony of the West – recently operationalized by Joseph Nye as 'soft power')[34] versus attempts to challenge it. It is also a debate about frames of reference and reference cultures. The PRC position in the 'Asian values' debate should be seen as a defence of the regime and the interests of the Chinese state.[35] Thus, the repudiation of Asian exceptionalism by Lee Teng-hui is an expression of alignment with the West – an approach that suits and coheres with Taiwan's political predicament regarding Mainland China. Institutional democracy for Taiwan is a means of gaining international recognition, an imperative of survival in an international order where the sovereignty of the Republic of China is recognized by only a handful of states. Democratic institutions form a contrast to Taiwan's political rivals across the Taiwan Strait and encourage positive attention from policy makers in Washington. Taiwan's strategy of attempting to influence perceptions of international sovereignty by highlighting the institutions of popular sovereignty is quite understandable given the exigencies of survival. Factor endowments in the asymmetry of power across the Taiwan Strait cannot be overcome through self-help alone.[35] Taiwan's adoption of democratic institutions parallels the adoption of western constitutionalism and a western legal system by the Japanese state at the end of the nineteenth century.

Regimes, Sovereignty, and the Issue of China's Participation in the WTO

The capacity of states to behave in a rule-bound, normative fashion regarding their rights and obligations is the implicitly understood basis of participation in international regimes. The compliance issue raised with respect to China's membership in the World Trade Organization (WTO) is fundamentally about whether this assumption is true.[36] Since regimes organize access to important resources, they are a good indicator of the importance of state sovereignty as an institutional form within a system of norms rather than a mere corollary of the exercise of power. Prima facie, the People's Republic of China is a sovereign state, with effective control over its borders and its legislative process. The domestic jurisdiction of the Chinese government is not in dispute. The question is whether the Chinese government is willing and capable of enforcing domestically what it has contracted internationally to do. The reason for skepticism is founded on the explicit anti-liberal foundations of the institutions and ideology of the People's Republic of China, confronting what is widely seen as an institutional representation of the 'embedded liberalism' of the international system of trade and investment.

State identities are at least partly shaped by international norms, including regime norms, and this process is crucial to understanding the process of China's accession to the WTO. Neoliberal regime theory implicitly assumes that regimes are established upon a distinctive form of liberal domestic governance. Few doubt that the government of the People's Republic of China will adjust its legislation to comply with the requirements of WTO membership. The issue is whether that will be translated into administrative action at the lower levels, and whether the Chinese government can get both lower and regional officials, as well as domestic enterprises to accept the norms of WTO membership.

Norms in Chinese society have been particularly unstable during the modern period. At least three separate and distinct normative systems have operated in modern Chinese history, with significant overlap. The traditional emperor-centred normative system did not recognize any authority outside China's borders. The legal sanctions associated with this normative system were eroded in the late nineteenth century and broke down completely following the overthrow of the Qing dynasty in 1911. For the rest of the twentieth century these norms were under challenge from revolutionary ideology, and at various times – in the 4 May era, during the land revolution of the Chinese Communist Party in the 1930s and 1940s and during the so-called Cultural Revolution of the 1960s and 1970s – under explicit attack. Nationalism and republicanism failed to congeal into a set of authoritative institutions and disintegrated into warlordism at the national level. The government established by Chiang Kai-shek in 1927 accomplished western-style legal reform on paper but failed to order social life in practice. Moreover, it was never free from internal or external military challenge, either from recalcitrant warlords, communist insurgents, or invading Japanese forces. The sanctioning power of the extended family, which always paralleled that of the imperial state in Chinese Confucianism, was weakened and then deliberately attacked and disrupted by Chinese communism.

The second normative system was that sponsored, fostered and enforced by the Chinese Communist Party. This is a system of ideology and organization, inculcated through mass political campaigns and enforced in small political groups. Initially, this system forged in the revolutionary insurgency was married to institutional forms copied wholesale and in detail from the Soviet Union after 1949. The pressure of internal development and external conformity broke down by the end of the 1950s, however. Increasingly, the formal institutions were challenged by ideological norms. This normative system was also disrupted during the chaos of the 'Cultural Revolution,' when organizational ties were disrupted and ideology came into dispute. The normative system of communism sought to replace ties of kinship with ties of ideological purity and organizational discipline centred on peer group pressure and hierarchic loyalties within the Communist Party. Constant campaigns were aimed at reinforcing ideological purity. These provided activists avenues of social mobility by attacking superiors who lapsed from the zeal demanded by the ideology. With ideology and organization in constant tension, norms and institutions were left in a state of permanent disfunction.

The regime that took shape under Deng Xiaoping after the death of Mao Zedong and that consolidated its power at the end of the 1970s sought both to rebuild domestic institutions and to take advantage of external resources to accelerate China's domestic development. Markets were initially favoured to accomplish cheaply what dysfunctional hierarchies could not. Neither the traditional normative system of dynastic Confucianism, nor the normative system of Communism were friendly to markets, property, or the contractual ethics of the marketplace.[37] Private law was absent in traditional China, and of course, communism was implacably opposed to markets and private property.

Private property relations have only gradually been legitimated in post-Mao China, and the role of the market only gradually recognized and approved of. Even if a substantial middle class is now emerging, there is no 'old money' in China to sustain and promote an ethos and an ethic of market relations and private property. Market relations are closely identified with a 'catch as catch can' attitude.

In the eyes of state officials, markets and property could only become accepted institutional norms so long as they functioned to increase the power and resources of the state. At an informal level, however, this also provided opportunities for rent-seeking by state officials, which, in the confusion of norms that has prevailed in the period of reform, they were only too happy to exploit. The dilemma and paradox of corruption is that it corrodes the legitimacy of the state while increasing incentives for individuals to enter state service.

In an ironic turn, the leadership of the Chinese state has increasingly turned to the 'rule of law' and norms of legal rule legitimated internationally to control the behavior of domestic officials, particularly those located at the sub-national or regional level. Increasingly, the norms of transparency and accountability preached by the WTO and international investors are being deployed to control local agents of the Chinese government. In this scenario, the norms of the WTO suit the instrumental purposes of China's central state elites. If WTO norms are institutionalized, it will not be solely or perhaps even primarily to secure the benefits of an open trading regime – the ostensible 'collective good' underlying the establishment of this multilateral organization – but rather, because the norms of WTO compliance suit the aims of state elites in shaping the evolution of China's domestic structures.[38]

Agents and Structures

Normative alignment and institutional constraints are not predetermined. To push this notion to the extreme would fall into the same conceptual trap that afflicted the earlier functionalist approaches to political science. Institutions and norms constrain – they do not cause or determine. The contrasting cases of China and North Korea are the best examples of the range of choice open to political leaders who started out with similar ideologies and world views. At the same time, the remaining distance between the institutions and normative practices of the contemporary Chinese regime and those of the developed western states also testifies to the gap between adaptive conformity to international regimes and changes in fundamental identity. Sovereignty is a remarkable institution, because although at one level it denotes a fundamental unit of membership in the international system, and establishes parameters for states to be recognized as such, it also serves as a fundamental marker of inter-state *competition*. The Chinese state holds fast to the institutions of sovereignty in order to protect its dissent from liberal norms of governance. At the same time, its effort to improve its power status in competition to the established liberal states in the international system leads China, much as Japan did previously during the nineteenth and twentieth Centuries, to adopt the institutions of liberal governance *including sovereignty itself*.[39] Ironically, therefore, sovereignty covertly promotes increasing institutional isomorphism against its ostensible purpose enshrined in the Treaty of Westphalia in 1648 – to protect normative (religious) *difference* within a community of states.

Notes

1 James N. Rosenau, 'The State in an Era of Cascading Politics,' in James A. Caporaso (ed.), *The Elusive State* (Newberry Park, Calif.: Sage, 1989), 19.

2 Anthony T. Kronnan, *Max Weber* (Stanford: Stanford University Press, 1983), 12.

3 Robert W. Cox: 'Gramsci, Hegemony and International Relations: An Essay in Method,' *Millennium*, 12 (1983), 162–75, and *Production, Power, and World Order: Social Forces in the Making of History* (New York: Columbia University Press, 1987). John G. Ruggie, 'International Regimes, Transactions, and Change: Embedded Liberalism in the Postwar Economic Order,' in Stephen Krasner (ed.), *International Regimes* (Ithaca: Cornell University Press, 1983), 195–231.

4 Stephen Krasner, 'Sovereignty: An Institutional Perspective,' in James Caporaso (ed.), *The Elusive State* (Newberry Park Calif.: Sage, 1989), 74.

5 Suisheng Zhao, *Power Competition in East Asia: From the Old Chinese World*

Order to Post–Cold War Regional Multipolarity (New York: St Martin's Press, 1997), 11.

6 For a good review of the territorial contours of the traditional Chinese state, see Michael D. Swaine and Ashley J. Tellis, *Interpreting China's Grand Strategy, Past, Present and Future* (Santa Monica: Rand Corporation, 2000), esp. 21–8 and 231–2. See also, Benedict Anderson, *Imagined Communities*, revised ed. (London: Verso, 1991).

7 Robert Keohane (ed.), *Neorealism and Its Critics* (New York: Columbia University Press, 1986).

8 See, for example, Alexander Wendt, has attacked this paradigm and reconstructed international relations theory by reasserting the value of ideas without abandoning epistemological realism. See, *The Social Theory of International Relations* (Cambridge: Cambridge University Press, 1999).

9 See Alexander Passerin d'Entreves, *The Notion of the State: An Introduction to Political Theory* (Oxford: Oxford University Press, 1967); on the western origins of the concept of sovereignty, see F.H. Hinseley, *Sovereignty* (New York: Basic Books, 1966).

10 D'Entreves was quite explicit on this score: 'Hobbes and Bodin emphasize unity and indivisibility of sovereignty. But sovereignty is first and foremost a legal concept not an attribute of power.' *The Notion of the State*, 110.

11 Morris Rossabi, in *China among Equals* (Berkeley: University of California Press, 1983), examined the problem of China's foreign relations during the period 900–1200, during which the Chinese Empire was divided and the weak Song administration had to contend with powerful Turkic and Tatar states encroaching on it. Rossabi made it clear, however, that pragmatic accommodation to powerful neighbouring states was not accompanied by an ideological readjustment in imperial rhetoric concerning the universality of the Chinese Empire or its linchpin role.

12 Michel Oksenberg, 'The Issue of Sovereignty in the Asian Historical Context,' in Stephen D. Krasner (ed.), *Problematic Sovereignty* (New York: Columbia University Press, 2001), 83–104.

13 Lanxin Xiang, 'Washington's Misguided China Policy,' *Survival*, 43 (2001), 10.

14 For an excellent review of the origins of the institution of extraterritoriality and its significance in the relationship between western states and non-western states see, Turan Kayaoglu, 'International Norms, Territorial Sovereignty and the Abolition of Extraterritoriality,' paper prepared for the annual meeting of the American Political Science Association, 31 Aug. 2001. For the institutions of extraterritoriality, see R. Willoughby Westell, *Foreign Rights and Interests in China* (Baltimore: Johns Hopkins University Press,

1927). See also, Wesley R. Fishel, *The End of Extraterritoriality in China* (Berkeley: University of California Press, 1952). For a treatment of extra-territoriality in China as a specific derogation of China's sovereign powers, see Valérie de Poulpiquet, *Le territoire chinois* (Paris: Librairie générale de droit et de jurisprudence, 1998), 96–107.

15 The genealogy and significance of this translation by the American mis-sionary W.A.P. Martin is discussed at length in Lydia H. Liu, 'Legislating the Universal: The Circulation of International Law in the Nineteenth Century,' in Lydia H. Liu (ed.), *Tokens of Exchange: The Problem of Translation in Global Circulations* (Durham: Duke University Press, 1999), 127–64.

16 Article XII of the commercial treaty contained this promise by Great Britain: 'China having expressed a strong desire to reform her judicial system and to bring it into accord with that of Western Nations, Great Britain agrees to give every assistance to such reform and she would also be prepared to relinquish her extraterritorial rights when she is satisfied that Chinese laws, their arrangement of their administration and other contents warrant her so doing.' Cited in G.W. Karlin, *The Development of Extraterritoriality in China*, vol. 2 (New York: Fertig, 1969), 12.

17 Fishel, *The End of Extraterritoriality in China*, 57.

18 Liu Jie, *Jingji quanqiuhua shidai de guojia zhuquan* [National Sovereignty in Times of Economic Globalization] (Beijing: Changzheng Chubanshe, 2001), 241–2.

19 Ibid., 242.

20 Jianfu Chen, *Chinese Law: Towards an Understanding of Its Nature and Develop-ment* (The Hague: Kluwer, 1999), 21.

21 Liu Jie, *Jingji quanqiuhua*, 244.

22 Ibid., 245–7.

23 On this point, see K.J. Holsti, 'Dealing with Dictators: Westphalian and American strategies,' *International Relations of the Asia-Pacific*, 1 (2001), 51–65.

24 Alastair Iain Johnston, 'China's Militarized Interstate Behaviour 1949–1992: A first Cut at the Data,' *The China Quarterly*, no. 143, (1998), 1–30.

25 Samuel S. Kim, *China, the United Nations and World Order* (Princeton, NJ: Princeton University Press, 1979), 410.

26 See Marius Jansen, *The Cambridge History of Japan*, vol. 4, *The Ninenteenth Century* (Cambridge: Cambridge University Press, 1989), 31–3.

27 Peter Duus, *The Abacus and the Sword: The Japanese Penetration of Korea, 1895–1910* (Berekeley and Los Angeles: University of California Press, 1995), 11–12.

28 For an explanation of this ideology and its eventual repudiation see, Andre

Schmidt, 'Decentering the "Middle Kingdom": The problem of China in Korean Nationalist Thought,' in Andre Schmidt and Tim Brook (eds.), *Nation Work: Asian Elites and National Identities* (Ann Arbor: Michigan University Press, 2000), 83–107.

29 Bruce Cumings, *Korea's Place in the Sun:A Modern History* (New York: W.W. Norton, 1997), 95.

30 Ibid., 102.

31 See Chong-sik Lee, *The Politics of Korean Nationalism* (Berkeley and Los Angeles: University of California Press, 1963), 101–26.

32 See Francis Fukuyama, 'The End of History,' *The National Interest*, (Summer 1989), 3–18.

33 For a perspective on the Asian values question, see Fareed Zakaria, 'Culture Is Destiny: A Conversation with Lee Kwan Yew,' *Foreign Affairs*, 73 (1994), 113–14.

34 Joseph S. Nye and William A. Owens, 'America's Information Edge,' *Foreign Affairs*, 75 (1996), 20–36.

35 This was the position enunciated by the Chinese delegation to the Bangkok Conference of February 1993: 'In the long process of history, the hardworking, brave and intelligent Asian people have created the splendid cultural tradition of respecting the rights of the state, society, family and individuals. This particular culture had played an important role in promoting the stability of the state and promoting the steady development of economy and society.' See, Sidney Jones, 'Culture Clash: Asian Activists Counter their Government's Restrictive View of Human Rights,' *China Rights Forum* Summer, (1993), 9.

35 For a full argument along these lines, see Christopher Hughes, *Taiwan and Chinese Nationalism: National Identity and State sin the International System* (New York and London: Routledge, 1997).

36 See, for example, Pitman B. Potter, *The Chinese Legal System: Globalization and Local Legal Culture* (New York: Routledge, 2001), esp. 125–42. Potter specifically warned against expecting specific compliance (p. 141). See also, Sylvia Ostry, 'China and the WTO: The Transparency Issue,' *UCLA Journal of International Law and Foreign Affairs*, 3 (1998), 1–22.

37 The debate surrounding Max Weber's *The Religion of China* engages both Chinese and western scholarship. The richness of traditional Chinese commercial culture is undeniable. Still there is no gainsaying that Dynastic China never underwent a process akin to that which Polanyi describes in *The Great Transformation* which systematically recast the state into a instrument favouring capitalist accumulation. The 'rise' of China has promoted domestic interest in the cultural basis of China's newfound economic

power. While most Chinese commentators are reluctant to accept the analysis put forward by Weber in the *Religion of China*, many acknowledge that the take-off in the Chinese economy has been predicated on an explicit break with the past. See, for example, Fan Yu, 'Qiangshi jingji yu wenhua de qiangshi' [A Powerful Economy and Cultural Power], *Zhongguo Guoqing Guoli*, (April 2000), 36–7.

38 The most succinct statement of this comes from China's chief negotiator for WTO accession, Long Yongtu: 'The market system is a rule of law system ... The first obligation and responsibility that we will have after we join the WTO will be to obey the rules.' Long Yongtu, 'On the Question of Our Joining the WTO,' translated in *The Chinese Economy*, 33 (2000), 15.

39 Chinese commentators and Chinese leaders have stressed the importance of China's 'global citizenship' and betrayed an anxiety about *forfeiting* China's global citizenship should China prove unable to adapt to emerging global norms and trends. See Lu Yi et al. (eds.), *Qiuji: Yige shijiexing de xuanze* [Global Citizenship: A Worldwide Choice] (Shanghai: Baiji chubanshe, 1989).

Studies in Comparative Political Economy and Public Policy